D0913541

THE POPULIST VISION

THE POPULIST
VISION

CHARLES POSTEL

OXFORD
UNIVERSITY PRESS

OXFORD
UNIVERSITY PRESS

Oxford University Press, Inc., publishes works that further
Oxford University's objective of excellence
in research, scholarship, and education.

Oxford   New York
Auckland   Cape Town   Dar es Salaam   Hong Kong   Karachi
Kuala Lumpur   Madrid   Melbourne   Mexico City   Nairobi
New Delhi   Shanghai   Taipei   Toronto

With offices in
Argentina   Austria   Brazil   Chile   Czech Republic   France   Greece
Guatemala   Hungary   Italy   Japan   Poland   Portugal   Singapore
South Korea   Switzerland   Thailand   Turkey   Ukraine   Vietnam

Copyright © 2007 by Oxford University Press, Inc.

Published by Oxford University Press, Inc.
198 Madison Avenue, New York, New York 10016

www.oup.com

First issued as an Oxford University Press paperback, 2009

Oxford is a registered trademark of Oxford University Press

Library of Congress Cataloging-in-Publication Data
Postel, Charles.
The populist vision / Charles Postel.
p. cm.
Includes bibliographical references and index.
ISBN 978-0-19-538471-0
1. United States—Politics and government—1865–1900.   2. Populism—United States—History—
19th century.   3. Social movements—United States—History—19th century.   4. Farmers—United
States—Political activity—History—19th century.   5. Working class—United States—Political
activity—History—19th century.   6. Middle class—United States—Political activity—History—
19th century.   7. United States—Social conditions—1865–1918.   8. Capitalism—United States—
History—19th century.   9. United States—Economic conditions—1865–1918.   I. Title
E661.P67 2007
973.8–dc22   2006051396

9 8 7 6 5 4 3 2 1

Printed in the United States of America
on acid-free paper

FOR MICHAEL

PREFACE

The global economy of the early twenty-first century has brought speculative booms, spectacular busts, and much questioning about what it all means. One thing is certain: the wrenching changes of the "new" economy bear a striking resemblance to changes Americans have experienced in the past.

This is a book about how Americans responded to the traumas of technological innovation, expansion of corporate power, and commercial and cultural globalization in the 1880s and 1890s. The advent of the telegraph meant that information that had taken weeks or months to cross continents and oceans now traveled at the speed of electric current. The telecommunications revolution and steam power made America, and the world, a much smaller place, facilitating large-scale organization and centralization. Corporations grew exponentially amid traumatic spasms of global capitalist development. Mark Twain called it the "Gilded Age." The rich amassed great fortunes, a prosperous section of the middle class grew more comfortable, and hard times pressed on most everyone else.

How did those on the short end respond to these changes? They organized protest movements the likes of which the country had never seen before. Populism—made up mostly of farmers but also of wage workers and middle-class activists—provided one of the most intense challenges to corporate power in American history. This book explores how the men and women of the Populist movement perceived and acted on the fast-moving changes of their modern world.

The conclusions drawn provide a cautionary tale about stereotypes of who is modern and who is not. During the Gilded Age, the corporate elite made exclusive claims on modernity. Captains of finance and industry, supported by economists and political scientists from the universities, held that the particular corporate model that they pursued conformed to unalterable laws of progress and development. They derided those who questioned corporate prerogatives as helplessly opposed to progress, bound by tradition, and intractably antimodern.

But were they? This work of historical excavation suggests otherwise. And that is what makes the experience of the Populists so relevant. The Populists challenged the corporate frameworks. They protested the inequitable distribution of wealth. They demanded more responsive government. But they, too, were modern. They embraced the Enlightenment notions of progress as firmly as their opponents did, and this allowed them to shape the weapons of protest out of the modern materials of technological, organizational, and ideological innovation. It gave the Populists confidence to act.

No attempt has been made here to resuscitate dead Populism for a living present. The movement's flaws should be a warning against any attempt at revival. The commitment of white Populists to white supremacy attests to the severity of those flaws. What does seem in order, however, is to seek a better understanding of the ways in which the Populists were influenced by modernity and sought to make America modern.

At the dawn of the twenty-first century, new structures of corporate prerogatives and control are being presented as the inevitable outcomes of new technologies and the new realities of a global economy. The Populist experience puts into question such claims of inevitability. The conclusion drawn in these pages is that the Populist revolt reflected a conflict over divergent paths of modern capitalist development. Such a conclusion is pregnant with possibilities. It suggests that modern society is not a given but is shaped by men and women who pursue alternative visions of what the modern world should be.

The Populists believed that the challenges facing their farms and homesteads required national solutions. In that populistic spirit, this book covers a wide territory. It looks at Populism as a national movement, focusing on farmers but also including wage earners and bohemian urbanites. It examines topics from education, technology, women's rights, and business, to government, race, religion, and science. Each of these topics deserves further scrutiny. Looking at the Populists with a wide lens points to the need for a many-sided reevaluation of what Populism meant. Hopefully, this book will contribute to such an effort.

A note to the reader: Populist men and women often lacked formal education. Except in those places where the meaning was unclear, quotes with unusual spellings and constructions have been left as in the original.

ACKNOWLEDGMENTS

In the course of this exploration I had the assistance of too many people to adequately thank. I would like to express my appreciation for the librarians who helped me navigate the archives and pointed me in unexpected directions. I am especially grateful to the diligent and generous people at the Center for American History at the University of Texas, the Chicago Historical Society, the Houghton Library, the Kansas State Historical Society, and the Bancroft Library. The overworked staff in the interlibrary loan office at the Berkeley Libraries deserves special thanks. I am also appreciative of a dissertation fellowship from the Mellon Foundation and a research and creativity award from California State University at Sacramento that allowed me to complete the project.

I am especially indebted to my teachers and colleagues. I had the wonderful good fortune of having Leon Litwack as my dissertation adviser. He encouraged me to take unbeaten paths, while his friendship and generous assistance and the example of his own scholarship and humanity sustained me along the way. Robin Einhorn also showed extraordinary generosity in terms of intellectual and moral support. Her sharp insights and her insistence on clarity of ideas proved invaluable. Michael Rogin, with his insatiable curiosity and formidable mind, helped me examine the big questions and spurred my thinking. I miss him. Henry Brady, David Brody, Eric Foner, David Hollinger, Laura Lovett, Mary Ryan, Seth Rockman, and Kim Voss provided sage advice and timely assistance. Jessica Tiesch and Wendy Wolford helped to brainstorm over early drafts. Joshua Howard, with his expertise in Chinese history, made me think broadly. Barbara Keys, Brian Schoen, and Lee Simpson provided helpful critiques of chapters. Peter Argersinger, Edward Ayers, James Hunt, Robert Johnston, and Glenna Matthews read the entire manuscript and provided invaluable suggestions, for which I am truly grateful.

Anonymous reviewers and Susan Ferber at Oxford University Press also helped make this book better. All of these people showed remarkable good will and thoughtfulness, and they share no responsibility for errors that I alone insisted on making.

I would be remiss to not acknowledge the memory of several teachers who set me to pondering questions of modernity and rural life. Robert Warden taught me about handling silage and hay, as well as a few things about the role of cooperative marketing, technology, and government regulation in the dairy business. I learned from Roger Ladd something about felling timber and the connections between a rock maple on a remote hillside and the global market for bowling allies. His partner, Pauline Ladd, provided lessons about the limits and possibilities for women in a rural environment. For his part, Oliver Chase, a carpenter by trade, taught me that houses are not built by architects alone, as the final product is always determined by a contest of wills between the designer and those who do the physical labor with hammer and saw. Perhaps that explains the theme of this study.

I owe particular thanks to Sam Postel and Rafael Postel, as well as Sableu Cabildo and Tony Fader. Their patient encouragement meant everything. Barbara and Sidney Cheresh showed less patience, but the same generosity of spirit. The fascinating and multitalented Michael Strange accompanied me on this journey from the beginning, providing the love and intellectual camaraderie that made it all worthwhile. This book is dedicated to her.

Berkeley, Calif.
2007

CONTENTS

ILLUSTRATIONS

THE POPULIST VISION

INTRODUCTION

Modern Times

On Bastille Day, 1894, the *Chicago Times* ran an item on a small revolution in American business. Under the headline, "Florists Nowadays Can Fill Orders in Any Part of the World," the story reported on the telegraphic trade in flowers: "Please send immediately to Mrs. —, at such and such an address in Paris, a dozen American beauty roses, and please have them there in time for dinner." It took several years of experimentation to make such orders a practical reality. "Now it is as easy and only a little more expensive," the *Times* noted, "to send flowers to an address in any part of the United States or Europe as to an address across your street."[1]

The telegraph had "annihilated time and space," to use the language of the day. The success of this new business, however, was only partly driven by technology. The decisive innovation was in the collective action of the florists, who embraced the new technology, regulated and standardized the flower market, and thereby revolutionized the flower trade. The flower sellers accomplished this through voluntary association—the International Florists' League and later the Florists' Telegraph Delivery (FTD)—reflecting the cooperative impulse coursing through American life.

Although the *Times* heralded flower sales by telegraph as "one of the remarkable business evolutions of the age," most Americans had far more pressing concerns during the summer of 1894. The country was suffering economic depression. The unemployed marched on Washington. Coal miners and railway workers struck to protect their livelihoods, only to be defeated by state militia and federal troops. Farmers faced another year of falling prices and despair. The great innovations in transport, industry, communications, and global trade had landed American capitalism in the proverbial ditch.

Yet the industrial and agricultural crises brought more than trauma and suffering. They also triggered innovative responses including the Populist revolt—one of the most powerful independent political movements in American history. The political, business, and intellectual elites greeted the Populists with equal shares of fear and derision. The Populists themselves—a broad coalition of farmers, wage earners, and middle-class activists—worked with self-confidence to challenge the status quo. Like the flower sellers, the participants in this movement believed that they could collectively wield new technological and organizational methods to serve their own interests. The power of the Populist movement lay in the efforts of common citizens to shape the national economy and governance. In the process millions of men and women at the lower rungs of society began, to use C. Vann Woodward's phrase, "to think as well as to throb."[2]

This book explores what these men and women were thinking. It examines protest thought in a time of technological transformation, incorporation, and globalization. Populism embodied a remarkable intellectual enterprise. It was known as "a reading party" and a "writing and talking party."[3] Few political or social movements brought so many men and women into lecture halls, classrooms, camp meetings, and seminars or produced such an array of inexpensive literature. The lecture notes, editorials, letters, diaries, and minute books left behind offer insights into the multiple layers of the movement: the leaders and theoreticians, the organizers and lecturers, and the participants and correspondents at the grass roots. They provide evidence of the Populists' mental world, of their strivings, of their designs for the future.

Most Populists sought economic and political reform, not the overthrow of existing systems. Culturally, too, the Populists, even those of an iconoclastic bent, tended to share common assumptions with many other Americans. The ethos of modernity and progress swept across the cultural landscape of late nineteenth-century America, driven by the winds of commercial capitalism. The Populists mainly shared this ethos. They mobilized to put their own stamp on commercial development. In doing so, the farmers and other reformers of the Populist movement were as committed to the notion of progress as any social group in post–Civil War America. A firm belief in progress gave them confidence to act. Because they believed in the transforming power of science and technology, they sought to attain expertise and knowledge for their own improvement. Because they believed in economies of scale, they strove to adapt the model of large-scale enterprise to their own needs of association and marketing. Because they believed in the logic of modernity, the Populist "clodhoppers" attempted to fashion an alternative modernity suitable to their own interests.

Recognizing these realities helps breach significant gaps in our understanding of the Populists. It helps explain the making of the Populist coalition, especially why so many women joined the cause, and why a large section of the labor movement turned to Populism for answers. It helps explain why the Populist constituencies so readily dissolved into the reform wings of the Democratic and Republican parties after the Bryan-McKinley campaign of 1896. It also sheds light on the continuities and discontinuities between late nineteenth-century Populism and early twentieth-century Progressivism. Populist visions of centralized government regulation make less anomalous the impulse toward Progressive Era state building. Similarly, Populist racial notions of social ordering help explain the consolidation of the separate and unequal system of American apartheid at the dawn of the new century. The callused-handed Populist shared much ideological ground with the university-groomed Progressive of the next generation.

How then to account for the *Sturm und Drang* of the 1880s and 1890s? Late nineteenth-century social conflict cannot be attributed to a cultural war of resistance against the commercial ethos of progress because this ethos was widely diffused among the contesting camps. This does not signify, however, that the contest lacked substance. Much was at issue.

Farmers' efforts at market regulation collided with the efforts of wholesale agents and other middlemen to accomplish similar ends. The demands of farmers for currency inflation—whether by printing greenbacks or coining silver—threatened the dogmas and profits of bankers and creditors. Workers' struggles for the right to build industrial organizations provoked virtual warfare, as industrialists claimed such rights exclusively for themselves. The capitalist elite pursued a corporate power that left little room for the organized power of the men and women of the fields, mines, or factories. Their corporate vision clashed with the Populist vision of an alternative capitalism in which private enterprise coalesced with both cooperative and state-based economies. At stake was who should be included and who should wield what shares of power—a conflict that all concerned understood as vital to the future of a modern America.

Our historical understanding of what the Populists thought is largely drawn from what they protested. We know that they assailed ruthless corporations and trusts. We know that they protested banking, railroad, and other "interests" that unduly influenced the political process and rendered state and federal governments corrupt, oppressive, and unrepresentative of the people. We know that they blamed the tight-money "goldbug" policies of the financial establishment for unemployment, low farm prices, and growing indebtedness. These targets of reform agitation were essential to the Populists' critique of what was wrong with late nineteenth-century America. Populism was an expression of protest against impoverishment and against the power of the corporate elite. Defining the Populists primarily by what they opposed, however, provides a limited and distorted picture of their movement and their times.

The source of this distortion lies within the master narrative of American history. The second half of the nineteenth century marked America's decisive transition to a modern, commercial, and industrial society. In the casting of this well-known story, the critics of the rising corporate order—especially those associated with rural life—have almost invariably played the part of Don Quixotes tilting at the windmills of modernity and commercial change. Such has been the fate of the Populists. In his celebrated 1893 essay, "The Significance of the Frontier in American History," the historian Frederick Jackson Turner described Populism as representing a "primitive society" incapable of appreciating the complexity of a "developed society." Since that time, "traditional" and similar adjectives have replaced the word *primitive*, but the essential narrative endures.[4]

What *has* changed dramatically over the decades is the assessment of what the "primitive" or "traditional" in Populism signified. Was it a source of good or potential evil? Was it a motor of progress or opposition to progress? In this regard, Turner, in describing the Populists as primitive, did not mean to denigrate but to redeem. In the Turnerian historical scheme, the primitive frontier formed the wellspring of America's democratic ethos, and the Populists were but one step from those frontier beginnings. Following Turner's lead, John D. Hicks and historians in the Progressive tradition placed Populism in the context of a democratic revolt of the frontier and the West against the city and the East. The Progressive historians also readily claimed the Populists as their own, as proto-Progressives anticipating the regulatory reforms of the Progressive Era and beyond to the New Deal. In so doing, Hicks and others overlooked much of what was unique in the earlier experience. But the logic was uncomplicated: democracy (with its primitive roots) and progress were but one and the same.[5]

The Second World War and its aftermath complicated that logic. The Holocaust and fears of totalitarianism placed popular upheaval and mass politics in a new and ominous light. Historian Richard Hofstadter at Columbia University and other mid-century scholars reexamined Populism to see if perhaps agrarian protest might contain seeds of irrational, intolerant, and anti-Semitic mass politics. Sure enough, they uncovered dangers lurking in the rural past. The menace of Populism, according to Hofstadter's Pulitzer Prize–winning *Age of Reform*, lay in the farmer's schizophrenic response to the status pressures of a modernizing society. On the "hard" side of the farmer's psychological duality he was a "harassed little country businessman," whose commercial self-interest pointed to levelheaded business strategies. On the "soft" side, especially during times of rural distress, the farmer saw himself as the injured yeoman of agrarian myth. It was this backward-looking delusion, Hofstadter warned, that led rural protest down the threatening paths of unreasoned radicalism and intolerance.[6]

The *Age of Reform* and its diagnosis of the farmer's mental state gained broad currency. It also provoked an impassioned response from other scholars, who toiled with much success to restore the Populists' democratic and progressive reputation. Significantly, the replies to Hofstadter skirted his key insight about the farmer as a businessman. Still, the scholarship of the late 1950s and 1960s did much to document that Populism represented a rational response to the new corporate order. In the process, the logic binding democracy and progress seemed to be reaffirmed.[7]

Quite different concerns animated the new social historians of the 1970s and 1980s. They did not share the old certainties about progress and development. To the contrary, they saw in Populism a movement of cultural resistance to the rising commercial order and to development itself. Lawrence Goodwyn, with his 1976 work *Democratic Promise: The Populist Moment in America*, blazed the trail for this cultural redefinition. Exploring the cultural dynamics of the farmers' movement, Goodwyn concluded that the old link between democracy and progress was historical fallacy. Populism represented the last best hope for democracy in America, he argued. But it did so as a direct challenge to the "creed of progress." Populism entailed a repudiation of what he characterized as the corporate culture of uninterrupted improvement. Goodwyn's work has cast a long shadow.[8]

Over the next quarter century, scholars continued to elaborate on the idea of Populism as a democratic revolt against progress and commercial change. They drew inspiration from the work of E. P. Thompson, who studied how traditional community in England responded to capitalist transformation. They discovered in the Populist farmer the premodern values that supposedly motivated resistance to the "market revolution" across the long nineteenth century. Steven Hahn, for example, located the origins of Populism in traditional rural economy and the cultural clash between the age-old "customs of mutuality" and the modern "cash nexus." Other historians have similarly stressed the role of premodern ideas in the shaping of Populist thought. John Thomas placed the movement's ideological underpinnings in the traditions of republican civic virtue and Protestant morality. Presumably, if nineteenth-century America was riven by the conflict between ancient republican values of the public good and modern liberal values of capitalist acquisitiveness, Populism represented the last stand of the former in resisting the commercial juggernaut. And if secular modernity threatened the Protestant moral tradition, the Populists stood their ground for evangelical piety.[9]

The social critic Christopher Lasch fashioned such assessments of the Populists into a linchpin of his analysis of American culture. Having studied history at Columbia University in the 1950s, Lasch once described Richard Hofstadter as the dominant figure on his intellectual horizon. But the mature Lasch would draw different—although no less problematic—conclusions about Populism than his mentor had. By the 1980s, Lasch had emerged as a prominent public intellectual, with his critique of consumer culture and modern life gaining the ear of a president. The marriage of market and science, in his view, had spawned a consumer society of insecurity and malaise. Modernity had stripped people of control of their work and families. This reality, he believed, put into question the entire Enlightenment project, a project that after three hundred years of promises had decidedly failed to deliver peace, equality, and human solidarity. New waves of technological and commercial progress at the end of the twentieth century offered Americans only further isolation and dehumanization.[10]

But Lasch also sought a usable countertradition in the American past. He found it in Populism. In his 1991 masterwork, *The True and Only Heaven: Progress and Its Critics*, Lasch explained the historical significance of what he called "the Populist campaign against improvement." The identification of democracy with progress, he wrote, "makes it hard to see that democratic movements in the nineteenth century took shape in opposition to innovation." The Populists defied the progressive imperatives of modernity, according to Lasch, and pointed to a future that would steer clear of both the market and the welfare state. Thus, he wove the Populists into an American legacy sustaining his critique of progress. A body of historical writing across a generation gave authority to this legacy and provided a structure of understanding: Populism was "the last outpost of the old America" responding in bold ways to the encroachments of modernity. Or, in the succinct language of David Thelen, late nineteenth-century social protest was driven by traditional people taking a stand to defend their world—family, community, and church —from an alien invasion of businessmen seeking development.[11]

This understanding has proven surprisingly durable. This is due, in part, to its simplicity and inner logic. It also enjoys the advantage of pervasive assumptions about who is modern and who is not, assumptions affirmed in the familiar casting of America's modernization story. It has been supported as well by English and European models of explanation, no matter how inapplicable they might be to late nineteenth-century America. Principally, however, this framework of historical understanding has been sustained by the skepticism about modernity that has shaped currents of recent scholarship. Such skepticism has led to a search for a firmly rooted and authentic past, as the commercialized and corporate present has turned the old confidence in Enlightenment ideals to ambivalence. In turn, scholars have projected this ambivalence on the unwitting farmers, laborers, and other common folk of the nineteenth century. But the framework can make for a poor fit. Its power

of explanation can wane dramatically on a close examination of its historical premises. This is especially the case with the Populists.[12]

The Populist world was too commercially and intellectually dynamic to resemble a traditional society in any meaningful sense of the term. This tells
us something important about the nature of late nineteenth-century reform:
the men and women of the Populist movement were modern people. The
term *modern* does not mean "good." Nor is it a value judgment across the
political spectrum from right to left. Moreover, to say that the Populists were
modern does not imply that they were more modern than, say, their Republican or Democratic opponents. Nor does it imply that all rural people shared
the Populists' modern sensibility. On the contrary, the Populists understood
that the transformations they sought required the uprooting of rural ignorance, inertia, and force of habit. Across much of America's rural territory,
Populism formed a unique social movement that represented a distinctly
modernizing impulse.[13]

Modern can be understood in a double sense: both as a condition or environment and as a disposition or striving. In both regards, the men and
women of the Populist movement experienced modernity much as described
in Marshall Berman's rendition of Marx. Modern economic relations shaped
their lives and they expressed a modern sensibility. The starting point of the
modern condition involved the rise of a world market, making production
and consumption increasingly international and cosmopolitan. Elements of
traditional nonmarket farming persisted, especially in remote Appalachian
communities and other isolated pockets of post–Civil War America. The
Populist country, however, was a commercial environment, bound to global
markets. It was an environment of boom and bust, which stretched across
most of a continent of commodity farming, mining, railroads, and urban
centers. "It is a mixed country in its productive pursuits," as a Farmers' Alliance newspaper explained, "and commercial throughout."[14]

Modernity entailed technologically sophisticated communications and mass
media. The telegraph, railroad, and steamship linked farm settlements with
Chicago, New Orleans, Dallas, San Francisco, Cincinnati, New York, Liverpool,
and London. Although farmers suffered rural isolation—an unmistakably
nonmodern feature of farm life—this isolation, paradoxically, grew with the
advance of railroads and farm mechanization that cast farmers across an ever-
wider territory. Yet commercially as well as intellectually, they lived in an urban
shadow. Second-class postage brought millions of pounds of inexpensive newspapers and pamphlets into the rural heartland and brought millions of men
and women into the national discussion of progress and reform.[15]

Modernity also implied a particular kind of people with particular types
of strivings. Modern men and women of all classes yearn for and demand

change. They delight in mobility, thrive on renewal, and, as Berman puts it, "look forward to future developments in their conditions of life and their relations with their fellow men." The Populists were just this kind of people. They sought to improve their domestic economy and their national government. They sought renewal in local schoolhouses and federal credit systems. They sought to refashion associational ties with neighbors and commercial relations with the world. They sought new techniques, new acreage, and new avenues of spiritual expression. To understand the full significance of these strivings it is necessary to look further than what the Populists were against— abusive railroad pricing, inequitable banking policies, and corrupt government—and to examine what they were for.[16]

This is a book about power and interest. More precisely, it looks at how American Populists engaged ideas about power and interest, because these ideas were central to their concerns. The men and women of the reform movement focused their attention on what they understood to be the economic underpinnings of political influence, wealth distribution, and commercial advantage. An Iowa journalist attributed the rise of Populism to this new preoccupation with economics. Prior to the Civil War, he wrote, talk of economics "would have cleared the benches of any town-hall." But the Civil War "obliterated" sentimentality, and the discussion of economics, finance, and revenue "are now heard with attention, intelligence and enthusiasm."[17]

When historical subjects directed their enthusiasm to the economic and the material, their focus poses challenges for historians who seek the exotic and the uncommon. It also presents thorny issues for scholars who have followed the "cultural turn" of recent years, with its emphasis on cultural explanations for historical developments. This turn has allowed historians to mine the past in search of cultural significance that expands our understanding beyond a narrow and empiricist materialism. In the case of Populism, however, it has also led down dead ends when it has failed to take into account a key element of the movement culture—the Populists themselves often looked at the world through a narrow materialist lens. From the vantage of the twenty-first century, much of what the Populists saw might be surprising and unexpected. But to explore what was truly remarkable in Populism, we need to examine how concerns about power and interest shaped the cultural and intellectual enterprise of late nineteenth-century reform.[18]

This is also a book about the idea of progress. The purpose here is not to evaluate the Populists by today's measurements of what is progressive or reactionary, forward-looking or backward-looking. Rather, the aim is to examine the role that the *idea of progress* played in Populist thinking. Looking at why the Populists embraced the notion of progress, and how they wielded the concept as a weapon of reform, tells a great deal about how they understood their times. In the nineteenth century the concept of progress played a central role in American social thought, although ambivalence about its meaning had grown by the end of the century. Take the railroad, for example. As Michael Kammen points out, prior to the Civil War the railroad represented unimagined progress, but by the late 1880s and 1890s it increasingly symbolized abusive economic power. This shift, however, must be qualified. For the Populists, the railroad rarely symbolized the destructive machine, the nature-devouring octopus. The concepts that linked railroads to unimagined progress continued to fire their imaginations. They were convinced that with new laws and regulations railroads would indeed deliver on their promise of faster, cheaper, and more equitable access to global markets. Hence they fused progress with reform.[19]

The inequities accompanying industrial and commercial development deeply troubled the Populists. Many of them experienced hard lives and crushing poverty as they witnessed the towering accumulation of capitalist wealth. The critique of such inequities, however, did not dampen the reformers' commitment to progress. Henry George's influential *Progress and Poverty* excoriated the growth of poverty and speculative wealth. But it is often overlooked that at the heart of George's critique was a "single tax" to unfetter urban and rural capital improvements—to make the promise of progress a reality. Like George and other late nineteenth-century reformers, the Populists sought improvement and they did so with what the novelist Hamlin Garland described as a "splendid optimism" about the future. "There is a kind of pessimism which is really optimism," he explained, "that is to say, people who believe the imperfect and unjust can be improved upon." Through the prism of the twenty-first century, belief in perfecting the human condition may appear naive. But it provides an essential element for understanding the Populist commitment and self-confidence. It also locates the Populists as men and women of their times.[20]

Like other Americans, farm and labor reformers carried the burdens of history and tradition. The Populists drew from the past that which was familiar and close at hand. They often cited biblical stories as well as Shakespeare, Cicero, Dickens, and other literary sources. They freely quoted personalities from the past—Washington, Jefferson, Jackson, Calhoun, and Lincoln—who loomed large in nineteenth-century oratory. In that sense, the Populists' ideas had roots in the traditions of their ancestors. The presence of the past in Populist thought may suggest a qualification to indicate that they were at once both traditionalists and moderns. Such a formulation, however, might erroneously suggest that the Populists were in some qualitative way less modern than their urban, academic, and other modernizing counterparts, who tended to be tied to the past in equivalent fashion. Also, it is often overlooked that much of the historical legacy that the Populists looked back to was also a modernizing legacy, with notions of innovation and progress having enjoyed a broad currency among eighteenth- and early nineteenth-century Americans. The characterization of the Populists as both traditionalists and moderns, moreover, fails to do justice to the type of determined certainty about progress and the future that gave strength to Populist commitment.[21]

Citing an Arab proverb, the historian Marc Bloch wrote: "men resemble their times more than they do their fathers." The Populists were no exception. They belonged to the new post–Civil War era, and the cataclysm of the war itself provided a backdrop for how late nineteenth-century reformers experienced rapid changes in national life. The expansion of the telegraph and railroad grids framed new ideas about reordering commerce and the flow of information. Pooling and the incorporation of business raised expectations about combination and economies of scale. Discoveries in the natural and social sciences, especially in evolutionary theory and electricity, provoked new ways of imagining economy, society, and spirit. New realities shaped the Populists' dreams and hopes for the development of their vocation, their community, their racial group, and their country.[22]

Reformers occasionally expressed doubts about a specific theory of Charles Darwin or Herbert Spencer. Or, more often, they protested the misuse of the new theories by defenders of the status quo. But the Populists were no less evolutionists than their "social Darwinist" opponents. The post-Darwinian ideas of development provided common points of reference within Populist debate, as Populist newspapers exposed their readers to the "evolutionary imagination." Such imagination helped the Populists make sense of their world of boosterism and rapid settlement. It also shaped the type of centralized organizations the Populists formed, the large-scale businesses they attempted, the state-centered reforms they pursued, the racial social ordering they sought, and the new avenues of religious expression they explored.[23]

Who were the Populists? Part of the difficulty in answering this question is that the Populist or People's party of the 1890s was less a typical political party than a coalition of reform organizations—what its founders envisioned as a "Confederation of Industrial Organizations." The national founding itself took place in "industrial conferences" held in Cincinnati (1891) and St. Louis (1892) attended by a battery of "industrial orders": the Farmers' Alliance and Industrial Union, the National Farmers' Alliance, the Colored Farmers' Alliance, the Farmers' Mutual Benefit Association, the Knights of Labor, the Women's Alliance, the Citizen's Alliance, and other reform groups. The numerical strength of each organization at least nominally determined representation. The precise configuration of the coalition varied at the state level, but the orders tended to fall into discrete categories: farmers' associations; labor organizations; women's groups; and an array of nonconformists, including urban radicals, tax and currency reformers, prohibitionists, middle-class utopians, spiritual innovators, and miscellaneous iconoclasts.[24]

Prior to the formation of the third party, the principal organizations of the coalition had been avowedly nonpartisan, with some members of the coalition hostile to the very existence of political parties. The People's party, even in the heat of electoral warfare, never fully shed its nonpartisan and antiparty origins. Such origins had two notable consequences. First, significant portions of the membership of the Farmers' Alliance, the Knights of Labor, and other groups rejected the idea of "going into politics." In practice, this meant refusing to follow their leaders into the People's party and instead pursuing reform through the traditional parties. In this regard, individual decisions about party allegiance and how to vote often had less to do with ideological divisions in terms of goals and aims, and more to do with the viability of a third party option in a given state or election. Second, the Farmers' Alliance and kindred organizations lacked trained or well-known political campaigners. This meant that when the "industrial orders" launched the People's party, they often relied on candidates who were professional politicians and other public figures from outside their ranks.[25]

Because of these peculiarities, any study of Populism must consider that all Populists were not equal. Take, for example, James B. Weaver, the People's party presidential candidate who polled over one million votes in 1892. His stature as a Civil War general and his long experience in Democratic-Greenback campaigns in Iowa provided the necessary credentials for the standard-bearer of the new party. But Weaver was a professional lawyer-politician, without close connection to the new ideas or organizations from which Populism sprang. In contrast, Farmers' Alliance leader Charles Macune had little faith in third-party politics and returned to the Democrats soon after the founding of the People's party. Yet scholars have quite rightly portrayed Macune as a "quintessential" Populist,[26] as he was the architect of the Farmers' Alliance, the "industrial order" at the ideological and organizational core of the Populist coalition. Accordingly, this study employs a concept of "Populist" that includes the confederation of organizations that lay at the foundations of the People's party. It focuses on the Farmers' Alliance because of its size and importance, but it does so without neglecting the role of the other farmer, labor, and reform movements that contributed to Populism's coherence.

To write about the coherence of Populism—a social and political movement that touched millions of lives and spanned a continent—is necessarily fraught with peril. Regional and local studies confirm the complex and constantly changing nature of the movement. Our understanding of Populism, however, has also been fragmented by limitations of the analytical approach. Scholars have invested considerable effort in distilling the regional essence of the Populist movement. John Hicks located the center of Populism among wheat farmers of the upper Midwest, downplayed the southern movement and its festering racial politics, and reduced the movement in the Far West to the influence of silver mining interests. C. Vann Woodward placed the vortex of Populism in the Cotton Belt, with its southern "rebel yell." Lawrence Goodwyn argued that authentic Populism rested on the cooperative experience of the Farmers' Alliance with its Texas roots, whereas most of midwestern and western Populism supposedly produced only an insidious "shadow movement" barren of authentic movement culture.[27]

This type of geographic analysis, however, breaks down upon closer examination. In electoral terms, the Populist vote for state offices in 1894 was as high in Colorado (41 percent) and Washington State (39 percent) as it was in Kansas (39 percent) and Texas (36 percent). In the same election, the California Populists (18 percent) doubled the Populist vote obtained in the southern states of Missouri (8 percent) and Tennessee (9 percent). Populism lacked a significant constituency in the northeastern states where the institutions of the two old parties were most deeply entrenched. In the rest of the country, the movement took root across a broad territory of cotton and wheat, staple crops and specialty crops, mining and railroads, white and black, rural and urban.[28]

Hence the necessity for examining Populism with a wider, more inclusive lens. This book responds to such a need. Although sensitive to regional, class, race, and gender distinctions, it casts a wide net to capture unifying themes that sustained a national movement with a national vision. No uniform doctrine prevailed within the Populist coalition, where a range of opinions coexisted. Perhaps, however, this was not for lack of effort, as the spirit of reform encouraged the search for orthodoxy. Reformers pursued inquiry and debate with the goal of revealing the incontrovertible certainties of "scientific" economy and government. Accordingly, Populist ideas tended to cluster into identifiable strands of accepted truths that bound together the networks of lecturers, editors, and activists of the Populist coalition, and that mobilized millions of ordinary citizens for what they perceived as a common cause.

Populism largely rested on the newly found organizational strength of America's farmers. In the 1880s and 1890s, farmers constructed organizations the likes of which had never before been seen in the country's history. The combined membership of the Farmers' Alliance and kindred associations numbered in the millions. The size and scope of this organizational movement, as observers at the time well understood, carried profound implications for America's social, economic, and political life. By the sheer force of numbers, organized farmers exerted leverage over state legislatures, and with their lobbyists in

Washington hoped to realize similar influence over Congress. Part I of this book examines the farmers' organizations that gave rise to Populism. The first chapter explores the origins of the Farmers' Alliance in the midst of the speculative boom and bust of the farmers' frontier. A promotional culture of "push and energy" accompanied the railroad into new terrain across much of the rural South and West. The Alliance movement took root in this environment, and rapidly emerged as an organizational power stretching from coast to coast.

The Farmers' Alliance brought a new quality to rural associational life. It organized farmers from "the business standpoint," believing that growers of wheat and cotton represented a business interest like any other in modern society. It demanded equity on the commercial playing field. And it offered a vision of improvement by means of business methods, education, and technology that gave rural Americans the hope of realizing the benefits of progress and development.

"Knowledge is power." This simple adage, attributable to the Enlightenment philosopher Francis Bacon, circulated widely in nineteenth-century America. Starting with its first lending libraries on the Texas frontier, the Farmers' Alliance defined itself as an educational movement. The second chapter focuses on the farmers' educational pursuits. The men and women of the Alliance demanded increased funding for colleges, agricultural stations, institutes, and other federal and state programs to disseminate business, technical, and scientific information. At the same time, Alliance members conceived of their own organization as potentially "the most powerful and complete educator of modern times." They spread a network of lecture circuits, literature distribution, and meetinghouse adult education across large swaths of rural America.[29]

The Farmers' Alliance had no monopoly on the educational enterprise. Urban and "New South" professionals held similar beliefs about the progressive power of education. For the rural reformers, nonetheless, education served as a great mobilizer. They placed their hopes on education as a means to close the gap between rural poverty and town prosperity. They seized on education as a weapon to break the corporate stranglehold on business "intelligence" that left the farmer at commercial disadvantage. They looked to education as a prerequisite to modernize farming by placing agriculture on a professional and scientific footing.[30]

Women joined the Alliance movement in numbers then unmatched by any mobilization of American women outside of the churches. This mobilization cannot be explained within the framework of a traditional people resisting modernity. Perhaps that explains the tendency to overlook women's presence in most accounts of Populist history. The third chapter is devoted to exploring the question of why so many women joined in the cause of rural reform. The partial answer is that rural women struggled with the same poverty that rural men did, and they wanted the same educational, economic, and political reforms. Many rural women also demanded voting rights and the suppression of the whiskey trade. But they saw these demands in the wider context of striving for a "better womanhood" through innovative changes in their role within the family, the farm, and the broader society.

Women also rallied to rural reform because they desired a more modern rural life and to gain greater access to opportunities within the modern economy. They wanted more equitable partnerships with men. They hoped for liberation from field labor. They sought updated methods and appliances to ease the drudgery of daily chores. They pushed for education and technical training. And they pursued economic independence as teachers, clerks, and telegraphers, and as employees and professionals in other careers then opening up to women. In line with then-prevailing notions of evolution, rural reformers also believed that by improving women's lives they would thereby improve the minds and bodies of their offspring.[31]

Chapter 4 explores business organization, what Farmers' Alliance members considered the heart of the matter. To understand Populist thinking about business and commerce, it is essential to return to Hofstadter's characterization of the "country businessman." This term implies neither curse nor praise, but rather it is how farm reformers of the time defined their own position. And it is the first premise of the economic ideas that they pursued. In the example of the flower trade, it could be assumed that the innovations in telegraphic commerce helped the florists' business but were peripheral to the workings of their neighborhood flower shops. Cotton or wheat farmers, however, engaged in a different kind of business because they did not sell their products in a neighborhood shop, as virtually every bale or bushel ventured into national and global trade. Farm reformers recognized that the survival of their operations depended on commercial innovation, including a more direct connection to national and international markets.

Rural reformers believed, as did many Americans, that the future lay with organizational consolidation and economies of scale. True, middling and small farmers made up the reform movement's largest constituency. True, farm reformers attacked concentrated wealth, and they had friends like the journalist Henry Demarest Lloyd, who wrote scathing exposés of corporate giants. Still, farm reformers recognized the advantages of size and concentration. They, too, believed that bigger was indeed better. To explain rural poverty they pointed to the farmers' late entry into the modern business world of combination: hence the necessity of the Farmers' Alliance and similar organizations. "Nothing could withstand their power," predicted Nelson Dunning, a national publicist for the Farmers' Alliance, "if the farmers of America would organize as intelligently and solidly as the Standard Oil Company has." Dunning's idea—repeated in Alliance editorials, letters to the editor, and lectures—reflected a conviction that spurred the agrarian revolt. Yet the significance of this idea remains hidden in the shadow of Lloyd's more famous exposé of Standard Oil's monopolistic misdeeds.[32]

It also remains hidden under the veil of romantic history that surrounds farmers' cooperatives. Cooperatives, according to Lawrence Goodwyn, laid the foundations for the subsequent democratic culture of Populism, as farmers learned to reject the centralized and hierarchical structures of the corporations by first taking part in the Texas Farmers' Alliance Exchange and similar cooperative enterprises. Critics have questioned this historical sequence of events. They have also argued that the experience with cooperatives was too limited to explain Populism's success. The quality of this experience is even more problematic.[33]

The Texas Farmers' Alliance Exchange represented a large-scale, centralized, and technically elaborate system to regulate cotton and other commodity markets. Farmers undertook experiments with such systems in virtually every sector of the rural economy during the 1880s and 1890s. What the farmers wanted from the Texas Exchange they also saw taking root in the valleys of California. The fruit and other agricultural exchanges formed on the West Coast, often with the involvement of Farmers' Alliance and Populist growers, showed much promise. These were (and still are) cooperative corporations of a special type. "Benevolent trusts," as the legal historian Victoria Woeste calls them, rested on the voluntary shoulders of thousands of farmers. They provided even the small producers access to economies of scale, standardization, technology, and regulated markets. Such was the faith that the members of the Farmers' Alliance and other hard-pressed farmers across the country placed in the power of organization.[34]

Part II of the book follows the Farmers' Alliances into the Populist coalition and the formation of the People's party. When the farmers "went into politics" they pursued the dramatic expansion of government regulation and control in the country's economic life. This included demands for the public ownership of railroads and the telegraph, as well as the distinctly Populist innovation of the "subtreasury," a proposal for a national system of farm credit, warehousing, and marketing. The Populists saw state action as a means to settle accounts with perceived enemies: corporate owners of railroads, telegraphs, and warehouses, and the eastern bankers dominating the financial and monetary system. Hostility toward corporate and financial power brought farm reformers to demand that the government act as a counterbalance. In so doing, as the political scientist Elizabeth Sanders demonstrates, farmers and their labor allies provided the impetus for the modern interventionist state that took shape in the late nineteenth and early twentieth century.

Within this process Sanders identifies "a major anomaly in American political development: social forces profoundly hostile to a bureaucracy nevertheless instigated the creation of a bureaucratic state." This apparent anomaly, however, rests upon two assumptions. The first assumption, widely shared in the scholarship, is that, as small producers, farmers were by nature adverse to centralized and remote institutions. In reality, the large-scale business organizations farmers built in the 1880s and 1890s pointed in the parallel direction of centralized and remote government institutions. The second assumption is that social protest movements, again by their inherent nature, were hostile to bureaucracy. "When has one seen protesters," Sanders queries rhetorically, "marching through the streets carrying signs that read, 'Give us an agency!'?" The answer lies in the peculiarities of the Populist movement.[35]

Most of the Populist "revolt" took place not in the streets but in lodge meetings and convention halls, where participants pored over problems of commerce and government and adopted resolutions for the creation or expansion of state and federal agencies, institutes, commissions, departments, and bureaus. The Populist coalition realized its first triumph on the national scene in 1890, with a successful lobbying effort by the Farmers' Alliance and the Knights of Labor to add a million dollars to the budget of the Census Commission. At the same time, the Populists cherished the one bureaucratic institution that they knew best: the post office. The postal service provided a model of large-scale, centralized, and efficient economy, inspiring and shaping Populist ideas of government as a force for progress, modernity, and equity.[36]

The Populists embraced a nonpartisan, managerial, and government-as-business vision of politics. This makes Populism's relationship to democracy complex. On the one hand, the movement was profoundly democratic in composition, mobilizing millions of often-marginalized citizens. On the other hand, in both practice and theory, the Populists pursued a "business politics" that was a far cry from the decentralized, localized, and consensual democracy of the late twentieth-century imagination. The Populists' notion of majority rule left little room for minority rights, and their vision of centralizing and managerial reform framed the internal political culture of their movement.[37]

Populist democracy must also be measured in the context of race. Race relations during this post-Darwinian epoch in American life turned especially menacing. The logic of progress built up the walls of segregation, restriction, and exclusion. Chapter 6 examines how this logic played out in the making of the Populist coalition. Historians have given different assessments of the Populist record on matters of race. The claims made by Richard Hofstadter and other scholars that the Populists were an ominous source of anti-

Semitism and intolerance have lost currency. The alternative claims made by historians such as C. Vann Woodward and Lawrence Goodwyn present white Populists as challenging racial taboos, only to have their courageous efforts at unity between whites and blacks collapse under the traditional weight of white supremacy. Contrary evidence provided by Barton Shaw, Steven Hahn, and other historians suggests that the white Populists' commitment to biracial cooperation was more rhetorical than substantive.[38]

Populist ideas about race reflected more than an inheritance; they had a strikingly up-to-date configuration. On race relations, too, the Populists sought modernity, progress, and innovation. They understood this as a mandate for Chinese exclusion and institutionalizing the system of "separate but equal." In practical terms, the presence of the People's party challenged the Democratic political monopoly in the South and thereby opened possibilities for African American political participation. This did not mean, however, that white southern Populists questioned core beliefs in white supremacy and the master race ideology. Across the South and beyond, the Farmers' Alliance, much like their urban "New South" counterparts, linked progressive reform with separating people by race and Jim Crow laws. In Texas, both white and black Populists sustained plans to segregate the prisons, asylums, and other state institutions. And within the Populist coalition itself, whites and blacks were separate and unequal.[39]

The People's party was conceived as an "Industrial Confederation," a multiclass alliance uniting "industrial orders" across the rural-urban divide. That Populism failed to gain traction in the urban and working-class centers of the Northeast points to the failure of such an alliance, a failure usually attributed to the cultural or ideological gap between rural Populism and urban and labor constituencies. However, as explored in chapter 7, such an explanation leaves unanswered why so many wage earners and middle-class reformers did join the Populist cause. In Ohio, Wisconsin, Idaho, and other midwestern and western states, the labor movement provided the People's party with its most reliable constituency. What is more, the successes that the Populist coalition did achieve were facilitated by the inspiration and cadre supplied by urban movements and middle-class activists.

Labor Populists gravitated toward coalition with rural reform in part because of their physical proximity to farmers. Farmers were often part-time coal miners, and coal miners often farmed to supplement their diet and income. Knights of Labor lodges welcomed cotton planters and railway mechanics alike. Proximity allowed for the cross-pollination of ideas, and labor Populists shared the faith of their rural counterparts in large-scale organization and state building. Only intervention by federal and state authority—regulatory commissions, mandatory arbitration, and ultimately government ownership—could restrain the chaotic lawlessness of the corporations. Railway employees acted together through centralized and uniform organization to advance their interests. Coal miners, facing the whipsaw effects of national price competition, experimented with "market unionism" to rationalize the coal market in much the way farmers attempted to rationalize cotton, wheat, and other markets.[40]

The combined force of labor detectives, state militias, and federal courts and troops repeatedly dismantled organization among the nation's railroad and mine workers. The labor movement languished at a time when agrarian organization ran high. Farmers exercised their citizenship rights and advanced their associations in ways that harassed, blacklisted, and unemployed workers could not. Especially with the onset of economic depression in 1893, the organized farmer appeared to the labor Populist as the best hope for political and economic reform.

Known to its detractors as the party of "cranks," Populism also enrolled a large contingent of the nation's nonconformists, iconoclasts, and freethinkers. It attracted advocates of every type of innovation and scheme that held promise of social renovation. Of these the most influential were the panacea and utopian movements, the Single Tax and currency reform leagues, the Bellamy Nationalist clubs, and the cooperative colonist societies. Derided by some scholars as middle-class inhabitants of the "shadow movement," such movements contributed ideas, personnel, and political energy to the Populist cause.

Nonconformist reform, often linked to the bohemian environments of Chicago, San Francisco, Denver, and other new cities, served as a meeting place for men and women from the workshop and farm, the middle class and working class, the declassed and deeply rooted. It brought together Farmers' Alliance organizers and Nationalist utopians, railroad workers and cooperative colonists. Such combinations provide insight into the making of the Populist coalition, where reformers with widely disparate agendas found in Populism a means toward the "Cooperative Commonwealth"—a perceived future of a progressive, modern, and equitable society.

Populism also represented an unusual coalition of religious belief and nonbelief. Although most Populists considered themselves Christians, the movement embraced an inordinate number of the religiously heterodox: spiritualists, Theosophists, Swedenborgians, mental scientists, agnostics, and other adherents of religious and spiritual reform. The enemies of Populism were quick to attack the "heretics" and nonchurchgoers who played a prominent part in the third-party movement. The agnostic Clarence Darrow was such an "infidel." Then a prominent figure in the People's party in Illinois, Darrow would later play a prominent role in the famous "Monkey Trial" of 1925, when he defended John Scopes, who was charged with violating the Tennessee law that prohibited the teaching of evolution. The best-known member of the prosecution was, of course, William Jennings Bryan, the Democratic-Populist presidential candidate in 1896. Ever since, Bryan's role has cemented the link in historical memory between Populism and fundamentalist religion. That it was Darrow, not Bryan, who had been a stump speaker for the People's party provides a warning against the facile identification of Populism with a traditionalist Christianity.

Populists, more often than not, were born in Protestant homes and came of age in an evangelical environment of revivals and camp meetings. The result was an "emotional-religious element" within the Populist movement that, as C. Vann Woodward noted, had become "subject of much rarified merriment" among secular academics in the first half of the twentieth century. Because of this element, scholars tended to dismiss the serious intellectual issues farmers engaged. By the 1970s, however, scholars no longer found merriment in Populist religion. Much as E. P. Thompson stressed the role of Primitive Methodism in shaping the English working class, American historians have emphasized the part of evangelical piety in late nineteenth-century social protest. The emphasis on traditional piety, however, has meant that historians have largely overlooked the new, dynamic ideas that shaped Populist religiosity, the focus of the eighth and last chapter of the book.[41]

Many Populists embraced a social Christianity that rejected the notion of salvation apart from overcoming poverty and inequities among the living. Reflecting post-Darwin understandings of human and social evolution, Populists tended to discard biblical literalism in their search for a cosmology suitable for a scientific age. And as the communications revolution made the world smaller, they probed the religions of Asia and elsewhere for clues to a better understanding of spiritual matters. These trends within Populist thought ran parallel to the liberal and modernizing currents coursing through the elite seminaries and universities at Chicago, Boston, and New York.

Across the spectrum of religious belief and nonbelief, what can be described as a creed of science served as a unifying strand within Populist thought. From Baptist preachers to agnostics, Populists shared with much of America a belief in the power of science. Empirical evidence and physical and biological principles provided the surest measures of morality and justice. The righteous, progressive, and modern society of the Populist imagination was to be built on empirically revealed and scientifically established truth. In their distinct fusion of moral faith and social reform, science served as the "morning star" of Populist strivings.[42]

In 1896, the People's party endorsed the Democratic presidential bid of William Jennings Bryan. With Bryan's loss, the election proved a mortal blow to the Populist cause. A small group of the Populist faithful soldiered on for several more years, but they did so without the Farmers' Alliance and the other "industrial orders" of the Populist coalition that had slid into oblivion. The future would bring renewed mass movements for social regeneration, renewed efforts at farmer-labor coalitions, and renewed variations of populist politics with a small *p*. Regarding the latter, Michael Kazin writes that populism remained part of the American political language across the twentieth century, "a flexible mode of persuasion" employed by both the left and the right, from Samuel Gompers to Joseph McCarthy, from Ross Perot to Jesse Jackson.[43] But late nineteenth-century Populism with a capital *P* was more than a language. It was a particular constellation of ideas, circulating within a specific coalition of reform, and set in motion within a distinct historical context. In that sense, the Populist vision was largely eclipsed at the turn of the century.

The old textbooks provide a standard epitaph to explain Populism's demise: the outcome was predetermined because its tradition-bound vision failed to match the requirements of a modern and industrializing society. Populism failed because Populism was wrong. At least that is how the winners explained the outcome. But the claim that Populism failed must be qualified by examining the impact it had on American life, and especially by the impetus that it provided for a wave of reform that carried into the new century.

As to whether Populism was right or wrong, the question must be framed in the context of historical possibilities. The Populists lived at a time of boom and bust characterized by spasms of technological change, combination, and globalization. It was a time of flux. In that regard, recent studies of American political development suggest that the particular configuration of corporate and state institutions that emerged from the late nineteenth century were not, as traditionally explained, predetermined by the requirements of capital formation and industrialization. The outcome was also conditioned by political forces and the ideas that drove them.[44]

If alternative models of capitalism were indeed possible, perhaps the example of telegraphic flower sales may have a broader significance. If the collective action of the florists successfully reoriented the flower trade, perhaps the Populists correctly assessed that cotton farmers, wheat growers, coal miners, railway employees, and other ordinary men and women could act similarly to effect a broad reorientation of commercial and state institutions. The following pages explore the notions of innovative possibility that inspired that effort.

PART I

Farmers

1

Push and Energy

Boosterism and Rural Reform

The Farmers' Alliance, the largest and most important constituency of what would become the Populist coalition, rose in the 1870s out of the dust and smoke of the central Texas frontier. The "honest, earnest, and brave" pioneers of the Alliance drove off the horse thieves, stood down the land sharks, built up law and order, and made central Texas safe for settlement and civilization. At least this is the account provided by official histories of the Farmers' Alliance, which also acknowledged that little evidence of these early days survived in the historical record. The reliability of the pioneer story of the 1870s, however, is less important than the reasons why the story was retold by Alliance historians in the 1880s and 1890s.[1]

Frontiersmen, as understood by every school child who knew of Davy Crockett and Daniel Boone, were invariably "honest, earnest, and brave." The Farmers' Alliance proudly claimed such a heritage. Frontier origins also carried a larger message about the historical role of rural reform. The Farmers' Alliance represented a civilizing force that stood on the cutting edge of progress and development; its frontier beginnings helped to explain why. In his widely circulated official history, Alliance publicist Nelson A. Dunning described the process in global context:

> The wave of civilization and development swept the world, from east to west; and when it reached the western border, it was reflected back as a great reform movement. It is the reflex wave of a higher civilization which promises to improve all existing countries, as the present civilization improved upon barbarism.[2]

The frontier had produced a reform impulse, according to Dunning, that would sweep back, from west to east, and bring a higher, more progressive civilization to America, Europe, and the world. The Farmers' Alliance published Dunning's vision about the frontier and civilization in 1891, two years before a much more famous scholar articulated a similar idea in what became known as "Turner's Frontier Thesis." The historian Frederick Jackson Turner argued that American civilization had been forged in the frontier experience. He also interpreted history from west to east, with the frontier reflecting its ethos on "the Atlantic coast and even the Old World." Years later, Turner's insight profoundly influenced the way that American academic and political leaders addressed the nation's past, whereas the Farmers' Alliance version gathered dust in the molding remnants of cheap reform literature.[3] This outcome, however, should not obscure the extent to which Populist ideas about the frontier and progress echoed, or anticipated, the ideas of Turner and other Progressive Era intellectuals.

The Populists' notions about progress and civilization were shaped by the demographic shifts in post–Civil War America, especially by the dispossession of the Native peoples, the so-called "savage occupants," and the rapid expansion of white settlement. The Industrial Revolution was filling cities with urban workers, a development that overshadows in historical memory the simultaneous process that was filling the continent with new farms. Between 1860 and 1890 the number of farms in the United States nearly tripled. Land under the plow rose from 407 million to 828 million acres, as farmers pushed into the Great Plains in search of commercial success in meeting the demand for grain and fiber on both sides of the Atlantic. For farm reformers, acquiring land and breaking new ground was a means of getting ahead. They also understood that it fulfilled a progressive and civilizing mission. Earlier generations of American agriculturalists had embraced the Enlightenment belief that they stood on the rungs of the historical ladder of progress. The torrent of rural development in the post–Civil War years confirmed this notion.[4]

Even more striking than the reach of the plow was the reach of organization. The white Farmers' Alliance alone counted over a million members from coast to coast. The Colored Farmers' Alliance claimed a similar number of black members in the rural South. Other farm associations organized hundreds of thousands of grain farmers in the Midwest and elsewhere. What is more, farm reformers organized from a professional and business standpoint, bringing a new modern quality to rural associational life. Organizational systems, Nelson Dunning observed, were "absolutely necessary for success in modern business" and produced "the astonishing results of modern undertakings." A product of the frontier and structured on modern business lines, the Alliance represented what Dunning described as "the most powerful" organization for progress and development in human history.[5]

The Farmers' Alliance was, indeed, born on the farmers' frontier. By most accounts, the first incarnation of the Farmers' Alliance appeared during the mid-1870s in Lampasas County, Texas, situated at the edge of agricultural settlement where farmers and their field crops butted up against the grazing lands of cattle ranchers. Little is known about the Lampasas Alliance, but it apparently served as a self-help and protective association, defending the small rancher and plowman against horse thieves and lawlessness. Although the Lampasas Alliance soon passed from the scene, by 1879 "sturdy frontiersmen" formed new alliances in Parker, Wise, and Jack counties of the Cross Timbers district of north central Texas.[6]

In the early 1880s, the alliances in Cross Timbers found themselves in the midst of a so-called "fence cutting war." Corporate ranchers had stretched barbed wire around tens of thousands of acres of grazing land, frequently closing off access to water and farmsteads. Gunmen protected corporate land claims and fences, while opponents of the fences organized in secret to cut the lines. The historian Robert McMath draws a parallel with the Cross Timbers fence war and the enclosure of the common lands of the English peasantry. In this interpretation, the precapitalist farmers of Cross Timbers, as with their English peasant counterparts, fought to defend a traditional culture based on mutuality, limited property rights in land, and self-sufficiency. The fence wars, according to McMath, reflected the resistance to the market economy that was "intruding more and more on Cross Timbers farmers." And out of this resistance emerged the movement culture of Populism.[7]

The conflict in Cross Timbers, however, looks quite different when it is taken into account that the district was at the epicenter of the boom of frontier speculation and development. The boom was driven by the farmers themselves and resulted in a conflict with cattle ranchers over competing claims to private property rights. Moreover, and this is the most critical element in terms of the genesis of the movement culture of Populism, the Farmers' Alliances played a key role as boosters of Cross Timbers development. The early Alliance members were acutely aware of the deficiencies of their relatively primitive and impoverished environment, an environment they strove to transform rather than perpetuate in the name of tradition. And they sought this transformation by boosting real estate values, strengthening links with the market, and developing the commercial structures of a modern agricultural society.[8]

Although the fence war in Cross Timbers was largely bloodless, the stakes were high in an environment of intense land speculation. A land fever gripped Texas. "Farmers are pouring into western Texas so fast," according to an 1886 newspaper report, "that ranchmen have just enough time to move their cattle out and prevent their tails being chopped off by the advancing hoe." The hoe advanced relentlessly, with a nearly tenfold increase in the state's improved acres between 1870 and 1890. In the Cross Timbers counties the population multiplied by a factor of six in the 1870s alone. Once settled, farmers boosted further immigration as the surest means for their own success. The furious pace of settlement came to a temporary halt when severe drought hit the Cross Timbers in the summer of 1886, a setback typical of the boom and bust of the farmers' frontier.[9]

Ranchers' fences posed a threat to landless cattlemen who wanted free grass for their cattle, and to cowboys who lost employment because of the new fencing technology. The sharpest conflict, however, took place where farm settlement pushed into grazing lands claimed by corporate land syndicates. The farmers perceived that the syndicates, based in New York and London, stood for alien land ownership, monopoly land grabbing, and lawlessness that impeded rural progress. The farmers, on the other hand, stood for law and order, affirmation of land titles, capital improvements, and dense settlement. Even worse than the ranchers' fencing, a Cross Timbers farmer testified, were the line riders who enforced with six-shooters the marked-off property lines claimed by the corporate landowners. "Line-riding is opposed to every interest in Texas," the farmer explained. "It opposes the development of the frontier; it is against the introduction of railways; it prevents the erection of churches; it is opposed to the building of schools."[10]

The fence war in Cross Timbers was part of a confrontation that extended up the Great Plains to the Canadian border. Farmers especially resented the ranchers' illegal fences on the public domain. The farmers did not view the public lands as a public commons of the traditional past, but as lands designated for private development. When Farmers' Alliance platforms insisted that the public land was "the heritage of the people," they meant that it should be parceled out as private "homesteads for actual settlers." By breaking the cattle monopoly over the public domain in eastern Colorado, a farmer reported, it was now possible to "get up a boom" for farming and town building. The end of the free range, the farmer was glad to note, presented new opportunities for the "homeseeker and investor," encouraging immigration by "actual settlers" with the assurance of "good and perfect title" to the land. Such was the context of the fence wars across the farmers' frontier, where two patterns of private property rights overlapped, one favoring the rancher, the other the farmer. Accordingly, the conflict resulted in a double enclosure of the open range. As a Kansas newspaper explained, the grazing controversy was "now being settled in favor of both parties by the barbed-wire fence." Cattle ranchers strung wire to keep their cattle in; staple-crop farmers strung wire to protect their crops and keep the cattle out.[11]

The farmer-rancher conflict took place within the larger context of expropriation of lands held by nonwhite peoples. In the cultural world of farm reform, civilization was by nature white or "Anglo-Saxon"; those communities that did not fit this category had little choice but to make way for the next stage of historical development. On the centennial of the U.S. Constitution, a Farmers' Alliance newspaper in North Carolina carried a front-page illustrated commemoration marking "Progress of 100 Years." Along with the railroad, the phonograph, the telegraph, and the Brooklyn Bridge, it depicted the opening of the West and "Indian Fighting" as milestones of the nation's progress.[12]

In the Indian Territory, white farmers pushed to open lands to white settlement. They made use of new fence laws to kill or confiscate Indian horses and cattle. Many white farmers also supported the Dawes Severalty Act of 1887 that divided up tribal lands into 160-acre private tracts for Indians and parceled the rest for private purchase by white settlers. The Farmers' Alliance endorsed the aggressive claims on tribal land. William Peffer, Alliance leader, editor of the *Kansas Farmer*, and future Populist U.S. senator, explained that "intelligent Indians feel the pressure of civilization" and would accept the dismantling of tribal property. But even if they did not, "the few Indians must give way to the common good."[13]

The Indians did have their defenders. Significantly, the Arkansas-based Agricultural Wheel voiced support for Indian treaty rights. This support reflected the Wheel's efforts to organize in the Indian Territory and the relatively inclusive racial outlook of its leader Isaac McCracken. Holding its national convention nine months after the passage of the Dawes Act, the Wheel expressed concern that railroad corporations and land syndicates would take advantage of allotment to seize Indian lands, and demanded that "the government shall protect the Chickasaws and Choctaws, and other civilized Indians of the Indian Territory, in all their inalienable rights."[14]

Thomas Bland and other reformers in Populist circles explicitly rejected the allotment policy. The Populist novelist Hamlin Garland also worked to preserve Indian lands. At the same time, Garland tended to accept that the logic of progress meant that Indians, "like children," needed fenced reservations for their protection. Nevertheless, views favoring the preservation of Indian land were always in the minority. William Peffer expressed the opinion of a broader Populist constituency when he declared that "the time for bartering with the Indians for their land is passed . . . we need all the land in this country for homes."[15]

New Mexico posed especially complex problems for the Anglo American settlers. Centuries of Spanish and Mexican settlement had left established patterns of land use and ownership. Cattle syndicates bought out vast individual land grants and also attempted to fence lands within the communal land grants. White Farmers' Alliance members occasionally made common cause with Hispanic farmers against the cattlemen. In San Miguel County

Hispanos organized a militant People's party in the midst of a bitter struggle to protect the communal holdings of the Las Vegas Community Grant from the land grabbing of Anglo ranchers. For most white farm reformers in New Mexico, as elsewhere, the privately held homestead remained the model of rural development.[16]

When the dust of the fence war settled in the Cross Timbers counties of Texas, the Farmers' Alliance turned its attention to the business of boosting real estate values. The key to success was attracting investors and white settlers. In the spring of 1884, William L. Garvin, then president of the Texas Farmers' Alliance, along with other prominent citizens in the district, organized the Commonwealth Immigration Society. The society contested the elections in Jack County on a platform of curbing land monopolies and "encouraging immigration and populating the lands of the state." Although Garvin gained the office of county treasurer, Joseph N. Rogers, the publisher of the state Alliance newspaper *Rural Citizen*, sought to avoid political experiments that might impede Alliance efforts to boost central Texas. The pages of the *Rural Citizen* promoted the "salubrious climate," "fertile soil," and excellent prospects for the immigrant in Jack County. "Our town has improvement written on every side," the *Citizen* boasted of the county seat; educators planned new institutions of learning, and farmers were "learning to handle their lands so they receive larger profits."[17]

Investing in Jack County involved the high-stakes gamble that development would entice a railroad into the district and thereby bring it "into connection with the business world." Without such a connection, investments were virtually worthless. The Farmers' Alliance lobbied hard to convince railroad managers that Cross Timbers would provide good sources of revenue. In the spring of 1886, the *Rural Citizen* organized a local "railroad meeting" in Jacksboro to offer railroad corporations "the hearty cooperation of our people to aid in the construction of a railroad," including "our willingness to contribute pecuniarily to the consumption of such an enterprise."[18]

The farmers of the Texas Alliances measured progress much as other boosters did. When the railroad arrived in the small town of Rockwall, the Farmers' Alliance press reported on new schools, county offices, churches, business houses, and the other signs of "push and energy." The establishment of the weekly *Rockwall Success* newspaper, with its featured Farmers' Alliance column, provided further evidence that the district was "wide awake" and promised new arrivals commercial success. The fusion of boosterism and reform that marked the Texas Alliance also characterized the rural movement in much of the West and the South, as Farmers' Alliances and similar organizations from California to the Carolinas promoted invariably healthy climates, fertile soils, and profitable prospects.[19]

Railroad corporations often shared interests with farm reformers in boosting new farm settlement. Luna Kellie, who would serve as the secretary of the Nebraska Farmers' Alliance, left St. Louis for a Nebraska homestead with images in her mind of the "Golden West" provided by the promotional literature of the Burlington & Missouri Railroad. The B&M assured potential settlers of the "Best and Cheapest Lands," and "Tremendous Crops!!!" What most attracted Luna Kellie was the promotional literature's promise of homesteads within four miles of the state capitol and the university, where she hoped to obtain a degree. Nothing in the B&M literature prepared her for the shock of the desolate and hard life she would find on the windswept Nebraska prairie. She would later conclude that the railroad engaged in deceptive and predatory promotion. Such practices by the railroads and other corporate promoters, however, only succeeded to the extent that the new settlers—and the farmers' organizations that they built—played their part in the speculative cycle.[20]

In Kansas, the symbiotic relationship between farmers and railroads produced frenetic development. During the 1870s and 1880s, the population doubled and nearly doubled again as the promise of railway access to newly opened lands drew farmers into the state. At the same time, calculating the wheat and corn shipments of newly settled farmers, railroads expanded from less than 1,234 miles of track in 1870 to 8,797 miles in 1890. Farm reformers such as William Peffer fully understood that farming and promotion went hand in hand. He recognized that the flood tide of development would have its ebb, and warned readers of his *Kansas Farmer* against going crazy about a "windy" boom. But neither Peffer nor his wide readership questioned new settlement and railroads as imperatives of progress. The *Kansas Farmer* featured front-page reports boosting the less settled districts of Kansas and Colorado, with their excellent water sources, irrigation prospects, choice soils, "neat and tasty dwellings," and plans for new schools, courthouses, railway connections, and other "innovation[s] of prosperity."[21]

In much of the South, too, the rapid extension of the railroad spread new rural settlement and new prospects. Leonidas L. Polk, the founder of the Farmers' Alliance in North Carolina, seized the opportunity. As a young man he had inherited a farm of marginal value in Anson County near the South Carolina border. When word spread that the Carolina Central Railroad planned to lay a new line through his property, he took the risk of turning the family farmstead into a prospective new town. He divided his acres into lots and converted his farmhouse into a post office, store, and printing office, from which he published a weekly newspaper to boost his plan for a new agricultural center. He called the proposed town Polkton and his *Ansonian* newspaper advertised for farmers to settle and take advantage of the district's fine soil and healthful climate. The promotion worked, Polkton took hold, and as a successful booster Polk launched his career as North Carolina's leading advocate of rural modernization.[22]

"The railroad—the American John the Baptist in the wilderness," commented one observer of southern development, is "sounding forth the oncoming of a Christian civilization. . . . New towns and settlements are springing up along its path, good families are coming in, and all the uplifting agencies of civilization are found where solitude or a life merging on barbarism had prevailed." Significantly, newly settled areas of the South and the West formed strongholds of the Alliance movement.[23]

As the Farmers' Alliance expanded nationally from its Texas base, the movement's publicists wrapped Alliance history in the legends of the heroic deeds of the sturdy pioneers of the Texas frontier. Such legends resonated across much of rural America. After all, millions of farmers had similarly taken great risks in the high-stakes world of new land claims, new settlements, and new hopes of success on the international commodity markets. The experience of such rapid changes in the rural environment was what Richard Hofstadter identified as the nub of truth in Turner's "Frontier Thesis": American society was powerfully influenced by a "fast-developing capitalistic agriculture expanding into a rich terrain." The rural dynamics of boosterism and expansion helped shape the intellectual world of the farmers' revolt.[24]

During its formative years, the Farmers' Alliance remained ideologically amorphous. The most significant influences on the Alliance movement came from organizations with which the farmers had prior experience. Alliance members were versed in the teachings of the Protestant churches and in the political doctrines of the Democratic party. To learn about organization and political reform the Alliance looked to two groups with northern and eastern roots: the Patrons of Husbandry (Grange) and the Knights of Labor. Although the Grange had fallen from prominence, for many farmers it remained—with its cautious methods and limited claims—the model of agrarian organization. At the same time, the daring and assertive methods of the Knights of Labor on the railroads of Texas and the Southwest drew the attention of the region's farmers. Alliance members often held joint membership in the Knights, and many others sought cooperation with the labor organization.

The Farmers' Alliance also inherited the legacy of the Greenback movement with its doctrines of currency reform and labor rights. As well, farm reformers often belonged to the Masons, Odd Fellows, and other fraternal societies, and were acquainted with their codes of organization and mutuality. All of these ideological currents coalesced within the loose framework of the Alliance. The Alliance itself, however, lacked ideological definition. Both friends and foes of the Alliance pondered its meaning. Was it an immigration society? Was it a resurrected Grange? Was it a new labor organization? Was it a fraternal or social order? Was it an attempt to create an independent political party? These questions begged for answers.

By the spring of 1886, the fledgling Texas Alliance, pulled in multiple ideological directions, had fallen into disarray. Many within the Alliance wanted to join with the Knights of Labor in an anticorporate political campaign. Other Alliance members sought to stay out of political and labor conflict. Into the breach stepped a new leader with new ideas. As the incoming president of the Texas state organization, Charles W. Macune forged a new consensus. He redefined the Alliance as chiefly a business organization that would steer clear of political and labor strife. The "business standpoint" of the Farmers' Alliance, as Nelson Dunning explained, meant that farmers organized "for the same reason that our enemies do": for "individual benefits through combined effort," and to protect "your business" in "a selfish world."[25]

With this emphasis on business goals Macune sought to ward off accusations that the Farmers' Alliance was a dangerous or radical organization. His strategy paralleled developments in the labor movement. Following the Chicago Haymarket bombing in May of that same fateful spring of 1886, the Knights of Labor and other labor groups bore the brunt of an antiradical witch hunt. In the eyes of Samuel Gompers and other trade union leaders critical of the Knights, the persecution showed the necessity for political caution and the need to put labor on a "business basis." Similarly, Macune put farm reform on a business footing. At the same time, he promised rapid and dramatic results. He articulated a bold strategy for transforming the Texas Alliance into a formidable business organization, national in scope and claiming a pivotal position within American commerce.[26]

Broad enthusiasm for Macune's strategy reunified and energized Alliance ranks and, at least for the time being, checked the impulse toward political action. In a few short years, the Alliance experienced phenomenal growth, rising from a small society of Texas farmers to a powerful organization spanning the continent, with a membership outstripping any comparable national order. From its rickety ideological beginnings, the Alliance also adopted a relatively structured vision of agrarian renewal. This vision—with its focus on commercial power and progress—was inseparable from the name of Charles W. Macune. What contemporary observers referred to as "Macunism" came to define one of the main currents of Populist thought.

Among the weathered and bearded faces of the men who accounted for most of the leadership of the Texas Alliance, the well-trimmed Macune stood out for what he was not. He was not a farmer. He was not a southerner. In addition, Macune, unlike many of his colleagues, was not attracted to the siren of third-party politics. Paradoxically, these salient features of his background go

Figure 1.1. Charles Macune, architect of the Farmers' Alliance movement (Center for American History, University of Texas, Austin)

a long way toward explaining why his reform message carried such weight among southern farmers. His proven loyalty to the Democratic party and to the racial codes of his adopted region removed any stigma of carpetbaggery or northern tutelage. At the same time, as the consummate professional, he was uniquely qualified to deliver a message of agrarian modernization and business progress.

Born in 1851 in Kenosha, Wisconsin, Macune was raised in Freeport, Illinois, by his widowed mother. His father had earned his living as a blacksmith before dying of cholera en route to California while Charles was still an infant. During hard times when he was about ten years old, Charles was hired out to a German family for a six-month stint of farm labor. From this experience he acquired knowledge of German and a lifelong interest in foreign languages. As with many young men of his time, the farm also taught Macune that farming was not for him. At the age of fifteen, he moved to Chicago, where he worked as a druggist's assistant by day and studied pharmaceutical literature at night. With the completion of the Pacific railroad, he traveled to California before arriving in Texas in the summer of 1871. He pursued the study of medicine after trying his luck in business, and married Sallie Vickrey, a college graduate and "a very estimable and accomplished" Texas woman. In 1879 Macune purchased a farm outside of Cameron in Milam County. He maintained his medical practice in town, however, and hired help to manage the farm.[27]

His medical practice put Macune in contact with the lives of the farmers of central Texas. Through the lens of his urban background and professional training he observed the farmers' isolation, their primitive business methods, their low professional status, and their lack of power as a commercial interest. He joined the Milam County Farmers' Alliance in the spring of 1886. Soon thereafter he quit his medical practice to work for the Alliance full-time. He committed himself to transforming the as yet ill-defined Alliance into a national organization for the professional progress of the farmer. Precisely why he made this commitment remains unclear. His detractors within the movement would accuse him of running the Alliance for his private gain. Although such charges were never proven, he gave the appearance of being attached to the salary and other amenities that his elevated position offered. Macune, however, was not just a mercenary. Especially during the second half of his life he displayed a passion to remedy both medical and social ills, serving for a time as a medic for an American mission in Mexico. But his direction of the Farmers' Alliance proved by far his most successful enterprise.

In the eyes of his fellow Alliance members, Macune's erudition, professionalism, and business savvy made him just the person to build the Alliance into a commercial power. His visions for the Alliance were also well served by his "true blue" loyalty to the Democratic party. Although as a child in Illinois he had once met Abraham Lincoln, the adult Macune clung to the southern Democratic ethos more firmly and more inflexibly than many of his southern-born colleagues. After settling in Texas, he showed no tolerance for either Lincoln's party or even for the ambiguities of multiparty competition. In 1874 Macune took over the editorship of the Burnett *Bulletin*, a Democratic weekly. He used the *Bulletin*'s editorial page to attack the Reconstruction governor Edmund J. Davis, warning that "the vitality of the South rests upon the issue between the carpetbagger and the honest Democrat."[28] Indeed, Macune exemplified the anti-carpetbagger. If other Alliance leaders—many of whom had taken part in Greenback, Union Labor, or other independent campaigns—could be accused of aspirations for turning the

Alliance into a political vehicle, his loyalty to the Democratic party was un-assailable. His confidence in Democratic rule was such that he saw no need to bring party affairs into the Alliance. This lent credibility to the ideal of build-ing the Alliance as a nonpartisan business association and allowed Macune to build bridges between loyal Democrats and third-party advocates.

By the fall of 1886, Alliance farmers elevated Macune, the nonfarmer with only months of experience in the organization, to the post of ex-officio presi-dent of the Texas Alliance. A year later, Alliance historians were already memorializing him as a "hero" and "a great leader" who had given expres-sion to "the spirit and principles which are struggling for life and expression in the popular mind." The following year, as president of the National Farm-ers' Alliance and Industrial Union (NFAIU), also known as the Southern Alliance, Macune moved to the nation's capital to direct the expansion of what was soon to become the largest and most powerful farm organization the country had ever known.[29]

The Farmers' Alliance expanded exponentially. In the three years between 1886 and 1889, the Texas Alliance grew from 38,000 to 225,000 members, enrolling into its suballiances 46 percent of the eligible population of the state. Eligibility for membership was defined as white persons over sixteen years of age engaged in agriculture and related pursuits, including country doc-tors, preachers, editors, and teachers (and excluding most nonwhite people, as well as most lawyers, bankers, merchants, and saloon keepers). In many rural districts the Alliance enrolled virtually the entire white community.[30]

From its Texas base, the Alliance spread rapidly across the cotton South, organizing unorganized farmers and successfully fusing with other groups. At its first national convention held at Shreveport in the fall of 1887, the Alliance merged with the Arkansas-based Agricultural Wheel. The Wheel had experienced its own spectacular growth across several southern states in the late 1880s, making the unified NFAIU a formidable organization. The Alli-ance also merged with Farmers' Unions in Florida and Louisiana and the Farmers' Clubs in North Carolina. Within a year of the 1888 merger, the North Carolina Alliance would claim 72,000 members in 1,816 local units.[31]

Macune's NFAIU or Southern Alliance soon reached north into the Wheat Belt. In Kansas, influential editors of the reform press, including Peffer of the *Kansas Farmer* and the Vincent brothers (Henry, Leo, and Cuthbert) of the *Nonconformist*, embraced Macune's project. By the spring of 1890, the NFAIU claimed 100,000 members in Kansas. The NFAIU also established a strong base in the Dakotas and successfully recruited in the Rocky Moun-tain states, enrolling some 15,000 members in Colorado. It enjoyed similar success on the Pacific Coast. In April of 1890, Texas organizer James S. Barbee set up the first California suballiance in Santa Barbara County with a total of eight members. A year and a half later, the California Farmers' Alliance claimed 30,000 members, enrolled in 500 suballiances, organized under 34 county alliances across the state.[32]

In the Northeast, Macune's Alliance organized farmers in New Jersey, Pennsylvania, and New York, but in much smaller numbers than elsewhere in the country. In much of the Midwest, the expansion of the NFAIU was slowed by the reality that many midwestern farmers were already organized. They divided their loyalties between the Grange and two other farm reform organizations: the Farmers' Mutual Benefit Association (FMBA), with its roots in southern Illinois; and Milton George's Chicago-based National Farmers' Alliance (known as the Northern or Northwestern Alliance). In Illinois, both Alliances maintained a following but neither matched the strength of the FMBA with its 50,000 members. Macune's negotiations to merge his Southern Alliance with the Northern Alliance and with the FMBA ultimately failed, despite the similarity of the three organizations. Nonetheless, the crusading energy of Macunism was duly felt within the other farm groups. Farmers experienced a new sense of organizational strength. As Alliance lecturer Lizzie Clark Hardy explained before a gathering in Oak Grove, Illinois, "power born of systematic organization" was opening "a new era" to the farmer.[33]

Macune emulated the organizational systems of other business and professional associations of the day. From his Washington office, he directed the Alliances' lobbying efforts on national legislation. He oversaw the network of reform newspapers under the auspices of the Rural Reform Press Association. And he edited the NFAIU's official newspaper, the *National Economist*, mailed to 100,000 weekly subscribers. Beneath the central offices, the organization maintained clearly delineated lines of authority. At the neighborhood level, suballiances—at times with as few as half a dozen members—gathered farmers in local schoolhouses and lodges. The suballiances organized under the direction of the county alliances that, in turn, sustained the powerful state alliances. Each level of the Alliance pyramid elected a president, business agent, secretary, treasurer, and other officers. Linking the organizations into a single whole, a system of Alliance lecturers, organizers, editors, and corresponding secretaries spread the organizational net over much of rural America.[34]

This level of organization required a dedicated cadre. Many Alliance organizers had professional experience as teachers, editors, ministers, or doctors. Men and women recognized for their intellectual or management skills held the more responsible positions. The Alliance cadre were more educated than their rural neighbors. They also harbored high expectations for a prosperous and culturally rich life, making the surroundings of rural isolation and poverty especially onerous. They responded accordingly to Macune's message of commercial prosperity through professional and intellectual improvement.

The dedication of these "local intellectuals" of rural America made possible a deep and broad organizational campaign, mobilizing both the schooled as well as the practically illiterate members of the Alliance movement.[35]

Macune had little patience for old agrarian nostrums. He rejected claims voiced at times by Grangers and other reformers that a special debt was owed to the farmers due to their elemental relationship to the soil. According to the old agrarianism, because the soil was presumed to be the source of all wealth, the nation was uniquely obligated to ensure the farmers' prosperity. Macune, however, dismissed the idea that farming played an exceptional place in the creation of wealth. He believed, citing Adam Smith's *Wealth of Nations*, that agriculture constituted a commercial interest like any other. He explained that Smith had refuted the fallacy that "agriculture was the only source of producing wealth, and that all other occupations only modified the wealth produced by agriculture, but in no way increased the volume of wealth possessed by the nation as the result of agricultural production."[36]

Farmers needed to organize not because of some primordial tie to the land but because they constituted a commercial interest on a par with the other commercial interests in modern society. "All the different classes and occupations of society," Macune noted, "are engaging in organization for mutual advancement and protection to a greater extent than ever before in the history of the world. In fact, we may say that every calling is organized. This thorough organization has created a new order of things." The new order made it imperative that the farmers also organize. To fail to do so would only perpetuate the farmers' relative poverty, ignorance, and lack of power.[37]

Macune's business ideology infused the Farmers' Alliance with a new sense of purpose. Like the Grange, the Farmers' Alliance adopted secret rituals to initiate new members and secure the privacy of its meetings. But whereas the Grange ritual focused on ancient lore to reinforce group identity, Macune stressed secrecy as the function of a "business organization for business purposes."[38] Leonidas L. Polk, who would succeed Macune as president of the NFAIU, noted that its meetings were secret for the same reason that meetings of bank directors or railroad executives were secret. "Business men who have succeeded," noted the Alliance in Bluff, North Carolina, "never made it a point to tell their plans."[39] Or, as a farmer from Colorado County, Texas, explained, physicians, lawyers, and every other vocation maintained a system of professional secrecy: "No member of any business firm would long retain his position if he should allow the community to know the means used to forward the enterprise." The Alliance farmer was no exception.[40]

Charles Macune believed that if farmers were to be organized on business principles they must do so on a strictly whites-only basis. Accordingly, ra-

cial exclusion was a foundational principle of Macune's organizational system. As widely understood in the modern, reform-minded business community in the American South, the future lay in strict segregation of the races.
The clubs, societies, and associations where white professionals and business-
people met and discussed matters of commerce and progress excluded nonwhite members. In the same spirit, Macune's Farmers' Alliance vigorously
pursued the whites-only principle. This had major repercussions for the
organization, especially in the rural South where in many counties blacks
and whites lived and worked in close proximity.

Black tenants and laborers frequently toiled on the farms of white owners. Occasionally the reverse was true. Black women often took in the laun-
dry or cleaned the homes of more prosperous whites. Black and white farmers
might conduct business with the same white merchants, creditors, and purchasing agents. Otherwise, blacks and whites usually moved in worlds apart.
They attended separate schools, prayed in separate churches, and created
separate fraternal societies. But a number of spaces opened in this wall of
nonassociation. Most notably, farm and labor movements made significant
experiments in biracial organizing.[41]

In the early 1880s, the Knights of Labor welcomed black members and
pledged "in the broad field of labor" to make "no distinction on account of
color." Although blacks usually belonged to separate lodges and sat in separate sections when in racially mixed meetings, black and white members also
made public displays of solidarity as they joined efforts in boycotts, strikes,
and parades. Moreover, the Farmers' Alliance, even with its whites-only
clause, initially allowed for dual membership in the Knights, a policy that
offered possibilities for cooperation across racial lines.[42]

The potential for such cooperation captured much public attention in the
spring and summer of 1886, when the events surrounding the Great Southwest Railway Strike unleashed a wave of protest. The Knights, often in conjunction with the Farmers' Alliance, sponsored political mobilizations across
Texas, and the conservative press sounded the alarm to the dangerous rise of
the Knights as a political force. The press took pains to alert whites to the role
of black section hands in the strike and especially to black participation in the
insurgent political conventions. Democrats warned white farmers of the danger posed by an "army of blacks" under the command of the Knights.[43]

Commenting on the racial abuse heaped on the southern Knights of Labor,
a black member of the order in North Carolina noted that whites "kept crying 'Nigger! Nigger!' until the two words 'Nigger' and 'Knights' became syn-
onymous terms."[44] This posed a dilemma for white farm reformers, who
weighed their options carefully. A coalition with the Knights and black labor
promised power in numbers. Isaac McCracken, of the Agricultural Wheel,
was among those farm leaders who wanted to test this power. In July 1886,

the Wheel called a meeting of delegates from Arkansas, Tennessee, Missouri, and elsewhere to organize a National Wheel and to strengthen cooperation with the beleaguered Knights. McCracken also proposed to drop the whites-only eligibility clause. After heated debate, the delegates of the white Wheels agreed to accept black Wheels into the order. Similarly in Florida, the Farmers Union also joined white and black farmers' clubs in a statewide organization.[45]

Charles Macune and the Farmers' Alliance moved in the opposite direction. The Alliance held to its whites-only clause and adopted a rule to prohibit dual membership with the Knights. Even collaboration between the two groups ran counter to the type of racial barriers the Alliance sought to build. In Robertson County, Texas, for example, blacks and whites made up roughly equal parts of the farm population. Nonetheless, as one white member of the local Alliance put it, to take "stock with the Knights of Labor will prove fatal," as the Farmers' Alliance was "strictly a white man's institution."[46]

When Macune negotiated mergers with the Agricultural Wheel and the Florida Farmers Union he demanded that these organizations exclude their black members, which they eventually agreed to do. [47] For Macune the ban on nonwhite membership was a strategic necessity, as he believed that the type of commercial combination farmers needed could not risk the perils of association with black laborers either in strikes or in political adventures. The whites-only clause also provided a message of sophistication expected of a modern and progressive business association. This message was especially important in the South, but it probably enhanced the Alliance's professional image in the North and West as well.

The Farmers' Alliance shifted the configuration of rural associational life. Rural Americans, much like their urban and small-town counterparts, tended to be "joiners" in an array of voluntary organizations. The act of joining, however, was also an act of exclusion. When members (whether black or white) attended their separate churches, met in their separate fraternal orders, or polled for their separate political parties, they did so as Baptists or Methodists, Freemasons or Odd Fellows, Republicans or Democrats, men or women. The Farmers' Alliance overrode such distinctions. It united entire districts by dismantling walls of exclusion based on religious creed, fraternal order, political party, or sex. The whites-only rule remained the salient marker of exclusion. Especially in the more remote districts, the Alliance often included virtually all whites in the neighborhood. African Americans might live over the hill or work the adjacent field, yet such neighbors had no place in the strictly white society of the Farmers' Alliance.[48]

Alliance bonds of mutual help among whites could and did translate into collective harm against blacks. Such was the case, for example, when the Centennial Alliance, in Bell County, Texas, called a special meeting to censure a local white employer for hiring and allegedly "giveing preforance" to black laborers. A local Alliance in Screven County, Georgia, ordered members to refuse leases to blacks to ensure that they would instead be compelled to work for white farmers.[49] In North Carolina, the Pitt County Alliance resolved to protest public funding for black schools, and the Churchill Alliance in Warren County sought legal restrictions to protect white landlords against "unfaithful" black tenants and field hands.[50] As a black member of the Knights of Labor put it, the Farmers' Alliance offered the black laborer nothing but "oppression and death."[51]

As the successes of the white Farmers' Alliance trumped efforts at biracial organizing, black farmers and laborers built their separate associations. These included several Colored Alliances that emerged in eastern and central Texas in the wake of the labor crisis of 1886. Andrew J. Carothers, a white Allianceman from Lee County, organized one of the two largest of these groups. The other started in Houston County and, although it had a black president, a black secretary, and a blacks-only eligibility clause, selected as its general superintendent the Reverend Richard Manning Humphrey, a white farmer who also ministered over several black Baptist congregations. Both Colored Alliances expanded rapidly in Texas and across the South. In January of 1890 the two groups merged into the Colored Farmers' National Alliance and Cooperative Union, reporting a combined membership of nearly 1.2 million black farmers including 300,000 women, although such membership claims tended to be inflated.[52]

The rivalry between the two Colored Alliances had bitterly divided rural black communities. To give thanks for the end of hostilities members took a Saturday off work to pray in their churches. General Superintendent Humphrey advised them to "spend no part of this, your sacred day, about the streets nor in idle gossip."[53] His admonition reflected Humphrey's own severe religiosity. It also corresponded to the reality that the Colored Alliance was a semi-clandestine movement based primarily in the black churches. The hostility and violence of white farmers compelled black farmers to organize out of the sight of whites and in the sanctuary of their churches. Whereas the white Alliance claimed secular and public space, issued demands from the steps of courthouses, and rallied on the county fairgrounds, black farmers carefully avoided public displays that would bring retribution from the white community. The presence of white officers in the Colored Alliance, including several state superintendents, also helped assure whites "that there is no danger of the present leaders advising [black members] to do anything wrong."[54] Humphrey, in particular, had the trust of white Alliance members who knew him as "a polished scholar, a Christian gentleman and honored minister of the gospel."[55]

Apart from a handful of white officers, the Colored Alliance barred whites from membership. It did so in response to the exclusionary policy of the white

Alliance. "If white organizations shall positively prohibit the [admission] of colored men to its membership," the Colored Alliance stated, "colored organizations shall prohibit the admission of white men to membership."[56] If local white alliances resolved against the hiring of black labor, a local alliance of black farmers in Alabama resolved "not to hire white folks."[57] The separate-but-equal doctrine had its advantages, as exclusive organization offered autonomy from white supervision. "We don't want social equality," explained J. W. Carter, a black spokesperson for the Georgia Colored Alliance. "All the Negro wants is protection. You white people attend to your business and let us alone."[58]

The Colored Alliance attempted to create organizational machinery that resembled the white Alliance, but the two organizations had starkly unequal possibilities. The tenuous structure of the Colored Alliance rested on a loose network of supportive ministers. Rural pastors often sympathized with the Colored Alliance, and its membership largely corresponded to their congregations. This relationship to the churches helps to clarify why the order could claim over a million members although it was virtually without literature, newspapers, lecturers, or other means of independent organization. Nonetheless, even the possibility that the desperately impoverished black cotton farmers had embarked on systematic organization was understood as a sign that dynamic developments were unfolding in rural America.[59]

"One thing is certain," observed Nelson Dunning, "organization as a factor of our modern civilization has come to stay . . . its benefits will be sought under all conditions and by all classes of people."[60] The farming business needed to be organized accordingly. Yet, farming was a special type of business. Even with its dynamic growth, much of the farming enterprise remained stuck in the rut of age-old routines. The technical state of agriculture lagged behind other industries. And rural life lacked material comforts and intellectual and cultural opportunities available in city and town.

In the South, new railroads, new towns, and new promise did little to change the regime imposed by the cotton crop. In the late nineteenth century, growing cotton still demanded intense and grinding labor that began in the spring when farmers turned the soil with one-mule plows. They chopped the weeds with hand hoes in the blazing heat of summer. The harvest, with its intense labor demands, lasted through the first winter frosts as men, women, and children picked cotton bolls until their hands bled. The drudgery of the cotton crop took a heavy toll on mind and body, and gave minimal returns. Bound up with a system of class and racial caste, the cotton regime left those at the bottom of the system in a vicious cycle of debt to merchants and landlords. Many cotton farmers struggled to provide shoes or proper clothes for their families, much less schoolbooks and a functional education. When the cotton farmers followed the railroad into new lands, they brought with them the old regime of overwork, ignorance, and poverty.[61]

In the West, farm mechanization held much promise for the ambitious grain farmer. The giant bonanza farms in the Dakotas showed that the "factory system" of large-scale mechanized farming could be applied to the production of wheat and small grains. The bonanza farm, however, mainly succeeded in boosting real estate values as settlers arrived in search of their private bonanza. Most western farmers had modest, family-based operations. Horse-drawn mechanical harvesters made it possible to cover more acres than harvesting by hand, but offered little relief from the dreary and exhausting cycles of field work, or from the dust, grasshoppers, and isolation that plagued the farmers on the newly opened Great Plains.[62]

Farm reformers believed that part of the solution was equity. The relative poverty and lack of progress in agriculture was the result of the railroad managers' discriminatory freight rates, the corporate purchase of corrupt legislators, and the bankers' control of credit and money. However, the reform imagination went beyond simply establishing a level playing field between industry and agriculture. Farm reformers also sought a more cultured, more productive, more modern life—a life that would transcend the limits of overwork, mud, and desolation, to realize a "higher civilization" in rural America.

American farmers in the 1880s and 1890s had little premonition of the drastic decline in the farm population that accompanied twentieth-century improvements in farm productivity. On the contrary, they often expressed optimism about a technology-driven rural renaissance. In 1891, the Princeton sociologist Walter Wyckoff recorded the thoughts of a Pennsylvania farmer about the relative position of agriculture and industry in modern society. The farmer noted that, in face of the encouraging advances in farm machinery and agricultural chemistry, farming was still "a long way behind" other industries. Farming still relied on human and animal muscle, "and a man's work or a team's work is pretty much what it was a hundred years ago." But he expressed confidence that "the farming business will soon catch up with the others" as agriculture adopted modern business practices and scientific methods. "I've got an idea that when the farming business is developed," the farmer told Wyckoff, "there'll be a big change in country life. Where there's plenty of brains and push and enterprise, there's likely to be excitement."[63]

The Farmers' Alliance movement embraced a similar hope for "a big change in country life." The movement would bring brains and push and enterprise to the rural districts. It would help close the urban-rural gap. It would stimulate the building of schools and colleges, putting a modern education within reach of Luna Kellie and the other young women and men of America's rural homesteads. As steam power had proved of limited value in agricultural applications, reformers such as William Peffer and Mary Elizabeth Lease believed that electric power would finally liberate farmers from the back-bending toil of farm work.[64] In short, for the farm reformers of the 1880s and early 1890s, nothing precluded the possibility that organization, business methods, education, and technology would place the rural countryside in the forefront of a modern nation.

2

Knowledge and Power

Machinery of Modern Education

In the winter of 1892, P. G. Temple set a modest proposal before the regular January meeting of the Gillespie County, Texas, Farmers' Alliance. He suggested that the Alliance send a memorial to the managers of the Columbian World's Fair in Chicago. The exposition, scheduled to open the next year, promised to put on display "the world's resources and progress in every department of human effort."[1] In Temple's view, justice demanded that the men and women responsible for producing this wealth also be represented at the fair. Temple proposed that the exposition managers

> take steps to represent the people who have created all this magnificense & luxury, with their surroundings in true life. Let the world of pleasure leisure & style, see the men & women in their jeans, faded calicos, & cotton checks who by their labor & handicraft, have made it possible for such an Exhibit. Let the farmers's cabin, the miners shanty & the tenement of factory hands be beside those magnificent buildings which represent the State &, the Nation.[2]

Temple's proposal captured much about how rural reformers understood the injustices and divisions cleaving American society. He gave expression to a social critique shared by millions of late nineteenth-century farmers: the submission of the laboring classes to the mounting burdens of debt, poverty, and overwork corresponded to the fantastic growth of monopoly, luxury, and ill-gotten corporate wealth.

Farm reformers understood that holding the World's Fair in Chicago—rather than in Berlin, Paris, or New York—presented an opportunity. Chicago formed the hub of a rail network that made attendance at the fair a practicality for millions of American farmers. Milton George, leader of the Northern Farmers' Alliance and editor of the *Western Rural*, expressed the optimism of his far-flung agrarian readership. "The opportunities for acquiring knowledge will be so complete, and the general thirst for knowledge will be so great," he predicted, "that nothing but an empty pocketbook will prevent people from going day after day." The fair would provide both spectacle and education, holding congresses of scientists, educators, authors, artists, religionists, reformers, mechanics, and agriculturalists. The exposition, George forecast, "will be a vast educational power."[3]

"Sell the cook stove if necessary," the novelist Hamlin Garland wrote to his father back on the family's Dakota wheat farm. "You *must* see this fair." Garland's father and invalid mother made the seven-hundred-mile trip, joining the pilgrimage to the "White City" on Lake Michigan.[4] Of the twelve million visitors to the fair, apart from Chicagoans, the largest contingent came from the farms and villages of the Mississippi Valley. The pilgrims came to satisfy their curiosity about "almost everything in which the human race is interested."[5]

In the Agricultural Building visitors learned of Russian wheat and rye, Japanese barley, Trinidadian sugar, and Javanese rice. They studied exhibits about the global commodity markets, demonstrating the position of American farmers vis-à-vis British, German, and other purchasers, as well as Argentine, Russian, Indian, Australian, and other competitive producers. The exposition displayed what M. J. Buchanan, editor of the *Prairie Farmer*, called "a composite picture of the natural and manufactured food resources of the habitable parts of the globe." In so doing it provided American farmers with lessons about the challenges they faced in the national and global economy. "There is no avoiding the fact that to succeed," Buchanan argued, "the farmer must take the same trouble to thoroughly know his business, must put in the same hours of close study, use the same skill, the same shrewdness and good management displayed by the successful broker, banker or manufacturer."[6]

The French, German, and other exhibits about agricultural education provoked pointed commentaries in the reform press. The exhibits, according to Buchanan, provided an "educational object lesson" for the American farmer. The United States lagged behind in agricultural knowledge. To compete, he argued, the public schools needed to provide relevant training, and the "country school house can, and should be greatly improved." American farmers also required the support of government experiment stations, agricultural colleges, and farmers' institutes.[7]

The World's Fair did not introduce the American farmer to the harsh realities of global commodity markets or to the inequities of rural education; rather, it reaffirmed lessons taught by swift changes in late nineteenth-century rural life. The systematic expansion of the telegraph and railroad networks, the "second information revolution," transformed America's agricultural heartland. The accelerated pace and volume of "business intelligence," as it was known at the time, shrank the commercial world of the farmer as never before. The telegraph turned the farmers' cotton, wheat, and corn into commodities on the modern mercantile exchanges in Chicago, New York, and St. Louis. Friday's closing prices at Liverpool and London markets became talking points in the villages of the Texas Cotton Belt and the wheat towns of California's San Joaquin Valley. The telegraph fed a national network of weekly rural newspapers, as the increasing speed of railroads brought early editions of metropolitan dailies to breakfast tables hundreds of miles from Chicago, Atlanta, St. Louis, and San Francisco.[8]

Declining freight rates and the low cost of second-class postage facilitated the paperback revolution and booming rural markets in periodical and inexpensive literature. The influx of books, magazines, and newspapers from the big-city publishing houses exposed many farmers to the latest in social thought. Knowledge once "too rare and precious for the common herd," the Alliance and Populist lecturer Mary Elizabeth Lease explained, "is in our day cheaper than coal and more common than pork and beans. Macauley, Huxley and Spencer are the daily companions of the coal heaver, the 'hewer of wood and drawers of water.'" At the same time, the exposure to modern schools of thought accentuated the limits that the farm environment imposed on intellectual and cultural development. Similarly, the emergence of land-grant colleges and other centers of scientific and technical research caught the attention of rural Americans, while underscoring the obstacles many poorly schooled farmers and their children faced in accessing scientific and technical knowledge.[9]

The Farmers' Alliance and kindred associations rested much of their hope for rural modernization on science-based education. The aspirations of the farm reformers occasionally clashed with those of academic officials and scientists when it came to decisions about curriculum and personnel. From the farmers' perspective, it was difficult to trust university officials who seemed to lavish resources on future lawyers, doctors, ministers, and other professionals, but showed little interest in training professional farmers. At the same time, academic administrators and scientists tended to read the farmers' resentments as confirmation that the rural population was indifferent to modern education.

In writing about farmer-academic conflict, historians have tended to cast academic experts in the role of modernizers battling to overcome the inertia of "reluctant farmers," who were mired in tradition and unconvinced of the value of education.[10] "Most farmers" embraced an agrarian traditionalism, as one historian explains, that led them to have "little interest in and some hostility toward the move to establish colleges."[11] Attitudes toward education, as another historian recently wrote of western farmers, were based on "deep-seated traditionalism, lack of education and understanding of modern science." Accordingly, "the farmers' antipathy toward new ways was directed against the just-founded land-grant universities, whose mission it was to improve agriculture."[12]

The ranks of farmers—as in the ranks of every other sector of American society—included people who lacked an understanding of modern science and distrusted "new ways." However, this was never the bone of contention in the farmer-academic conflict. The Farmers' Alliance and other organizations involved in this conflict led the movement for "new ways" in agriculture and put a premium on science-based education. Both farmers' organizations and college personnel agreed, as Alan Marcus has pointed out, that "making modern farmers or farmers modern stood as the *raison d'etre* for agricultural education." Where they disagreed was over the methods the universities should use to deliver on this promise, with farm organizations stressing the business side of scientific farming, and scientists stressing laboratory research skills.[13]

Farm reformers believed that closing the rural education gap was a prerequisite for improving rural life. Like many other Gilded Age Americans, they subscribed to the notion of progress through education. They shared this notion with urban reformers as well as with prosperous and politically conservative farmers. Education may not at first appear to be an effective fulcrum for a protest movement in that the reformers' commitment to education afforded points of confluence with the political and business elite. The Farmers' Alliance often enjoyed quite conservative company in its campaigns to expand state aid to education, land-grant colleges, experiment stations, and federal and state agricultural departments. Given such company, one might assume that expectations about education would diffuse protest, not sustain one of the most powerful social and political movements of the late nineteenth century. But education served to agitate, mobilize, and organize at the grass roots.[14]

P. G. Temple and his fellow Alliance members felt strongly about the injustice of the farmers' poverty and the capitalists' opulence, as demonstrated by his proposal to display farmers' cabins and workers' tenements at the World's Fair. But he also felt strongly about educational progress. His county Alliance gave him the responsibility of preparing a report on the Blair education bill, a proposal by the conservative New Hampshire Senator Henry W. Blair to expand federal support to public schools and colleges. Temple's report concluded that the bill "would be of more general benefit to the population of the U.S. than any now before Congress."[15]

For Senator Blair and the comfortable upper classes, the notion of educational progress provided succor. For Temple and his fellow farmers, it fanned the spirit of protest. Educational progress, they believed, constituted the great equalizer in commerce, technology, and social standing. And it conformed to their understanding of power within the dynamics of a modern world. Among their collective grievances, agrarian reformers bitterly assailed the monopolists' grip on "sources of intelligence" and access to knowledge. Believing in a progressive future, Farmers' Alliance members looked upon education as their most effective implement to shape the contours of that future. A young Texas woman, writing to the *Southern Mercury* under the pen name Country Girl, recommended that education was the one thing for which it was worth going into debt. After all, Country Girl argued, "Knowledge is Power."[16]

This axiom—"Bacon's famous direction," as another Texas woman put it—carried weight within the ranks of the farmers' movement. As Francis Bacon had "sounded the modern note" in Renaissance inquiry with his utilitarian stress on innovation, enterprise, and human improvement, farm reformers looked to education as a means to renovate, improve, and modernize rural life.[17] They sought to liberate rural people from what they perceived as the burdens of ignorance, mental inertia, and unsound habits. From its early stirring, the Farmers' Alliance defined itself as an educational movement. In 1881, at a rally on the steps of the Parker County, Texas, courthouse, S. O. Daws, the state lecturer for the Alliance, explained to the crowd that the organization's primary purpose was "the intellectual improvement of the farmers." By bringing neighbors together and establishing lending libraries, the Alliance could help overcome the farmers' "limited opportunity for mental culture."[18]

Farm reformers knew from harsh experience that the farming business was growing increasingly untenable for those lacking the latest in business and technical know-how. Without up-to-date methods, farmers simply could not keep pace with other commercial interests. Working smarter would mean having the ability to devote more time and energy toward improving the mental and cultural world of the farmer. "The old fashioned idea that farming does not require an education," Blanch McGarity lectured to her fellow Alliance members in Leesville, Texas, was a "false ignorant notion of the Dark Ages." Farmers needed both private and circulating libraries "where the best literature and information about farming can be gotten."[19]

By the late 1880s, the Alliance had grown to an intellectual enterprise that stretched across much of rural America. Its president, Charles Macune, articulated a philosophy of business education that gripped the imagination of the rural schoolteachers, ministers, doctors, and the often self-educated men and women who served as the cadre of the Alliance movement. This cadre built lecture circuits across some thirty states, and a network of approximately one thousand weekly newspapers.[20]

Hundreds of thousands of rural men and women took part in Alliance education, coming off their farms to attend Alliance lectures and classroom instruction. The regular biweekly or weekly meetings of the suballiances, often held in the local schoolhouse, were mainly educational functions. In a presentation on the proper agenda for a suballiance meeting, Florence Olmstead reported to her Alliance in Douglas County, Kansas, that "the educational part of our work is the most important of all, because upon that depends all the rest." The organizational side of the work, she proposed, should be reserved for the first part of meetings. Typically the balance was devoted to lectures, instruction, or research across a wide array of topics from science and history, to legislation and finance.[21]

Macune's educational system focused on professionalism and improved business methods. Just as his own diligent study of medical literature had raised his professional status, so too could farmers elevate their position. Farmers needed to sharpen their competitive edge. They needed to arm themselves with up-to-date knowledge of marketing and accounting. Typically, the Lone Tree Alliance in Jewell County, Kansas, followed its regular meetings with evening lessons in bookkeeping.[22] Farmers needed to exert control over information about crop yields, prices, interest rates, and other business intelligence. They needed a more acute understanding of their economic and political position vis-à-vis the other interests within modern commercial society. They needed to bring themselves up to an intellectual par with other professions by building up the Alliance movement as an agency of intellectual progress. The Alliance system of business education promised tangible improvements in the hard lives of farmers. As farmers seized this promise with passion and urgency, Macune projected that the Farmers' Alliance would soon be "the most powerful and complete educator of modern times."[23]

Macune's message of business education drew the attention of another important rural constituency: the progressive farmers dedicated to scientific farming. Leonidas L. Polk exemplified this constituency. Next to Macune, Polk was the Farmers' Alliance's most vital leader. In 1889 he succeeded Macune as the president of the National Farmers' Alliance and Industrial Union (NFAIU). He rose to national fame and many observers expected that he would be the People's party's presidential candidate in the 1892 elections. Unlike Macune, a new arrival to the South and a relative stranger to farming, Polk was a native southerner with a lifelong commitment to scientific farming and agricultural education.[24]

Polk was born in 1837 on a North Carolina cotton plantation situated on the edge of the coastal plain near the South Carolina line. His father died when he was thirteen years old, leaving the young Leonidas title to his share

Figure 2.1. Leonidas Lafayette Polk, president of the National Farmers' Alliance and Industrial Union (Southern Historical Collection, Wilson Library, University of North Carolina, Chapel Hill)

of two cotton gins, 1,848 acres of farmland, and thirty-two African American slaves. The Polk name had carried weight among the landholding gentry of the Carolinas since before the American Revolution. Perhaps it was also from his ancestors that he inherited his interest in agricultural innovation, a subject that had preoccupied planters in the region for generations. As a teenager he read agricultural journals that promoted "system" in managing slaves, soil enhancement, seed selection, and other problems of scientific farming. To pursue his interest, in 1855 he entered Davidson College, where he avoided the classical languages to study agricultural chemistry and other courses he found more worthwhile.[25]

After serving as a lieutenant in the Confederate army, Polk returned to farming and strove to put into practice the latest in agricultural know-how. But his stint at farming did not last long, as Polk soon sold his family farm in a lucrative real estate promotion, allowing him to pursue new opportunities as a merchant, cotton broker, and newspaper editor, and new efforts to modernize agriculture in North Carolina.

Polk campaigned to arouse his state from what he perceived as its post-war lethargy. It needed more "skill and energy and enterprise" if it was to "keep step with the progress of the age." To centralize the state's modernization efforts he lobbied for the establishment of a state department of agriculture. The legislature created such a department in 1877, appointing Polk as its first commissioner. "Our work means improvement, progress—or it means nothing," emphasized the new commissioner ensconced in his office in the state capital. In that spirit he promoted crop diversification and intensive cultivation. He standardized the chemical fertilizer industry. He launched experiments with Indian jute, German millet, sugar beets, chufa, and silkworms. Showing a special interest in upgrading the profitability of fish stocks, he imported "artificially impregnated" salmon eggs from California, releasing 589,000 Pacific salmon into North Carolina rivers.[26]

Polk's department also led the effort to enact new fence laws. For generations, North Carolina farmers constructed zigzag wooden fences around their crops to keep out free-roaming cattle and hogs. Building fences around crops may have been profitable in a time of abundant timber and slave labor to maintain the fences, argued the commissioner and his allies. But "from a modern point of view" this system was wasteful and inefficient. "In truth, in civilized life, nothing is absolutely or permanently stable, because civilization itself is too progressive," noted one of Polk's colleagues. "Its demand is always something new, something better." In this case, better meant replacing the long fences around crops with smaller fences around cattle and hogs, an innovation that would improve both livestock and soil, raise efficiency, and conserve forests. Polk cautioned that the new system must not be imposed on certain less settled regions where it would "doubtless work hardship and damage." But over time the people "must ultimately revolutionize long-established habits."[27]

The problem of immigration also weighed on Polk's mind. North Carolina needed an influx of settlers with capital and drive to develop underutilized farmlands. Polk hoped to stem the flow of white farmers heading to Texas and Arkansas seeking to "grow rich raising cotton." At the same time, he believed that without the gang system of slavery, black labor could never prove profitable. Like his schemes to replace Atlantic fish stocks with Pacific ones, he hoped for a solution to the labor problem by replacing African Americans with white immigrants from Europe and the North. Although previous efforts of the immigration societies and land companies had failed, Polk's Department of Agriculture systemized publicity to boost the state to potential settlers.[28]

Polk resigned his state office in 1880, took a position as the head of the state agricultural society, and went into business as a cotton broker and farm implement dealer. He sold farm equipment to make money, but he also subscribed to the imperative of equipping farmers with steam-powered machinery and the latest innovations in farm technology. As a sideline he manufactured and sold a patent medicine under the label "Polk's Diphtheria Cure." Although a later historian suggested that his patent medicine venture exemplified preprofessional quackery in American medicine, Polk desired professional legitimacy. He had his medicine chemically analyzed at the Agricultural Experiment Station in Chapel Hill, and took his patent business to New York where he organized a stock company and sought recognition from the French Academy of Medicine.[29]

Polk led the campaign for building an agricultural college to promote scientific farming. North Carolina reformers had been pushing for such a college since the 1850s, and Polk took up the cause as early as 1872. Fifteen years later his Farmers' Clubs helped make a state agricultural college a reality. The Farmers' Clubs were grassroots educational societies that usually met in local schoolhouses. The guiding hand of the clubs was Polk's *Progressive Farmer* newspaper. With the first issue in February of 1886, its editorials focused on the lack of "system" in agricultural education. At the time, the University of North Carolina received funding for this purpose under the federal land-grant laws. But the university had failed to offer a systematic curriculum for the scientific farmers of the future. "Give us a *system*," demanded the *Progressive Farmer*, as Polk's Farmers' Clubs lobbied for a new college. In 1887 the legislature voted to build a "College of Agriculture and Mechanic Arts," and Polk's reputation rose throughout the region as the founder of what is known today as North Carolina State University.[30]

That same year, the Interstate Convention of Farmers, representing the powerful cotton-growing interests of the South, held its first meeting in Atlanta. Recognizing Polk's contributions to scientific farming and agricultural education, the convention elected him as president, and he would hold that post until 1890. Henry W. Grady, editor of the Atlanta *Constitution*, and other leading lights of the New South business and educational elite also attended the convention. The wealthy planters who set much of the agenda for the meeting had little tolerance for the crusading spirit that attracted the debt-strapped poor to the Farmers' Alliance and agrarian protest. Yet Charles Macune, as one of the Texas delegates, felt quite at home in Henry Grady's company. Macune also made an impression on Polk, who recognized in the Farmers' Alliance a means to realize his lifelong goals of rural improvement. Macune and the membership of the Farmers' Alliance felt similarly about Polk. He may have stood at the pinnacle of the elite "agricultural-political complex." Within the Alliance movement, however, this was perceived as a strength and not as a weakness. The ranks of rural reform roiled with disputes about political alliances, women's rights, temperance, business strategies, and boycotts and labor strikes. But from "mudsill" to plantation owner,

Alliance members held remarkably noncontentious views about technology and scientific farming—staples of Alliance education.[31]

The rural reform press provided farmers with extensive reporting on developments in science and technology. Macune's *National Economist* set the pace. Its "Applied Science" columns informed readers of Louis Pasteur's latest work on rabies and the Royal Society's explorations in germ theory. Much of the reporting had immediate, practical implications. From Texas to the Dakotas, many farmers were new arrivals or were working with new soils and new crops under new marketing conditions. The *Rural Californian* and similar reform papers associated with the Alliance movement on the West Coast carried information about the production of citrus, figs, and subtropical fruits. For farmers in the Corn and Wheat Belts, newspapers such as Milton George's *Western Rural* and William Peffer's *Kansas Farmer* supplied exhaustive information about soda nitrate, fungicides, soil fertility, irrigation, tile drainage, and discoveries in horticultural and veterinary science.[32]

Through the clamor of enthusiasm for technological innovation rose occasional voices of concern. Any reader of farm literature would have been impressed—and possibly alarmed—at the possibilities for applied science on American farms. Writing under the headline "Progress and Its Troubles," a contributor to the *Western Rural* expressed anxiety about advances in strain selection and stockbreeding. The appearance of potato rot and other new blights, he argued, was proof of the dangers involved in man's ability "to change the domestic animals, fruits and vegetables from the original size, beauty and worth." Despite such reservations, the writer fully subscribed to the progressive mission. "Man was so constituted, both in his physical and mental make-up to be a progressive being," he concluded. "His five senses, his cerebrum and cerebellum, his muscles and mental foundation all center on one truth, that he must of necessity be progressive."[33]

The Farmers' Alliance and kindred organizations looked to state institutions of higher education as sources of scientific and practical knowledge. They lobbied long and hard to ensure that the land-grant colleges remained true to their original mission as centers for agricultural research and expertise. They demanded that colleges provide more access to farmers, and offer courses and build facilities more relevant to the business and scientific needs of future agriculturalists. Farmers accused the University of California of "teaching rich lawyers' boys Greek with the farmers' money." Colleges should teach the science of farming rather than draw the children of farmers to other professions. "Then what shall higher education be?" queried the resolutions of the Texas Farmers' Alliance at Cleburne. "Shall it be such as to lead the young man away from the farm and all other industrial pursuits, or shall it not rather be such as to make them better farmers?"[34]

General Stephen D. Lee, president of the Agricultural and Mechanical College of Mississippi, contributed regularly to Macune's *National Economist*. According to Lee, the "recent discoveries of science and art" had rendered the old literary curriculum obsolete. Charles Francis Adams had posed the problem at Harvard University, Lee noted, and public pressure had compelled the gradual introduction of chemistry, business, and other professional subjects into the college curricula. Only agriculture remained ignored. Under conditions of the world transportation revolution this neglect threatened the farmers' very existence. "The facility and cheapness of transportation has done away with all local competition," Lee argued. "In 1880 it cost 18 cents to transport a bushel of grain from the West to New York, or from New York to Liverpool. Now [1889] it only costs about 2 cents. So thrifty farmers in any country have not only to compete with each other, but with thrifty farmers in the West, and, in fact, all over the world." As a solution, Lee looked to the system of agricultural schools and colleges in Germany and France, where the education of the farmers had restored soil fertility and effected "a complete revolution in agriculture." By contrast, American yields declined and American farmers languished in relative ignorance. Without better education the American farmer would be left off the train of world progress.[35]

The new colleges must, as one midwestern farmer demanded, "bring science down out of the sky and hitch it to the plow." Farm organizations supported university extension services, agricultural stations, and other mainly state-centered institutions for the spread of technological knowledge. The Farmers' Alliances and Grangers lobbied for the Hatch Act of 1887 establishing federally funded agricultural experiment stations, which they hoped would serve as "general bureaus of information" in the farming districts. Reformers also looked to the experiment stations for modernizing innovations. William Peffer, for example, proposed federal funding for an experiment station to determine "if electricity can be profitably used and applied" to farm machinery.[36]

The Farmers' Alliance and other farm groups collaborated with state universities and state agricultural commissions to spread a system of lecture forums known as Farmers' Institutes. The institutes flourished on the Pacific Coast, where farmers in unfamiliar surroundings hungered for information about "what, where, and how to plant," and in the Southeast, with experts delivering papers on chemical fertilizers, orchard crops, dairy, and stock raising. In Alabama, Alliance leader and state agricultural commissioner Reuben Kolb used the institutes to promote experimental farming and his own political ambitions. As a hybrid organization linking the grass roots with the "agricultural-political complex," the Farmers' Institutes embodied a variant of the statist models for technical education that shaped the direction of agrarian protest.[37]

In some localities the Farmers' Alliances held aloof from the Farmers' Institutes to avoid accusations of misusing state funds or because of political and organizational conflicts. But in much of the South and West the Alliance cosponsored the Farmers' Institutes. William Peffer considered Farmers' Institutes a "great need" and, with the help of faculty from the State Agricultural College, organized them across Kansas. In California, the Alliance leader John S. Dore organized the first institute in Fresno County, and his Alliance neighbor and fellow raisin grower Douglas T. Fowler joined the faculty of the University of California as the state supervisor of the Farmers' Institutes. Similarly, in North Carolina, D. Reid Parker, the state lecturer of the Farmers' Alliance and a professor at Trinity College (now Duke University), organized the state's Farmers' Institutes, in which Leonidas Polk also played a prominent role.[38]

Scientific farming had its limitations. The depressed condition of agriculture was due to "discriminating and unjust national legislation," Polk explained to the Ocala convention of the Farmers' Alliance in December 1890. "Were it due to false or imperfect systems of farm economy, we would apply the remedy by improving systems of our own devising."[39] Farmers understood that their economic distress made improving farm technique that much more difficult. Clara Egan of the Kansas Alliance submitted a poem to the *Kansas Farmer* to this effect. The poem noted bitterly that "I'd try some self-improvement some," if it were not for the burdens of mortgage debt, and "I'd study modern farming from a scientific view," if it were not for lack of time and money.[40] Such complaints, however, signaled discontent with economic and financial conditions—conditions that impeded the use of improved methods. As reflected in the pages of the *Kansas Farmer* and the other rural newspapers associated with the Farmers' Alliance, the improvement of technique and scientific farming were topics of keen interest to their readers.

Although grounded in business and technology, Alliance education also promised to bring a general "mental progress" to farm districts. The new modern farmers required a comprehensive understanding of their economic, political, and intellectual position. In regard to the last of these, Macune's educational ideas offered a means to obliterate the intellectual gap between rural and urban Americans. This gap—whether perceived or real—was painfully felt among farmers, and the prospect of realizing intellectual equity proved an important force driving the reform movement.

Lecturing before the Bell County, Texas, Alliance at its May 1888 meeting, Mrs. J. Morton Smith called on her fellow Alliance members to claim their rightful place in the van of "the grand march of American intellect." Farmers "must aim at the loftiest things," Mrs. Smith urged, "not content with occupying secondary position."[41] The Bell County Alliance appealed to its members to make farmers "the peers in intelligence of those that sneered at them as ignoramuses."[42] In such appeals farmers voiced a deep resentment—that registered at the level of both occupation and class—against the stigma of intellectual inferiority. Yet, particularly among young people, it also reflected a discontent with farm life and its intellectual and cultural restraints.

"What is to become of the boys that are now growing up on the farm?" This question was deposited in the Alliance "query box" in Cottonwood, Texas. A young man using the pen name of Ox Driver responded to this question in the *Southern Mercury*. The Alliance being a nominally secret society, a correspondent to the Alliance press normally used a pseudonym. In Ox Driver's case, his pen name reflected his dissatisfaction with the intellectual prospects of a young farmer. "I am but a youth of twenty summers; my opportunities for getting knowledge have been few and ill-used. I am neither a Socrates nor a Plato," he wrote the *Mercury*. "I view this subject as one of immense magnitude," especially because of the prejudiced attitude of young women, who "turn their noses at farmer boys." Young women "see our condition and are aspiring to become the wife of a lawyer, banker, merchant or some other ten-cent dude." Dispirited, the young Ox Driver was quitting the farm business.[43]

Ann Other of Ennis, Texas, one of the *Mercury*'s most influential correspondents, counseled Ox Driver that quitting the farm was not the sure means to satisfy his "aspirations for a higher life." In regard to study and knowledge, she argued, farm boys had advantages over the young men of the city. She suggested that Ox Driver save his tobacco money to purchase a higher quality of literature. She recommended travel books "revealing the wonders of foreign lands." She especially favored George Bancroft's *History of the United States* and other works of "deep research and profound thought."[44]

Along similar lines, Rural Widow, another *Mercury* correspondent, took Ox Driver and other farm boys to task for their failure to act "like an intellectual being and treat the girls as such." Instead of discussing literature or current events "of vital importance to intelligence," when they called on young women, young men discussed the weather, invoked the piano, and followed that with small talk. Their talk was "so small that no microscope could make it visible." After "the intellectual banquet is over," Rural Widow noted, "the youth of twenty (forty) goes home to complain that the girls turn their nose up at him." She recommended to Ox Driver that he read Shakespeare, Charles Dickens, Sir Walter Scott, and George Eliot. "I hold it true that not to know Shakespeare, the keen and mighty prober of the deep heart of humanity," Rural Widow concluded, "is to live in a mental darkness most deplorable."[45]

Ox Driver remained unconvinced. Farming, he believed, was incompatible with intellectual development: "The very nature of our surroundings is detrimental to self-culture." Poverty put works of "deep research" out of a farmer's reach. Fourteen-hour workdays precluded more than an hour of reading a day, which meant that "it would require one hundred years to acquire a practical education." Although "farm life is, indeed, a happy and independent one," Ox Driver reasoned, "it is at the same time the most non-progressive."[46]

Ann Other and Rural Widow—and probably Ox Driver, too—enjoyed an educational level above the average farmer or Alliance member. Their letters indicate that they were part of the schooled or self-educated farm population, whose homes might have a piano as well as a parlor library stocked with Bancroft's volumes. Nonetheless, ideas about rural enlightenment extended beyond the more educated group, resonating from top to bottom of the Alliance movement. "The great trouble with the farmers," Alliance lecturer Harry Tracy would exhort his audiences, "is they cultivate their muscles too much and their brains too little." Tracy's plain speaking earned him the reputation as the "Sam Jones of Texas," as he spread the gospel of mental cultivation. "No intelligent people has ever been enslaved," Tracy preached, "no ignorant people have been found in any other condition than slavery."[47]

Tracy's slavery metaphor carried a specific meaning for farmers struggling to make sense of their hard lives. As one Texas cotton farmer put it, the political bosses compelled farmers to "work harder, plow deeper, economize clouser, eat less, put fewer rags on our children, grow them up in ignorance." But the farmers would never suffer such a regime: "God has implanted in the human heart an unquenchable thirst for knowledge & for liberty." Knowledge was not only a condition of liberty; it was, in itself, fundamental to the realization of human potential.[48]

Education was a means toward higher and more modern conditions of life. This supposition, as much as any other, drew rural Americans toward the agrarian movement. Putting pen to paper was a new challenge for many correspondents with the reform press. Hard-pressed farmers found little time to write except between chores, or when rain kept them out of the fields. In the case of Little Bobby, a farmer from Jack County, Texas, it took the pressure of his wife and her aunt to convince him to take up the pen, and "go smarting down the literary line." "Mr. Editor," Little Bobby explained, "what we want is more 'literary men.' We want to be educated":

> If the farming class would work a little less, and train their minds a little more, they would soon discover their rights. . . . We do not expect every one to

become a MaCune . . . but we do say that the Farmers Alliance . . . has made the improvement of the mind the duty of all, and unless we comply with this decree of progress we can never fulfill our mission."[49]

Alliance farmers viewed this "decree of progress" a public responsibility. The progress of the farmer lay with public education. It was not sufficient to bring books and papers into the home, explained Allie Marsh to her Randolph County, North Carolina, Alliance, because to awaken a thirst for knowledge required schools with competent teachers, teachers who "should make teaching as much of a profession as the college professor."[50] Mrs. J. Morton Smith reiterated the necessity of professionalizing the public schools in a lecture before the Bell County, Texas, Alliance. "Appreciat[e] the supreme importance of the public school system and its relation to the advancement of the great body of farmers," Smith implored her fellow Alliance members. "I cannot too strongly urge you to direct such attention to this question as will guarantee to the youth of your land the advantage of a thorough education. Secure if possible persons of high intellectual ability, combined with purity of character and morals, to take charge of your schools."[51]

For Alliance members, the public schoolhouse was a point of local pride. Nothing spoke better of a community's progressive outlook than a well-built schoolhouse. The schoolhouse often doubled as the Alliance meeting place, even if that meant suspending classes for the children. The public schoolhouse served as a metaphor for the Alliance movement as an educational enterprise, and provided the movement with civic legitimacy. Alliance farmers believed that public instruction was inseparable from the rights and duties of citizenship. "Education is not only a function of the State because the State is pledged to administer its affairs for the welfare of the people, but because its own safety depends upon the education of its citizenship," argued a Louisiana farm reformer in the pages of Macune's *National Economist*. "The intelligence of the people is a desideratum of the government itself. It is not a question as to whether the State may or may not educate. The State must educate, or the State itself is the sufferer," the reformer from Louisiana concluded. "What we ought to do is to build up our public school system. . . . Nothing can exceed in importance, the cause of general education."[52]

Yet in the rural districts of the American South a modern public school system remained an aspiration. A federal study estimated that in 1892 a third of school-aged children in the South were "in no useful connection with anything deserving the name of school." Rural schools suffered from lack of buildings, underpaid teachers, and sporadic terms of instruction. In 1890, the rate of illiteracy among white persons over nine years of age hovered around 5 percent in the North and the West. White southerners suffered illiteracy rates three times that high, and in North Carolina and Louisiana it

was 23 and 21 percent respectively. More than 60 percent of black southerners could not read or write. Lon Livingston, president of the Georgia State
Alliance, decried public education in the rural South as "largely a farce,"
leaving the region's inhabitants with less opportunity "for thought and study
than any people in modern history." This took a heavier toll on the people
than the railroads and land monopolies. "Of all the burdens a people can
bear," Livingston argued, "ignorance far surpasses all others."[53]

The Texas school system suffered ailments common across the South.
Coming into office in 1871, the Democratic Redeemers effectively stymied
the Reconstruction-era efforts to build up state-supported schools. By the
late 1880s, the Texas legislature authorized funding for four months of public
instruction a year. A shortage of trained teachers, however, combined with
the demands of farm work, meant that students often attended for less than
four months a year, if at all. The state, moreover, did not fund school construction, which meant that more than half of all Texas schools were located
in vacant barns, outbuildings, or churches.[54]

The politics of public schools for farm children proved problematic for
agrarian reformers. The decentralized structure of the Texas school system,
for example, tended to keep school reform at the district level. Farmers' Alliance members, however, focused on government regulation of textbook
publishers and similar state and national remedies, perceiving that their problems flowed downward from state and national legislation. White supremacy
also complicated the politics of elementary education. The proposed Blair
Bill ignited passionate debate across the South, partly because it stipulated
that the millions of dollars it would provide in federal assistance to southern schools would be divided equitably between schools for black and white
children.[55]

To fund schools attended by black children, even segregated schools, carried political liabilities. "Men have pleaded for increase of schools and more
education as essential to progress of any kind," noted an Alliance newspaper in North Carolina, only to be "silenced by the terrible scare-crow of
'nigger.'"[56] At the same time, the Pitt County Alliance reflected a wider sentiment among the white farmers of the Tar Heel state when it adopted a resolution denouncing "oppressive, unjust, and iniquitous" school taxes that
provided funds for educating black children.[57] Supporters of school taxes,
as one Texas Democrat put it, wanted "the women of the South picking
cotton to pay taxes to educate negroes."[58] At the height of the Texas fence
wars a note was posted in Coleman County that included the demand of "no
monopolies and don't tax us to school the nigger."[59] Especially in multira-
cial districts, white property owners opted to forgo building schools rather
than build them for black children. "The greatest weakness of the district
system," a Texas school superintendent explained, "is the mixed races. A

voluntary district taxation that required two-thirds approval of the property owners will do well where the population is all white; but if you have one white and one colored school, the whites owning ninety-nine one-hundredths of the property . . . many districts will refuse to vote the tax."[60]

In spite of such obstacles, the Farmers' Alliance served as the rural South's most effective champion of public education, at least for white children. A resolution adopted by the Cabarrus County, North Carolina, Alliance expressed the commitment of its members to the public schools. The Cabarrus County Alliance required that every suballiance appoint a special school committee to work in the local school district, and to "require the committee to visit the homes and see that the children are kept in school for the full term" and "to visit the school at least twice a month and see that the school is properly provided for and the teachers do their duty."[61]

Amory Dwight Mayo, a northern-born educator, spent his professional life studying southern schools. Sharing no sympathy for the "crude and suicidal theories" espoused by the leaders of the Farmers' Alliance, he nonetheless believed that the prospects for southern modernization lay with the success of the Alliance movement. He viewed the Alliance as being representative of the "great masses of the plain white people" and their aspirations for improved schools for their children. "The most hopeful feature of the movement," Mayo observed, "is that it has everywhere been accompanied by an imperative demand for better common school facilities."[62]

Even more than the white Farmers' Alliance, the Colored Alliance focused its energies on education. The Colored Alliance also sought to improve the segregated public schools, although its demands on public resources were often muted out of concern for white retaliation, and it stressed "self-help" educational efforts. The educational work of the Colored Alliance gained broad support in the rural South at a time when the schooling of black children suffered woeful neglect, when schools lacked teachers and books, and when rudimentary church structures often doubled as schoolhouses. Local Alliances pooled community resources to set up schools and raise "the intellectual moral grade of their pastors and teachers." Although its general superintendent Richard Humphrey complained bitterly about the failure of members to pay Alliance dues or to purchase the Colored Alliance newspaper, he reported that members did make small tuition payments for teachers' salaries and for extending the duration of school sessions. The ability of rural blacks to sustain such payments amid dire poverty indicates that they had their own ideas about knowledge and power.[63]

Black farmers and laborers hoped that the ability to read, write, and calculate would provide leverage in their negotiations with unscrupulous landlords, creditors, and legal authorities. What is more, as many whites feared, blacks viewed education as a means toward political and social justice.

Through the educational efforts of the Colored Alliance they sought to re-cover the rights lost with the overthrow of the biracial Reconstruction gov-ernments. Reconstruction "placed weakness on the top of power, and power did what it always will do—shook it off," explained Reverend J. L. Moore, the black superintendent of the Colored Alliance in Putnam County, Florida. The educational work of the Colored Alliance, he believed, was laying the foundation for the next trial, when "moral, intellectual and financial strength [will] come to the top [and] we will come to stay."[64]

White southerners were deeply suspicious of educational efforts in the black community, recognizing a potential danger to the racial caste system. As Richard Humphrey explained, whites "look[ed] upon themselves as spe-cial favorites to Heaven," and were "violently opposed to the education of the colored race in any form." In the face of this opposition, the Colored Alliance presented itself as amenable to white interests. It accepted the prin-ciple of segregation, and encouraged members to educate themselves to be "more obedient to the civil law." Such at least was the mask the Colored Alliance presented to the public as it raised funds for teacher salaries and quietly pursued dreams of improved schools across the South.[65]

The Farmers' Alliance movement recognized that the future of rural educa-tion lay with the state colleges and the common schools. But the task could not be left to the future. In the present, the farmers needed to organize for self-education to better engage the complex problems of modern society. "To induce the people to read is the first step," Macune reasoned. "When people will read they will think, and whenever they begin to think the battle is more than half won." To get people reading and thinking required what he de-scribed as a modern educational machine. The engine driving this machine was the reform press, and as editor of the *National Economist* and president of the National Reform Press Association, Macune was its chief engineer.[66]

Farm reformers attacked the corporate stranglehold over the newspapers and publishing houses. Farmers' Alliance lecturer Harry Tracy explained to his audiences that the control of the "channels of thought" via the newspa-pers was "responsible for the greed, tyranny, and flunkyism" that ruled the country. Similarly, Alliance lecturer Ben Terrell regularly made the corpo-rate-dominated press a focus of his critique of monopoly. "The men who produce [the] wealth are decreasing in power, influence and comfort day by day," Terrell told a farmers' meeting in Fulton County, Georgia. "They are falling into ignorance. Their curse is want of education and refinement and the desire for a higher life." The responsibility for this situation lay mainly with the newspapers. "The press is the greatest power in the land," Terrell argued, "because it makes the laws." The "power of the press" had grown "beyond computation" in the struggle between monopoly and the farmers'

HERE IS WHAT DID THE WORK—THE SECRET IS OUT.

Figure 2.2. "Economic Circulating Library," in the *People's Paper*, Stafford, Kansas, October 13, 1892 (Kansas State Historical Society, Topeka)

progress. Thus, Terrell posed the question: "Shall we control it, or will we leave this, the greatest of all weapons, in the hands of others?"[67]

Only the development of the reform press and other farmers' institutions could break the corporate grip on the "channels of thought." "From education comes evolution," the columnist and lecturer Merlinda Sissins exhorted her fellow Texas Alliance members. The "progress of this great movement to equalize men's opportunities, depends almost entirely upon the rapidity of their education." Therefore, Sissins concluded, "every Alliance should urge its members to substitute a good industrial paper for the capitalistic one they are now taking. This is the great necessity."[68]

The publishing system of the rural reform movement failed to match the capacity of the big metropolitan publishers. One Texas farmer attributed this inability to farmers' poverty and their "lack of knowledge of the power of the press."[69] Nonetheless, a striking number of farm reformers did understand this power and sustained a remarkable system of rural newspapers. Led by Macune and his *National Economist*, the National Reform Press Association combined the efforts of some one thousand newspapers with a total circulation in the hundreds of thousands of copies. Milton Park's *Southern Mercury*, Polk's *Progressive Farmer*, Peffer's *Kansas Farmer,* and the *Nonconformist* published by the brothers Henry, Leo, and Cuthbert Vincent, among several other reform newspapers, enjoyed broad statewide and regional readerships. Most reform presses, however, served rural counties. Large or small, the reform newspapers relied on reprinting from one another, creating a network of shared information, offering weekly readers "the essence of the brains of the world."[70]

At a meeting of the Gillespie County, Texas, Alliance, when the Alliance president called on the members to stand if they received a reform newspaper, the whole assembly rose to its feet. Some of those members possibly only stood up out of a sense of obligation. That would confirm, however, the extent to which the farmers understood that a successful battle for rural progress would be waged by means of the printing press, the telegraph, and second-class mail.[71]

Macune's educational system diffused knowledge by way of a centralized plan, and from the top down. As editor of the *National Economist*, Macune tried to frame the curriculum. The Washington office of the National Alliance sought to ensure "a properly regulated lecture system," and state alliances screened lecturers and editors for their adherence to "Alliance principles." The didactic nature of Alliance pedagogy conformed to precepts of business efficiency. It also reflected the conviction within the reform movement that the mental world of the people could be readily shaped, channeled, and directed toward reform goals. As one rural correspondent suggested, by setting fixed and uniform topics for discussion at the national level, "a vast number of minds could be brought to bear simultaneously on one topic."[72]

Charles Macune must have concurred. In the winter of 1892, the *National Economist* launched the publication of weekly lesson plans "for use in Alliances, debating societies, lyceums, and to disseminate a correct understanding of the economic questions of the day." The lessons included history, statistics, finance, economics, and government. Macune provided detailed instructions on how to properly conduct blackboard exercises among often poorly educated farmers who may not have "handled chalk for ten or twenty years." This particular lesson scheme never bore fruit. Nonetheless, it reflected both the exceptionally democratic and the highly centralized and didactic ideas motivating Alliance pedagogy.[73]

The Alliance curriculum covered the economic and political systems of Europe, Asia, and Latin America. It addressed the latest theories of social, economic, and political science. It also paid special attention to the farmers' role in history. Two Alliance historians, Nelson Dunning and W. Scott Morgan, wrote widely circulated histories that articulated reformers' notions about the historical place of the agricultural classes. Dunning stressed the technical side of this history and the contributions made by the development of the farmer's vocation to "bringing about the civilization of the present." In the early years of the United State, he observed, the attention that Washington, Adams, and Jefferson paid to agricultural experimentation had produced the marvel of American farming. Although the end of the nineteenth century brought years of neglect, American agriculture was yet "in its infancy." Under "kindly laws," Dunning predicted, mechanization would place American farmers "at the head of the world's producers."[74]

For Dunning, progress was reflected in the model plow that a French agricultural society had presented to Thomas Jefferson. For Morgan, on the other hand, the French had provided American farmers with a revolutionary model. Morgan's *History* stressed that, as in France a hundred years earlier, the United States suffered from corruption, fettered commerce, strangled competition, foreclosed mortgages, and decaying barns, fences, churches, and schoolhouses. As in France, conditions were being laid for a revolution. In America this revolution would be a peaceful and evolutionary one, prepared by education, and wielded by "the power of Opinion."[75]

Herein lay the significance of Alliance history lessons. The "advancement of civilization," as Ann Other explained to her *Southern Mercury* readers, passed through "vigorous organic action," leading to "decay," only to again give place to "higher development" when people reclaimed their rights against concentrated wealth. The American *sansculottes*—the clodhoppers, the hayseeds, the plain people—were inevitably going to assert themselves. New and clear ideas would prepare their triumph. Such was the spirit of Alliance education. No matter how defective or limited their previous education, reformers believed, every man and woman—or at least every white man and woman —had the capacity to absorb the highest achievements in human knowledge. In absorbing such knowledge, the lowly and discounted could make a fundamental change in their status and power.[76]

Under the Alliance umbrella, farmers organized a wide array of educational activities. Alliance lectures and symposia became a regular feature of rural life. The Alliance sponsored social science clubs, literary societies, and lending libraries. Taking up the slack from the regular schools, the Alliance gave farm children classroom instruction in reading and arithmetic. At times, their semiliterate parents and grandparents joined the young people, making for a remarkable experiment in adult literacy. It was in the regular meetings of the suballiances, however, where most of the work of Alliance education took place. From outlying farms, men and women traveled to the local schoolhouse or other Alliance halls to take part in research or literary exercises, and to hear lectures and papers covering a wide array of topics. The closed meetings could be suspended altogether, replaced by a public lecture on history or science, legislation or finance.[77]

Alliance education reached deep into the farmers' ranks, and by that measure it was indeed a profound and democratic upheaval. It "brought the agricultural and laboring people to comprehend their importance in the world of political thought," noted a resolution of the Centennial Alliance in Bell County, Texas. And it thereby equipped farmers for "independence of thought and action."[78] The Vincent brothers similarly noted the impact of Alliance education in Kansas and beyond. "General reading became more universal," they observed, as "the education furnished in Alliance halls stimulated the latent energies of the rural classes."[79]

Alliance lecturers reminded their followers that education served time-tested patriotic ideals. To "labor for the education of the agricultural classes" was an imperative of citizenship. "Heed the charge of Moses to the Levites," a lecturer before the Bell County, Texas, Alliance exhorted her listeners, "that 'all children should be instructed in everything which would qualify them for good citizenship,' thus inaugurating a system that will give your people happiness and your state wealth, position and honor."[80] Education, Olia Jones explained to the Harbin, Texas, Literary Society, was "the germ of true patriotism," the principle that "makes our glorious old republic rise high in the scale of civilization." American farmers, like most Americans, were well versed in the language of patriotic obligation. Alliance education, however, tended to define obligation in a decidedly Macunist—that is businesslike and commercial—spirit.[81]

Struck by the commercial energy animating the rural districts, the educator Amory Mayo attributed this force to the educational work of the Farmers' Alliance. In his 1890 address before the American Social Science Association, Mayo characterized the Farmers' Alliance as the "Third Estate of the South," the "mighty army of the common people" signifying the end of the old, hidebound order. "Hereafter, the South follows the North in the rush to the front of the fittest who survive," he predicted. "And the contest for place will be on industrial lines."[82]

Mayo's "Third Estate" analogy echoed northern myths about the supposedly feudal nature of southern society. Furthermore, a good Alliance member would never locate the South in the North's footsteps. Farm reformers deplored the inadequacy of rural education on both sides of the Mason-Dixon Line and usually looked across the Atlantic for educational models. Hence, the lament of Ox Driver that in America young men lacked an educational system such as in England, "where they turn a fellow out at twenty-one with a fair education and master of a trade." Hence, the enthusiasm of Macune's National Economist and George's Prairie Farmer for French and German rural education.[83]

But a kernel of truth lay within Mayo's observation. The Farmers' Alliance spread an innovative and dynamic message that took hold especially in the newly settled and expanding farm districts of the South and West. It was a message of efficiency, applied science, modernization, and progress. In that sense, the Alliance movement marched in parallel with New South and other mainly urban and elite constituencies of reform. It was also a message of business: farmers engaged in commodity agriculture needed to think and act as economic agents within national and global commerce. This was the course of instruction taught month after month in the Alliance's schoolhouse meetings. This was the unifying principle of the lecturing system and the network of the rural reform press. When America's farmers filed through the Agricultural Building at the Chicago World's Fair, they may have been in awe at the spectacle, but they had left their homes well prepared for its lessons.

3

A Better Woman

Independence of Thought and Action

The women of the Farmers' Alliance disagreed about women's rights. Their letters to the *Southern Mercury* revealed the extent of the disagreements. A correspondent writing under the pen name Ann Other, an agile polemicist for women's suffrage, leveled the following set of questions at her opponents:

> If independence of thought and action is good for the development of man, why would it not be for women? Can we have the full development of mind in children when mothers are trammeled by inconsistent laws and dictates of fashion, and society that dictates to her in dress, in thought and in action? . . . Have women an equal right (with their husbands) in law to their children? Have women a right to property acquired before marriage, and have they an equal right with the husband to that acquired after marriage?[1]

For Ann Other, equal rights meant equality in politics, too, and political rights were essential for women's independence. Charitie from Ruston, Louisiana, disagreed, articulating the anti-suffrage argument. Although her own husband favored women voting, she argued that entering the dirty business of politics would deprive women of their moral advantage and their "influence over men" in the household. Charitie held a minority viewpoint, as most letters to the *Southern Mercury* supported women's voting rights.[2]

Their disagreements over voting notwithstanding, the two women coexisted quite comfortably within the "sisterhood" of the Farmers' Alliance. This was because Charitie, as much as Ann Other, subscribed to ideals of women's progress that were widely held within the Alliance movement. Female suffrage supporters such as Ann Other shared with Charitie key assumptions about the problems facing farmwomen. Charitie, for example, believed that women had to gain "the right to be independent" profession-ally and financially and that they should "compete with man in the highest branches of science and art." Charitie appealed to the Alliance for assistance in providing women with professional training. "To teach girls printing, te-legraphy, shorthand writing," and other occupations, she reasoned, was the "parents' actual duty to their daughters, more binding upon them than such training for their sons." For Charitie, "business education and instruction" was the essential prerequisite of female independence.[3]

The dialogue in the pages of the reform press about what they called the "woman question" provides a clue as to why hundreds of thousands of women joined the Farmers' Alliances and the Populist revolt. "No other movement in history," the novelist Hamlin Garland observed, "not even the anti-slavery cause—appealed to the women" as much as did Populism.[4] Why did the movement have such an appeal? To begin with, women joined the Farmers' Alliance for the same reasons that men did. "All things that are of interest to men are of like interest to women," Mrs. M. E. Clark lectured the Shawnee, Kansas, Alliance. "Their interests should be, and are, to a marked degree, identical." Rural women farmed, taught school, pursued professions, and faced many of the same societal issues that rural men did. Not surpris-ingly, they embraced with similar enthusiasm the Alliance's message of rural progress.[5]

The Farmers' Alliance offered women extensive rights within the orga-nization, rights that stood in stark contrast to those offered by other insti-tutions in American life. To encourage their attendance at meetings, the Alliance imposed no dues on women members. Otherwise, women enjoyed the same membership rights that men did in terms of speaking, voting, and holding office. Whereas the Grange had offices specifically designated for women, the Alliance opened all positions to women without distinction. This stated policy of equality set the Alliance apart. Political parties barred women from political affairs. The churches also excluded women from deliberative positions. Women enrolled in the Farmers' Alliance because it offered them remarkable opportunities of expression on formally equal terms with men.[6]

Formal equality fell short of equality in practice. The burdens of childcare and household chores limited women's ability to participate in reform work. Once at the meetings, women bore responsibility for decorating the halls, pre-paring refreshments, providing good cheer, and the other "social enjoyments of the occasion." Few women held positions of higher authority in the move-ment despite their considerable numbers in the ranks of local lecturers, secre-taries, and treasurers. Men also monopolized the business functions of the Alliance. Many Alliance members, both men and women, accepted the no-tion that women's place was as the "helpmeet" of her husband.[7]

Yet by opening its ranks to women, the Farmers' Alliance provided a forum for the discussion of the "woman question" and its solution. Its meetings and newspapers allowed for debates about the meaning of equal rights for women and for expressions of women's consciousness and solidarity. Historians have connected the beginnings of such expressions to modern development and the growth of cities in the first half of the nineteenth century. Commerce, industry, and the urban environment made for a physical separation of work and home. Women thereby came to inhabit a "separate sphere" and, with the assistance of the popular press, womanhood realized a vocational identity within urban society. Rural life, by contrast, often lacked the physical separation of work and home, as well as the autonomy of urban life. The formation of women's consciousness, therefore, did not proceed according to the urban pattern. It did, nonetheless, proceed. Inexpensive popular literature brought the precepts of women's consciousness even to remote rural districts. At the same time, women sought progress in their "sphere" and the rural world.[8]

For many rural reformers, both women and men, political equality was a requirement of women's progress. The commitment to women's voting rights was strong in the West, especially in the Mountain states where, under Populist auspices, women won the right to vote in Colorado in 1893 and in Idaho in 1896. In North Carolina, and elsewhere in the South, the public discussion of women's voting rights was held in check. In Texas, however, the debate erupted in the pages of the reform press, with most participants in the debate supporting female suffrage. Even with such regional discrepancies, the Farmers' Alliance represented a potentially powerful constituency for achieving the vote, with a vocal minority of its members actively campaigning for suffrage as the key to elevating women's status.[9]

It would be misleading, however, to measure the spectrum of ideas on the "woman question" by the polarity of opinion about the vote. Suffrage formed only one axis of the debates, while the economics of women's status took an even more prominent place in the discussion. Economics weighed heavily on late nineteenth-century thought, and Farmers' Alliance women believed, no less than men did, in its transforming power. Many Alliance women conceived of women's progress primarily in terms of the type of work they performed on the farm and the careers they might pursue in town. Progress meant domestic and garden work instead of heavy fieldwork. It meant self-reliance and capacity for gainful employment. It meant training and skills for a place in education, medicine, accounting, telegraphy, and other new and expanding occupations.

Much of the discussion of the "woman question" focused on the home, family, and motherhood. The economic burdens of falling farm prices, mounting debts, and repossessed farms did indeed place stress on the domestic order. At the same time, domestic institutions cried for reform. Although farm reformers disagreed about specific remedies for improving homes, marriages, and families, they shared a notion that the family structure was in need of renovation and renewal. They lamented women's "enslavement" and "close confinement" on isolated farmsteads. They decried the liquor trade as the destroyer of homes and marriages. To improve women's lives, they sought changes in marital relations, domestic economy, parenting, and community life. Inspired by evolutionary and racial theory, they believed that a more independent woman—strengthened in mind and body—would produce offspring similarly bright and strong.[10]

Such was the potent mix of strivings that brought hundreds of thousands of women to the Farmers' Alliance. The common denominator in these efforts, taking account of differences of shading and focus, was to make better lives for better women. The farmers' movement offered rural women hope for an expanded social and cultural environment, improved methods in the kitchen and garden, a more just configuration of marriage and family relations, and increased opportunities for education, employment, and perhaps participation in political affairs. In short, the Alliance movement attracted large numbers of women because it raised the prospects of a more independent and modern life. This vision is difficult to reconcile with the historical framework of rural protest representing tradition-bound farmers heroically defending their communities and homes from the encroachments of modernity, a framework that has left largely unanswered the question of why women played such a pivotal role in the farmers' movement.

The Farmers' Alliance attracted an accomplished group of women leaders to its ranks. When the supreme council of the National Farmers' Alliance and Industrial Union (NFAIU) assembled in Indianapolis in November 1891, it included the popular author Sarah E. Emery of Michigan, along with editor Annie L. Diggs of Kansas and later of Washington, D.C., where she joined with Charles Macune to direct the National Reform Press Association. The Council also included two of the small number of women lawyers in America: Mary Elizabeth Lease, the famous orator from Kansas, and Marion Todd of Illinois. Although enjoying less renown than Lease, Todd was more accomplished both professionally and as a theoretician of the Populist movement. After her studies at Hastings School of Law in San Francisco, Todd went on to become one of the first women to pass the California bar. She set up a law practice in San Francisco and entered politics in 1882 as the Greenback candidate for state attorney general. Returning to the Midwest, Todd lectured for the Farmers' Alliance, struck fear in the hearts of her conservative opponents who saw her as "a sort of she-devil," authored several popular works on economic reform and women's rights, and served as an editor of the *Chicago Express*, an influential Greenback paper with a national circulation.[11]

Todd, like Lease, Diggs, Emery, and other women leaders of the Alliance movement, was educated, professional, and more accustomed to living in town than in the farming districts. In that regard, her career and that of other leading women of the Alliance resembled those of Macune, Polk, Peffer, and other male editors and leaders of the farmers' movement, and for similar reasons these women proved well suited to deliver the Alliance message of rural modernization. Their professionalism and erudition provided examples for less eminent women of the reform movement, especially for the rural schoolteachers, postmistresses, doctors, and other professionally oriented women who joined the Alliance's educational work as lecturers, editors, essayists, secretaries, and bookkeepers. The women leaders of the Alliance may not have lived on the farm. Yet women and men who did avidly studied what they wrote. And when leading women of the Alliance spoke in the rural districts, even at the height of the harvest, thousands of farmers traveled from remote homesteads to hear and applaud what they said.[12]

Two nonprofessional women attended the supreme council meeting at Indianapolis. Miss L. E. Roberts served as the state lecturer of the Illinois Farmers' Alliance, but was relatively unknown out of her home state. Bettie Gay of Columbus, Texas, enjoyed a much broader reputation. She was the only southern woman at the supreme council and, unlike Diggs or Todd, who built their reputations with voice and pen, Gay was neither an outstanding orator nor writer. Yet she took a prominent place in the Alliance movement. More than her professional sisters, she represented an Alliance ideal of womanhood. An enlightened and successful farm manager, her life exemplified the progressive woman of the future.

Born in Alabama, two-year-old Bettie Munn (Gay) arrived in Texas in 1836 as part of the great westward migration from the Atlantic and Gulf states. As a young woman Bettie married Rufus King Gay, a wealthy planter and slaveholder. Gay occupied her time on the plantation studying philosophy and natural science. But the Civil War and its aftermath interrupted the plantation's prosperity, and Gay left her studies to direct the work of the farm. As with many Alliance women of her generation, Gay experienced the war and its aftermath as a time of hardship and responsibility. This legacy weighed especially heavily on the consciousness of southern Alliance members, but in the North, too, the exigencies of war were a formative experience for reform women. Anna Ferry Smith, for example, the California Alliance's indomitable organizer, came into her own as a Civil War nurse in Pennsylvania. War widows, too, as Marion Todd noted, were called on to display "remarkable executive and administrative powers." In the discussion of the "woman

Figure 3.1. Bettie Gay, prominent Texas Alliance member and Populist (Center of American History, University of Texas, Austin)

question" within the Alliance, the Civil War was the common point of reference for the emergence of the self-reliant woman.[13]

When her husband died in 1880, Bettie Gay took over his debts and a deeply mortgaged plantation. She soon proved an efficient manager. After paying off the mortgage, she held 1,776 unburdened acres and became one of the more successful cotton planters in Texas. She did not remarry and only gradually relinquished management of the plantation to her son Jehu Bates

Gay. Her independent course, unusual for a propertied widow, won her ac-claim within the reform movement. As her Alliance colleague Annie Diggs stressed, she demonstrated energy, industry, and "executive ability."[14]

Gay lived on the stagecoach road a few miles outside of Columbus, the seat of Colorado County in central Texas. She participated actively in the Baptist church, but felt that in "most of the churches women have been al-lowed no voice." By the mid-1880s she found her own voice in the farmers' reform movement. She also took a prominent place among the women cor-respondents to the *Southern Mercury*, the newspaper of the Texas Alliance.[15]

Bettie Gay shared little in common with most of her fellow Alliance mem-bers in terms of wealth and education. Unlike Gay, few Alliance members could be counted among the elite cotton planters of the South. Most Alli-ance members were also unlike the farmhands and sharecroppers who pro-vided the labor on the big cotton estates. Typically, the male members of the Alliance were married property owners. If they did not own their farms, they still tended to not be among the poorest tenants. Thus Alliance women were mainly the wives, mothers, and daughters of middling farmers. Unlike Gay, most farmers had few opportunities for study. Cash poor and pressed by the relentless demands of fieldwork and chores, Alliance members struggled to achieve more than a rudimentary education.[16]

Despite her elevated economic and educational level, Bettie Gay found in the Farmers' Alliance a community of like-minded women and men, in-cluding those who shared her vision about women's progress. Many of her colleagues sympathized with Gay's advocacy of women's suffrage, although this sympathy was far from unanimous and the Texas Alliance itself avoided taking a position on the question. But Gay and other suffragists saw more in the Alliance than a means toward the vote. They saw a movement commit-ted to the liberation of rural women from the social and economic constraints that held them in isolation and ignorance. "The Alliance had come," Gay believed, "to redeem woman from her enslaved condition."[17] The success of the Farmers' Alliance, lecturer Harry Tracy told his audiences across the rural South, "means the emancipation of the farmers' and laborers' wives, daughters, and mothers from the isolated slavery that now environs them."[18] In response to such appeals, women joined with men in making the weekly or biweekly trek to the suballiance meeting halls, where women's participa-tion was a frequent topic of discussion.

The 1891 "Ladies' List" of the Centennial Alliance in Bell County, Texas, noted the names of ten married and seventeen unmarried women, account-ing for 40 percent of the membership. Having women on the rolls, however, did not guarantee their participation in Alliance activities. The deliberations of the Centennial Alliance repeatedly returned to this problem. In one meet-ing the Alliance resolved to set aside every third Saturday of the month as

"Ladies' Day" devoted to women's essays. In another meeting it adopted a sharp protest against a proposal to start charging women dues. In yet another meeting the Alliance adopted a five-cent fine on husbands who failed to bring their wives to meetings without an adequate excuse.[19]

Not all men welcomed women into the Alliance. Dianecia Jones of Cedar Hill, Texas, charged that the men of her local alliance objected to "woman's rights" and female participation. "The brethren go regularly to every meeting," Jones noted, "but they manage to leave the women at home to pail the cows and watch the little brats."[20] Men occasionally voiced opposition to the inclusion of women who "know nothing about business."[21] Other men actively encouraged women to attend meetings. "Those farmers who regard their wives, mothers and daughters as unsuitable persons to associate with themselves as members of the Sub-alliance," warned an Alliance paper in Kansas, posed the question "whether such men are themselves suitable persons for membership."[22] The leadership of the Texas Alliance exhorted its local alliances to "get in your women," and most did so. Two of the three suballiances in Gillespie County, for example, reported a membership with equal numbers of women and men.[23]

On average, women filled a fourth of the benches in Farmers' Alliance meetings. By 1890, approximately 250,000 women had enrolled in the NFAIU. Women also joined the Northern Alliance, the Grange, and other farmers' organizations. The farmers' movement organized women on an unprecedented scale, surpassed only by America's churches. More women joined the Farmers' Alliance than the Women's Christian Temperance Union (WCTU), which, with 160,000 members in 1890, was by far the largest women's organization in the country. At the same time, members of the rural-based Farmers' Alliance and the more urban-based WCTU shared similar concerns and ideals. If many Alliance women embraced the WCTU's beliefs about temperance and moral uplift, many women of the WCTU, including its dominant personality, Frances Willard, were drawn to Alliance ideals of financial and economic reform. In the spectrum of women's reform, however, the Alliance offered rural women unique possibilities.[24]

Most immediately, women joined the Alliance as a means to escape the lonely monotony of the farm. If the "faculty of social intercourse" distinguished human beings from the lower animals, then the isolation of farm life reduced farmers all too closely to the level of brutes. Such was the reasoning of Horace L. Deford, a Texas farmer from Palo Pinto County. He criticized the "close confinement" of farm life. He decried the lonely rounds of toil that prevented farmers from "scarcely going beyond the boundaries" of the farm. Rural life, Deford believed, was particularly detrimental to women. The Farmers' Alliance offered a means of "social intercourse" that would spring wives and daughters from the dreary cages of lonely farmsteads.[25]

Farmers' efforts to overcome social isolation through voluntary association resembled similar efforts among professional and middle-class city dwellers. Historian Robert Wiebe attributes this urban associational impulse with a search for order as city people lost the connectedness of the "island communities" of rural and small-town America. In this endeavor they were not alone. Robert McMath also emphasizes that rural America had a tradition of associational life—churches, granges, and fraternal orders—on which the Farmers' Alliance built. But if farmers enjoyed the embrace of social networks that city dwellers lacked, why did farm reformers decry rural isolation in such poignant terms? Why did the farmers build a professional association with the self-conscious aim of overcoming the detached loneliness of farm life?[26]

The answer to this paradox lies in part with the rigors of commercial farming. Farmers' Alliance leader W. Scott Morgan of Arkansas made a harsh indictment of the dreary life of the farm. Even on prosperous farms, he observed, the treadmill routines of housework obliged a woman "to make a slave of herself, working from daylight to bedtime," and suffer premature old age. He attributed this work regimen to the demands of commodity agriculture. "The tendencies have been for the farmers to transform themselves and families into wheat, corn and cotton producing machines." In the world of the modern farmer, the time and energy of the farm household was measured on the same calculus as the mules and horses, "as capable of producing so many bushels of wheat or corn or so many bales of cotton." And, as Morgan noted, social connections were one of the casualties of this calculus.[27]

During the course of the nineteenth century, a great migration from communities on both sides of the Atlantic dispersed millions of prospective farmers across the trans-Appalachian West. Some groups enjoyed more success than did others in resuscitating or reinventing elements of communities left behind: Germans and Czechs in Texas and Kansas, for example, and Norwegians and New Englanders in the Upper Midwest. But the booms and busts of wheat, cotton, and other commodities buffeted even the more stable communities. Such is the story of Hamlin Garland's family, which abandoned the Wisconsin valley of his New England ancestors for the lure of bonanza crops in the Dakota Territory. Garland himself escaped farm life to become a writer, but was tormented by the solitude and drudgery that wheat farming imposed on his mother and sister. This torment brought Garland back to the Great Plains as a champion of the Farmers' Alliance and its efforts to emancipate women.[28]

The vicissitudes of commodity agriculture contributed to the remarkable mobility of farm families and to the transitory nature of their social networks.

The restless movement toward new opportunity tended to dissolve neighbor-hood and social ties as quickly as it formed them. This was especially the case in regions of new settlement, but even in older communities the solvent of continual migration took its toll. In farm settlements in central Illinois, for example, the majority of farmers were often new arrivals who would soon launch out again for new land. This left a minority of stable families to hold together the social networks. Such networks, however, often revolved around male-centered work, politics, and entertainment, leaving women secluded on their prairie homesteads.[29]

Farmers' efforts to build voluntary associations faced the daunting challenges of the boom and bust nature of their business and the shifting dynamics of the rural environment. Even the most formidable organizations proved ephemeral. The Grange boom of the early 1870s collapsed a decade before the Alliance boom of the late 1880s, which also lasted only a half dozen years. Alliance members may have known about the Grange boom of the 1870s, or had other experience with organization, but their own farm districts often had only rudimentary neighborhood networks. The fleeting nature of rural association may help explain why the members of the Farmers' Alliance experienced the deficiencies in "social intercourse" so acutely. The very impermanence of social networks meant that reformers did not take them for granted, but were acutely aware of the need to build them. And women were at the center of these concerns.

In Hamlin Garland's Populist novel, *A Spoil of Office*, Ida Wilbur represented "advanced" and "modern" womanhood as a young lecturer in the farmers' movement. Wilbur pointed to the decline of the Grange as another sign that the farmer had not learned about organization and the need to stand with others. "Well, I suppose he must suffer greater hardships before he learns his lesson," the young lecturer noted. "But God help the poor wives while he learns!"[30]

William Garvin and S. O. Daws drew a similar conclusion. As founders of the Texas Alliance, the two men had spent years organizing in the rural districts and had observed firsthand the "lonely and secluded lives" of the farmers. They stressed that the monotony of farm life took an especially heavy toll on women. Farmers "rarely go beyond the limits of their own farm," Garvin and Daws noted, "except to attend the election, go to market or the country store." As men did the voting and much of the trading, this left women even more confined. Meanwhile, migratory patterns often separated extended families. A visit to relatives could mean a trip to "a distant part of the country [that] is planned for years."[31]

Women's chores further amplified the monotony of farm life. The wash-tub and cook stove were "essential to the life and comfort of every human being," explained Bina Otis of Kansas, "but they form a combination that makes a slave of the majority of the farmers' wives and sends many of them to a premature grave." Annie Diggs described "drudging women" on a treadmill of churning, baking, sewing, washing, cooking, and scrubbing. And she blamed the "toilsome, dreary" life of the farm for sending so many women to insane asylums. If a woman's burdens did not send her to the asylum or an early grave, she soon was reduced to "wrinkled and stoop shouldered" exhaustion.[32]

Women who actually lived on farms tended to use more buoyant language when discussing their lives. To endure hardship without complaint was a valued quality in a farm woman. "For a good, everyday household angel, give us a woman who laughs," a Kansas woman wrote the *Nonconformist*, affirming that a desirable woman "has a uniformly cheerful spirit and is able to discover the silver lining to every dark cloud." Untiring good cheer—like childbirth and cooking—was women's obligation and duty. At the same time, Alliance women believed they had reason to cheer the future. Their work may have entailed excruciating drudgery. But striving to make a successful farmstead carried the hope of a better tomorrow—hope raised to expectation by the ideals of rural reform.[33]

The Farmers' Alliance offered "a glimmer of a way out," as Hamlin Garland put it. It helped farmers "forget mud and rain and cold and monotony." It allowed them to share the images painted in Ida Wilbur's mesmerizing talks. This was a future where rural citizens enjoy "lectures in beautiful halls, erected in every village"; where farmers have "time to read, and time to visit with their fellows"; where "cities ris[e] near them with schools, and churches, and concert halls, and theatres"; and where "happy men and women . . . sing to their pleasant tasks." Such sanguine images of the modern future were standard fare of Farmers' Alliance agitation, an agitation that spread because it resonated with the overworked and exhausted women of rural homes.[34]

Luna Kellie was such a woman. She would gain renown as the state secretary of the Nebraska Farmers' Alliance, an editor of reform newspapers, and a "middle-of-the-road" Populist. Unlike other leading women of the Farmers' Alliance, Kellie spent her adult life on rural homesteads. In the 1920s, she penned her memoirs on the back of old Farmers' Alliance certificates, leaving an account of devastating mental and physical hardships and equally intense hopes for the future. Born in 1857, she passed her childhood in Minnesota railroad towns, where her father worked on the Northern Pacific Railroad. After a failed stint at farming in Minnesota, the family relocated to St. Louis, where Luna's mother died and where she soon married James T. Kellie, her father's foreman on the railroad.[35]

Kellie had plans for her new family, plans that could not fit within their rented and crowded quarters in St. Louis. She wanted at least twelve children,

Figure 3.2. Luna Kellie, secretary of the Nebraska Farmers' Alliance (Nebraska State Historical Society, Lincoln)

"fifteen would be better," and a large home and a healthy environment in which to raise them. At eighteen years of age, she set out with a newborn son for a homestead outside of Hastings, Nebraska, "the worst looking little town [she] had ever seen." Her dream of a bright large home turned into the dark and claustrophobic nightmare of a sod house, where she suffered in terror of a collapsed roof, and where winter snows kept her family trapped for months in an eight- by twelve-foot room.[36]

The combination of overwork, the trials of childbirth, and the strain of losing two children left Kellie on the edge of physical and mental collapse. At the depths of exhaustion and unable to stand, she did her washing and other chores in a sitting position. She nonetheless remained optimistic about the future. She hoped that "before many years" the family would take a vacation. She calculated that if the farming business took hold the family would go see the geysers and other wonders of Yellowstone described in a *Harper's* magazine. "Our trip never materialized," she reported in her memoirs, "but we put in some happiest hours of life planning it."[37]

Schools and churches were few and far between. The critical lack of schools introduced Kellie to the question of women's political rights, as the school district debated whether women should be allowed to vote on school-related issues. Although as a child she had feared the drunken violence of Election Day, her husband, James, assured her that the Farmers' Alliance would clean up the polls. While James did his best to enlighten Luna about politics and the Farmers' Alliance, Luna tried to win him to religion. One of Luna's most satisfying moments came when the family joined a Methodist church, the only church within range of their home. The preacher was also a farmer, and the Kellies struck a neighborly agreement to pasture his cows in exchange for milk. But the lack of choices in terms of neighbors and churches proved problematic. When the cows failed to produce, James attacked the preacher for making false claims, and never entered a church again except for funerals.[38]

The Kellies ran their homestead as a joint enterprise. James worked the fields and spent the profits from corn and wheat to purchase machinery to expand acreage. Luna tended the garden, the chickens, and the cows, and she controlled the income earned from eggs and chickens to sustain the household. She took pride in her earning power and its contribution to the future prosperity of the farm. She also enjoyed an exceptional level of financial autonomy. Many women complained about men's exclusive control of the money. In a letter to the *Nonconformist*, a Kansas woman wrote that "inter-dependence" was rare on the Plains. In the "partnership between men and women called marriage," a wife has "to go on the knees of her soul to ask [a husband] for two cents for a postage stamp." The letter writer proposed to put the matter before a vote of readers, predicting that women would report that nine out of ten men claim the "wife is only entitled to what is given her." As this letter indicates, the Kellies' situation approached a reform ideal rather than a widely practiced reality.[39]

Luna Kellie faced a steep learning curve on the farm. Her grandfather back in Wisconsin had taught her something about growing fruit, yet her repeated efforts withered in the unforgiving Nebraska climate. She had better luck with chickens. James had even less farming experience and "only knew fruit as it came on the table." He had some success with spring wheat, harvesting such a fine crop that he delivered a paper on the subject before the local Farmers' Alliance. But the scissors of declining grain prices and rising interest rates left the Kellie farm in pitiless debt.[40]

The Kellies lost their farm after seven years of desperate toil. Without croplands, the family struggled to make a living by raising chickens, sheep, and other livestock. But now Luna increasingly turned her energies to the success of the reform movement. It was through the movement that farmers would realize their dreams of education, good homes, and the prosperous Nebraska that she had imagined as a girl reading the promotional literature of the B & M Railroad. By 1892 the Nebraska Farmers' Alliance affiliated with the National Farmers' Alliance and Industrial Union (NFAIU) and elected Luna Kellie as state secretary. She tirelessly corresponded, edited, and set type, driven by the hope that, even if not her family and her generation, at least the next generation would gain "industrial freedom." Although she performed her Alliance functions from her rural home, she was now at the hub of a great network linking farmers across the state and the nation.[41]

Even at the grass roots the Alliance movement linked its members to a broader network of reform. Partly this was a community of face-to-face encounters. The meetings of the suballiances, although frequently having a dozen or fewer participants, served an array of practical social functions. They provided a means of neighborhood mutual assistance for the sick or widowed. They allowed farmers' daughters and sons to socialize with potential husbands and wives. Suballiance meetings also facilitated the much-anticipated picnics, parades, and seasonal encampments that brought Alliance families together across the county and even from neighboring counties.

The Farmers' Alliance—mainly through its network of newspapers—took on multiple functions as a community at the remote and distant level. Depending on the circumstance, the Alliance represented a community of cotton growers, a community of southern farmers, and a national community of rural producers. And in all of these permutations it included a community of rural women. "What is the sisterhood of woman," a Kansas woman asked, "or, rather, what will it be, since it does not exist in its true state at present. What does it mean, and in what will it differ from what now is?"[42] The reform press provided a forum for articulating an answer. Women contributed as editors, columnists, and correspondents, and most reform newspapers carried features that were intended to be of special interest to women. This included serialized novels, as well as columns on health and childcare, the kitchen and garden, and "ladies' departments" for exchanges of letters.

The "ladies' department" of the *Southern Mercury*, the Dallas newspaper of the Texas Alliance, published letters from a particularly devoted corps of correspondents. Their letters usually discussed the problems confronting farmers as farmers. But they also addressed letters to one another as women. At times, they penned their correspondence as if to distant relatives whom they had never met. "Charitie, I am very glad that you, for one, have deigned to recognize me in this family circle," Birdie from Corn Hill, Texas, wrote her Alliance sister in Ruston, Louisiana. "I feel quite complimented by the pen picture you drew of myself. . . . Here is the picture in my mind of you." By such means, the *Mercury* served to extend ties of solidarity among women readers.[43]

That Birdie would describe such ties in terms of the "family circle" reflected a widely held opinion that women's position within the Alliance was analogous to their status in the family. As Bettie Gay explained this relationship, women's place in the Alliance was the same as it was in the family—"the companion and helpmeet of man." But women debated what it meant to be such a "helpmeet." They discussed the terms on which the family was to be organized. And they probed the extent to which the Alliance watchword "equal rights to all" applied to women. Women's letters to the reform press argued widely divergent opinions on these and related questions. Correspondents drew "pen pictures" of one another. They also sketched their aspirations for the future of the family, the society, and the nation—and women's place in that future.[44]

No less than other late nineteenth-century Americans, farmers debated the "woman question" largely in terms of how to define the "woman's sphere." This debate, however, needs to be understood in its rural context. For urban middle-class Americans, the doctrine of "separate spheres" loosely corresponded to a physical separation between men, who went off to their daily employment, and women, who stayed home and attended to their domestic affairs. On many farms, by contrast, the women and men worked in close proximity. The nineteenth-century farm, as agricultural historian David Danbom puts it, remained "a business as well as a home." Wives and daughters often pitched hay, chopped cotton, and performed other fieldwork along with husbands and sons. Even where a division of labor was more clearly drawn, as in the case of Luna and James Kellie, women and men often worked on complementary lines. The farmers' discussions of idealized notions of "separate spheres" ignored these farmstead realities, focusing instead on the future possibilities for rearranging domestic life. This explains why farmers often embraced concepts of the "woman's sphere" that were no less rigid and constricting than those upheld by their urban counterparts.[45]

Some women within the Alliance argued that the "woman's sphere" was fixed by the fireside and the home. Women might provide moral support to reform, but they should leave the political and economic battles to the men. "While we may not enter the arena of politics, or mingle in the busy commercial mart with the sterner sex," explained a lecturer to the members of the Morris County, Texas, Alliance, "in our sphere at home, by the fireside, and in the social circle, we can make our influence felt for the good of our noble Order." Other woman cited Eve's transgression in the Garden of Eden to justify restricting women's roles.[46]

Biblical arguments against expanding women's rights provided a lightning rod for critics. Marion Todd rejected the idea that the Bible could be used as an authority for defining women's place, as the Bible was only man's interpretation. Mrs. L. Canfield argued a similar position before the Farmers' Institute at Dufur, Oregon. "Woman's sphere is beyond the ken of man to fix," she asserted. "Ever since Adam's time men have been watching and fearing, lest woman should assess and maintain her own individuality." Progress would pull down all barriers, Canfield believed, so that "the work of each individual will be given as he or she is able to bear." Only "when this state of civilization is reached, the bone of contention 'women's sphere,' will have been buried with the musty traditions and barbarous customs of an undeveloped age."[47]

Writing to the *Kansas Farmer*, Jennie F. Kungle relegated "woman's sphere" to the dead era of "superstition and idolatry." Lester C. Hubbard's *Farmers' Voice*, a Chicago-based paper with a rural readership across the upper Midwest, similarly attacked the doctrine of separate spheres—"ice walls of nonintercourse between the sexes"—as a "relic of the barbarous middle ages." Southern reformers also engaged in the debate. Among the correspondents to the *Southern Mercury*, Ann Other led the way. Bluntly summing up her studies of the problem, Ann Other concluded that woman's "proper" place was "what ever the state of society dictates to her."[48]

If the notion of confining women to domestic roles provoked debate, a broader consensus prevailed about the necessity for better homes and improved domestic life. "Let us look to the upbuilding of our homes," Addie McCaskill entreated her sisters in the Texas Alliance. "Let us brighten up our intellects, attend our sub-Alliances and gain information from every possible source . . . to the best interest of our home." The home was a critical site for farmers' progress. "The true history of the world," Mrs. J. Morton Smith explained to the Bell County, Texas, Alliance, "is the record of the home life and the characteristics of its people. It is to women . . . we look as the 'star of Bethlehem,' to light the way to a higher and better life."[49]

The Farmers' Alliance made improved homes a particular imperative. It carried the promise of liberating farmers and laborers from the coarse environs of boardinghouses and tenements, of sod houses and rural shacks. Alliance members viewed bank mortgages on homes as especially onerous and threatening. And they saw home ownership as the critical test of a civilized life. "A man who owns a home is a patriot," Harry Tracy warned his audiences, "a man in a boarding-house is a tramp," who was only passing "another mile post on the road to barbarism."[50]

The "home and garden" sections of farmers' newspapers added fuel to the rural impulse for better homes. So did the inevitable comparisons with the tidy and prosperous homes that the farmers would pass on their trips to town. Home improvement also touched on essential notions of rural progress. As

Luna Kellie experienced, proper child rearing required a safe and clean environment. A well-lit sitting room was seen as a prerequisite for education
and study. And putting the household economy on a businesslike footing
demanded a well-organized kitchen and garden. Improving farm life, putting the rural home on up-to-date lines, preoccupied the women and men
of rural reform. A generation before the Country Life Commission of 1908,
rural families had organized a similar domestic modernization movement
under the auspices of the Farmers' Alliance.[51]

The reform movement also sought to reorder family life within the home.
Alliance women discussed this problem in two ways. First, they saw the need
to augment women's moral influence so as to safeguard the virtue of daughters and to protect husbands and sons from liquor and licentiousness. Second, many Alliance women understood that domestic progress required a
new relationship between women and men. Bettie Gay and other advocates
of women's rights connected the hopes for better homes with women's aspirations for equality. A woman, Gay observed, "demands that she be allowed
to render service in the great battle for human rights, better conditions, happier homes, and a higher civilization." For Gay, this was a struggle for a "better
womanhood," a womanhood with equal opportunities, "acknowledging no
master and accepting no compromise." Similarly, the California Alliance
leader Annette Nye of rural Los Angeles County appealed to her sisters to
join the struggle for homes and equal rights, "this battle for our homes, our
children and our own right to stand side by side with our brother."[52]

Carrie Ashton of Illinois also stressed the link between domestic improvement and equality between the sexes. In her regular contributions to
the *Farmers' Voice* she encouraged her readers to "strive to make happier
and more pleasant homes." To make an ideal home, according to Ashton, required "perfect equality" between husband and wife. Equality meant women's
political rights, rights pertaining to family finances, and striking the word
"obey" from marriage vows—demands that, along with the equalization of
marriage and divorce laws, echoed within the ranks of the farmers' movement. She also went beyond the formalities of law, suggesting that men and
women should share an equal burden of the housework. Although her views
on housework were unusual, many women embraced Ashton's argument
that fundamental changes in women's status were needed to realize the Alliance promise of better homes.[53]

In the idealized rural home women enjoyed the time and energy to attend
to the moral and educational needs of the family. For most women, however, the demands of kitchen chores and farm work made it difficult to fulfill this idealized role. Confronting the realities of women's work, therefore,
shaped much of the discussion about women's progress. Their long and

debilitating labors in the fields, reformers believed, meant that women were neglecting the home and the cultivation of the young. They saw the liberation of women from field labor as a precondition of a civilized and modern existence.[54]

The burdens of fieldwork weighed with special force on the women of the cotton region, where a majority of women on farms spent at least some of the year chopping and picking cotton. Mrs. S. J. Morrow of Fayette County, Alabama, wrote the *National Economist* to dispel "some superstitious idea that women don't work out on farms." With her four children she had spent the summer working hard in the cotton patch, and she reported that other women had done the same on nineteen of twenty farms in the county. "I hope that all the women that work on the farms will join in with the Alliance and pray to our State officers for relief for the poor, toiling, suffering woman and children."[55]

The Alliance leadership voiced concern for the plight of the Mrs. Morrows in the cotton patch. More accurately, they expressed concern for white women, as the Alliance showed indifference to the plight of African American women, who even more universally worked the cotton crop. Compelling women into the fields defied the progress of history. William Garvin and S. O. Daws described it as a throwback to the "savage mode of life" practiced by "the aborigines of this country."[56] Other Alliance leaders likened women working in the cotton fields to slavery. For her part, Bettie Gay pledged the Farmers' Alliance to overthrow this condition of "industrial serfdom."[57] The Cabarrus County, North Carolina, Alliance resolved to "relieve the women of the burden of farm labor, and allow more time for the education of the children."[58] The liberation of women from fieldwork required the success of the Alliance program of rural uplift and progress. This included small but important practical steps such as substituting corn for cotton.

To underscore the ruinous effects of cotton growing, B. F. Ellis, a Texas farmer, compared the labor used in planting an acre of cotton versus an acre of corn. Women and children worked both crops. With corn, they harvested in September and threw the ears into a crib. Hoeing and picking cotton, however, meant that women and children bent their backs under the "scorching rays of a July and an August sun, and they must continue to bend them until the bleak November winds makes them shiver." The added profit amounted to "the pitiful gain of $4.78 per acre," a sum that could not compensate the absence of women from the home nor children from school. Under the cotton regime, Ellis concluded, there could be no "happiness for our homes," and only "slavery for our children."[59]

Another Texas farmer, Anna Rester, hoped that through the efforts of the Alliance, "the daughters will be sent away from the fields to the more quiet and pleasanter duties of household life." She recalled the "peace and sunshine of other days" before women were driven "to the corn field and cotton field, there to take her share of the labor with the hard-handed man of strength." Of course, black women had worked southern fields for centuries and poor white women had also shared the burdens of fieldwork. But with the dislocation of Civil War and the abolition of slavery, followed by the hard times of the 1880s, white women spent increasingly long hours hoeing and picking cotton. For Rester, white women working the crops violated her notion of natural order and the proper sexual division of labor.[60]

Similarly, when Bettie Gay and other reformers characterized women's labor in the fields as a form of "serfdom" or "slavery," they shared a common point of reference in the experience of chattel slavery. Having spent her early years on a large cotton plantation, Gay had intimate knowledge of the slave labor system that compelled black women and children to spend their waking lives hoeing and picking cotton. During hard times after the war Gay had herself gone into the fields. For a white woman to go into the fields out of dire necessity was acceptable, even noble. As one young woman wrote to the *Southern Mercury*, she was not ashamed to "plow, hoe, plant, pick cotton, etc." There was "no disgrace" in fieldwork, she claimed, because "Papa has no boys big enough to help him, and therefore his girls must help."[61]

With emancipation, the black freedmen had struggled to keep their wives out of the fields. A generation later, the white farmers of the Alliance did much the same. Some of their mothers had worked in the fields during the time of slavery. Older Alliance women may themselves have worked the crops before the war, if not during it. Despite their personal histories, however, the stigma of slavery and racial inferiority hung over women and children working in the cotton patch. Izora Barlow, a young schoolgirl from Corn Hill, Texas, expressed concern that hoeing and picking cotton hurt her studies. Izora understood that for the whole family to be compelled to such labors was "like they say the negroes did in slave time."[62]

White women working the same fields as black men stirred particular anxieties about sex and race. Populist leader James "Cyclone" Davis exploited these fears in his 1892 campaign for Texas attorney general, noting that a "sweet white girl" might hoe cotton in the same cotton field with black laborers. Placing a "precious Anglo-Saxon girl down on a level with a burley negro in a cotton row. Oh, my God!" Davis protested, "and this in free America!"[63] Presumably, women's freedom meant work segregated by race. Although white farm reformers found fieldwork especially objectionable, they also viewed as degrading other types of labor that put white women in too close proximity with African Americans.

Polk's *Progressive Farmer* urged its readers to diversify their crops so that women could be free of cooking for the black laborers needed for cotton farming. If a farmer only chose the Alliance route of diversification, "his wife, dear devoted woman, instead of wearing out her life in cooking for a lot of negroes to work cotton, has time to look after the adornment and the beautifying of her home" and other more appropriate duties. In the North and West, no less than the South, women desired relief from the debilitating routines of the farmyard and kitchen. Yet these routines grew especially oppressive when marked by the taint of servitude and racial caste.[64]

The women of the Alliance strove to shed the stigma of slavery, but they also wanted to discard the discredited image of the pampered and dependent southern belle. Southern women, as much as northern women, aspired to productive activity and self-reliance. This is what Sue Huffman Brady, a Texas public school official, told the Woman's Congress at the Chicago World's Fair. The hardships and responsibilities imposed by the Civil War and its aftermath had produced "changing ideals" about a new woman—a woman with prodigious "mental and moral force" and "executive ability." Alliance women shared Brady's assessment, including her enthusiasm for opening up educational and professional opportunities for women.[65]

"If civilization pays, if education is not a mistake, if hearts and brains and souls are more than the dress they wear," a Texas woman wrote the *Southern Mercury*, then "give the girls the widest and highest education we have dreamed of." Another correspondent using the name "Country Girl" urged parents to "educate your daughters that they may be independent." Through education "our country homes will be a paradise."[66] A woman writing a North Carolina Alliance newspaper similarly noted that "the better education of women" meant "a better and happier world."[67] Indeed, rural reformers looked at women's education as a cure-all for the hard lives and social ills that women endured. Education would rescue women from overwork and financial dependency. It would allow women independence of thought and expanded visions. Practical education would also train women as industrious, businesslike, and self-reliant managers of rural enterprise.

Improved womanhood demanded innovations in the farm and domestic economy. Part of the solution lay in new appliances, especially modern cook stoves and sewing machines. A typical newspaper advertisement for a hydraulic clothes washer boasted that it relieved women of the "killing labor" over the washtub and saved "labor, time, and money." Improved efficiency mainly depended on women gaining expertise in the running of the household. Rural reformers pushed for state universities to expand course offerings on "Household Management," "Domestic Economy," "Nursing the Sick," and other subjects pertaining to domestic science. "It will be a glorious day for the South," Leonidas Polk predicted, when practical education shall make young women "of equal proficiency in the management of the household and the flower-garden." If women were to be liberated from drudgery, they would need to be trained as systematic workers. By introducing "the same methodical principles that control outside establishments," the editors of the *Prairie Farmer* explained, women could "triumph over the helter-skelter methods that render home-keeping and other occupations such unprofitable employment."[68]

The efforts of the Farmers' Alliance to promote scientific farming carried particular significance for women. In the sexual division of labor, men bore responsibility for staple crops and draft animals. For men to purchase machinery or invest in new breeds of stock required relatively large sums of money. In the case of the Kellie family, for example, the debts that James incurred for horses and machinery eventually crushed the farm. By the same division of labor, Luna grew fruits and vegetables, churned butter, and marketed eggs and chickens. Although less capital intensive, such products played a vital role for household consumption and cash income. Women labored to put the raising and marketing of their products on an efficient footing. When Luna set strawberries or planted an apple tree, she closely followed the instructions provided by rural newspapers that covered the latest science and provided technical advice regarding pomology, apiculture, dairy, poultry, and vegetable gardening—essential parts of the farm enterprise for which women bore responsibility.[69]

Women also turned to Farmers' Institutes and university extension programs for agricultural expertise. At a Farmers' Institute held in Brown County, Kansas, organizers set aside one day for a women's department where farmers read papers on gardening and other women's interests. The women's department was such a success that the Brown County farmers decided to reserve half of the next year's institute for its work.[70] Women paid special attention to the potential for new crops. "There are 62,000 women in the United States interested in the cultivation of fruit," estimated Macune's *National Economist.*[71] When the agricultural extension at the University of California offered its first class, "fully three-quarters of the applicants were ladies."[72] Also in California, a "Woman's Parliament" in Pomona held special sessions on women in agricultural pursuits. Addressing one such session, Theodosia Shepherd expounded on the benefits that the horticultural business offered women, allowing them to "go into the field and work without being ostracized or thought to be out of their sphere." It also provided women with an independent source of income. And to better the condition of women, Shepherd stressed, "no factor is so important as the economic."[73]

The primacy of economics underlay much of reform thought about women's progress. Most important, liberating women meant equipping them with an independent means of livelihood. Farm reformers recognized that there was "a large and growing class of intelligent, unmarried women."[74] This did not imply that women should march off the farms to earn a salary on their own. It did mean, however, that they must have the training and capacity to do just that. Clara Smith of Pottawatomie County, Kansas, had mixed feelings about women's suffrage. But she expressed certainty about the need for practical training and industrial schools for girls: "Yes, and a thorough business education, and the trades and professions."[75]

Prostitution, farm reformers believed, loomed as the all too likely result of unexpected death or sickness of husbands and fathers. Women on farms needed to be prepared so as to avoid the fate of desperate widows, abandoned wives, or orphaned daughters. But even within marriage women needed to have the capacity of self-reliance. Economic dependence deprived women of the freedom to negotiate a compatible spouse, turning marriage into "a synonym for lust and property owning." Lack of potential earning power, Marion Todd explained, compelled women "to sell themselves by the day, month or for a life-time to some man for support."[76]

The Farmers' Alliance looked to rescue women from dependency by expanding their professional opportunities. Small towns and rural villages offered few choices. But the choices appeared to expand rapidly in the late nineteenth century, especially in the fields of clerking and teaching. Where "brain and tact are necessary for success," noted Jennie Kungle of Kansas, the educated woman had opportunities that were making her "the mistress of the school-room, and the pride of the counting-house."[77]

Rural reformers put a premium on careers that were considered socially proper for educated, native-born, white women. Telecommunications provided one such environment within a workforce sharply segregated by race and sex. In 1870, only 355 women worked in telegraphy. Twenty years later, 8,474 women made up 16 percent of the total number of telegraph and telephone operators. Their ranks included women from the farm who worked in railroad depots and rural offices. Although the number of rural women telegraphers was small, their stories were serialized in magazines and were topics for novels with titles like "Wired Love," and thereby entered the popular imagination.[78]

The South presented especially limited career options for women. Even so, in the South, as much as in the North, changes in employment patterns inspired visions of future possibilities. The number of women employed as schoolteachers in the southern states increased by 100 percent during the 1880s, reaching 60 percent of the teaching force. To meet the demand for teachers, in 1891 the Farmers' Alliance successfully lobbied the North Carolina legislature to build a teachers college for white women. Less dramatic gains in other professions also fueled expectations of change. By the mid-1880s, for example, telephone service started to arrive in southern towns, and women operated the switchboards.[79]

The opening of employment possibilities caused Jennie Dixon, the editor of the *Southern Mercury*'s "Home Circle" page, to pronounce the arrival of the "woman's century." Women were "coming to the front" as lawyers, doctors, dentists, reporters, merchants, jewelers, clerks, and city officials. A salaried profession, according to Dixon, was a young woman's best alternative to "unwomanly" labor in the fields. Farmers should, therefore, keep their boys on the farm. But they should send their daughters to college and "fit them for some business." In the case of drought, or worms, or foreclosure, or expensive machinery purchase, a daughter with a career would be best situated to help with the family fund.[80]

California Alliance member Flora Kimball expressed similar enthusiasm about the "new departures made by women in the fields of work." She noted that "nearly every postoffice has lady clerks, and a large number serve as postmistresses."[81] Positions within the burgeoning postal service provided an example for women's future possibilities as clerks, managers, and office-holders. Dissenters held that "a good, true wife, mother or daughter" was "too good for office life."[82] Other reformers stressed the positive impact of women's role in the office, bringing a much needed "purification" of the social atmosphere.[83]

Ann Other observed that modern inventions and mass production had allowed men to wrest from women her former occupations as weavers, soap makers, and midwives in the old economy. "Thus crowded out of her old fields of labor by men's intrusion and invention," she concluded, women "must demand a more useful and energetic life." Such a life, however, was not to be recovered with the spinning wheel of the past, but in the commercial and technological realities of the present. Even picking cotton to earn cash was preferable to the interminable and unprofitable labor of carding and spinning cotton by hand. If the schooled doctor had replaced the midwife, women needed access to medical education. Women's future was in medicine, dentistry, shorthand, telegraphy, photography, printing, and other "light employments" associated with the new technologies of the day.[84]

Factory work also held promise. The big city was no place for a farmer's widow or daughter, with its vicious slums, degraded immigrants, and predatory "white slave trade." But rural reformers enthusiastically welcomed factories to the countryside. Industry would bring both prosperity and employment opportunities for women. William Peffer argued that Kansas needed to catch up with the industrial progress of New England. Markets would expand for farm products, he estimated, "as fast as men and women become permanently engaged in mechanical work that requires all their time." The North Carolina Farmers' Alliance saw industry as a prerequisite of progress. "The salvation of the South is in manufacturing," noted an editorial in the *Caucasian*, a leading newspaper of the Tar Heel Farmers' Alliance whose local alliances adopted resolutions in favor of building textile mills and canneries that would "give an electric thrill to every branch of industry."[85]

The authors of such proposals usually envisioned women as potential factory operatives. One factory booster in the North Carolina Alliance argued that "a $10,000 knitting mill would give employment to about 100 hands, mostly women and children."[86] Another Carolinian explained that with "our own families" doing the work in the mills, that is farmers' wives and daughters, strikes and labor troubles could be avoided.[87] Millwork also offered white women distance from African Americans, as management segregation policies meant only white employees worked in the machine rooms of the cotton mills. Leonidas Polk saw industrialization as a particular benefit for white women, providing them with "honorable" employment. While visiting a tobacco factory, he was especially impressed by the "wonderful regularity, precision, and rapidity" with which the women performed their tasks.[88]

New economic possibilities for women bolstered the arguments for voting rights. Eva Sims, an Alliance member in the Indian Territory, wrote in support of Ann Other's pro-suffrage position. "This day and time women clerk, work in telegraph offices and a great many other public places," she noted, "and if voting is a disgrace, those places are disgraceful, too."[89] As progress opened the way for economic opportunities, the vote would inevitably follow. "The only true way to look at the question of [women's suffrage] is in the light of the general progress of the human race," observed Juliet Martin of Pauline, Kansas. "The growth of the competitive system has caused the advance of women to the front." Now was the time for women to wield the ballot.[90]

Rural women were also drawn to politics as they played an increasing role in the public terrain of social regulation. Farmers' Alliance women advocated a variety of legal restraints and state initiatives to regulate private activity in the name of protecting the morals and health of women and minors. Kansas women wanted the opportunity to vote on "moral questions," Juliet Martin reasoned, because of their responsibilities in the protection of sons and daughters from moral dangers. Women thereby expected "at least an equal right to say what conditions shall surround her children from infancy to maturity." Among these conditions she listed gambling restrictions and age of consent laws.[91] In North Carolina, the Farmers' Alliance initiated legislation to bar the sale of tobacco to persons under the age of seventeen.[92]

The women of the Farmers' Alliance discussed suffrage as a means to "vote against the saloon and in favor of clean men."[93] They advocated prohibition, however, not because of an abstract morality, but in pursuit of government controls to regulate improved social health. Men's drinking binges left families in poverty. Intoxicated men abused women and children. Liquor corrupted the polls. And men poisoned by liquor blocked effective temperance laws. Only rural women, who mainly did not drink, could successfully take the fight against liquor to the ballot box. A correspondent wrote to the *Western Rural* explaining that women sought the vote because "we simply want the gratification of living in a land where the destructive work of alcohol is unknown."[94] Many Alliance women, including Annie Diggs and Bettie Gay, were inspired by the ideal of the government taking prophylactic measures to protect the nation's health. The urban leaders of the temperance movement correctly gauged the rural movement when *The Voice* of New York, the national newspaper of the Prohibition party, reported, "The Prohibition movement has no more outspoken and consistent friend than the National Farmers' Alliance."[95]

Rural reformers also helped pioneer state welfare systems. They embraced the ideals of "scientific charity," as it was known, stressing rationality, planning, and business efficiency in the care of those who could not care for themselves. The Farmers' Alliance in North Carolina, Texas, and elsewhere pushed for new consolidated state organizations for orphans, the blind, and the insane. "As civilization advances," noted the *People's Party Paper* of Georgia, the care of orphans "can no longer be left to the church and the street," but required state institutions. As part of the state consolidation of social welfare, the care and treatment of dependents and delinquents increasingly fell under the authority of state boards of charity. Significantly, Mary Elizabeth Lease served as the head of the Kansas State Board of Charities under a Populist administration. Lease appointed another woman reformer, Emma Pack, as the matron of the State Insane Asylum. Rebecca Hampton served as the police matron in Kansas City, Kansas, and another Populist woman, Eva Blackman, served as the secretary of the Metropolitan Police Board in Leavenworth, where she introduced a reporting system designed to check every half hour "the whereabouts of every man on duty," as well as other measures to modernize the police force.[96]

Education also drew women into politics. In rural districts the Farmers' Alliance played an important role in supervising the public schools. They discussed curriculum, the hiring of teachers, and the maintenance of schoolhouses. Committees of suballiances worked to persuade neighbors to keep their children in school, and kept watch over the moral and professional quality of instruction. As the presumed moral guardians of the next generation, Alliance women shouldered much of the responsibility for the supervision of the common schools. When it came to education, women's "sphere" was decidedly public.[97]

Yet women lacked the right to vote on educational questions. Luna Kellie became aware of this inequity when a neighbor, a single mother with eight school-age children, could not vote to improve the schools in the local school district. The local Farmers' Alliance intervened, and women with children or who paid taxes gained the right to vote in the local school district. Much later, the People's party nominated Kellie for Nebraska state superintendent of public instruction. Reformers considered women as at least as qualified as men to supervise education at the local and state level. But it was the right to vote on educational issues that first convinced Kellie that women needed to be in politics.[98]

By the early 1890s, it appeared that the farmers' movement would soon place women's suffrage on the national political agenda. The pro-suffrage positions of the likes of Marion Todd of Illinois, Annie Diggs of Kansas, and Annette Nye of California had the sympathy of farm reformers throughout the West and Midwest. The Northern Farmers' Alliance reiterated its support for the women's vote at its 1892 convention, as did the state conventions of the National Farmers' Alliance and Industrial Union from Kansas to California. The women's vote provoked more controversy in the South. In Texas, Bettie Gay and assistant state lecturer Mary M. Clardy campaigned hard for suffrage. With an interesting twist on post–Civil War debates about national commitments to voting rights, one Texas woman argued that the women's vote would receive "protection from Uncle Sam."[99]

The reform movement failed to deliver. At the 1892 founding convention of the People's party in St. Louis, pro-suffrage delegates from the Farmers' Alliance took part with hopes that the new party would endorse female suffrage. Temperance leaders also lobbied for a prohibition plank. The presence at the convention of Frances Willard of the Women's Christian Temperance Union personified the connection in many delegates' minds linking women's suffrage and prohibition. But Herman Taubeneck of the Farmers' Mutual Benefit Association and other leaders of the new party feared that these interconnected issues would split the reform vote. The St. Louis convention took the path of least resistance and deferred women's suffrage to the states. Annette Nye reported that her Alliance sisters "went home saddened and disappointed, but not discouraged."[100]

Women's suffrage fell to political expediency. It lacked support in the South and was too closely associated with prohibition. This association, it was believed, would have political costs. The new national political party needed to appeal to Catholic and immigrant farmers whose cultures accepted the drinking of beer and wine, as well as urban voters who rejected prohibition. "It would be a suicidal policy," as an editorial of the *Southern Alliance Farmer* explained, "to espouse outside issues that are not germain to our platform."[101] A resolution of the Valley Center Alliance in California summed up a broad sentiment when it called for dropping the demands for women's

Figure 3.3. Annie Diggs, Populist orator and editor (Kansas State Historical Society, Topeka)

suffrage and temperance, unburdening the Alliance of "too much of minor details, to the injury of our cause in matters of so much more weight and importance."[102]

The notion that women's suffrage was but "a minor detail" provoked controversy. Some women agreed. Luna Kellie argued that the suffrage plank would divide the Alliance in the face of larger issues. Mary Elizabeth Lease, the "Queen Mary of the Alliance," left St. Louis ridiculing the demands for prohibition and suffrage as "absurd" when compared to the economic reforms needed by the farmers. Lease would later earn a reputation for erratic and vindictive positions. But on this point she shared ground with those who believed that suffrage and politics were secondary to the economics of women's liberation.[103]

The view circulated widely among rural reformers that women's economic independence must be realized before the vote would be meaningful. It was popularized with Laurence Gronlund's evolutionary socialist treatise *The Cooperative Commonwealth*. John A. Tetts, president of the Louisiana Farmers' Union, among others, echoed Gronlund's argument within the farmers' movement. In the broader circles of the People's party Charlotte Perkins Gilman—who would soon emerge as a leading feminist—embraced similar concepts about the priority of economics. A year after the St. Louis conference, she described the People's party as "the advanced movement of the age. It means more to the real profit of civilization than all other issues of the day together." As for suffrage, although "reasonable and necessary," she believed that it paled in importance when compared to the economic tasks of women's equality.[104]

Marion Todd, Annette Nye, Bettie Gay, and other Alliance women dissented. They viewed political equality as a prerequisite for women's progress. Nonetheless, many of these dissenting women remained committed to the Populist cause. They did so because of the rare opportunities the movement offered women, and because the People's party still held out more hope for suffrage than the established parties. Even staunch advocates of suffrage shared the conviction that women's equality was bound up with the Populist vision of economic and social renovation.

The agitation for women's suffrage troubled Elles Fisher, a member of the Comfort Alliance in Bastrop County, Texas. Although she described herself as "a strong advocate of woman's rights," she believed that by entering the political arena women would be placed on level and competitive terms with men. In this regard, she charged Ann Other and the advocates of voting rights with philosophical confusion, misrepresenting Herbert Spencer. "I do not think Spencer intended the element of which he speaks [the competitive struggle], should be injected by women at the ballot box," she argued. "We, as sisters, must wield our influence at the fireside." Although Ann Other had not explicitly cited Spencer, Fisher touched on an important element of the discussion within the Alliance: evolutionary doctrines about competition and social progress shaped the imagination about women's future.[105]

Post-Darwin notions of evolution provided the foundation for Charlotte Perkins Gilman's ideas about women and society. She drew inspiration from Lester F. Ward, who in an 1888 article in *Forum* magazine placed women in the center of human evolution. "True science teaches," Ward wrote, "that the elevation of woman is the only sure road to the evolution of man." For Gilman, "true science" composed a mixture of evolutionary concepts that derived from diverse theorists, including Darwin and Lamarck, and Spencer and Ward. By the turn of the century, this mixture of ideas would propel Gilman into the intellectual leadership of the women's movement. But a decade prior, when she lectured before Farmers' Alliance audiences, a similar mixture of ideas about women and evolution already resonated within the ranks of rural reform.[106]

As Elles Fisher suspected, Alliance members used Spencer's doctrine of the competitive struggle to pursue their own agenda of sexual equality. By breaking down barriers between the sexes, they believed, women would enter into a freer association with men in the race of life, and thereby place society on a higher and more harmonious plane. This evolutionary argument underlay a treatise on women's rights that Marion Todd wrote under the irreverent title *Professor Goldwin Smith and His Satellites in Congress*. Smith, a renowned professor of history at Cornell University, warned against the "mixing" of male and female roles that would make women "competitors" with men. Todd's response, serialized for a largely rural readership in the *Chicago Express*, subjected the professor to ridicule. She noted that society already placed women in competition with men in the fields of labor and the professions. For men, she suggested, being replaced by women with superior talents might weaken their "great faith in the survival of the fittest." For women, however, the untrammeled competitive struggle offered liberation. "The warfare of sex will continue and grow stronger," she predicted, "until it reaches the climax when women shall go free."[107]

Catherine G. Waugh, another Illinois reformer, placed similar emphasis on unfettering competition between women and men. She challenged the claims of political economists that the struggle for existence took place between families rather than individuals. Women and men lived as individual beings and therefore should be treated as such. As to the objection that this would undermine marriage, she replied, "let marriage compete on equal terms with other occupations." The Chicago *Farmers' Voice* popularized her work among rural readers. Lester Hubbard, the Populist editor of the *Voice*, explained that freeing women from every "handicap in the race of life" would open the evolutionary path to human improvement. "The true symmetry of human life," he contemplated, "must be found in the free and equal association of the sexes in all possible relations, for thus are two hemispheres welded into a perfect globe."[108]

The evolutionary imagination also framed the discussion of motherhood, as Alliance members stressed the connection between women's rights and the mothering of future generations. "Has not a slave mother," Ann Other asked, "produced a slave offspring in all time?" This query echoed older ideals that historians have described as "republican motherhood."[109] Flora Kimball of the California Alliance, for example, made explicit connections between women's rights and the raising of patriots in service of the country. "The women of the next half century will be mothers of a superior race of men," she suggested, "because, being patriots and statesmen, they will teach their children patriotism and statesmanship." But her idea that patriots breed patriots as like breeds like indicated that she had also assimilated distinctly late nineteenth-century ideas about evolutionary science. "In consequence of woman's enlarged sphere," she concluded, "her children will inherit greater intellectual power, finer physiques and moral tendencies."[110]

Marion Todd, citing the latest scientific data drawn by biologists, informed her readers that men inherited power of mind and character from their mothers. Females formed "the trunk of the tree of life," whereas "the males [were] but a subsidiary force in the world of genesis." Like Charlotte Perkins Gilman, Todd may have drawn this "Gynaecocentric Theory" of inherited characteristics from Lester Ward's *Forum* article. Whatever its source, it led Todd to believe that every step of women's progress meant stronger and smarter children. "The offspring" of the advanced woman, "like the whelps of the lioness, shall be brought forth heirs of her own kingdom of power and dominion."[111]

Bettie Gay stressed even more emphatically the link between women's social progress and biological evolution. "It is an acknowledged principle in science," Gay reasoned, "that cultivated and intelligent mothers produce brainy children." And she also understood this process in terms of mothering a better race. "To strengthen, by cultivation, the intellectual capacities of the mothers," she observed, was the only means by which "a mentally great race may be produced." She did not specify which scientific principles established the link between cultivated mothers and brainy children. Had Gay examined Lamarckian theories of acquired characteristics? Or was Gay relying on Spencer directly? She did not explain. But she wrote with the confidence that her Alliance sisters were acquainted with the basics of evolutionary theory.[112]

Similarly, the multiple meanings of Gay's exhortation to produce a "mentally great race" would have been well understood by her readers. Farmers' Alliance lecturers and writers frequently invoked the cause of the "human race" as the reform movement advanced humanity as a whole. These same lecturers and writers also accepted the notion that humanity itself was divided by biologically determined racial types. By "great race" Gay may have meant "Anglo-Saxon race," "American race," or "white race." She left this to the imagination of her readers, an imagination influenced by the racial assumptions that were intrinsic to late nineteenth-century "acknowledged principles of science."

The Populist discussion of racial improvement corresponded with the focus on heredity in other women's reform movements. In 1881, Jenny Beauchamp, who later served as president of the Texas Women's Christian Temperance Union, argued that women's lack of rights produced "a prog-

Figure 3.4. Mary Elizabeth Lease, Populist orator (Kansas State Historical Society, Topeka)

eny of slaves who grow into a nation of imbeciles."[113] In 1885, the Chicago chapter of the WCTU initiated a *Journal of Heredity* devoted to proto-eugenic subjects. The Kansas Sanitary Convention the following year held a session on the principles of heredity and the scientific improvement of the race. The featured speaker was Mary Elizabeth Lease. "The two great objects of the best men and women of this life," she told the convention, "should be first to improve the race morally and physically; secondly, to make this earth a fit abode for the superior people who will then occupy it."[114] She returned to similar themes as a Populist agitator. "The race will be mentally and physically healthier, happier and handsomer," she wrote for the Populist press in 1893, "because the mothers of the race, no longer dependent upon man, will be freed from his bestiality." With women controlling reproduction, "our jails and almshouses, streets and alleys shall no longer swarm with the spawn of degraded men."[115]

For Lease, women's improvement was part of a global problem of racial hygiene. Her book, *The Problem of Civilization Solved*, published in 1895, elaborated on the larger context of inherited characteristics by setting forth a plan to "revolutionize the world" through racial social engineering. The plan called for a system of colonial partition to ensure that the "gifted white race" gained "stewardship of the Earth." The United States would annex the rest of the Western Hemisphere, drain the swamps and clear the forests of the Amazon and Orinoco basins, put scientists to work on vaccinations for tropical disease, and divide the South American continent into two hundred-acre plantations for white settlers. Since white people were supposedly "unable to perform manual labor in the tropics," Lease proposed that the government provide each white family with three families of "negro or oriental tenants" to do the work. In the process, colonization would "rescue victims of hereditary failure," as only those whites with "inheritable incapacity" would be sent to the tropics. In turn, the superior racial stock remaining in the United States would contribute to "national greatness."[116]

Although not as grandiloquent as Lease, George E. Bowen, writing in the *Southern Mercury*, made explicit the connection between making better mothers and American nationalism. He explained that for America to wax strong in the world, rural women needed to have more children. In his evolutionary imagination, the extremes of poverty and wealth were leading to low urban birth rates and possible extinction. Farmers, by contrast, had large families and long lives. If the government improved rural education, farmers could produce more "intelligent human stock," and thereby "enhance the power, strength and intelligence of the nation."[117]

Few Populist women spoke as forthrightly as Lease did about supplanting the inferior peoples of the earth with superior ones. Nor did many women show concern for the biological problems of the "human stock" of American power. For rural women the global problems of racial improvement may have seemed remote from their quotidian concerns. They joined the farmers' movement because they were farmers seeking financial relief in the face of hard times. And they joined because they were women with aspirations for educational and professional opportunities, economic independence, and, at least for many of them, political equality.

At the same time, notions of progress and evolution played a part in women's mobilization. There was a grim side to these notions, especially as they coalesced with the endemic scientific racism of the day. But belief in evolutionary progress gave a remarkable cadre of Alliance women certainty and confidence in their actions. It spurred the quest for new forms of social ties, better homes, and innovations in the relations between women and men.

And it gave life to a search for a "better womanhood" that provided a sense of solidarity and purpose to the momentous efforts of hundreds of thousands of rural women to study, debate, and improve their lives.

The women of the Farmers' Alliance yearned for change. To paraphrase Marshal Berman, they were not merely open to changes in their family, community, and economic lives, but positively demanded them, actively sought them out and struggled to carry them through. They embraced the symbols of motherhood and family, not to defend the "fixed, fast-frozen relationships" of the past, but in search of personal and social innovations.[118] In doing so, they shared much in common with the urban women's movement. Farmers' Alliance women formed what might be best described as a rural contingent of the women's movement, a contingent whose aspirations for a more modern existence helped define the meaning of late nineteenth-century agrarian protest.

4

A FARMERS' TRUST

Cooperative Economies of Scale

In the early spring of 1889, farmers gathered at a convention in Fulton County, Georgia, to discuss solutions for low cotton prices and hard times. The featured speaker was Farmers' Alliance lecturer Ben Terrell of Texas, who spoke on the meaning of cooperation. "Here is how cooperation will work," he explained. "Kentucky sells mules; you need them and buy them, paying $125 for a mule that can be bought in Kentucky for $60. You have no option. You must now buy in your home market. You should buy in Kentucky." As for marketing their cotton crop, he told Georgia's farmers that by pooling their resources they could "fight capital with capital" and leverage the price of cotton on the world market. "Keep cotton from Europe sixty days," he said, "and the price will run up."

Through combination they could do more than resist their enemies, Terrell assured the assembled farmers; they could bring rational order to the commercial system. "Everything will be in proportion," as he put it. The railroads made it cost-effective to purchase draft animals from out-of-state stock-breeders and supplant the local market in mules. The telegraph and steam-ship allowed for the organization of the nation's cotton crop. By means of combination farmers could insert themselves more directly in regional, national, and global markets, putting commerce on efficient and proportional lines. To the accusation that a combination of farmers amounted to monopoly, Terrell replied: "If it is a monopoly we shall create a grand one. It will be a philanthropic monopoly. It will distribute wealth among the people."[1]

Terrell's cooperative vision offered farmers hope. During good harvests and bad, global competition placed a steady downward pressure on the price of cereals and fibers. The price that Georgia farmers received for a pound of cotton fell from a high of 10.6 cents in 1881 to a low of 5 cents in 1894. Over the same time period, the price paid to a farmer in downstate Illinois for a bushel of wheat fell from $1.22 to 45 cents. For many farmers, one-mule-team operations and debt-strapped homesteads offered scant prospects of sustainability, much less prosperity. Year after year the high cost of fertilizer and capital improvements made for more debt than profit. Depressed rural districts lost population as creditors foreclosed on mortgaged homesteads and farmers migrated in search of new land.[2]

Yet, rather than despair, reform-minded farmers had confidence in their ability to reshape the nation's economic life. Despite their hardships they held an abiding faith that the American farmer was destined to enjoy the fruits of the nation's progress. They therefore attributed the hard times for farmers to the speculations of middlemen and the undue influence of railroad corporations, banks, and other monopolistic interests. Farmers' suffering, they believed, was far from inevitable. It was but an aberration, a deviation from the natural working through of social progress.

The meetings and lectures of the farmers' movement instilled confidence in the idea that farmers had the power to create a more just and prosperous future. Reformers insisted that such a future was neither a utopian scheme nor a theoretical possibility; it was a practical matter of business, to be achieved on the basis of studying existing realities. Significantly, farmers looked to the burgeoning corporate institutions for models of empowerment. This is what gave them confidence in what they described as "large-scale cooperative enterprise." For Charles Macune of the Farmers' Alliance, large-scale business cooperation stood for "the very essence of justice, fairness and equity." It "possess[ed] the elementary forces . . . for breaking the power of monopoly," and represented "a mighty lever that would lift the burdens and weight from labor and the productive industries of the country." Macune's cooperative ideal inspired the economic experiments of the Farmers' Alliance. Similar ideas also guided the Illinois-based Farmers' Mutual Benefit Association and the other farmers' movements at the foundation of Populism.[3]

Macune's system of large-scale cooperative enterprise marked a departure from the often local or community-based cooperative stores or workshops that typified earlier cooperative experience. In terms of territory and volume, Macune and other farm reformers launched vast undertakings on a state, regional, and even a national scale. These enterprises required centralized direction, rapidly coordinated communications, bureaucratic organization, and salaried agents and lobbyists. Farmers' efforts at centralized purchasing paralleled the experiments in the warehousing and direct shipment of goods and supplies undertaken by Montgomery Ward and other corporations. Similarly, farmers' attempts to organize markets for cotton, wheat, dairy, fruit, and other products aimed to align supply and demand, standardize production, centralize distribution and marketing, and set prices —mirroring corporate innovations in the manufacturing and transport industries that fostered cooperation and suppressed competition.[4]

"What can be done to stop the trusts?" a cotton farmer from Delta County in northeast Texas queried the readers of the *Southern Mercury*, except for the farmers themselves to "unite and form a trust." The morality of this proposition was unambiguous. "Does anyone ask, where is the consistency of those who are crying out against trusts, and professing to abominate them, and yet advocating them? Ah, you say, 'circumstances alter cases.' Yes, they do. It is a great crime to take the life of a fellow creature, but if he is attempting to take yours . . . it is not only your privilege but your duty to kill him. How else," he concluded, "can we save ourselves from ruin?"[5]

For farmers to unite in a functioning trust, however, they had to overcome formidable obstacles. Success required the resources to hold products off the market. As the Delta County farmer pointed out, this excluded many small and indebted farmers, at least initially. By his estimate, "not more than one third of the farmers" had the necessary means to combine in a trust, although "the men composing that third are by far the largest farmers." If these large farmers controlled enough of the market to enforce a general rise in prices, he speculated that eventually the number of small farmers "who will be able to join in the trust will be greatly increased."[6]

In practice, rural poverty and indebtedness, hostile merchants and bankers, and the inexorable pressure of global markets effectively limited the participation of many poor cotton and other staple-crop farmers in cooperative experiments. Unlike the educational work of the reform movement, which claimed a broad following and drew in large numbers of the rural poor, the cooperative campaigns had a narrower base. Cooperative experiments tended to expose the chasm between those growers who had the resources to make marketing decisions, and the debt-ridden and land-poor farmers who lacked such resources. For African American farmers, poverty and white hostility condemned their separate black cooperatives to failure, and the color of their skin barred them from membership in the cooperatives of the white Alliance. To the extent that they were allowed access to buy and sell through the white cooperatives, the dependency of black small farmers and sharecroppers on landlords and merchants often meant they had insufficient control of their crops to give cooperative marketing practical significance. The same applied to some poor whites. From the perspective of the poorest farmers and farm laborers, the cooperative experiments of the late 1880s and early 1890s often appeared remote and unaccountable.

Among commercially viable farmers, along with those having more immediate hopes of viability, many saw their future prosperity in large-scale cooperation. The prospects for controlling agricultural markets appeared especially promising in California, where fruit and other products were shielded from global competition. By the turn of the century cooperatives had emerged as key players in California agribusiness. As a Stanford University historian observed at the time, cooperative enterprise in the Golden State arose on the principles of the business corporation, existing "solely because it can earn greater profits for its members than can be obtained by any other marketing arrangement." But this was not peculiar to the Pacific Coast. Across the Populist country, the same business principle animated farmers' efforts to establish large-scale cooperative enterprise. When farmers in Kansas or Texas spoke of uniting in a trust, that was precisely what they meant. Farming was a business, and large-scale cooperation was a business enterprise writ large.[7]

The cooperative vision, however, represented more than the Stanford professor allowed, as farm reformers understood that large-scale coopera-tion carried large-scale social implications. The Farmers' Alliance held that cooperative business principles "may be successfully applied to most, if not all, the business pursuits and enterprises of the country."[8] For some reformers this possibility opened the doors to the future social harmony of a "coop-erative commonwealth." Marion Todd, Annette Nye, Mary M. Clardy, and other prominent Farmers' Alliance women endorsed this idea with their appeal to introduce "the principle of cooperation in every department of human life to its fullest extent."[9] Perhaps only a minority of farmers who engaged in cooperation desired the full program of such a "cooperative com-monwealth." But by way of cooperation they did hope to organize agricul-ture on a par with manufacturing and other commercial interests. They sought to forge a more direct integration in national and international mar-kets. And they looked on cooperative business principles as an essential part of a more rational, dynamic, and modern path of development.

In December 1890, delegates to the supreme council of the National Farm-ers' Alliance and Industrial Union (NFAIU) met in Ocala, Florida, a small town in the center of the state with big aspirations to become a commercial metropolis. Ocala's boosters had lured the organizers of the supreme coun-cil with offers of cheap passenger fares, free lodging, tourist excursions, and the opening of a carnival-like "Semi-Tropical Exposition" boosting Florida produce. Basking in the December warmth, delegates from the icebound agricultural heartland spent their free hours strolling through orange and lemon groves and admiring what the ambitious locals had accomplished. The Ocala farmers had focused on specialty crops in a national market protected by a tariff barrier against imported citrus. They also realized, with the help of a New York business agency, striking successes in large-scale marketing techniques. The assembled Alliance members saw in the small paradise that farmers had carved from the Florida wilderness a validation of their own visions of future prosperity.[10]

In North Carolina, Leonidas Polk and the Farmers' Alliance criticized the "all cotton" system and pushed for experiments with crops that would provide higher yields and profits. Why plant cotton to earn $20 per acre, queried Polk's *Progressive Farmer*, when grapes would earn $150?[11] When Marion Butler took over the presidency of the state Alliance, he declared that "cotton is a failure." In its place he advocated producing fruits and vegetables (truck farming) for New York City and other metropolitan markets. Success in the New York market, however, required effective organization. Butler welcomed the formation of the North Carolina Truckers and Fruit Growers' Association as "a big step in the right direction." The key lay in standardized packaging, quality control, and centralized marketing. The trucking business would soon be the most important industry in eastern North Carolina, he predicted, if only the farmers realized sufficient organization.[12]

In Georgia, too, ambitious farmers sought to bring order to the fruit and vegetable industry. They organized a joint-stock company with headquarters

Figure 4.1. John Cunningham (left), chair of the Georgia People's party and president of the American Fruit Growers' Union, and Tom Watson (right), Populist member of the U.S. Congress (Southern Historical Collection, Wilson Library, University of North Carolina, Chapel Hill)

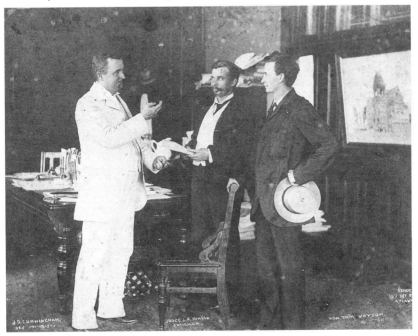

in Macon to regulate shipping and marketing and to centralize information about supply and demand in an effort to prevent gluts and sustain profits. Some of the biggest names in the farm reform movement took part. They included Tom Watson, who was elected to the U.S. Congress on a Farmers' Alliance platform and emerged as a prominent leader of the People's party. Watson joined his fellow farm owners near Augusta in diversifying into fruit production and had a personal stake in the problems of marketing and transportation. John Cunningham, the chair of the state People's party in Georgia, was one of half a dozen of the state's leading Populists involved in organizing the fruit business. Cunningham, who owned 110,000 fruit trees on six farms, served as the president of the Georgia Fruit Growers Association and the American Fruit Growers Union. With headquarters in Chicago, the American Fruit Growers Union sought to establish centralized marketing, storage facilities, and legislative lobbying efforts for the nation's producers of perishable crops. Its participants included the Southern California Fruit Exchange, the Chautauqua Grape-Growers' Association in New York, and similar organizations in Alabama, Georgia, Illinois, Missouri, Oregon, and Texas.[13]

In the Midwest, as the price of wheat and corn collapsed, farmers invested in alternative crops. Meetings of the Farmers' Mutual Benefit Association in southern Illinois discussed fruit cultivation and marketing, as farmers planted fruit trees in their unprofitable wheat fields and turned the region into a major supplier of orchard crops to Chicago, Detroit, and other metropolitan markets. Meanwhile, dairy cooperatives emerged as the stronghold of midwestern agricultural cooperation. By the 1890s, the Illinois State Dairymen's Association held a functioning regional monopoly representing a combined capital of $300 million. Although efforts at a national dairy union proved unsuccessful, the cooperative dairies of Minnesota soon proved the efficacy of national dairy marketing. Dairy farmers enjoyed a relative prosperity and mainly steered clear of the Farmers' Alliance and similar reform movements. But members of the reform movements took part in the cooperative creameries and the reformers were duly influenced by the results. They also paid close attention to the rapid developments out West, especially in California where the future of large-scale cooperation seemed to be rapidly taking root.[14]

Marion Cannon's steam-powered mechanical thresher was large even by California standards. The machine measured fifteen feet high, twelve feet wide, and forty feet long. It took fifty-two men, thirty-eight horses, and fourteen wagons to tend the machine as it harvested and separated the Fordhook lima beans on Cannon's Ventura County farm. As with many agricultural experiments in California, the thresher cost more than one farmer, even a prosperous farmer, might venture. Cannon entered a partnership with neighboring farmers to have the thresher built for the bean crop of 1890. No stranger to machines and the benefits of the economy of scale, he had worked for twenty years as a hydraulic miner in Nevada City applying steam power and industrial methods to harvest gold from the Sierra foothills. Gold allowed him to move to Ventura County in 1873 and to become an important booster of the county's progress. He was a founder and director of the Bank of Ventura (which later merged with the Bank of Italy/Bank of America) and served as chairman of the local school board. His primary interest, though, was farming. Lima beans proved a profitable crop for Cannon and his Ventura County neighbors, and they planted thirty thousand acres of them.[15]

Ventura County farmers, however, lacked leverage in marketing their bean crop. The Southern Pacific Milling Company, a subsidiary of the railroad corporation, controlled bean warehousing, marketing, and shipping throughout the region. Cannon emerged as one of Southern Pacific's most dedicated opponents, and he carried the fight against the corporation into the farmers' reform movement. His position as the Grand Steward of the California Masons helped build his reputation as a substantial farmer with leadership skills and "executive ability." He was therefore a natural choice to head the newly formed California Farmers' Alliance. At their November 1890 state convention in San Jose, Alliance members elected Cannon as the president of the state Alliance. For the next two years, he personally directed much of the work of the Farmers' Alliance and the People's party in California, his Populist career culminating in a successful run for the U.S. Congress in the 1892 election.[16]

Cannon's star rose quickly in the ranks of rural reform. Elected as the chairman of the St. Louis Industrial Conference of reform organizations in February 1892, he helped steer that gathering toward third-party action. In addition to his pointed and uncompromising oratory, Cannon's reputation benefited from representing the farmers of the Pacific Coast, whose recent agricultural boom attracted considerable attention. When he attended the Indianapolis meeting of the supreme council of the NFAIU in 1891, he brought a railroad car laden with nuts, raisins, lemons, and limes. California farmers had provided the gifts with the intention of advertising their products. Farmers in the heartland, however, showed less interest in purchasing exotic products from the Golden State than in keeping up with its progress in agricultural methods. In terms of mechanization, Marion Cannon's giant bean thresher typified a trend in California farming. Bonanza farmers in the San Joaquin Valley employed wheat combines of legendary proportions. And horticultural experiments and the development of specialty crops promised exceptionally high profits per acre.[17]

California farmers pioneered modes of group action. By pooling their resources, wheat farmers, even those with the smallest holdings, purchased

Figure 4.2. Marion Cannon, president of the California Farmers' Alliance and Populist member of the U.S. Congress (Ventura County [Calif.] Museum of History and Art)

modern machinery and applied state-of the-art methods. The valleys of the Golden State provided laboratories for cooperative innovations for irrigation projects, mechanization, purchasing supplies, and marketing. Studies of these cooperative experiments have noted that most of the farmers involved had little interest in the Farmers' Alliance or Populism. They focused their attentions on the technical and marketing problems involving their particular crops. At the same time, Farmers' Alliance members played an active part in cooperative enterprises. Cooperative growers of raisins, beans, citrus, and other specialty crops formed the principal rural leadership of both the Farmers' Alliance and the People's party in the state.[18]

Figure 4.3. Lima bean threshing machine (Ventura County [Calif.] Museum of History and Art)

Marion Cannon displayed unlimited optimism about the possibilities for transforming California into an agricultural and industrial empire. He showed particular enthusiasm for a future metropolis in the Los Angeles basin. Already "the recognized emporium of southern California," he believed that the construction of a deep-water harbor would allow Los Angeles to rapidly overtake San Francisco. And he predicted that the successful completion of the Nicaraguan Canal, cutting months off the sea routes to Europe, would ensure prosperity to Los Angeles and the whole West Coast that "the most vivid imagination can scarcely picture." Cannon had plenty of company in making these predictions as the rural reform movement put great stock in regional boosterism. In Cannon's case, the intensive cultivation of specialty crops inspired his imagination about commercial prosperity in national and international markets.[19]

In 1887, a farmer who had emigrated from Indiana reported an income of $550 per acre from his Santa Clara prune orchard, a yield that a hundred acres on an eastern farm might not match. "It is a conceded fact," a rural editor observed, that fruit growers "making homes on 10 or 20 acres save more money, live better and are more prosperous" than farmers growing cereal crops on one hundred sixty acres in the Midwest. Such reports produced predictable results. California farmers plowed under their wheat fields to plant vineyards and orchards. Between 1886 and 1893, the state's output of dried prunes rose over 600 percent, from eight million to fifty-two million pounds.[20]

The citrus industry grew exponentially as the development of the ventilated freight car and ice bunker made it possible to sell California lemons in the national market. Between 1880 and 1893, farmers expanded the state's citrus orchards from three thousand to forty thousand acres. Marion Cannon, while sticking with lima beans for his own farm, invested capital in the citrus boom as one of the original shareholders of the Limoneira Ranch. Formed by Cannon's Ventura County neighbors, Limoneira was a privately held corporation that would soon emerge as one of the largest lemon producers in California. Few farmers hoped to match the scale of the Limoneira operations, but even small farmers scrambled to invest in crops that promised high profits as well as more modern conditions of life.[21]

The citrus boom provoked a marketing crisis that compelled farmers to experiment with large-scale cooperative enterprise. The farmers suffered from price wars as packers, purchasing agents, and other middlemen took advantage of glutted markets. Citrus growers had attempted to form regional cooperation as early as 1885 to bolster their market position. But their cooperatives failed to gain traction until the "red ink years" of 1890 to 1893, when mounting debts and high packing and transportation costs pushed farmers to unify in the Fruit Growers Exchange.[22]

The dried-fruit industry took a similar route to cooperation. In Santa Clara County, the center of the dried-fruit business, local drying cooperatives proved ineffective in organizing the market, giving rise to repeated attempts at large-scale combination. This included the formation of the Fruit-Driers' Association and the Alliance Co-operative Milling Company, which formed in 1890 and 1891, respectively. But the breakthrough came with the establishment of the Santa Clara Fruit Exchange. In May 1892, four hundred farmers gathered in San Jose to set up the exchange, which put a temporary end to price cutting. It standardized grades and launched experiments in collective marketing, beginning with an exhibit at the Chicago World's Fair.[23]

Wheat and sugar beet farmers and other more traditional farmers also joined the cooperative campaign. The wheat farmers of San Luis Obispo County were among the most hard pressed in the state. When the Farmers' Alliance built a cooperative flourmill in the county, a ceremony to lay the mill's cornerstone drew a crowd of over a thousand spectators. Marion Cannon commended the gathered farmers for their cooperative heroism in the face of the obstructions of the Southern Pacific monopoly, and the San Luis Obispo flour mill came to symbolize the Alliance's efforts on behalf of the victimized wheat farmer. The future, however, lay in fruit growing, and poor wheat farmers planted orchards and vineyards as quickly as their finances would allow. The Farmers' Alliance was often in the middle of this transitional process, building cooperative businesses in the new agricultural industries. In 1892, for example, farmers in Tulare County marketed four thousand tons of raisins through the Alliance Packing Company.[24]

Three of the most important leaders of the California Farmers' Alliance rode the raisin boom in Fresno County. John S. Dore, Douglas T. Fowler, and James L. Gilbert had much in common. They all had university educations, with Fowler and Gilbert being scholars as much as they were farmers. Dore served as the chairman of the state executive committee of the California Farmers' Alliance, and Gilbert followed Cannon as Alliance state president while serving as vice president of the National Farmers' Alliance. They shared a deep ideological commitment to reform and dedicated themselves to the People's party. They also grew raisins, which meant that the Alliance ideals of cooperative enterprise directly impacted their lives. When not lecturing about cooperation and pomology at the University of California, or directing Farmers' Institutes, Fowler managed one of the largest vineyards in Fresno County. Dore and Gilbert managed their own large vineyards.

Dore proved particularly successful and suffered the consequences of his success. In 1890, only seven years after his arrival in California, his mainly Chinese labor force produced 170 tons of raisins. Harvesting grapes and curing raisins on that scale was a high-risk investment. During the 1892 harvest Dore wrote to his Populist colleague Thomas Cator about his economic worries. Hiring a hundred men at $1.55 per day meant high outlays, while cool weather threatened to spoil the curing process. Even if successful, "the combinations of packers, commission men & R.R. freights leave very little." Two harvests later, the situation had deteriorated. With the commission packers setting the price, Dore's indebtedness increased with every crop. "I guess I should have gone crazy had I given all my thoughts to my financial affairs the last two years," he lamented. "I can see no hope for the raisin business till times are changed." Alliance leaders such as Dore, Gilbert, and Fowler thus committed themselves to changing the market structure. Unless the growers combined to regulate prices, the fruit boom would lead to bust.[25]

California farmers faced an outstanding question: how to organize broadly and completely enough to control an entire market. The Farmers' Alliance made sporadic attempts at cooperative packinghouses and other enterprises. The California Grange had experimented with cooperatives since the 1870s, employing the tried methods of the Rochdale consumer cooperatives pioneered by English weavers. The producer cooperatives among California farmers, however, required considerable capital that they raised by selling shares to members. The abuses of this "joint-stock" system drew bitter criticisms, as farmers complained about the small cliques of shareholders who controlled the votes and manipulated such enterprises for their own profit. The cooperatives also suffered from untrained and incompetent management. Ultimately, the "joint-stock" methods proved too narrow to organize a whole class of producers, an essential prerequisite for regulating markets.[26]

In its pursuit of a broader and more professional system of cooperation, the Grange popularized the example of London's "Civil Service Supply Association," a consumer cooperative among employees in the London post office. The Supply Association offered several advantages of interest to American farmers. It removed the potential for abuse by shareholders by eliminating all shareholding. By charging only a nominal entrance fee it facilitated membership by the whole class of civil servants. Every officer of the association was required "to learn the ABC of commercial business," and the "corporate nature" of the post office, "a vast and complex business," provided excellent commercial training. California reformers were probably acquainted with the Grange literature about the London Supply Association, or they derived related ideas from English and European precedents.[27]

By the mid-1880s, California cooperativists began experiments to organize whole categories of farmers. Some cooperatives stipulated that shareholding be reduced to a small and equal number among all members or, even more promising, they eliminated stock shares altogether. Farmers arrived at the conclusion that by removing the contentious issue of shareholder profits they could build a system that was "most likely, in practice, to prove permanent, incorruptible, and likely to offer equal benefits to all members." The Farmers' Alliance lobbied for state legislation mandating equal or no shareholding in cooperative enterprise. Even before the passage of such legislation in 1895, however, farmers put various combinations of these principles into practice, making California's agricultural markets among the most highly organized in the country.[28]

The formation of the California Fruit Growers' Exchange in the summer of 1893 provided evidence of the viability of this new type of agricultural organization. The citrus industry posed formidable technical problems in terms of irrigation, frost protection, disease control, packing, and refrigerated shipping. Most important, it faced the marketing challenge of regulating and expanding sales across the continent. To accomplish these tasks, citrus farmers required highly centralized, bureaucratic, and professional services. They also needed an inclusive organization broad enough to establish an effective monopoly.

Both corporate growers and struggling poor farmers needed the Fruit Growers Exchange to function in the national market. The cooperative provided an array of essential services, including statistical and technical information and a tightly regulated system of packing, grading, and marketing. Members paid for the services according to how many carloads of fruit they shipped. The division of votes was made by the same criteria. At least nominally, the many small farmers with five or even fewer acres enjoyed the same service and the same rights as did the big fruit ranchers. This proved the key to success for the exchange. At the same time, with more carloads of produce and more votes, the corporate growers dominated the cooperative's executive board. By the turn of the century, Charles Teague, the manager of the Limoneira Ranch, the largest of the corporate citrus ranches, presided over the California Fruit Growers' Exchange. He additionally directed the Walnut Growers' Exchange and the Lima Bean Exchange.[29]

Corporate and cooperative enterprise blended in myriad ways. Marion Cannon, for example, sold his lima beans through the cooperative Lima Bean Exchange, whose director also managed the Limoneira Ranch, a private corporation that dominated the board of the cooperative Fruit Growers' Exchange. Cannon had no qualms about the intermingling of corporate and cooperative interests. Cooperatives formed incorporated enterprises and private farm corporations were often at the fore of cooperative undertakings. This made perfect sense for farm reformers who sought agricultural progress through combination. In an editorial titled "Corporate and Cooperative Orcharding," A. T. Dewey of the *Pacific Rural Press*, and an ally of the Farmers' Alliance, expressed doubts about cooperatives owned by "city people or others unacquainted with the fruit business," and he favored domestic corporations over foreign-owned ones. In its multiple forms, however, combined capital augured well. "There is no reason," Dewey believed, "why wise enlistment of capital in co-operation or in corporation in orchard planting should not prove of great value in the progress of the State and in the prosperity of individuals."[30]

Marion Cannon drew the line with the railroads. When he took rhetorical aim at corporations he meant, in the first place, railroad corporations, not agricultural enterprises. The practical logic of cooperative and corporate combination, however, blurred such distinctions. Leland Stanford, for example, one of the "Big Four" magnates behind the Southern Pacific Railroad, was an outspoken enthusiast for farm cooperatives. Starting in the 1880s, the Southern Pacific maintained symbiotic and often close relations with the growers' exchanges. Joint railroad and farm cooperative marketing campaigns culminated at the turn of the century with formal agreements between the Southern Pacific and the citrus, prune, and other cooperatives. The railroad also sponsored cooperative farm settlements. In 1889, the Southern Pacific set up a corporate department, the Southern Pacific Colonization Agency, to assist cooperative farming on railroad lands. With or without railroad corporations, California farm reformers saw in the intermingling of cooperative and corporate enterprise the best hope for the agricultural empire of the future.[31]

"We are today . . . in the midst of a mighty social revolution," John F. Willits told his fellow members of the Jefferson County, Kansas, Farmers' Alliance,

"and the watchword—organization and practical cooperation—is the shib-
boleth of every successful business enterprise that marks the progress of this
enlightened age. The word, co-operation, means more to us than any other
word in the English language." But precisely what did the word mean for
the Grain Belt farmers of northern Kansas? In part, it involved the small-
scale trade in coffee, tobacco, butter, and eggs that business agents of local
alliances conducted both close to home and as far away as Colorado and
Missouri. Cooperation meant building warehouses, creameries, grain elevators, supply stores, and other local ventures.[32]

But above all, cooperation meant experiments in large-scale enterprise.
There were no local or small-scale solutions for Kansas wheat farmers, who
had too many debts, too little cash, and too many isolated operations spread
over too much territory, and who competed in a global market without protection of tariff or geography. The successful organization of every farmer
in Jefferson County, or in the entire state, would gain scant leverage in the
international wheat trade. Farm reformers sought a means to "divert the great
stream of farm products from its present channel" and thereby bring the
Kansas wheat farmer into direct relations with the Liverpool grain mills and
other consumers. Reformers imagined a range of solutions, all of which
pointed to the need for centralized enterprise on a gigantic scale.[33]

Jefferson County, Kansas, farmers contrived one solution. They called it
the Farmers' Trust, an experiment initiated in the spring of 1888 by Walter
N. Allen, president of a local farmers' club. Its stated aim was to centralize
control of warehouses, grain elevators, stockyards, and other strategic points
of agricultural trade, giving the trust "a monopoly in the commission business and power to control shipments and regulation of the price of farm
products." In the process, it planned to "wipe out ninety per cent of the re-
tail men," replacing them with a system of buying and selling coordinated
by central bureaus in "direct communication with local shippers by telegraph
and telephone." For the trust to be effective it sought exclusive rights to the
purchase of all farm products not just of Jefferson County, or of Kansas, but
of all states and territories of the Mississippi Valley. Its conventions were
attended by delegates from a dozen wheat-growing states in the Midwest,
and from as far away as Oregon.[34]

The word *trust* in the name was a source of unease, even among supporters
of the movement. Walter Allen attributed this to a failure to understand that
trusts were "modern institutions" that protected "the weak against the strong"
by enforcing uniform standards. He insisted that a trust's centralized power
was the key to success. Farmers' efforts at mutual protection had failed, according to Allen, "owing to the decentralized principle of their organization."
The Farmers' Trust, by contrast, was "founded in the very opposite principle,
and has therefore centralized power with concentrated business energy."[35]

The Farmers' Trust movement received extensive coverage in the newspapers of the Kansas Farmers' Alliance and provoked debate among reformers about the meaning of a farmers' monopoly. William Peffer spoke at its conventions and argued that it may be impractical, but if successful "will have done a great good." As it turned out, the Farmers' Trust formed a central bureau but lacked a presence in the farm districts outside of Jefferson County. A farmer wrote to the Meriden *Advocate* to report that he had wanted to sell his nine hundred bushels of wheat to the trust but was frustrated by the absence of a trust business agent in his county. The Farmers' Trust failed to convince farmers to buy shares of its $20 million of chartered stock. And three years after its incorporation, a Farmers' Trust brand of mail-order wheat was all that was left of the movement.[36]

Illinois wheat farmers developed similar designs for conquering the market, although their efforts were more deeply rooted in a mass organization. In the early 1880s, Johnson County farmers launched experiments in cooperative marketing to bypass the local grain buyers and realize a better price on the Chicago market. These attempts at pooling led to the formation of the Farmers Mutual Benefit Association (FMBA), which by 1887 had organized fifteen thousand farmers in southern Illinois. The organization aggressively pursued centralized systems of large-scale cooperation. This included a system of farmers' exchanges, whereby FMBA state business agents marketed farmers' cereal crops and organized direct purchases from wholesalers and manufacturers.

The exchange system led to the creation of the Industrial Cooperative Society of Illinois. Much like the Farmers' Trust, the purpose of the society was to realize control of the marketing of the crops as well as the purchase of supplies for the rural districts throughout the state. This ambitious plan floundered for lack of capital and expertise. In its wake, however, the FMBA gained the reputation as the midwestern flagship for the reform ideal of cooperation.[37]

A Texas experiment provided the most widely imitated prototype of large-scale cooperative enterprise. The Texas Farmers' Alliance Exchange was the brainchild of Charles Macune. From its Dallas headquarters the exchange system would offer Texas cotton growers all the advantages of a centralized and regulated market, with a rational structure and direct access to credit and to the commercial centers of New Orleans, New York, Liverpool, and Hanover, Germany. It would also organize the direct purchase of supplies and consumer goods on a scale beyond anything Montgomery Ward or other corporations had yet attempted. Farmers' Alliance lecturers spread the word about the Texas Exchange as the organization expanded from its Texas base. From Georgia to California, the Farmers' Alliance set up state exchanges and floated plans for a national exchange system. At long last the nation's cotton, tobacco, and cereal farmers had found the true road to business combination and commercial power.

Some members of the Farmers' Alliance expressed doubts about the commercial viability of the exchange system and had misgivings about the centralized and remote economy it signified. The more ideologically committed members and cadres of the Alliance, however, tended to strongly support Macune's cooperative system and to grasp its significance. Mary B. Lesesne of Llano County, Texas, an ardent supporter of the Farmers' Alliance, had a discussion with a prominent lawyer about the organization's business principles. The lawyer asked her, "What is the platform of the Farmers' Alliances?" She responded, "They are opposed to monopolies." To which the lawyer tellingly observed that the Alliances "are forming one of the grandest monopolies that the world ever saw." Lesesne conceded the charge. "It may become a great monopoly," she replied, "but we predict that it will use its power wisely."[38]

In its first major trial of strength, the Farmers' Alliance wielded its power not against monopoly but against the merchants and other commercial middlemen within the local community. Texas farmers viewed middlemen

Figure 4.4. Headquarters of the Texas Farmers' Alliance Exchange (Dallas Public Library)

as largely responsible for the low price they received for their cotton. The Texas Alliance did the arithmetic at its celebrated Cleburne convention in August 1886. European and New England spinning mills paid $80 million a year on Texas cotton. Texas producers only received $64 million for their crop. The $16 million difference was the crux of their problems. Part of it went to pay exorbitant transportation costs. Most of the loss, farmers believed, went to the middlemen who used false weights, defective samples, and other devices to drive down prices. The local merchants, with their comfortable town existence created at the farmers' expense, played the markets by forming "cliques and corners." To defeat the middlemen, the Cleburne convention appealed for farmers to form cooperative cotton yards and other means of pooling and combination.[39]

Texas farmers knew about cooperation from the Grange that operated some fifty cooperative stores in Texas and a central purchasing agency in Galveston. The Grange maintained a cooperative fire insurance association, a publishing company, and several small textile mills. Archibald Johnson Rose, the Worthy Master of the Texas Grange, ran the cooperatives on careful business lines. He stressed that "all who become members of this form of Co-operation become members of a firm," and must pay due consideration to capital and profits. Although by the 1880s the Grange had lost its previous energy, under Rose's direction its cooperatives carried on and they provided the model for most of the cooperative stores, cotton gins, and other "joint-stock" enterprises sponsored by the Farmers' Alliance. Reform editors and lecturers made such cooperative efforts a key point of their appeal to potential recruits. Many farmers responded sympathetically.[40]

The farmers of Gillespie County struggled to make a living on the dry, western edge of Texas cotton farming. Soon after the Cleburne convention, the men and women of the county joined the Farmers' Alliance and sought relief in combination. The Gillespie Alliance approved an array of cooperative experiments. Its members, however, had little direct contact with or participation in these experiments. They voted in favor of participating in a joint-cotton yard, for example. But the yard itself was set up in Bexar County, nearly a hundred miles to the southeast. The Gillespie Alliance approved an Alliance manufacturing center and other enterprises that were even more distant. Responsibility for taking part in these far-flung cooperative efforts fell upon the well-traveled shoulders of the Alliance's business agent.[41]

Closer to home, the Gillespie Alliance formed a cooperative store in Fredericksburg. The store ran on "joint-stock" principles and the Alliance empowered a separate board of directors with control of its management. Such Alliance stores usually lacked the capital to supply farmers with seeds, fertilizer, or other farming inputs, and often traded on a cash basis in smaller items such as buttons, thread, lamp oil, and coffee. They conducted business much like other businesses. Management was neither democratic nor participatory. Directors were selected for one-year terms and their subordinates were excluded from cooperative governance.[42]

Employees working in cooperative stores were considered to be clerks (a subcategory of merchants) and therefore were ineligible for membership within the Farmers' Alliance. I. H. Dilly, a Texas farmer and Alliance member, took a job as a clerk in an Alliance store only to be informed that "I cannot attend an Alliance lodge on account of my occupation." Dilly appealed his exclusion to the Farmers' Alliance leadership, which confirmed that only the selected director of an Alliance cooperative store, and not his subordinate employees, could attend Alliance meetings.[43]

The cooperative experience for most Alliance members entailed education about the latest innovations in cooperative business enterprise and raising funds to make them possible. Women might lecture on the virtues of cooperation. Or they might make largely symbolic gestures of financial assistance. On Independence Day, 1889, Bettie Gay and other prominent Alliance women declared their intent to sell eggs and butter to help finance cooperation. When it came to the practical workings of cooperation, however, women, along with most rank-and-file Alliance members, stood apart while selected managers and business agents directed business.[44]

The experience of the cooperative cotton gin in Buda, Texas, southwest of Austin, underscores the obstacles the Farmers' Alliance faced in broadening the foundations of cooperation. According to the rules of the Buda Cooperative the members of the association met once a year and, in the interim, a committee of seven members ran the business. Any member of the Alliance could attend the annual meeting, but only those members who owned stock had the right to speak. This represented a significant barrier to participation by nearly moneyless farmers as shares sold for the considerable sum of $5 each. The number of shares that farmers owned also determined the number of votes they had within the association. Although no single member was allowed to own more than one hundred shares, control of the gin rested with several large investors.[45]

In 1890, the three men holding a full hundred shares—M. S. Ward, Joe Biles, and R. C. Barton—served as president, business manager, and secretary of the Buda Cooperative committee. Four other large shareholders filled out the ranks of the committee. Of the two dozen remaining shareholders, eleven held five shares or less. By 1897, the small holders had all left the association. At the same time, Annie Ward, Mrs. Joe Biles, and Mrs. R. C. Barton joined the short list of top shareholders, putting control of the gin in the hands of the Ward, Biles, and Barton families.[46] Such a cooperative enterprise, as the Farmers' Alliance recognized, provided a breeding ground for "neighborhood factions . . . individual or local jealousies, [and] family or political differences"—a far cry from the Alliance ideal of the modern business organization.[47]

Farmers addressed stinging letters to the *Southern Mercury* attacking the joint-stock system of cooperative business. "In the last analysis," a farmer from the Prairie Lea Alliance in Guadalupe County wrote of the cooperatives, they "are but joint stock corporations" to make money for shareholders. Accordingly, he and his neighbors had attempted a cooperative experiment that barred dividends to shareholders, eliminated profits, and sold at cost plus expenses. They sought to solve the "middlemen problem" and provide "cheap goods," thereby placing "the poorest 'nigger' and the meanest white man" on an equal footing with "the best farmer in the land." Reform leaders quickly attacked the heresy of the Prairie Lea experiment.[48]

John A. Tetts decried Prairie Lea's elimination of dividends as a transgression against "the human nature of men." Without the profit motive, he believed, cooperative enterprise would never realize the concentration of capital necessary to establish effective monopoly. At the time, Tetts sat on the board of directors of the Farmers' Union Commercial Association of Louisiana, a cooperative corporation seeking to control both marketing and purchasing in the state's rural economy. To launch its operations, the directors had solicited a quarter of a million dollars' worth of capital stock, selling shares at a hefty $50 dollars apiece. An investment of this magnitude reflected the new thinking about the cooperative future: to eliminate the middleman and match the power of the corporation required the creation of even larger and more powerful combinations.[49]

In an editorial titled "Economic Evolution," Tetts placed farmers' cooperatives within the context of the social evolutionary doctrines of the day. "As the human mind is continually progressing toward perfection," he theorized, "so the economic principles are tending in the same direction." As proof, he pointed to monopolies and corporations. "By combining capital and wisdom," they built steamships and railroads, "furnishing means for the cheap distribution of the products of labor," and allowing the laborer to "enjoy the comforts and luxuries produced . . . at the other extreme of our continent." But the unregulated corporations "which were formerly obliging friends have assumed the role of despotic masters." The solution, he believed, lay in recognizing that "monopoly is the outgrowth of a beautiful principle of combination," a principle that only required proper direction.[50]

Texas farm reformers sought to direct combination along two tracks. On one track they strove for industrial diversity. The Farmers' Alliance championed manufacturing as a key to progress. Gillespie County's P. G. Temple, for example, saw building factories as a means to cut transportation costs and strengthen the nation's balance of trade. Regional industries would also undermine the position of the middleman in the rural economy. Whereas the North had the advantage of more concentrated capital, southern Alliance members saw cooperative "large stock companies" as a means to pool resources for regional industrialization. In this spirit, the Co-operative Manufacturing Alliance launched a farm implement factory in Dallas and textile mills in New Braunfels and Marble Falls. Farmers looked hopefully to the success of these enterprises. Both individuals and local alliances purchased $5 shares in their capital stock. Yet, undercapitalized and lacking expertise, all of the Texas Alliance's manufacturing cooperatives failed prior to full operation.[51]

The other track of Alliance combination led toward organizing agricultural markets. In the reckoning of William Garvin and S. O. Daws, American farmers held "a practical monopoly" in the global cotton supply, producing three times the combined output of India, Egypt, and other competitors. To make that monopoly effective, however, farmers needed to engage "the combination system of doing business." It "became an absolute necessity," Garvin and Daws argued, to establish combination "national in character, with a central head, extending its branches and striking its roots into every nook and corner of the land."[52]

Charles Macune's design for a Farmers' Alliance Exchange provided a model for a centralized and complete system of organization. It would organize "the whole class" of cotton producers by combining capital while reducing barriers to participation. The Texas Exchange, with Macune as its business manager, authorized half a million dollars in capital stock to be raised through a $2 assessment on every member of the Texas Alliance. At the same time, Dallas officials, hoping to turn their city into the cotton capital of the nation, provided the Exchange nearly $100,000 in cash bonuses and city property, including a prime city lot fronting the railroad.[53]

Contemporary observers took note of the resemblance that the Texas Exchange bore to the modern syndicate or trust. In a *Popular Science Monthly* article titled "A Lesson on Cooperation," Clarence Ousley pointed to Macune's Exchange as a leading example of the spread of centralized combination among the nation's farmers. "The commercial method of the times seems to be the merging of competing enterprises into syndicates and trusts under a single management. Naturally enough a similar tendency is becoming manifest among producers as well as among manufacturing and transportation agencies." The Texas Exchange, according to Ousley, represented the effort to form "gigantic farmers' pools" under the control of a single bureau.[54]

In the early stages, the prospects for the Texas Farmers' Alliance Exchange looked promising. It put in place a rationalized and uniform system of sampling, numbering, and weighing cotton bales. Under this system, business agents across the state—communicating with headquarters in Dallas by specially encoded telegraph messages—maintained a united front in the face of local purchasing agents. Standard classification also facilitated direct sales to England, France, and Germany. In so doing, as Macune explained, the Exchange "brought the markets of the world into competition with the local buyers in the purchase of cotton." This marketing service cost the farmer a minimal 25 cents a bale, plus telegraph charges. With the initial success of the Texas Exchange, confidence grew that it represented the future of organized cotton markets. The outstanding questions were whether it could sustain control of a sufficient percentage of the Texas harvest, and whether it could successfully enroll the rest of the nation's cotton farmers.[55]

The plans for the Exchange also called for centralized purchasing. It would eliminate the furnishing agents and other middlemen by organizing direct purchases for all of the farmer's needs: everything from coffee and cook stoves to plows and harness. Economy of scale served as the guiding principle. Farmers believed that if they placed cooperative purchasing on a large enough footing it would render equivalently large benefits. "It is not far distant," an Exchange enthusiast predicted, "until we will want to handle coffee by the cargo, salt by the train load, wagons by the thousand, bagging by the million yards."[56]

To handle such a volume of business required a fitting headquarters. The Exchange building in Dallas stood four stories high, contained an "acre-and-half hall," and covered an entire corner lot. Macune objected to the plans for the headquarters as too expensive and impractical. Nonetheless, built of solid brick and costing $45,000, the building served as a monument to the reformers' intentions. "It is a fact," asserted John McFall, a Delta County farmer, "that we have one of the best buildings in the state, one that every Alliance man in this great state should be proud of." With its businesses in full operation, he predicted, the Texas Exchange would emerge as "one of the greatest commercial powers in the world."[57]

Poverty posed the most intractable obstacle to this power. Crop liens too often left the crops of indebted farmers in the hands of merchants and other creditors. To provide debt relief, the Exchange adopted a system of joint-bank notes, whereby the members of a suballiance pooled collateral for the purchases of individual members. The joint-bank notes, however, only intensified the cash shortages crippling the Exchange. Macune's original plan obligated all Alliance members to purchase their first $1 share in the Exchange by October 15, 1887. A month after the deadline only eighteen hundred members had purchased their share. The vast majority of the nearly three hundred thousand members of the Texas Alliance failed to make the assessment. Subsequent appeals realized similar results. The dearth of cash among Texas farmers partly explains the failure to collect even these minimal assessments.

Explanation, however, must also be sought within the mix of opinions among Alliance members about the Exchange.[58]

Alliance president Evan Jones evangelized the cause of large-scale cooperation with special eloquence. In his address to the national convention of the Farmers' Alliance held in St. Louis, December 1889, Jones placed the fate of civilization with the success of the exchange system. "The advancement of civilization, the development of the natural resources of our country, the promotion and perpetuation of our free institutions," he stressed, depended on "the creation and successful operation of all our gigantic enterprises." Hence the necessity to adhere to the "business principles" of true cooperation. As Jones told the convention, this left no room for idealistic experiments in cooperation with a capital C, or overly charitable systems that undermined diligent attention to accounting, investment, outlays, profits, and interest.[59]

Farmers sent into the *Mercury* a steady stream of letters expressing their determination to make the Exchange a successful business. D. F. Redding, the secretary of the Baldwin Alliance in Pickens County, Indian Territory, penned one of the most poignant of these letters. "We are all poor, and made short crops last year," he explained, and "do not own as much as an acre of land to call home." Even so, of the thirty men and ten women of the Baldwin Alliance, only one had failed to make the $2 assessment for the Exchange. These impoverished farmers joined the Texas Alliance "for convenience in business matters." In their view, failure to support the Exchange marked a failure to understand commercial realities, and they were determined to "put to shame the oft repeated assertion that 'farmers have not sense enough to do business.'"[60]

D. F. Redding and the Baldwin Alliance members belonged to the Chickasaw Nation. Their experience with the local cooperative store—a store that "gives sixteen ounces to the pound, and treats a resident of the Indian Territory just like they do white folks"—gave them confidence in cooperative enterprise. They responded with dismay to the failure of Texas Alliance members to provide more than 15 cents each to support the Exchange. "If the brethren of Texas do not do better," Redding noted, "we Chickasaws will be forced to conclude that 'white man heap talk.'"[61]

J. A. McDonald, a farmer from Wilson County in southern Texas, lost all sympathy for the local cooperatives that, he believed, bore responsibility for the weakness of the Exchange. He had a point. Funds that might have been directed toward headquarters in Dallas flowed toward dozens of local "joint-stock" enterprises. Local cooperatives also undermined the efforts of the Exchange to control and regulate the market. "Six months ago I was as zealous for co-operative stores as any man," McDonald admitted, "but to-day I wish there was not one in existence. Why? Because they do not work in harmony with the Exchange." Cooperation could only succeed, he believed, if organized from top down. "Don't you know that one hundred co-operative stores working on an independent basis . . . would ruin the Exchange? . . . Don't you know that a body without a head is dead?" The Alliance needed to first secure the success of the Exchange that could in turn "build branches enough throughout the state to reach us all. Then everything will work in harmony and be altogether lovely."[62]

Other Texans lacked McDonald's faith in the ability of the Exchange to reach them. A member of the Griffith Alliance in Red Oak, Texas, using the name Poor Gal expressed her doubts regarding the assessments sent to the Dallas headquarters. She wanted to know "what becomes of our money, and when do we get it back?" This question troubled her, especially given that "we never see Dallas, never do any trading there in any way, shape, form or fashion." To reach Dallas from Red Oak required farmers to drive their horse-drawn wagons over forty-four miles round-trip, a prohibitive distance for convenient marketing. For most Alliance members, trading with the Dallas Exchange meant relying on a system of Alliance business agents connected by telegraph and railroad.[63]

The Exchange stood removed from those too poor to take advantage of its services. By adopting the joint-note system the Exchange made a gesture to gain the business of debt-strapped farmers. The joint-note system, however, collapsed prior to the 1888 harvest, and all Exchange business was once again placed on a cash basis. Other workings of the Exchange alienated the poor. The Exchange denied full benefits to the nonshareholders, who composed the large majority of Alliance members, and even charged them an extra 5 percent commission. One farmer warned that, if "those who were better financially situated" received better treatment, the less fortunate "will be very apt to turn their backs to the Exchange." Such discrimination "makes me lose my enthusiasm and love for the Exchange," he lamented. "As soon as we begin to be selfish all harmony and brotherly love will soon play out."[64] In a similar vein, a young woman writing under the name La Belle protested against the Exchange's high-handed treatment of the poor. She believed that those capable of investing in the Exchange should do so, "and not stand and blow about the unable not being willing to help them." La Belle posed the question, "If they work with the same spirit as monopolists what will monopoly be? Is the order for the benefit of the poor and needy or not?"[65]

The color line formed another barrier to the success of the exchange system. The system of segregation between the black and white Alliances meant that the Colored Farmers' Alliance opened their own cooperative enterprises, including farmers' exchanges in Houston and other southern cities. These enterprises, however, lacked the resources necessary to function. The Colored Alliance recruited black farmers who owned land, but their farms were often so small and debt strapped as to be only marginally viable. The majority of rural blacks worked the land of white owners as tenants, sharecroppers, or wage laborers. Crop liens on their debts meant that even more successful black tenants lacked independence when it came to marketing and purchasing. Most commonly, blacks worked on shares whereby they received only two-thirds or a half of the crop. Dependent on the landowner for housing, supplies, and mules, sharecroppers usually owed their share of cotton well before harvest and might not even touch money from one season to the next.[66]

Cooperative marketing and purchasing had little chance of success in the midst of this level of poverty and dependency. As superintendent Richard Humphrey observed, "With no money, no credit, [and] few friends," the prospects for the Colored Alliance businesses remained grim.[67] The Colored Alliance organized separately and with few friends in the white community, and was always aware of the deadly potential of white hostility. In the summer of 1889, white opposition to black organizing resulted in violence in Leflore County, Mississippi. The Colored Alliance had organized a boycott of white merchants to protest unfair treatment. Whites attempted to break the boycott with threats and intimidation. Three companies of the Mississippi National Guard arrived on the scene to restore order, after which a posse of two hundred whites shot and hung over twenty blacks, driving the Colored Alliance from the county. The combination of poverty and white hostility precluded effective cooperative organization among black farmers.[68]

The financial difficulties of the Texas Farmers' Alliance Exchange produced accusations from the *Mercury* editors of incompetence or possible malfeasance. Alliance members grew increasingly unsure of the enterprise's viability. The members of the Gillespie County Alliance, for example, initially sold their cotton through the Exchange and adhered to Exchange regulations for wrapping and weighing cotton bales. Yet a proposal to purchase stock in the Exchange "consequenced quite a discussion." The Gillespie farmers eventually passed a motion that the county Alliance "cease to discuss the affairs of the Exchange until the institution went down or up." In the fall of 1889, after two years of precarious existence, the Exchange went down. The Dallas headquarters was auctioned to a group of Alliance members, who struggled to maintain it as the Farmers' Alliance Commercial Agency, a private trading business.[69]

As the Texas Exchange failed, the power of the Farmers' Alliance turned upon a new enemy: the jute bagging trust. The jute trust controlled the market in the jute bagging that farmers used to wrap their cotton bales. In the spring of 1889, it raised the price of bagging from 8 to 12 cents a yard. The Farmers' Alliance responded with a boycott. It campaigned to substitute cotton bagging for jute, negotiating with southern mill owners to produce cotton bagging at competitive prices. Henry Grady and other boosters of southern industrialism heartily welcomed the Alliance's efforts. The Alliance also attempted to create its own bagging mills in Alabama and Texas. In Mississippi the Alliance leased a building at the state penitentiary in Jackson to produce cotton bagging. The idea for using convict labor to produce bagging may have derived from California, where farmers had successfully lobbied the legislature to put convicts in the San Quentin prison on round-the-clock shifts in the prison mill to reduce the price of jute bagging used to ship California wheat. Although the plan to substitute cotton bagging was only marginally successful, the threat of success drove down the price of jute. This victory provided a powerful moral impetus for the spread of organization.[70]

A similar boycott galvanized farmers in the Midwest. During that same spring of 1889, farmers rallied to protest when the National Cordage Company threatened a 50 percent hike in the price of the twine used for binding cereal crops. National Cordage represented the archetype of the modern monopolist, dominating the national market in rope and twine. It was also a power behind the jute trust. Reformers wasted no time in attacking the monopoly. In Illinois, farm organizations throughout the state agitated for a boycott by substituting hemp twine with straw to bind their grain. The threat of a boycott forced the mighty twine trust to back down its prices. By the end of the year, the agitation against the jute and twine trust had subsided. The farmers had triumphed over monopoly—"organized evil had been met with organized good."[71]

The jute wars, however, soon gave way to an intimate peace agreement between the National Cordage Company and the farmers' organizations, a peace that reflected the extent to which reformers' ideals of large-scale cooperation were shaped by the modern business model. The ungainly collapse of the Texas Exchange failed to cool the enthusiasm for large-scale enterprise. Besides the ongoing campaign to build exchanges in other states, farm reformers were increasingly drawn to schemes for cooperative businesses on a national scale. The National Alliance Insurance System represented such a scheme. Approved by the 1889 St. Louis convention of the Farmers' Alliance, the national system capitalized on the successes of Alliance business agent Alonzo Wardall of South Dakota, who had established an effective system for marketing fire, hail, and life insurance policies. The proposed new system would organize the Alliance's National Insurance Department on a scale unmatched by other mutual insurance companies. Its Washington headquarters would install Wardall as the national superintendent and director of the National Board of Insurance, overseeing state superintendents and county agents throughout the country.[72]

The National Alliance Insurance System, however, was a modest proposal compared to the National Union Company (NUC). The NUC grew out of the "national exchange movement," an attempt by Charles Macune and the Farmers' Alliance to replicate the Texas Exchange experience on a national scale. Oswald Wilson, the business agent for the Florida Alliance, played a key role in its formation. A veteran of the Texas Alliance, Wilson had made a name for himself marketing fruit for Florida citrus growers. In January 1889, he opened an office in New York City and started to shift his energies from marketing fruit to organizing a national purchasing and marketing agency. His plan for the National Union Company entailed a national whole-sale agency that would provide farmers with all of their needs from "a knit-ting needle to an elephant." Under the plan, the company would serve as the national bank for farm loans, and the central office in New York would control a network of four thousand Alliance cooperative stores to be located in rural counties across the country.[73]

For the National Union Company to function, it needed the backing of outside capital and the business connections that the Alliance itself lacked. Wilson found the solution in a business partnership with the National Cord-age Company—the same corporation behind the twine and bagging trust. In return for 8 percent of the profits, National Cordage promised the Alli-ance financing and cheap goods, including jute bagging at pre-1888 prices. Backed by the Farmers' Alliance, the Farmers' Mutual Benefit Association, and the resources of National Cordage, the National Union Company initi-ated business in 1891 with some forty stores. This fell short of the original plan, but marked the beginning of yet another remarkable experiment in centralized commerce in the farming heartland.[74]

The business arrangement between the farmers' organizations and the National Cordage Company defies explanation unless the nature of the twine and bagging trust is taken into account. Incorporated in 1887, the National Cordage Company represented an innovation in monopoly organization with its more than forty mills controlling production within the United States. It also cornered the global market in raw hemp as well as the marketing of rope, twine, and bagging. National Cordage emerged as one of America's "great industrial corporations" by the sheer force of combination. What set National Cordage apart was that it realized a monopoly on the cheap, un-like the railroad or steel corporations that required enormous capital out-lays. Its promise of future profits rode on a single premise: with enough of the market, even hemp twine could be turned into gold. This belief drew millions of dollars of speculative investment from New York bankers.[75]

The same belief pulled in the leaders of the Farmers' Alliance and other farm reformers, who expected that the future prosperity of the farmer lay precisely in the type of organization that the twine and bagging trust repre-sented. They looked to a partnership with National Cordage as a means to realize the economy of scale and market share that would undercut the middlemen and reduce prices farmers paid on twine, bagging, and other supplies. What the trust did for manila hemp it could undoubtedly accomplish for cotton, wheat, and other staple crops.

The outlines of the plan for the NUC gained approval from President Leonidas Polk and the supreme council of the NFAIU at its Ocala meeting in December 1890. The deal was struck in July of 1891, when Charles Macune, Alonzo Wardall, and other Farmers' Alliance officers from across the country met secretly in a New York City hotel with National Cordage executives. The agreement was then put before the state Farmers' Alliances, where it gained a broad endorsement. In Kansas, for example, "an overwhelming majority" of the state Alliance supported the new business venture. The secretary of the Kansas Alliance Exchange observed that "it would be an easy thing to throw" the business of the Exchange into the NUC, which would allow the Alliance to control the Kansas grain market. Such pronouncements did not go unnoticed on Wall Street, where business reporters speculated on the potential of the NUC to centralize the vast rural market. "IT'S A BIG THING ON PAPER," announced a *New York Times* headline, "A SCHEME TO REVOLUTIONIZE THE COUNTRY."[76]

The merger with the twine and bagging trust provoked opposition. The state Farmers' Alliances in Virginia and Georgia rejected the plan, and dissent was voiced in the Midwest as well. The nature of the opposition defies simple categories. In Illinois, for example, Milton George of the Northern Alliance accused the NUC of attempting to set up a monopoly that would destroy the independent country stores. In making his argument, however, George only revealed that he was a reformer of the old school who had yet to assimilate the modern doctrines of cooperation. Reformers of the new school like Michael D. Coffeen and John P. Stelle, Illinois leaders of the Farmers' Alliance and Industrial Union and the Farmers Mutual Benefit Association, respectively, both embraced the NUC as an effective tool against middlemen. If the twine trust's millions could be used to destroy "oppressive commercial systems," Stelle argued, "must the aid be rejected simply because of the source when it comes?" The divisions over the NUC did not fall along any particular political lines, as opponents and supporters of third-party action stood on both sides of the NUC controversy. Milton George, for example, had little enthusiasm for political experiments, whereas Stelle was making a name for himself as an early champion of the third-party movement.[77]

The National Union Company's sharpest critics came from the ranks of the rural newspaper editors led by W. Scott Morgan, Annie Diggs, and other officers of the National Reform Press Association. Morgan warned that the NUC contemplated a "full-fledged trust" that would "freeze out the small dealer, who is doubtless trying to do a legitimate business." Stephen McLallin, editor of the *Advocate* newspaper of the Kansas Farmers' Alliance, similarly cautioned that the NUC represented a "gigantic monopoly" that would "destroy all competition in trade."[78]

It struck an odd note for the editors to protest against the dangers of combination. Morgan, McLallin and the other Populist editors had vigorously promoted similar schemes, from the Farmers' Trust to the Texas Alliance Exchange, all of which had the explicit purpose of establishing monopoly control of the market and destruction of the small traders. Perhaps the partnership with National Cordage set off alarms as to the meaning of a farm monopoly. It is also likely that the editors recoiled in fear of what the NUC threatened to do to newspaper advertising. The NUC proposed to cut costs by reducing advertising expenses, a step that editors warned would result in the "muzzling of the press." Morgan predicted that the NUC "would be a fatal blow to reform newspapers, as they cannot be sustained without advertising patronage."[79]

Although the editors protested in defense of the "small dealer," their own newspapers played a part in eliminating the local merchants and connecting rural homesteads with the burgeoning direct-marketing corporations. The post office carried millions of pounds of mail-order advertising into remote rural districts. In rural Mississippi, a study of postal records showed that by the 1890s both men and women were "much addicted to shopping by mail."[80] Farmers' Alliance editors fed the addiction. Newspapers such as McLallin's *Advocate* and Polk's *Progressive Farmer* carried advertising for both local suppliers and merchants, as well as for Baltimore, Chicago, Cincinnati, and Philadelphia mail-order operations. And the out-of-state advertisements tended to be larger. Philadelphia's Thornton Barnes wholesale house, for example, carried prominent offers to the farmers of Kansas and North Carolina to "buy direct at wholesale prices and save the middleman's exorbitant profits." Such firms provided free catalogs, a wide variety of goods, and usually an endorsement by a Farmers' Alliance business agent.[81]

The Chicago editor Lester Hubbard showed where advertising agreements could lead. His *Farmers' Voice* enjoyed the reputation as the foremost reform newspaper in rural Illinois. But its motto "Opposed to All Monopolies and Trusts" carried a selective meaning, as the *Farmers' Voice* was financially controlled by Montgomery Ward, a company doing its best to establish a monopoly in the rural mail-order trade. The company had carefully groomed support among farm reformers from the time of its close ties with the Grange in the early 1870s. The *Farmers' Voice* regularly ran eight full pages of Ward's advertising until in the heat of the election campaign of 1892 the company removed the Populist Hubbard from the editorship of the newspaper. Prior to this political falling out, the five-year marriage between rural reform firebrand and mail-order giant made sense to all involved. For Montgomery

Ward it provided effective advertising and cheap second-class postage rates. For Hubbard it provided financial backing for his newspaper, making it possible to deliver his Populist message to sixty thousand to a hundred thousand rural readers a week. And for the readers it allowed them to stay up to date on developments in the reform movement, while at the same time do their trading with a company whose business model they appreciated: direct sales, no middlemen, and equitable and anonymous treatment.[82]

At the same time, Farmers' Alliance leaders did, in fact, have reason to be alarmed about new assaults on the local merchants and other small-town business interests. In November of 1892, Marion Butler gave a speech to a Memphis audience expressing concern about the "imaginary line of supposed antagonism of interests which has grown up between every town in America and the country adjacent." As the new president of the North Carolina Farmers' Alliance, Butler viewed the distrust between the farmer and the "business and professional man of the small cities and towns" as the greatest obstacle to the political goals of the farmers' movement. Responsibility for this "feeling of hostility" lay in part with the Alliance itself, Butler noted, as it had allowed country people to lay the blame for their woes on neighbors close at hand. He might have added that the Farmers' Alliance had mobilized hundreds of thousands of farmers behind a business strategy that had the explicit aim of destroying the town merchants and other small dealers.[83]

Farmers' innovations in large-scale cooperative enterprise proved to be high-risk ventures. Local cooperative grain elevators, cotton gins, supply stores, warehouses, and insurance companies occasionally had staying power. Dairy farmers and fruit growers established durable monopolies. But the experiments in marketing monopolies among staple crop farmers—experiments on which the grain and cotton belt rural reformers rested so many of their hopes—quickly succumbed to the combined pressures of poverty, the global market, and the organized opposition of merchants, bankers, and railroad managers. The great gamble with the National Union Company followed the pattern of precipitous rise and fall experienced by the Farmers' Trust, the Illinois Cooperative Society, the Texas Alliance Exchange, and similar innovations. The National Union Company would suffer the added humiliation of the spectacular collapse of its once powerful business partner. In May of 1893, an overextended National Cordage Company lapsed into receivership. The corporation had embodied the speculator's pure faith in the economy of scale. Its collapse shook that faith and precipitated a stock market crash from which it took Wall Street much of the decade to fully recover.[84]

The Farmers' Alliance also fell on hard times. In the midst of the ruins of failed cooperative enterprises and an acute economic depression, reformers focused their energies on politics and the electoral campaigns of the People's party. But the Populists continued to embrace the business doctrines learned from the Farmers' Alliance, and the concept of large-scale cooperative enterprise remained an essential part of their appeal to the nation's farmers. Luna Kellie, in a celebrated speech to the 1894 convention of the Nebraska Farmers' Alliance, stressed the role of cooperation in winning farmers to the reform cause. "If we wish the farmers to join," she told the delegates, "we must convince them each and every one that it will benefit him individually." She knew firsthand about the benefits of business cooperation, as her now invalid husband sold insurance policies for the Alliance insurance agency. She stressed to the delegates the potential of large-scale purchasing and marketing, including the pooling of the state's crop to negotiate better prices at foreign markets.[85]

At the top of Luna Kellie's list of "co-operative work" she placed the construction of a north-south transcontinental railroad. Farm reformers in the upper Plains had long sought a short and cheap link to Europe and South America by way of the Gulf of Mexico. Among numerous proposals for cooperative "farmers' railroads," they devised a plan to build a new railway system from a Gulf terminal such as Galveston, across the Plains states, and into Canada. The plan originated with Alonzo Wardall, who used his extensive contacts as a Farmers' Alliance business agent to organize a "people's railroad convention" in Lincoln, Nebraska, during the summer of 1893. Out of the convention emerged the Gulf and Inter-State Railway Company. Known as the G & I, the corporation required between $30 million and $50 million to begin operation, a sum to be raised by the cooperative pooling of stock, prepaid user fees, and public financing by state and county governments.[86]

The G & I never laid a section of track. That Alonzo Wardall, Luna Kellie, and other Populist stalwarts placed so much faith in its success, however, said a great deal about the cooperative impulse that shaped their movement. Theirs was not a warm and fuzzy cooperativism of neighborhood mutuality or communal interdependence. Their cooperativism did not stand for the small-scale, face-to-face world of tradition against the modern world of impersonal relations. Rather, Populist cooperativism took inspiration from the giantism and dynamism offered by steel rails, steam power, telecommunications, and bureaucratic organizational technique. It focused on large-scale institutional structures capable of placing national and global commerce on alternative tracks.[87]

Therein lay the significance of the G & I railroad: it represented an alternative path of large-scale capitalist development. If realized, the G & I would be a "second Illinois Central." The tracks of the two companies would have required a similar scale of operations, concentration of capital, organizational system, and technology. But the G & I would have tens of thousands of farmers subscribing to the company, giving it a much larger investment base.

Additionally, the directors of the G & I would have to answer to "people's railroad conventions" and other mainly rural constituencies instead of answering mainly, or exclusively, to the financial magnates in New York or Chicago who held the largest bloc of corporate stock.

Perhaps most significantly, the G & I was conceived as a semipublic corporation, partly owned by state and county government, to be eventually integrated into the nationalized railway system of the future. The Populists' conception of cooperation necessitated a greatly expanded state function in the economy. In that sense, large-scale cooperative enterprise was often perceived as something of a hybrid or transitional phase between the chaos of competitive capitalism and the organization of state monopoly. As Charles Macune put it, the business enterprises of the Farmers' Alliance represented "passive combination to temporarily perform the functions of true government." If government were "to do its whole duty and assume control of such lines of business as are essential to all," he reasoned, it would render farmers' monopolies superfluous.[88]

In the reform vision of the Farmers' Alliance, private, cooperative, and state-based economies interacted in fluid and dynamic ways. The logic of this interaction drew rural reformers inexorably toward political action. They realized that without the political levers of control, even the best-laid business plans would come to naught. By that measure, Richard Hofstadter was only half right about agrarian protest. He quite correctly identified the farmer as a country business person whose commercial self-interest pointed to level-headed business strategies. But he was mistaken to attribute the farmers' passions for government ownership and third-party experiments to "soft-headed" delusions.[89] Rather, convictions about state monopolies and political action flowed directly from business strategies based on commercial interest. As Luna Kellie understood, it was precisely a farmer's belief in what "will benefit him individually" that led to support for large-scale cooperation, state ownership, and the other business innovations of the agrarian protest.[90]

PART II

Populists

5

Business Politics

State Models and Political Frameworks

John W. H. Davis grew cotton and shouldered the burdens of poverty and family sickness in the piney woods of Grimes County, Texas. In 1894 he campaigned as the People's party nominee for county tax collector. When on the stump he articulated to his fellow farmers the relationship between local and national politics. Although concerned about the role of "political trixters and town rings" in local affairs, he explained that the problems farmers faced were primarily national. They flowed downward from Washington, where the politicians had produced the most "vissous and viloness class legislation . . . on reccord in any country at any time." He further explained that this political record had to be understood within the context of national commerce. To the charge that Populist demands for national reform had no place in a contest for county tax collector, Davis responded:

> When they tell you that your county affairs have nothing to do with national politics they simply dont know what they are talking about, they had just as well say individual hicks has nothing to do with commerce, it is each individual hick, that piles up the cotton on your walses so each individual opinion makes national politics.[1]

As a young man Davis had served as a private in the Confederate Georgia Infantry, and with little formal schooling he penciled his notes with a rough and untrained hand. Yet for seven years he had devoted himself to the cause of Alliance education. "The day for slush and nonsense has passed," Davis and his Grimes County colleagues believed, "and the time for facts reasons and proper deduction has come." The Alliance had kindled within its ranks a "general desire for information and almost universal effort at research." They poured over census data and reports from the Secretary of the Treasury and the *Congressional Record*. Their studies corresponded to a political understanding that prioritized the possibilities, and dangers, of government action in national (and global) commerce and finance.[2]

The Grimes County Populists embraced a national political vision that pointed to a radical departure from the way politics was widely understood and practiced in late nineteenth-century America. By the 1880s, two firmly entrenched parties dominated the political scene. At the national level, Democrats and Republicans held much in common as they shared a conservatism that was acceptable to the financial and corporate establishment. With so little separating them, the two parties appealed to voters on the basis of party and sectional prejudice. In much of the North and West, Republicans waived the "bloody shirt" to remind voters that the Democrats, the "party of rebellion," bore responsibility for the Civil War, just as Democrats in the South played on white fears of the Republicans as the party of carpetbaggery and "Negro rule." Meanwhile, the national party leaders stirred the electorate with their election-year battles over the tariff. Otherwise, they mainly succeeded in keeping issues of substance from the national agenda.[3]

The real political action took place at the state and local level, where party organizations mobilized voters in fervent campaigns about liquor and lotteries, public schools and public services. The warring sides tended to divide on cultural lines. Among other such divisions, mainly Protestant and native-born Republicans often saw Catholic and immigrant Democrats as their political enemies. Whomever the enemy might be, late nineteenth-century politics invariably orbited around party organizations. Party bosses directed operations of the party caucuses, legislative committees, and urban machines. Corporate favors, kickbacks, and the "spoils system" of rewarding party loyalty with government jobs and contracts augmented the power of both machine and boss. At the same time, the political system rested on party men in urban neighborhoods and rural towns and villages, where face-to-face negotiations over promised services and patronage often determined political outcomes.[4]

The highly localized and partisan political system presented difficult choices for reformers. One option was to seek influence within the Democratic and Republican parties. Advocates of civil service laws, greenbacks, labor rights, temperance laws, and women's suffrage made inroads into the two dominant parties, especially at the state and local levels. Frustrated by the intransigence of national party leaderships, reformers also experimented with going outside of the traditional parties, organizing the Independent, Greenback-Labor, Prohibition, and other third parties.[5]

For the Farmers' Alliance, limited successes in local and state politics only strengthened the conviction that the solution to the farmers' problems lay at the national level. In rural districts of the South and West, the Alliance compelled Democratic and occasionally Republican candidates to pledge support for farmers' demands. However, whether Democratic or Republican, presidents, congressional leaders, and their loyal party functionaries stood in the way of national reform. This brought many members of the Farmers' Alliance and associated organizations to the conclusion that they needed a new independent political party to achieve the economic and financial reforms that they envisioned. The result was the People's party, the most powerful third-party movement since the formation of the Republican party prior to the Civil War. Its stated goals focused on reconfiguring national commerce. However, it also strove for a new type of politics that would deliver rationalized, nonpartisan, and businesslike governance.

Davis and his Farmers' Alliance neighbors believed in nonpartisanship as a political ideal. The organization's primary purpose, according to the Alliance's declaration of principles, was "to labor for the education of the agricultural classes in the science of economical government, in a strictly nonpartisan spirit." Alliance members viewed party prejudice as the enemy of reform and sought to supplant loyalty to a political party or its candidates with "the advocacy of principles and interests." More than that, they viewed the party caucus, the legislative committee, the patronage system, and the "spoils of office"—the essential nuts and bolts of the existing political process—as inimical to their conception of a clean and true politics.[6]

"Though non-partisan," Davis explained, "the Alliance is political to the core." Its politics, however, was of a rare type, rooted in the "science of government" and based on knowledge of the "relationship of the government to finance, commerce, agriculture and transportation." For Davis and the Farmers' Alliance movement, government was both a knowable science and a technical and administrative mechanism for the rational and equitable regulation of finance and commerce.[7]

To the question "what is politics?" an editorial in the *Dakota Ruralist* replied: "The science of government. The regulation of our own affairs as a commonwealth."[8] As Leonidas Polk put it: "We have at length learned the difference between partyism and politics. Politics is the science of government: partyism is a little collar with a chain on it."[9] Accordingly, the Farmers' Alliance was political in the "broader and higher sense of the term," Polk explained, in that it "seeks to inculcate those principles which are essential to a proper balance and symmetrical growth in our national progress."[10]

Charles Macune reduced the theory of government to naked essentials: government "is a business organization for carrying on the public business in a commonsense, business-like manner." He believed that government functions "should be reduced to business terms, placed upon a business basis and attended to by business agents." As commerce suffered at the hands of middlemen, bankers, and corporate lawyers, the government suffered from politicians and their acolytes. Just as he did in Macune's system of large-scale cooperative enterprise, the professional business agent was to take the central role in the business of government.[11]

Such antiparty politics partly explains why Macune was so troubled when the Farmers' Alliance placed the organization's weight behind the People's party. For Macune, "going into politics" violated sworn pledges of nonpartisanship, and he joined the sizable ranks of Alliance members who stuck with the traditional parties (although without recognizing the partisan nature of their traditional loyalties). Macune stayed with the Democrats, a commitment that by 1892 compelled him to withdraw from the Farmers' Alliance. But even with Macune's departure, the Macunist notions of "businesslike" and nonpartisan politics continued to hold sway within the movement and the new People's party.

Stephen McLallin of the Kansas Farmers' Alliance argued that independent political action would educate the people "to ignore party, to rise above it" to a "higher and nobler and purer politics."[12] Annie Diggs noted of the newly forming People's party: "We call it a party, but it is not right so. It is a great uprising of the people" aimed at a new regime where the nation's business agents did the work of the people they served.[13] Leonidas Polk saw the emergence of a higher politics in the growing recognition among the people of the "duties, functions and powers of the government as their general agent."[14]

Perhaps William Peffer best captured the meaning of the antiparty politics of the new party in his widely distributed treatise *The Farmer's Side*. He noted that "the Government of the United States is simply the agent of the people," adding that if the nation's farmers were to have this agent properly serve their commercial interests they must project political power. As a model for political action he pointed to the bankers, manufacturers, railroad companies, and cattle dealers, all of whom understood the need to unite their separate and distinct organizations for their common interest. "Now, let the farmers and their co-workers learn from the lessons which these things teach." What was needed was not a traditional political party. Rather, the Farmers' Alliance and like organizations should maintain their individuality just as the railroad associations did, while at the same time combining into a "grand national body for political purposes." "Let us organize for business," Peffer counseled, "and let that business be one of intense political power."[15]

The stress on the business or commercial side of political power indicated what was innovative about the politics of Populist reform. Distrust of parties as political institutions had motivated third-party movements at least since the Know-Nothing movement of the 1850s. The Populists inherited this antiparty tradition. The People's party, according to Annie Diggs, represented "a protest against the dangers and tyranny of permanent party organization."[16] The Populists, however, were also trailblazers, participants in what sociologist Elisabeth Clemens describes as a "flurry of political invention" in which new "interest group politics" challenged partisan dominance in the late nineteenth and early twentieth century. Antiparty reformers of an earlier era had stressed putting country above party; when stumping for votes the Populists did the same.[17] But as Peffer so succinctly explained, this was a new type of antipartyism: the political power of business interests.

The quest for political power inspired the "industrial conferences" in Cincinnati (1891) and St. Louis (1892) that gave birth to the People's party. The new party plunged into the work of putting the nation's political life on

Figure 5.1. William Peffer, editor of the *Kansas Farmer* and Populist U.S. senator (Kansas State Historical Society, Topeka)

the proper commercial footing. It focused on government action to provide low-cost and efficient transportation and telecommunications that would bring western and southern farmers into closer connection with northeastern and European markets. It pursued national reforms to reduce the cost of credit and expand the money supply and thereby cheapen the cost of agricultural inputs. The demands in the People's party platform—from cheap farm credit to currency inflation—provided telling evidence that rural reform had indeed "organized for business."[18]

Populist politics, however, represented more than the sum total of its business demands. It also represented an alternative notion of what freedom meant in America, as the reform movement displayed considerable skill in translating the commercial politics of the Farmers' Alliance and kindred organizations into the familiar historical idiom of American liberty. On the lecture circuit Jefferson and Jackson figured as the historical godfathers of Populist reform, with Wall Street and the railroad corporations replacing King George and Nicholas Biddle's bank as the symbols of tyranny. Of course, to claim the heritage of Jefferson and Jackson demanded resort to rhetorical alchemy. How, for example, could the old ideals of states' rights, decentralized power, and limited government be reconciled with the Populist demands for a vastly expanded role for centralized government monopolies in the rural and national economy?

The explanation for such contradictions lies neither with deceit nor delusion. Rather it lies with the protean nature of the American watchwords of liberty. From the Revolutionary generation to the present day, jeremiads about imminent threats to freedom have remained a constant of American political life. The Populists proved masters of the art. They could cite with great facility from Jefferson and Webster, Jackson and Lincoln to warn their constituents about the threats to their freedom and "industrial liberty." Such was their political heritage. But, as historian Eric Foner reminds us, the meanings of freedom changed from one generation to the next. Consequently, the Populists' deference to the freedom claims of their political ancestors often appeared oddly out of sync with the substantive content of the "industrial liberty" that they sought.[19]

A close look at their hopes for "scientific government" shows that the Populists were acutely aware of the new conditions in which they lived. Their conceptions of government and politics took inspiration from the new materials at hand, including the emerging possibilities offered by combination, centralization, bureaucracy, and state-centered economics. The Populists paid homage to the democracy of their political ancestors. But theirs was a new type of political ideal, a majoritarian vision shaped by and in service to the commercial, managerial, and antiparty requirements of business politics.

The postal service provided a model for the Populist vision of government as business. The new innovations in American society provided J. W. H. Davis and his Grimes County Alliance colleagues with blueprints for restructuring society. As Davis explained, they "made a close study of political economy which deals with the most common things of life." Few things were more uniformly common in the life of the farmer than the post office. The Post Office Department represented the largest branch of the federal government, the nation's most extensive bureaucracy, and the singular institution in America with which farm families had a regular connection. The striking success of the federal postal service in delivering the nation's mail fueled reformers' imaginations about the viability and necessity of state-run enterprise.[20]

"The American people are quick to apply new inventions to lessen the expense or increase the profits in private enterprises," noted the Populist editor Cuthbert Vincent, but "have been woefully slow to adopt new ideas in government." He predicted that with the "object lesson of the postoffice before us," in a few years "the next step in evolution will be the recognition of business methods in attending to the affairs of society." The same model of administration that worked for national mail delivery could also organize a national weather bureau, labor and farm statistics, and warehouse, marketing, and credit services, as well as postal banking, postal package express, and postal telegraph and telephone.[21]

The rapid expansion of mail service in the years after the Civil War made a salient impact on American life, especially in rural locales. A former postal clerk in North Carolina reported on the wonders of the "ubiquitous" mail system that could reach every person in the United States for 2 cents a letter. In "rough and jagged" backcountry it might cost the government $5 or $10 to deliver a letter, "yet the aggregate whole reduces the expense of all." In contrast to the apparently arbitrary rates and abuses of the railroad and telegraph companies, the post office was a model of uniform, fair, and equitable business practices.[22]

"Hardly any feature of modern civilization is more striking," reported Lester Hubbard's *Farmers' Voice*, "than the development and present extent of communication by means of the mail." Cheap rates had ushered in the "modern idea" that mail service was no longer a luxury for the few. With fifty-seven thousand offices, handling three and a half billion pieces of mail a year, "there is no department of Government with which as large a part of the people has to do, and none which the people has to deal so often, as the post-office." Of course, Hubbard had special reason to welcome this "modern idea." The newspaper postal rate of 1 cent per pound made it possible to connect the *Voice*, doubled in weight by Montgomery Ward price lists, with tens of thousands of rural readers.[23]

The postal subsidy providing free delivery within county limits also played a role in rural politics by augmenting the influence of small newspapers in remote districts out of reach of the railways. The town of Comanche, Texas, for example, lay sixteen miles south of the closest railroad depot. This put Comanche's citizens out of range of the *Dallas Morning News* or the *St. Louis Globe-Democrat*. But the postal subsidy allowed the local reform leader Thomas Gaines to turn his *Pioneer Exponent* newspaper into an effective vehicle of political insurgency. He realized a countywide readership and, despite meager resources and a remote location, kept *Exponent* readers in close contact with national developments. Among other things, he established a postal subscription partnership (another subsidized service) with the *Chicago Express*, keeping county farmers abreast of the latest postings from the headquarters of the greenback reform movement. The postal system served as a political and intellectual lifeline for Comanche reformers, who duly lauded the virtues of the system. As one local farmer put it: "If a correct picture could be taken of all the post offices in the U.S. during business hours, it would be the grandest sight ever seen and would make many men feel proud of the system."[24]

Farm reformers did, indeed, feel proud of the system. Alliance women pointed to the post office, which employed a number of female clerks and postmistresses, as an example for female advancement. With the mail service's reputation for scrupulous fair treatment, Populist farmers in Merced County, California, favored the idea of resolving their transportation problems by simply expanding the postal system to accommodate "sending farm products by mail."[25] A farmer visiting the nation's capital found the small stature of the Post Office Department building a cause for concern. Writing to Charles Macune's *National Economist* under the pen name Civis, the visitor observed that the post office was the "one department in which every citizen of this grand country is interested." The building, however, failed to "comport with the dignity of the Nation," and threatened "to affect its perfect operations." He recommended extending the Post Office Department to the west and raising it two stories higher so that it might be "rescued from its dwarfed condition."[26]

Tom Watson noted something else about the post office on his arrival in Washington in 1891 as a newly elected congressman: "The Mail Carriers are uniformed in Confederate Grey," he reported to his Georgian constituents.[27] For many southerners the mail service provided evidence that centralized administration at the federal level could transcend the sectional divide. This was unlike the federal government's other "giant system" of that era, the pension bureau that provided benefits for Union veterans of the Civil War. The Populists showed sympathy for soldiers' pensions, and occasionally expressed hopes that they would be extended to Confederate veterans, too. But the pension system never grabbed the Populist imagination as had the post office, partly because of its sectional limitations and partly because of the perception that the "political bum" earning an officer's pension plundered the system at the expense of the common soldier.[28]

The mail service, of course, suffered from its own inequities. Farm reformers demanded that mail carriers deliver mail to rural customers, just as they did to urban ones, so that farmers would not be compelled to trek to town to receive their mail. In the name of "equal rights for the country and town," Tom Watson made rural free delivery into a political campaign. The farmer in his remote homestead had the same right to timely information as the city dweller. "Literature is a civilizer wherever it goes," Watson noted. "Quick mails encourage it; slow mails retard it." In 1893, the U.S. Congress appropriated $10,000 to experiment with rural free delivery, a bill that Watson called "the first purely and distinctively Populist measure." The Populist Marion Butler of North Carolina worked along similar lines in the U.S. Senate.[29]

Apart from convenience for the farmer, rural free delivery also posed a direct challenge to the localized system of political patronage in favor of centralized administration. The Post Office Department's 77,000 rural postmasters represented the nation's largest pool of federal patronage jobs. The local postmaster often owned a local store and belonged to the "town rings" of local political organizations. Rural free delivery shifted responsibility from these local political brokers to a network of mail carriers directed from Washington. The Populists may not have been the prime mover of this shift, as officials within the Post Office Department itself also looked to undercut the power of the local postmasters to put the bureaucracy on a more rational and modern footing. But farm reform provided a powerful rural constituency for squeezing out the political influence of postal patronage and instituting more uniformly bureaucratic principles.[30]

"Anachronisms in a civilized age," "relics of barbarism," and "the statesmanship of the cowboy engrafted on the appetite of the coyote"—such were the charges that the Vincent brothers directed at the system of postal appointment. The Populists proposed several solutions, including reducing salaries and other plums of post office jobs, electing postmasters by direct vote, and extending civil service law to all postal employees. As the Vincents argued, "the people generally don't care a straw whether the men who hand them their letters, or do other routine matters for them, belong to the republican, democratic, Populist or prohibition parties, so long as they do their work politely and well." Delivering the mail should be done exclusively on the basis of merit "ow[ing] nothing to politicians of any party."[31]

Extending uniform civil service rules through the ranks of the post office would produce a more rational system of bureaucratic organization. The reform editors of the *Pacific Rural Press*, for example, saw permanent appointments and promotions on the basis of efficiency as the key to putting the postal service "on a right basis." By applying the same "business methods" of permanent organization used by railroad corporations, the post office would remove the "exceedingly bad influence" of politics. As the editors noted, it would also provide a test for farm reformers' visions of "large governmental administration in a continuous line."[32]

The example of the post office supplied the Populists with their most potent and widely applied argument for nationalizing what they considered "natural monopolies," especially the railroads. Farm reformers aimed much of their political fire at the railroad corporations. In Kansas, California, and other states where railroad controversies loomed large, resentment against the railroad corporations provided impetus for the Populist revolt. Grievances against the railroad capitalists and their managers, however, rarely translated into antipathy toward railroads as an essential technology and organization. Farm reformers, understanding that railroads provided the lifeline that made farming commercially viable, often rested their hopes for progress on expanded and improved railway lines. Charles Macune considered the railroad one of the "greatest creations of genius for the furthering of the progress of enlightenment."[33]

Herein lay the rub. The farmers' recognition of their dependency on the railroads led them to the conclusion that railway systems were dangerously susceptible to monopolistic abuses. For their part, the railroad capitalists were no less dependent on farm shipments for their profits, a reality that helps explain the relative stability of freight rates. Nonetheless, farm reformers believed that corporate control thwarted the dynamic potential of rail transport, frustrating their hopes for cheap, rational, and efficient connections with national and world markets. They especially resented evidence of arbitrary charges and unfavorable routes, as well as stock-watering, political favors, and other nefarious business dealings. The railroads practiced such abuses with impunity because, as Macune would stress, they were in a line of business essential to all, allowing for monopoly and "extraordinary power over the masses."[34]

The Populists viewed the railroads as public highways, which, like canals and post roads, provided a means of public communication and transportation. Reformers considered railroads to be public institutions because of their social function, including large federal contracts to carry the mail, as well as the extensive use of public funds in railroad construction. To stimulate railroad expansion—often with the support of farmers' organizations—town and county officials, state legislatures, and the U.S. Congress authorized untold millions of dollars in subsidies, bonds, and grants to the corporations. In Kansas alone, railroad companies held over eight million acres of land granted by the state and federal governments. Public facts belied the corporate claims of private rights of ownership and led the Populists to demand public control.[35]

By what means was this public control to be exerted? At least initially, the Farmers' Alliance campaigned for state railroad commissions. Through regulatory boards and commissions, reformers hoped to establish "rigid, honest, and just" supervision and a centralized authority for adjudicating conflict and removing abuses. Enthusiasm for state railroad commissions ran high within the Farmers' Alliance in Texas, North Carolina, and elsewhere in the South. In Kansas, William Peffer offered effusive praise. "The Commissioner system, with ample powers vested in the Commission," he informed the readers of the *Kansas Farmer*, "is the best method of dealing with and regulating railroads. The Railroad Commissioners of Kansas have been able, without friction or serious difficulty . . . to amicably adjust a very large number of controversies."[36]

For reformers such as Peffer, railroad commissioners and their bureaucratic power represented the possibilities of governance by businesslike public agents. The commissions, however, often failed to live up to the promise when corporate managers defied or circumvented their rulings or crippled them by legislative action. State commissions also faced the daunting task of regulating interstate railroad traffic. The failings of the commission system provoked a mixed response. In North Carolina, the Farmers' Alliance fought back with demands to strengthen the machinery and efficiency of the commission. The Texas Farmers' Alliance grew doubtful that the commission system was adequate and increasingly discussed the need for state and national ownership. "Government ownership of railroads," reasoned reformers in Comanche County, "would enable people to travel for enlightenment, information and pleasure, and would go farther to break the bonds of prejudice than any other one thing possible to be done." By December of 1890, concerns about the efficacy of the commission system were expressed in the platform adopted at the Ocala, Florida, meeting of the National Farmers' Alliance, which called for government railroads in the case of the failure of the commission system.[37]

In California, where the railroad corporations had run roughshod over the railway commissioners, the Farmers' Alliance sought more immediate action. The state president of the Alliance, Marion Cannon, had a long-standing feud with the Southern Pacific Railroad, whose private control of transportation posed the main obstacle to realizing his dreams for the development of southern California. Cannon focused on the region's three acute needs for improved infrastructure: the dredging of a deep-water harbor at Los Angeles, digging a Nicaraguan canal, and expanded railway access. He believed that the Southern Pacific managers would not or could not meet these needs, and that private corporations fattened on public subsidy choked regional prosperity. Only federal ownership of the "agencies of public transportation and communication" could unlock the potential economic dynamo of the Los Angeles basin.[38]

Cannon doggedly campaigned for government ownership of the railroads. He issued directives to the lecturers of the California State Farmers' Alliance that they must restrict their speeches to only six points, five of which pertained to the railroads and the related Nicaraguan canal. His stubborn insistence on government ownership of the canal fostered unease within the ranks of the state's farmers, many of whom feared that a conflict over nationalizing the canal would slow practical progress on its construction. Although Cannon embraced the Ocala platform of the National Alliance, he rejected the platform's formula of government ownership of the railroads only if the commission system failed to correct the abuses. At his urging the state Alliance adopted the demand for "absolute and unconditional" government ownership of the railroads "as speedily as possible." He repeated this demand at the 1892 Omaha convention of the People's party, where he provoked a roar of approval when he stood up to attack the policy of asking the railroads for discounted passage for convention delegates. Why request favors from the corporations, he queried the assembly, when within a decade the people would own their own railroad?[39]

By this time Cannon was preaching to the converted. The reform movement had already endorsed government ownership at the St. Louis conference held earlier that year, and reform editors and lecturers turned their attention to defeating the critics of a nationalized railway. To the objection that it would give the government too much power, the Minnesota Populist leader Ignatius Donnelly noted that it was the political power of the railroads that made it "an impossible thing" to "regulate the roads by law." To remove the fear of political abuse of federalized railroads, the Omaha Platform called for a constitutional amendment to extend civil service protection to all federal employees.[40]

Farm reformers also pointed to international developments as evidence that government railways were not only efficient but marked a higher and more progressive stage of civilization. The Kansas Alliance leader Percy Daniels pointed to the Australian example, where the government ensured a rational rate structure, fewer train accidents, and peaceful labor relations. He also espoused "The European Plan" whereby "natural monopolies" provided similar advantages to the public. That the United States stood nearly alone in rejecting government control only stood as testimony to the country's lack of progress.[41]

American railroads languished in primitive backwardness because the corporations "keep back the clock of civilization." This was the message that Tom Watson delivered to a packed audience at the Degive's Opera House in Atlanta during the spring of 1894. By comparison, he noted "the German Empire is to-day the mightiest civilized force . . . that this world ever saw." The evidence of this civilization lay with its cheaper, safer, and otherwise superior railroads. "In Germany," Watson explained, "when the Emperor travels he pays his way like a gentleman," whereas in America senators beg for corporate passes and do the corporate bidding.[42]

European models captured the imagination of Marion Todd. Her 1893 treatise *Railways of Europe and America* confirmed Todd's reputation as the reform movement's leading authority on the railway question. She undertook her study with the help of fellow Illinois farm reformer and national People's party chairman Herman Taubeneck, who provided translations. She found that of all the railroad systems studied, the Hungarian "zone system"

Figure 5.2. Marion Todd, Populist orator and theorist (Doe Library, University of California, Berkeley)

MARION TODD.

offered the best model, a means to rationalize national rate structures that would "revolutionize the Railway system of the world if adopted." Among its other measures to reduce costs and improve service, the "zone system" used post offices as ticketing agencies. Todd noted that in the best railway system, "profit or loss in dollars should be as foreign as the same in connection with the Post Office Department."[43]

Tom Watson's *People's Party Paper* expressed similar enthusiasm for the Hungarian system and its use of postage stamp ticketing. With such a system, the post office would eliminate the ticketing and advertising agencies that in America cost $200 million a year. The system adopted in Hungary and elsewhere, the *People's Party Paper* noted, represented "the kind of centralization we need in this country." By cutting the rates and increasing the efficiency of transport, "it centralizes bread and meat into the mouths of the workingman's children and clothes on their backs." Nationalized railways would also improve mail service and cut in half the tens of millions of dollars a year that the Post Office Department paid private rail lines to move the mail.[44]

Along with the railroad system, the Populists viewed the banking and monetary systems as antiquated, premodern obstacles to progress. The so-called money question lay at the heart of the Populist understanding of the "science of government." Whether in the local Farmers' Alliance lodges or People's party clubs, the study of the money supply had a regular place on the agenda. Farm reformers believed that through their efforts at statistical calculation, research, and investigation, they could put the nation's governance on the secure footing of rapid and equitable development. This proposition appeared to reformers as especially indisputable in regard to devising remedies for the tight money supply and deflationary price spiral of the 1880s and 1890s.[45]

The reform press published dozens of books with titles such as *Metallic Money and Hard Times*, *A Better Financial System*, *Our Money Wars*, and *Science of Money*. Among these, perhaps two works best captured the Populist outlook. Reform editor Seymour Norton's *Ten Men of Money Island* appeared in 1891, providing an exposition of the greenback doctrines of a government-issued paper currency and low-interest loans. The work popularized the financial theories originally developed in the 1840s by Edward Kellogg, who wrote about the need for a flexible and centrally issued "legal tender" paper currency freed from the chains of gold and silver. He also advocated government control of interest rates and "land-loans" to farmers and manufacturers. An expanding currency and cheap credit would ensure economic growth, close the gap between rich and poor, and make for internal improvements "in a perfection unexampled in the history of nations."

Ten Men of Money Island was part of a broader revival of Kellogg's theories in the 1880s and 1890s, and contributed to Populist ideas about "scientific money."[46]

The *Seven Financial Conspiracies*, written by Sarah Emery of Lansing, Michigan, sounded a Populist jeremiad about the dangers of currency contraction. With the first of its many editions published in 1887, it recounted the seven acts of "Shylock's tragedy" in which the nation's fate was sacrificed to bondholders and bankers and their mounting "hordes of gold." The Civil War served as the prelude to the tragedy, a national trauma encouraged by the "money kings of Wall Street" who only feigned concern for black slaves to satisfy their own "thirst for human gore" and to seize possession of the national finances. Implicating Shylock in the fratricidal bloodletting served a nationalist theme that resonated with Emery's many readers on both sides of the Mason-Dixon Line. Before the guns had cooled, she explained, the federally chartered national banks plotted to destroy the greenbacks issued to finance the war and to redeem their war bonds in high-priced gold. The conspiracies climaxed with the "Crime of '73" and the demonetization of the silver dollar. The resulting contraction of the currency, according to Emery, produced "more misery and crime to the people of this country than all the wars, pestilence and famine with which they have ever been afflicted."[47]

Emery's tale of conspiracy contained an eclectic mixture of currency theories. Those reformers who favored a greenback solution—the printing of legal tender notes without regard to a metallic standard—may have disagreed with Emery's preoccupation with the "Crime of '73" and the silver question. On the other hand, dedicated silver enthusiasts such as William "Coin" Harvey focused on the single issue of coining silver to the exclusion of greenbacks and other possibilities. Within the movement, however, divergent solutions to currency expansion circulated broadly and lists of Farmers' Alliance and People's party demands—from the first national meeting of the Farmers' Alliance at Shreveport, Louisiana, in 1887 to the Omaha convention of the People's party in 1892—invariably included some combination of both paper money and silver remedies. Even among strong supporters of greenbacks, pragmatic considerations of the politically possible tended to compel a grudging acceptance of silver inflation. The California Populist leader Thomas Cator explained to a colleague in the Farmers' Alliance why it was necessary for the People's party to endorse both paper and silver. Although he personally preferred greenbacks as "ultimate money," he advised that "the people are *not* yet ready" for a nonmetallic currency, and therefore "we better press close along the Omaha Platform."[48]

Cator's advice reflected the reality that rural constituencies demanded currency expansion by any means. Either by silver or paper, or a combination of both, farmers hoped that an inflated money supply would help raise farm prices and make farm credits more available and easier to repay. Charles Macune and other reformers looked to the French experience where the government had broadly inflated the currency with both paper money and silver coins. The result, according to the *National Economist*, provided "a lesson to the world that should be studied with profit by all nations." By putting a per capita volume of currency in circulation that was three times that of the United States, France saved itself from the "financial distress and disaster" and achieved "wonderful prosperity and business vitality," while America suffered.[49]

Marion Cannon also looked to French progress as a model for monetary reform. He had made his own fortune mining gold and sat on the board of the Bank of Ventura. Nonetheless, he firmly supported greenback demands. In 1891 he presided over the Los Angeles convention of the state Farmers' Alliance that condemned a currency based on gold and silver as a "dangerous exercise." The convention conceded that until the people "become sufficiently enlightened to abandon this relic of barbarism [a metallic standard], each article so used should be equal in its privileges." Accordingly, France showed what could be accomplished with an enlightened silver policy. In discussing the money question at the Los Angeles Chamber of Commerce, Cannon predicted that by following the French example of coining silver, America would surpass France's glory and achieve "commercial and monetary supremacy."[50]

Whatever their particular views about greenbacks or silver inflation, the Populists shared a common belief about money as a science. They pursued monetary reform with the conviction that, as Macune explained, an adjustable and regulated money supply was essential to "keep pace with the growth of the country's population and the expansion of her business interests."[51] Or as the Texas Populist and money theorist Harry Tracy put it, an expanding currency was a precondition for "evolving a higher civilization." Progress required adjusting the volume of money "to the demands of business at all times and places."[52]

The reformers' claims to "scientific money" did not always produce well-grounded, carefully reasoned, or humane arguments. Although the Populists' soft-money treatises were usually superior to the formalistic arguments about the alleged virtues of gold, tracts such as *Coin's Financial School* imitated the worst in the pedantic dogmatism of the "goldbug" bankers and their academic and political allies. On both sides of the money debate—Sarah Emery versus John Sherman, for example—writers portrayed their opponents as conspirators threatening to subvert the pillars of civilization. The Populists often shared with the business elite implicitly anti-Semitic views about the role of "Shylock" in the economy. In California, farm reformers also used the money question as a "scientific reason" to persecute the Chinese. They calculated that the Chinese bore responsibility for the tight money supply because their presence decreased the per capita volume of currency and, worse, they sent money out of the country. But whether the topic was silver coins, paper notes, bank conspiracies, or Chinese exclusion, the Populists embedded their arguments in statistical tables, legislative chronologies, and other incontrovertible evidence required by the businesslike, efficient, and rational demands of the "science of economical government."[53]

Soft money would provide relief from the downward price spiral that drove the nation's farmers into poverty. It left partially unsolved, however, the dual problems of marketing and credit. Initially, Charles Macune hoped that his Alliance Exchange business system would both regulate markets and provide cheap loans. As the original Texas Exchange faltered, he launched his quest for a national system of cooperative marketing and credit. He also looked toward the national government and elaborated one of the most innovative proposals for federal intervention in the economy ever to enter American politics. First proposed in the fall of 1889, it was known as the "subtreasury" system. With subtreasury offices established in the farming districts, a bureau within the Treasury Department in Washington could provide low-interest loans secured by cotton, wheat, and other staple crops, and centralize and regulate marketing.[54]

The subtreasury idea represented an enormous undertaking. It entailed the construction of federal offices, warehouses, and grain elevators in over one thousand American counties where farmers raised staple crops. As estimated by Harry Tracy, the subtreasury's most able advocate, it would cost $17 million to "erect every one of the elevators and warehouses upon the most modern plan and with the most substantial appliances." With a perfected national system of crop statistics, the central bureau in Washington would set price standards on the cotton, tobacco, wheat, and other staple crops stored, weighed, and sampled in subtreasury facilities. The bureau would provide farmers with receipts for their stored crops on which they could receive 2 percent loans paid out in flexible legal-tender notes. In so doing, the subtreasury system would liberate farm commerce from the twin curses of tight money and speculation.[55]

Instead of shipping crops long distances to storage where seasonal gluts favored speculators, the subtreasury provided for controlled and direct commerce in the global market. "Since the country has been gridironed with railroads, telegraphs and telephones," Harry Tracy explained, "nine-tenths of the wheat, corn, oats, cotton and tobacco that enters into commerce, is bought and sold by wire, hence these products, stored alongside a railway and telegraph office in the interior are as practically on the market as if stored in St. Louis, Chicago or New York. They can be delivered at any seaport on our coast at from three to ten days."[56]

The subtreasury system offered hope to farmers who watched their incomes disappear in the speculative web of the cotton and grain trade. Reformers from the cotton and wheat belts campaigned hard for subtreasury legislation in Congress. But some farmers showed less enthusiasm. The subtreasury did nothing to help regulate the markets in hogs, milk, fruit, and other produce that could not be stored in grain elevators or cotton warehouses. As one Kansas Alliance member put it, "Those who are raising corn and feeding it to hogs and cattle could not derive any benefit from it whatever."[57] In Illinois, the leaders of the Grange, the Northern Alliance, the Southern Alliance, and the Farmers' Mutual Benefit Association (FMBA) all opposed the scheme. Farmers in the West also objected. They wanted cheap credit but they wanted land, not stored crops, to serve as collateral. Hoping to gain rural support for a presidential bid, California's Senator Leland Stanford drafted an alternative system of 2 percent loans on land. Populist leaders struck a compromise by adding land-loans to Macune's original system.[58]

The subtreasury proposal entailed centralized government involvement in the rural economy without an American precedent. For inspiration, farm reformers once again looked to Europe. Tom Watson pointed to Swedish prosperity and its farm loan system. American reformers also knew of a law in czarist Russia that resembled the subtreasury plan. In 1888, the Russian government, concerned about the falling value of grain sales that it depended on for revenue, issued an imperial decree for state regulation of farm credits and marketing. News reports of the Russian decree circulated widely in the months before the Farmers' Alliance adopted the subtreasury plan. American reformers, however, showed special interest in the highly centralized credit system adopted by the Bank of France.[59]

In their original proposal for the subtreasury, Charles Macune, Leonidas Polk, W. Scott Morgan, Lon Livingston, and other members of the Farmers' Alliance Committee on the Monetary System pointed to the French example as "proof positive" of what the subtreasury could accomplish. They quoted at length from a report on the impact of an 1848 French decree mandating that warehoused farm products be accepted as security on low-interest loans. In so doing, "the great institution" of the Bank of France "had placed itself, as it were, in direct contact with every interest of the community, from the minister of the Treasury down to the trader in a distant outpost. Like a huge hydraulic machine [the central bank] employed its colossal powers to pump a fresh stream into the exhausted arteries of trade." Macune and his colleagues cited the success of this "huge hydraulic machine" as evidence of what a centralized financial and monetary system could do for the American farmer. They also noted that in the time elapsed since 1848, changes in rapid transportation and "the instantaneous transmission of intelligence" made a centralized system "easier managed and more necessary."[60]

For Charles Macune the subtreasury represented "the entering wedge" and "the one most essential thing" in reform politics. The Farmers' Alliance adopted the strategy of subjecting political candidates to the subtreasury litmus test. Opponents of the system, whether Democrat or Republican, would face the farmers' wrath at the polls. In the South, the Alliance leadership expected that this strategy would purge the ranks of the Democratic party of those politicians who failed to attend to the business interests of the farmers. The strategy, however, produced a chain of unintended consequences, including a crisis within the Farmers' Alliance and the reorientation of rural reform toward third-party action.

Although Tom Watson and other southern Democratic politicians embraced the subtreasury, much of the Democratic leadership stiffened their resistance to Alliance pressure. This provoked a crisis within the Alliance itself, as some members started to question their lifelong loyalties to the "party of their fathers." It turned out that the nonpartisan pledge that Macune had once wielded so effectively to keep the Alliance within Democratic ranks could also work in the opposite direction to loosen party ties. As a North Carolina farmer put it, "The test of heresy hereafter must not be the mere adherence" to the Democratic party, "but the advocacy of principles and interests . . . to which every party ought to subscribe."[61]

The nonpartisan logic of reform moved inexorably toward a rupture with the traditional parties. Especially in the South, where Democratic loyalties tightly intertwined with the politics of white supremacy, the move proved messy and acrimonious. In Georgia, Lon Livingston and other leaders of the Farmers' Alliance went to the edge of independent politics only to return to the Democratic fold. In North Carolina, Leonidas Polk moved more surely toward a new party. But in his first steps Polk tried to straddle the divide, with his *Progressive Farmer* arguing that since "our complaints are mostly national, hence we can afford to divorce State and National politics." For the 1892 elections Polk's paper counseled members of the Tar Heel Alliance to split their tickets, voting nationally for the Populists and in the state for the Democrats. On the national level the *Progressive Farmer* demanded the subtreasury and related reforms. But on the state level it advised that "we cannot afford to risk negro supremacy here."[62]

The prospect of a break proved too much for Charles Macune, the chief architect of the Alliance movement, who in 1892 returned to the ranks of the Democratic party. *Southern Mercury* editor Milton Park and other leaders of the Texas Alliance, meanwhile, formed a halfway organization known as the Jefferson Democrats that originally tried to work within the Democratic party, but eventually joined with independent party activists such as Comanche County's Thomas Gaines in the Texas People's party. In Alabama, the Jeffersonians maintained a similar halfway position until 1894. Each tortured step toward political independence made by southern reformers elicited charges of racial and regional treason and rendered much of the white South, including the Farmers' Alliance itself, into bitterly warring political camps.[63]

In the Midwest and West, farm reformers made a quicker and initially cleaner break with the traditional parties. In Kansas, the November 1889 triumph of a "People's ticket" in Cowley County helped precipitate the break. Greenback reformers of Union Labor, a self-styled "party of progress and advanced ideas," played a key role in the Cowley County insurgency. Part of their success was due to Union Labor's commitment to a nonpartisan ideal of a "people's movement," the success of which they understood would put the existence of their own party into doubt. "What a sacrifice for many," observed a farmer from Vilas, Kansas, "to fall away from party, even for a little while!" Yet he appealed to his fellow farmers to make Cowley County a national example for nonpartisan reform: "I think Cowley county, in the late election, has solved the problem, where, irrespective of political creeds, *the people* united." "Are you ready for this great coming together of the people?" the farmer asked reformers of all parties. "Or do you intend to stand firm to party tho' heavens fall?"[64]

In June of 1890, Kansas reformers met in Topeka to form a state People's party pledged to the principles of the Farmers' Alliance. Political enthusiasm swept the farming districts. When at the height of the harvest season Mary Elizabeth Lease visited Westmoreland, Kansas, over seven thousand farmers traveled from miles around to hear her speak. The fact that farmers would leave their fields to listen to a three-hour discourse on Populist demands carried its own message. "It means that there is a screw loose somewhere in our political machine," reported a participant. "Sister Lease told us where a good many parts of the machine were badly out of order" and required the "repair shop" of political action.[65]

By the fall of 1891, the movement for the new party had crested on the West Coast. On October 21, delegates met at the Hazard Pavilion in Los Angeles, and with Marion Cannon and Leonidas Polk presiding, solemnly renounced "all former allegiance held or claimed by us in either the Republican, Democratic or other political party."[66] The Farmers' Alliance, in pursuit of its antiparty politics of business interests, had given rise to a new national political movement. In the process, the Alliance itself splintered and declined. "But if the alliance is dead," J. W. H. Davis explained to his fellow Grimes County, Texas, farmers, "she died giving birth to the people's party . . . and brought a nation from the midnight of ignorance to the morning light of reason."[67]

From its first steps the People's party teetered on the wobbly legs of nonpartisanship while it struggled to transform farm reformers' notions of "politics-as-business" into a viable political force. Party campaigns required leaders with special skills in political tactics, debate, and agitation. A number of prominent rural editors and farm leaders successfully remade themselves as party officials and candidates. But the new party also drew on the talents of lawyers and politicians with experience in party politics. These included skilled campaigners like Tom Watson in Georgia, and powerful orators like James "Cyclone" Davis and John Rayner in Texas. The party also attracted well-known politicians like Iowa's James Weaver, who had experience as the Greenback candidate for president in 1880 and who received over a million votes as the Populist presidential candidate in 1892.

Ignatius Donnelly, the novelist and veteran political campaigner from Nininger City, Minnesota, also played a role in refashioning rural reform as a political creed. He was known in some reform circles as "the father of the People's party" because of the striking political rhetoric with which he supplied the movement. A man of many hats, to his critics Donnelly's multiple enthusiasms rendered him comic. But to his admirers, the wide spectrum of intellectual, business, and political projects he pursued, and the energy and dynamism with which he pursued them, only strengthened his value as a spokesperson of reform. Born in Philadelphia in 1831, Donnelly was the product of the big city. His Irish father had left the Catholic Church, practiced medicine, explored scientific literature, and inspired in his son a lifelong passion for the works of Francis Bacon and the English Enlightenment. The young Donnelly studied law and speculated in urban real estate before leaving Philadelphia to make his fortune in the West.[68]

Arriving in Minnesota in 1856, Donnelly formed a partnership to boost the new town of Nininger City, seventeen miles downriver from St. Paul. He published a journal to promote immigration, hoping to profit from the speculative fever that had gripped the state. As Nininger's boom faltered, Donnelly decided to farm his unsold properties. Although he had no experience, and his intentions to go into farming met ridicule from his neighbors, he sought to gain a reputation as a progressive and scientific farmer. He planted fruit trees and diversified his crops, applied the latest methods for computing profits, and employed the newest machinery. Later, he invested in large-scale bonanza farming, purchasing several thousand acres of virgin prairie. His farms, however, always remained a sideline and were mainly worked by hired help.[69]

Donnelly's preoccupation was politics. After the Civil War he served three terms in Washington as a Republican congressman. He sat on the House Committee on the Pacific Railroad and immersed himself in the politics of railroad promotion. Although he lobbied for several lines, he mainly worked for the interests of Jay Cooke, the Philadelphia banker and railroad magnate. As Martin Ridge, Donnelly's biographer, observed: "The business of government for him was business—big business." After losing his congressional seat, Donnelly spent the rest of his political career in the trenches of Minnesota politics, and his interests in business and politics shifted to the farmers. Among other projects, he joined the Farmers' Alliance and collaborated with Alonzo Wardall to promote cooperative life and hail insurance.[70]

With each election cycle Donnelly aligned himself with a new political formation—Liberal-Republican, Independent, Greenback-Democrat, Farmer-Labor, Anti-Monopoly, Union Labor—while he also moved back and forth between Republicans and Democrats. "Let no one accuse us of vacillation or inconsistency," he replied to charges that he lacked political conviction. "No party owns us. We adhere to principle and follow where it leads. We propose to make our life a protest against the slavish rule of caucuses and rings which now afflicts this country." In short, Donnelly was a consummate politician whose distrust of the party system left him a political nomad. Not surprisingly, he found a home in the antiparty politics of Populism.[71]

Between political campaigns Donnelly wrote books. The inspiration for most of his writing came from his reading in scientific journals about the latest news of discovery. His most celebrated work, *Atlantis*, drew from a wide range of literature to establish evidence of an ancient civilization that sank beneath the Atlantic Ocean. First published in 1882, *Atlantis* was a spectacular success. By 1890, it had gone through forty-nine editions and won Donnelly membership in the American Association for the Advancement of Science. Meanwhile, he labored on with other ventures, including publication of *The Great Cryptogram* in 1887, the product of his efforts to prove that Francis Bacon authored the plays produced in Shakespeare's name. Two years later he wrote *Caesar's Column*, a futuristic and dystopian novel.[72]

Donnelly brought his literary talents to bear in translating the grievances of rural reform into a potent political language. He authored the celebrated preamble to the Omaha Platform adopted by the People's party convention on July 4, 1892. The preamble evoked the nation's birthday, General Washington, the Constitution, and "free government." Populist editors christened the party's platform as a "Second Declaration of Independence."[73] Donnelly's passionate and incisive indictment of the millionaires and corporations echoed Jefferson's charges against King George. In 1892, just as in 1876, Americans faced the loss of liberty and a looming "absolute despotism."[74]

Although the preamble followed well-worn rhetorical lines, the content reflected the harsh new realities of modern times. Post–Civil War developments had produced both fantastic fortunes and alarming poverty. The preamble gave voice to the fears among many late nineteenth-century reformers that the course of liberty now turned on the distribution of wealth. The growing gap between the rich and poor provided Donnelly with his central indictment: "From the same prolific womb of government injustice we breed the two great classes—tramps and millionaires." Liberty hung in the balance because, through currency contraction, high interest rates, and other means, the "fruits of the toil of millions" were stolen for the "fortunes of the few."[75]

The preamble offered a remarkable political solution to economic inequity. In the name of defending American liberty it called for the rapid increase in the centralized power of the state. "We believe that the power of government—in other words, of the people—shall be expanded," the preamble advised, "to the end that oppression, injustice, and poverty shall eventually cease in the land."[76] The first Declaration of Independence located the danger of tyranny in the extension of the powers of government. Its 1892 version recognized despotism in economic oppression and looked to the extension of government to secure liberty.

Donnelly was not the first to frame the Populists' financial and commercial demands in terms of the traditions of American liberty. His preamble borrowed heavily from Sarah Emery's warnings about a bankers' conspiracy to impose despotism. It also echoed the report from Charles Macune and his Committee on the Monetary System, which concluded the argument for a centralized state machine of "colossal" financial power with an appeal to return to the old watchword of "Liberty!" Donnelly pulled these strands of thought into one piece and created a powerful statement about how the Populists understood freedom in the modern conditions of late nineteenth-century America.

In writing the Omaha Platform, Donnelly had the assistance of James "Cyclone" Davis, a Texas lawyer and politician who barnstormed across nearly every state in the country for the Populist cause. He earned the name "Cyclone" with his knack for overwhelming his debating opponents with quick rejoinders and a relentless debating style. Tall, lean, and tanned, he cultivated an image of physical vigor and daring. For much of his life he woke at five in the morning for a special regimen of calisthenics, a practice inspired by reading about diet and exercise in the *Scientific American*. In public he donned his trademark Prince Albert coat, broad-brimmed hat, and a scarf in lieu of a tie. He had a passion for public speaking, although he rarely ran as a candidate. He worked the Chautauqua lecture circuit, stumped for Texas Democrats in the 1880s, and emerged as the Populists' star debater in the 1890s when he gained a broad following among audiences in the Prairie states and the Far West.[77]

In 1894, Davis compiled his political arguments in a rambling book titled *A Political Revelation*. He sought to demonstrate that Populism followed "in the line laid out by the revolutionary fathers." The result read like a tortured legal brief proving that the Constitution provided a mandate for the full Populist platform. Government ownership of the railroads, the income tax,

JAMES H. (CYCLONE) DAVIS

Figure 5.3. James "Cyclone" Davis, Populist orator (Doe Library, University of California, Berkeley)

and the subtreasury system, according to Davis, all flowed from the original intent of the Founding Fathers. Revealing his southern Democratic heritage, Davis showed special deference to Jefferson and Jackson. The Populists, he reminded his readers, adhered to the "Jefferson theory of Democracy." Just as in Jefferson's confrontation with Alexander Hamilton, the Populists represented the people against aristocracy. "Every plank in the People's Party Platform that came from Thomas Jefferson was true Democracy," Davis explained. "The crowd that takes their politics from Alexander Hamilton is the crowd that we have to beat."[78]

The claims to the Jeffersonian mantle often required considerable rhetorical skill. Whether it was nationalizing the railroads or "raising a billion dollars from a graduated income tax," Davis and other reformers did their best to reconcile Jefferson's views about limited government with the Populist platform. The Jeffersonians and Populists also had different sensibilities about the meaning of popular government. Jefferson and his colleagues considered representative institutions sacrosanct and viewed encroachments on the sovereignty of state legislatures as the surest sign of tyranny. The Populists, however, in light of the corrupting power of corporate lobbyists over the political process, grew skeptical of the very notion of representative government. At the local level, they viewed town councils as warrens for dishonest cliques and rings that, even if cleansed of corruption, were impotent in matters of importance. If anything, the state legislatures were worse.[79]

Nebraska farmers distrusted the "silvery-tongued office-seeking lawyers" who inhabited the state house because, as Luna Kellie explained, the legislature was where the people's interests were "tabled by a committee appointed by some scoundrel in the shape of a speaker."[80] Tom Watson made a similar assessment, arguing that the credit system should be vested exclusively in the federal government, as "we should greatly fear the corrupting influence of large sums of money, control of which was left in any degree to State legislatures."[81] The Vincent brothers posed the question in an editorial in the *Nonconformist*: "Is Representative Government a Failure?" And they answered with a conditional affirmative. "We are the worst governed country on the face of the earth," they noted. And the fault lay with the legislatures. More than the venality and ignorance of those in office, the problem lay "in the organization itself." The legislatures had to be "shorn of much of their power. Their wings must be clipped."[82]

From distrust of the legislatures grew the Populist demand for the direct election of U.S. senators. They also called for direct legislation by way of the initiative and referendum to check the "legislative behemoth." Cyclone Davis saw the referendum as the "complete power of the people over their lawmakers."[83] Luna Kellie looked to direct legislation as a guarantee that "no power higher than the vote or veto of the people can exist in a free country."[84] By clipping the wings of the legislatures the Populists hoped to make government "accountable to the people themselves, and the people only." In doing so, they attempted an important innovation in the nation's governance. The messy political horse-trading typical of representative bodies would be replaced by nonnegotiable mandates of the majority. And government would move closer to the antiparty ideal of a business agency kept in check by the popular vote.[85]

Cyclone Davis and other Populists claimed the heritage of Andrew Jackson who, on behalf of the plain people, waged war on the "monster bank." But with Jackson, too, they had to stretch. The Jacksonians favored hard money and states' rights, whereas the Populists wanted soft money and distrusted the notion of state sovereignty. Jackson vetoed the federal charter for the Bank of the United States in Philadelphia, seeking to devolve the banking power to the decentralized state and territorial banks. The Populists fought the federal bank charters for the sixteen hundred banks in the National Banking System and demanded a centralized banking system located in the federal bureaucracy in Washington.[86]

Most significant, the Populists wanted to dispense with the Jacksonians' main contribution to democratic practice: the mass political party. The Populists articulated specific demands to dismantle a party system that relied on face-to-face and personal party loyalties and patronage. They campaigned for civil service reforms to eliminate party appointments in government service. They also demanded the secret "Australian" ballot and other reforms in the voting process. The Populists hoped that a nonpartisan secret ballot would free their insurgent third party of the cost of printing and distributing party ballots. It might also facilitate ticket splitting, or "fusion" between Populists and one or the other major party, a practice essential to Populist electoral success. The secret ballot might curb the endemic corruption that too often "counted out" a reform candidate, and it might tame the civic wars that climaxed at the polls. Election Day, with its turbulent and intoxicated displays of party strength and personal loyalties, was anathema to farm reformers who believed in businesslike government.[87]

By reducing partisanship, the Populists hoped to realize a more enlightened politics of careful deliberation and political education. The "modern educational machine" built by the Farmers' Alliance—with its centralized networks of newspapers and lecturers—served as a foundation. The Populists wanted to shift the business of politics from the smoke-filled rooms of party bosses and local political brokers to a more impersonal and transparent system. By undercutting the role of local party organizations and the personal allegiances they fostered, the Populists looked to make the political process more rational and scientific, less fraudulent and corrupt, and more closely disciplined by the popular will. As a means to realize "clean politics" and to select "good officers," the People's party in Ventura County, California, proposed that primary elections be conducted through the U.S. mail, a proposal indicative of a wider Populist striving for a more anonymous and equitable politics.[88]

Unfortunately for the Populists, as historian Michael McGerr explains, the Democrats and Republicans responded to nonpartisan and third-party challenges with their own "educational politics." The traditional parties still relied on processions and fireworks and other partisan displays. But in the late 1880s and early 1890s, they developed centralized systems of political education to win over potential voters under the nonpartisan sway of the Farmers' Alliance or other reformers. Both Democrats and Republicans built war chests to finance the mailing of literature and other weapons of political persuasion. Ironically, the People's party lacked the resources to compete. In the highly competitive business of "educational politics," a business that the Populists helped launch, they were no match for the well-financed machines of their political enemies. The Populists had few options but to run their campaigns the cheap and old-fashioned way, with marches, bands, stump speeches, and other methods of partisan mobilization. In the heat of such campaigns the Populists proved themselves capable of partisan abuses they abhorred in their opponents.[89]

Their claim to the democracy of Jefferson and Jackson contained the perplexing irony that the Populists demanded the evisceration of the very institutions that previous generations had viewed as central to democratic theory and practice. At the same time, they failed to articulate a coherent alternative model of democracy. As a new third party, they protested electoral fraud, influence peddling, ballot restrictions, political intimidation, and other antidemocratic practices of the two parties in power. The Populists' preoccupation with "scientific government," however, usually fastened on the business question (money, markets, transportation), although at times the democracy question did come to the fore. Especially in the thick of the labor conflicts of 1893 and 1894, a significant strand of Populist thought focused on the problems of democracy in a complex, modern, and corporate society. The influential Populist jurists Frank Doster of Kansas and Thomas Nugent of Texas, for example, explored the new meanings of democracy at some depth.[90]

Thomas Nugent's views are especially instructive. He believed that the previous "Jeffersonian simplicity" of small government was unsuitable for the complex and modern present. As the People's party candidate for the governor of Texas, he played a major role in Populist politics, although he was more of a philosopher than a politician, and gave voice to political heresies that were rarely publicly discussed. Dispatching Thomas Jefferson to the historical dustbin was such a heresy. Nugent candidly explained that in the early years of the American republic, Thomas Jefferson "taught an extreme individualism," relegating government to its minimal functions. "'The less governed, the better,' became an adage that appealed at once to the statesman, the demagogue, and the private citizen." He observed, however, that the railroad, telegraph, and corporation, and the resulting interdependence and "interchange of thought and intelligence," had transformed the role of government in society. From a distrusted and minimal agency, the government was now "reaching out and touching every part of the social fabric." The task of reform was to give direction to this inexorable process, placing the expanding state on rational and scientific lines.[91]

Farm reformers looked to Europe for prototypes of the "scientific government" of the future. The Populist Carl Vrooman of Kansas noted that the principles of the movement "have had as their champions such statesmen as Bismarck, Gladstone, Chamberlain . . . and the greatest college professors and economists of England and Germany." Populists often expressed enthusiasm for the Swiss system of initiatives and referenda. Tom Watson admired progress under the limited monarchies of Scandinavia and Holland, and especially the "advanced civilization" of imperial Germany.[92]

Watson also drew lessons from Napoleon. In the 1890s, a Napoleon revival spread in the United States, as many Americans hoped for a strong man to deliver the nation from its multiple ills. Reporting on the so-called "Napoleon craze," *Century* magazine reported that "the interest in Napoleon has recently had a revival that is phenomenal in its extent and intensity." Muckraking journalist Ida M. Tarbell and Princeton Professor William Milligan Sloane contributed serialized Napoleon biographies in the *Century* and *McClure's Magazine*. Politicians preened themselves in Napoleon's image. *Harper's Weekly* reported that then Ohio governor William McKinley, known as "the Napoleon of Protection," also "looks like Napoleon and knows it." The fascination with the French emperor corresponded to a broad discontent with corrupt and impotent political institutions, as well as strong currents of militarism and nationalism in American public life. The Populists were not immune to these currents. Tom Watson and the Populists, however, were drawn less to military valor and patriotic glory than to the example of Napoleon's administrative systems and energized state power.[93]

After the Populist Waterloo of 1896, Watson made his own contribution to the Napoleon revival, researching and writing two massive books on French history. The first, *The Story of France*, ran over a thousand pages and culminated in Napoleon's triumph. The second, *Napoleon*, provided a seven hundred-page defense of the "great Corsican's" reputation. Combined, these works represent one of the most systematic elaborations of a leading Populist's ideas about history and governance. In Watson's treatment, Napoleon towers as "the peerless developer, organizer, [and] administrator," who had applied the science of government to build a centralized and rational system of law and education, the Bank of France, and a strong state. Napoleon not only knew how to destroy opposing armies, he "delighted in improvement, in embellishment, in the growth of commerce, agriculture, and manufactures." The general, Watson noted, was a "master builder" with a "modern tone."[94]

"Lawless as was Napoleon's seizure of power," Watson reasoned, "it gave France just what she wanted." The Napoleonic order, confirmed by popular referenda, rested on the foundation of universal suffrage and the overwhelming support of the people. Even at the end of his career, Napoleon showed "the same love of system" under which "no real despotism could be possible." Despite his imperial trappings, Watson wrote, the emperor remained "the highest type of democrat" because of the civic equality embodied in his systems for state education, civil service, the army, and science.[95] Napoleon's career, Watson would later observe, "affords the most striking illustration of what can be done, under modern conditions, by giving intelligent direction to the democratic impulse of a nation."[96]

The historian C. Vann Woodward made an acute observation about Watson's *Napoleon*. "One has the feeling upon closing the book," Woodward noted, "that an author who can use the term 'the great Democratic despot,' without consciousness of paradox is reconciled to a union of Caesarism and democracy." Woodward tried to dismiss this union as aberrational, a product of Watson's "naïve childhood identification" with the French hero. After all, according to prevailing assumptions the Populist Watson was a radical democrat and Jacobin and therefore a natural antagonist of emperors and dictators. Even so, Watson's Napoleon worship left Woodward questioning: "Could it be that the Israelites worshiped the same gods as the Philistines?"[97]

Marion Cannon shared Watson's appraisal of "the great Napoleon" and the benefits he brought France and the world. He explained to the Los Angeles Chamber of Commerce that America was in need of its own "lordly figure." The times cried out for "that leader, who, grasping the situation with firmness and a high resolution, and a commanding patriotism, shall step to the front and lead the great industrial millions of the world to freedom and happiness."[98] Similarly, Mary Elizabeth Lease wrote that "we need a Napoleon in the industrial world," who will lead the people to "fulfill the hopes of humanity and the promise of the ages." This type of overblown rhetoric provided a good measure of the oversized ambitions of Cannon and Lease. However, it also corresponded to that strain of Populist opinion that desired the liberation of politics from the burdens of electoral partisanship and legislative deal making, and to thereby bring singleness of purpose to the business of state—to energize and modernize government administration.[99]

Other Populists believed that the enthusiasm for Napoleon was misplaced. John Davis of Junction City, Kansas, twice elected to Congress on the People's party ticket, a member of the national executive of the Knights of Labor, and a dedicated Greenbacker, published a scathing biography of Napoleon in *Arena* magazine. He set out to demonstrate that on matters of finance the French general was neither modern nor scientific, but "an untaught barbarian." Napoleon's use of metallic currency to equip his armies, according to Davis, made him "a child of the past, a meteor from the dark ages" attempting to "roll back into paganism and slavery the wheels of an enlightened Christian progress." The British, Prussian, and Russian armies, the victors in the Napoleonic Wars, proved the superiority of the paper currency issued by the Bank of England. Conversely, "the one great lesson of Napoleon's career," Davis concluded, was that no nation was safe "with a shrinking volume of money."[100]

Although John Davis and Tom Watson differed in their evaluations of Napoleon, they shared the view that the key measure of the French emperor's career lay with the success or failure of his managerial and administrative systems. That Napoleon crushed representative institutions and established a one-person dictatorship remained on the margins of their considerations. In the Populist imagination, the ballot box and universal suffrage were important for ensuring a government of the people. They sought the power of the majority confirmed in fair elections and referenda. The purpose of politics, however, was not simply clean and majoritarian government, but "scientific government"—government founded on modern and businesslike systems of education, transportation, communication, trade, credit, and money.

The internal functioning of the Farmers' Alliance and other reform organizations reflected the broader reform visions of businesslike administration. On the one hand, the Farmers' Alliance showed a strong commitment to a majoritarian democracy. All members had a vote and all officers of the local alliances—from doorkeeper to president—were selected by the majority of members. State and national officers, in turn, were chosen by majority vote of local, county, and state representatives. Decisions of the state and national executives were frequently sent down to the membership for approval, where local suballiances debated contentious issues large and small. On the other hand, the elected officers, especially at the state level, often wielded broad "executive authority" within the centralized pyramid of the Alliance structure. The parameters of debate and discussion within the movement were often sharply circumscribed. And the majoritarian imperative of the movement culture frequently allowed for little tolerance for dissenting opinion.[101]

At each step of the organizational pyramid, a small number of individual officers directed the centralized work of the Farmers' Alliance. At the county level, the president of the Alliance was vested with powers of appointment and often played a pivotal role. Under the constitution of the Alliance of Wake County, North Carolina, for example, a county president held broad responsibilities to supervise and direct the organization's work. The president resolved disputes, appointed committees, called county meetings, and ordered their proceedings. The president also bore responsibility for directing the "secret work" of the Alliance, as the requirements of secrecy provided additional impetus for centralizing Alliance business in the hands of its leading officer. In recognition of the potential for abuse of such powers, the rules also included term limits for county presidents.[102]

At the state level, annual conventions selected the state officers of the Alliance and reviewed their work from the previous year. Between conventions, however, collective and representative bodies either lapsed or barely functioned, leaving wide discretion to a small number of state presidents, business agents, and other executives to direct the centralized work of state organizations. This allowed top Alliance managers to accumulate extraordinary authority within the system. In Georgia, the work of the state Alliance was dominated by the "Alliance Moses," Lon Livingston. In Texas, when Charles Macune attained the presidency of the state Alliance, he was hailed as a "hero," a "great leader," and the new "Napoleon of finance." Marion Cannon tried to direct the California Alliance as a virtually one-person operation.[103]

In North Carolina, Leonidas Polk enjoyed an unmatched prestige and authority that only grew with his elevation to the presidency of the National Farmers' Alliance and Industrial Union. The reform press paid due respect to the honorary "Colonel" before Polk's name, and cultivated Polk's image as "our ideal of an intelligent Southern gentlemen"—a latter-day Robert E. Lee—directing the army of reform. Military imagery played a major role in post–Civil War public life. But the portrayals of Polk, Livingston, Macune, Cannon, and other top officers as the level-headed commanders of the Alliance army also reflected the key role played by a relative handful of executives within the Alliance movement.[104]

Centralization also served the efforts of the Farmers' Alliance to check centrifugal ideological forces and affirm a singular message of "Alliance principles." The state lecturing system provides an example of how this worked. State officers centrally recruited and screened lecturers, drew the itineraries of their lecture tours, and supervised the financing of those tours. In Kansas, the Alliance lecture system was directed by the Kansas State Lecture Bureau. Because the bureau itself met only once a year, the responsibility for the practical direction of the statewide lecture system lay with one or two officers in charge.[105]

In California, Marion Cannon personally supervised the activities of the lecturers. "I sent out my proclamation putting in force the lecture system," as Cannon explained, "giving instructions to the lecturers throughout the state." His instructions included detailed talking points, as he sought to assert his one-man leadership over an especially diverse and fractious state Alliance.[106] Indeed, Cannon personally directed much of the work of the California State Alliance. Placing "power in the hands of one man," as one disgruntled (and former) Alliance lecturer put it, Cannon appointed officers, settled local disputes, and issued rulings to guide the activities of the state organization from top to bottom.[107] In regard to the editorial policy of Alliance newspapers, Cannon ruled that he enjoyed the authority to exert "complete control over all our organs." Although Cannon's methods were heavy-handed, similar practices throughout the Alliance movement ensured the careful screening and supervision of lecturers and a broad uniformity of the Alliance message.[108]

The efforts to focus the message influenced discussion and debate at the grass roots. From its inception, the Farmers' Alliance had prohibited certain types of speech in meetings, including partisan politics and religious doctrine. It was also against Alliance rules to publicly criticize another member of the order. Moreover, members were expected to adhere to "Alliance principles," especially the platform positions adopted by the state and national conventions. Accordingly, on issues deemed tangential to the essential principles of the organization, such as women's suffrage and temperance, reform newspapers at times carried open-ended debates. On questions pertaining to key points of Alliance doctrine, by contrast, discussion was often sharply limited. Moreover, as the political demands on the Alliance intensified, the possibilities for dissent diminished.

The subtreasury issue underscored how external political pressures took their toll on dissenting opinion within the Alliance. At the outset, the subtreasury provoked considerable discord, especially among Alliance members who produced crops unsuitable for the proposed subtreasury warehouses. Despite strong dissent, Alliance majorities ratified the subtreasury. The leadership then used the subtreasury as a political battering ram, refusing Alliance support to any political candidate who failed to endorse the scheme. In this climate, disagreement about the subtreasury posed an acute problem: if the Alliance attacked a political candidate who expressed doubts about the subtreasury, what about the Alliance member with similar doubts?

The Alliance leadership turned support of the subtreasury (and its use in politics) into an internal loyalty test of Alliance principles. President Polk issued a national directive for members of the Alliance to "guard with untiring vigilance" against disloyal members. He warned especially against those who went public with their criticisms. "Such an offense is a violation of his obligation and should merit expulsion," Polk warned. "The will of the majority is the law of the order, and if he cannot acquiesce in the decision of the majority . . . he should first divest himself of his alliance uniform."[109] North Carolina Farmers' Alliance President Marion Butler echoed Polk, calling on Alliance members to be vigilant and watch for potential spies who were "constantly finding fault" and criticizing the subtreasury platform. "Look out for such men," he cautioned, "they are in many lodges."[110]

By the fall of 1891, conflicts over the subtreasury and related "Alliance principles" were exacerbated by disagreements about whether or not to endorse the emerging People's party. Over the next months, these disagreements led to defections and schisms that cut sharply into Alliance rolls. The crisis, however, was long in the making. The Alliance had always proved

Figure 5.4. The Alliance school of nonpartisanship, in the *People's Advocate*, Hill City, Kansas, January 21, 1892 (Kansas State Historical Society, Topeka)

awkward in its accommodation of divergent currents of opinion within its own ranks. As a movement "of principles not of men" it had struggled to develop "firm principles" that would still allow for a broad membership. Wrapped in a majoritarian ethos, the movement culture of the Alliance had limited capacity for internal debate and minority rights that were often viewed as antithetical to majority decision making and businesslike leadership.

Many of these same attributes carried over into the People's party. The top officers of the party, forming what historian Peter Argersinger describes as a "party oligarchy," defied the limits of their authority, negotiated political deals without the consent of the membership, and exploited a hierarchical organizational system to curtail democratic decision making. A dissenting Populist described the chair of his party's state committee as "a dictator, whose power is absolute; who in practice of corrupt and disreputable political methods has out done all other political managers that have ever risen." The criticisms only grew louder and more widespread as the political pressures intensified on the new party. In part, this reflected the sense of betrayal among reformers who hoped that the People's party would liberate politics from political bosses and their backroom deals. As Argersinger demonstrates, the structural requirements of party competition erected barriers to the democratic aspirations of many supporters of the third party.[111]

At the same time, much of the People's party leadership arrived at their positions from farm organizations where they had served as powerful executives with broad mandates. Top party managers—including those who drew considerable criticism from below, such as Marion Butler, Rueben Kolb, and Marion Cannon—acquired their organizational ideas and practices as state presidents of the Farmers' Alliance. Similarly, the much-maligned national party chairman, Herman Taubeneck, received his training as the leader of the Farmers' Mutual Benefit Association. These continuities suggest that the rise of a "party oligarchy" had roots within the farmers' movement itself. They also suggest that agrarian democracy did not fall from grace after biting the forbidden fruit of politics and political deal making. Rather, the democracy of the Populist organizations was limited from the outset by the complex administrative systems that they required, and by the reform visions they pursued of majoritarian authority, scientific administration, and business power.

In her study of the rise of interest group politics in the United States, Elisabeth Clemens examines how the democracy of rural Populism of the 1880s and 1890s devolved into the "economic corporatism" of farmers' organizations in the 1910s. She points to the speed of this transition as one of the puzzles of American political development. "Economic corporatism" she defines as a type of nonpartisan "business politics" involving the pursuit of commercial interests through close relations with state agencies and "bureaucratic beachheads" at both the state and federal levels. Examining the paradoxical nature of Populist democracy itself offers at least part of the answer to the puzzle of what came afterward.[112]

Here it is instructive to return to J. W. H. Davis's campaign as the People's party candidate for Grimes County tax collector. The presence of an unschooled Texas cotton farmer such as Davis on the Populist ticket showed evidence of the grassroots nature of the movement. Similarly, the efforts of the Texas Populists to break the grip of "town rings" by organizing on the basis of neighborhood school districts underscored a commitment to popular politics. Perhaps most significant, when the local farmers met and deliberated in the suballiances and People's party clubs, they formed part of a democratic rural milieu that made Davis's political campaign possible.

Yet, when Davis explained the goals of his campaign he stressed two important realities about Populist objectives. First, the campaign centered on national not local politics. Davis did not present himself as a leader of a local town hall or village democracy defending itself against outside encroachment. Rather, he campaigned in the name of "individual hicks" whose interests could only be advanced through national politics. Second, Davis emphasized that as "individual hicks" pile up cotton they act as commercial agents in a national market and must act accordingly in national politics. Commerce, he explained, connected farmers to the Populist platform.[113]

The result: a broadly democratic rural movement embraced a vision of business politics that focused on centralized, bureaucratic, and state-centered reform. Perhaps it would be anachronistic to describe Populism as a variant of "economic corporatism." Farmers pressed for the subtreasury and other proto-corporatist projects when the government bureaucracy was yet too thin to support them. More than that, in the 1880s and 1890s, the attempts of rural reform to make "bureaucratic beachheads" at the state and federal level were often frustrated by the stronger business politics of the corporations. But the Populists' lack of success in this regard was surely not due to lack of imagination or lack of effort.

6

RACE PROGRESS

Shaping a New Racial Order

The formation of the People's party posed a racial dilemma. In the early 1890s, African Americans still clung to the right to vote in much of the South. Their choices, however, were growing increasingly narrow. The Republican party had lost its former strength in the South, and what remained often adopted "lily-white" policies of racial exclusion. At the same time, the Democratic party offered the black community small concessions in exchange for votes, with the understanding that blacks would acquiesce to the Democratic doctrines of white supremacy. For the new People's party to have any chance of success at the polls it had to attract a section of the black vote without undermining its support among white farmers. This was a politically difficult and dangerous undertaking for the emerging People's party across the South. In Texas the task largely rested on the able shoulders of John B. Rayner.

Rayner's trajectory was similar to that of other Populist leaders. Born in 1850, he was the son of U.S. Congressman Kenneth Rayner, whose North Carolina plantation fell on hard times after the Civil War. John studied the classics, labored in county politics, and eventually moved to Calvert, Texas, where he taught school. Along the way, he trained as a Baptist preacher and much like Harrison Ashby, S. O. Daws, and other Protestant ministers in the ranks of Populism, he took a skeptical view of both church and creed and looked to improve people's lives in the here and now. In 1892 Rayner joined the People's party. With his gift for public speaking, he gained renown as he campaigned across the remote country districts of eastern Texas. By 1895 he served on the party's state executive committee. Soon thereafter, as the Populist fires cooled, he devoted his attention to farmers' technical education.

Rayner also turned to eugenics, seeking racial improvement through the latest discoveries in social hygiene.[1]

But something separated Rayner from the other leaders of Texas Populism. He was born chattel, his mother the slave property of his father. Despite his light complexion he lived on the black side of the American color line. This reality influenced his Populist vision. Although Rayner and other black Populists shared with white Populists a common set of assumptions about social progress, they had their own preoccupations and emphasized a distinct set of Populist ideas. Black Populists looked to the movement with limited expectations. Whereas white Populists hoped for a broad reordering of the nation's economic and political priorities, black Populists often focused on immediate life-and-death issues of legal justice and political rights. Whereas white Populists pursued racial uplift with the confidence of innate superiority, blacks pursued racial improvement with the bitterness of having all other paths closed by the debilitating combination of extreme poverty and the restrictions imposed by white power. In the multiplicity of Populist thought the racial chasm produced two Populisms, black and white.

The color line mocked the Populist promise of equality. "Equal Rights for All, Special Privileges for None!" was the slogan the Populists emblazoned across their newspapers and convention halls. The slogan was usually applied in the Macunist business spirit of fair play in commerce. Even so, its egalitarian implications spurred the imagination, especially about women's rights. Explorations into the rights of the former slaves, however, remained sharply curtailed. Discussion among white reformers usually started and ended with the pat formula that blacks should be allowed economic equality, and possibly political equality, but not "social equality." This formula masked deep political and economic inequities. It also justified separation. Instead of racial equality, white farm reformers envisioned a future of expanded distance between blacks and whites.

White Populists understood that they lived in a "white man's country." American society, however, refused to divide neatly along the color line. Farm reformers grappled with who was white, who was not, and what to do about it. Did German immigrants belong in the Farmers' Alliance with the native-born and English-speaking farmers, or should they be shunned as aliens? The Chinese carried the double burden of being nonwhite and alien, yet what about the farmers' needs for their labor? Were Mexican farmers nonwhite, or simply unfortunate captives of a nonprogressive culture and religion? Did Native Americans make for good Alliance members, or did progress require their imprisonment upon reservations? White Populists shared concerns of this type with much of the rest of Anglo-America and, like other Anglo-Americans, their ideas about race ran the spectrum from relative tolerance to lynch-mob oppression and forced exclusion.[2]

Populism emerged at a time of dramatic innovations in American race relations: the Chinese Exclusion Act of 1882, Jim Crow laws, and then the disfranchisement of black voters. Contemplating the ominous changes in the racial order, John Rayner observed that "the momentum of our progress calls for sudden innovations and many upheavals and convulsions in sociological affairs." He had a point. The separate but equal system of American apartheid arrived on the wings of progress. True, the "moss-backed" economic conservatives also took part. But the self-styled progressives of the New South movement bore special responsibility. Mainly comprising urban businessmen, lawyers, educators, and editors, the New South movement sought to renovate and modernize southern life. In line with the widely accepted assumptions of the day, they viewed white supremacy as scientific and modern. And separation of the races formed an essential part of the New South doctrine of progressive development.[3]

Henry W. Grady, editor of the *Atlanta Constitution*, popularized the New South doctrine across the region and the nation. In a speech in Dallas at the opening of the 1888 Texas State Fair he set forth a vision for a new racial order. "I declare that the truth above all others," he told his largely rural audience, "is that the white race must dominate forever." Recognition of Anglo-Saxon supremacy, he explained, would bring about reconciliation between the North and South. Further, racial distinction, rooted in biology, had created "an impassable gulf" that made necessary a strict separation of racial types. He would later clarify that this meant "separate accommodation everywhere": schools, theaters, railroads, streetcars, and literary clubs. Segregation, Grady explained, did not reflect a lack of sympathy toward racial inferiors. If the black man accepted the principles of white supremacy and separate development, he could share with whites the benefits of progress and prosperity. "His interests and the interests of the [white] people of the South are identical."[4]

Twenty-five thousand Texas farmers had gathered to hear Grady's Dallas speech. According to press reports, they greeted his words "with rapt attention and the keenest delight."[5] The following year, with Farmers' Alliance leader Leonidas Polk at his side as his specially invited guest, Grady repeated the same racial principles on Alliance Day at the Piedmont Exposition before twenty thousand members of the Georgia Farmers' Alliance. He struck a chord with Farmers' Alliance audiences because they shared the same vision. In North Carolina, Farmers' Alliance president Marion Butler lauded Grady as the greatest southerner of the postwar era, and Polk's *Progressive Farmer* extolled Grady as "America's most brilliant orator." White Populists would come to disagree with Grady and the urban New South leaders on certain political and economic questions; their ideas about race, however, closely adhered to Grady's precepts. No less than their urban counterparts, white rural reformers believed in white supremacy, sectional reconciliation, an identity of economic interests between whites and blacks, and racial progress predicated on the strict separation of the races. White Populists, especially in the South but not exclusively so, embraced this mix of ideas. They might elevate one element above the others given personal inclination and political circumstance, but they usually applied these principles in combination as mutually reinforcing notions of racial progress.[6]

For different reasons, African Americans also adopted elements of the New South doctrine on racial matters. A black preacher from Tennessee believed that Grady's speech in Dallas pointed to "the coming future, where the two races would walk in peace and union and yet distinct, contented, [and] prosperous."[7] The same ideas echoed in Booker T. Washington's famous address to the 1895 Atlanta Exposition. "In all things that are purely social," he reassured the white South and the nation, "we can be as separate as the fingers, yet one as the hand in all things essential to mutual progress." Many blacks resigned themselves to segregation as a means of survival. For black Populists like John Rayner, separate racial development also opened possibilities for racial uplift.[8]

The Populists saw themselves as shaping the modern society of the future —a future in which racial separateness would be further institutionalized and defined. The Farmers' Alliance laid a foundation by spreading the principle of racial distance as it organized across rural America. The subsequent entry of the Alliance movement into third-party politics led to politically driven experiments in biracial cooperation. For a brief moment, white and black Populists succeeded in finding patches of common political ground. But even at the height of cooperation, white and black Populists often pursued separate goals. The color line held. Historians have stressed that the reform movement had few choices given the weight of the white supremacist tradition in the American South and the virulence of the backlash against any and all challenges to this tradition.[9] The reformers, however, were not mere victims of an intractable tradition. From the strivings of the Farmers' Alliance through the campaigns of the People's party, the Populists played an active part in shaping the racial order that proved such an immovable political object.

The white Farmers' Alliance was a driving force behind the new Jim Crow segregation laws adopted across the South in the 1890s. Historians have debated whether these laws were truly new, given de facto practices of segregation widely adhered to in the years following the Civil War. Farm reformers, however, believed at the time that drawing clearer lines of separation was innovative, progressive, and essential for the modern development of both blacks and whites. The whites-only clause of the Farmers' Alliance was understood in these terms. Racial separation would protect white women, ensure white supremacy, and spur progress for the white race. It would also facilitate black progress. Explaining the positive good in the Alliance's whites-only clause, a Texas farmer reasoned, "It is better for both white and black to keep their orders separate." Otherwise, "Mr. Negro will soon be playing second fiddle with only one string to it." By the perverse logic of white superiority it was assumed that blacks would find themselves "playing second fiddle" in a biracial setting. By this same reasoning, separating the races gained currency as a humane and generous means to allow blacks to climb out from under white supervision.[10]

The latest discoveries in biology, white farm reformers believed, confirmed the need for establishing racial distance. Evolutionary science supposedly demonstrated that, among other perils, "racial mixing" threatened mental and physical degeneration. M. G. Elzey, the editor of the "Applied Science in Agriculture and Rural Economy" column in Macune's *National Economist*, alerted readers to the dangers. The old idea that "crossing breeds or races *per se* strengthens them" had reportedly been disproved by the experiments of modern animal breeders. "Mr. Darwin to the contrary," Elzey noted, "mixed races are as a rule inferior races." He also cited the findings of a professor at Johns Hopkins University indicating that "the negro has more of the animal and less of the man in his nature." To fail to recognize the significance of the latest discoveries in physiological knowledge, he warned, could only hinder "the mutual progress of both races in the path of modern civilization."[11]

The Farmers' Alliance put this understanding of "modern civilization" into a political campaign for segregation laws, realizing some of the most sweeping legislative victories in the movement's history. The Jim Crow laws of the 1890s turned the de facto realities of segregation into an increasingly rigid legal system of racial separation and racial control. The old systems of social control had rested on the personal power of the master or landlord over his slaves or dependent laborers. Emancipation broke the chains of slavery, and commercial development had further eroded the old order, creating a more autonomous and mobile black population. The new Jim Crow system reflected the fears of white southerners about "uppity" blacks as a restless and assertive generation of African Americans came of age outside of slavery and under increasingly modern conditions.[12]

The Jim Crow laws often pertained to urban settings: streetcars, libraries, theaters, and public parks. But the impulse toward further segregation also had its rural logic. White farmers objected to white women working in fields and kitchens in the proximity of black men. White communities demanded the segregation of the textile mills and processing plants in the rural districts. White rural patrons expressed outrage at the appointment of black postal clerks. Perhaps most important, rural whites were concerned about the racial management of the railroads. Steam power and steel rails brought modernity and its possibilities to the countryside and had a profound impact on rural life and the rural imagination.[13]

More than any other institution, train cars and railroad stations exemplified the modern dilemma of the racial order. They were places where mobile, unsupervised, anonymous travelers met in close quarters. Making the situation more explosive, those whites, including most farmers, who could not afford a first-class ticket met blacks on equal terms. In contrast to the workplace where blacks served white employers, or in the supply store where blacks owed debts to white merchants, in a railroad car blacks and whites paid the same fare for the same right to a seat. Accordingly, whites made the railroads a primary target of the new segregation laws. Reform-minded southerners considered these laws a mark of modern and progressive race relations.[14]

The Farmers' Alliance provided a powerful rural constituency for the new laws. In a typical resolution, a local Alliance in Franklinton, North Carolina, voted in favor of adopting a new railroad law "with separate cars for white and colored." An Alliance newspaper in North Carolina ridiculed black objections to separate railroad cars as only confirming their necessity.[15] Jim Crow legislation also merged with demands for reform. "When it comes to making a separate car for the negroes to ride in," explained a young Texas woman and member of the Farmers' Alliance, the demand for public control of the railroads would ensure that white farmers "would have our own way" in segregating them. Starting in 1890, white farm reformers would have their way as Alliance-backed "farmers' legislatures" in Georgia, Louisiana, and other states initiated "separate accommodation" laws on the railroads. Samuel Adams, the leader of the Alabama Farmers' Alliance, only reluctantly accepted the constitutional necessity of including the word *equal* in the 1891 bill requiring "separate but equal" facilities, and Alabama's segregation law passed with the unanimous approval of Alliance-supported legislators.[16]

The Colored Farmers' Alliance attempted to make the most of the new "separate but equal" regime, pressing on the "equal" side of the equation. At the same time, black farmers had few illusions about the intentions of their white counterparts. The question of black voting rights showed the depths of the distrust between the black and white Alliances. The Colored Alliance supported a proposal by Senator Henry Cabot Lodge of Massachusetts for federal legislation to prevent voter fraud. Black farmers viewed the Lodge bill as a means to safeguard black voting rights in the face of white intimidation and ballot stuffing. "We want something guaranteeing every man a free vote and an honest count," the Reverend J. L. Moore emphasized, and the "fed-

eral election bill . . . point[s] in that direction." The white Alliance promised black voters "perfect justice," but vehemently opposed the federal measure. White farmers viewed the "Force Bill," as they called it, as a throwback
to federal Reconstruction and "Negro domination."[17]

In this climate of mutual distrust, the black and white Alliances developed only minimal contacts despite the similarity of their names and stated
purposes. White Alliance leaders claimed with a paternalistic spirit that white
farmers were the "best friends" of black farmers. Such claims, however, did
not translate into assistance to the black Alliance. To help with the printing
needs of the Colored Alliance, for example, a proposal for aid came from
Milton George's Northern Alliance office in Chicago, but not from Macune's
Farmers' Alliance and Industrial Union. Even if aid had been offered, it would
have been rejected by the black membership because of the intense level of
distrust. In North Carolina, Walter Pattillo, the black state organizer of the
Colored Alliance, accepted $10 from Elias Carr, the state president of the
white Alliance. But he did so in strict secrecy, warning Carr that if black
members knew that he had received "one cent" from the white Alliance, "they
would not follow me." In a step toward improved relations, acting on a proposal from the white leadership of the Colored Alliance, the white Alliance
adopted a resolution in the fall of 1889 favoring business cooperation between the two Alliances. Cooperation meant little in practice, however, as
the two orders quietly feuded over outstanding differences.[18]

As the farm reform movement "went into politics," the white Alliance
leadership adopted a more conciliatory policy toward the Colored Alliance.
When in December of 1890 the supreme council of the white Farmers' Alliance held their annual meeting in Ocala, Florida, the Colored Alliance held
its national council in Ocala at the same time. As their mutual exclusion rules
dictated, they did not attend each other's sessions, but representatives from
the white Alliance visited the black hotel to meet with their black counterparts. The result was a succinct statement by the white Alliance on racial
matters. "We recommend and urge," read the Ocala resolution, "that equal
facilities, educational, commercial and political, be demanded for colored
and white Alliance men alike, competency considered, and that a free ballot
and a fair count be insisted upon and had for colored and white alike, by
every true Alliance man in America."[19]

The wording of the Ocala resolution may have seemed generous at the
time. Over the course of the ensuing decade it grew increasingly apparent
that the same promise of "equal facilities" justified profoundly unequal
schools, train cars, and public services. Similarly, the rhetoric of a clean ballot would provide a pretext for stripping blacks of their voting rights. At the
time, however, the national meeting at Ocala offered promise—or so superintendent Richard Humphrey reported it to the Colored Alliance membership.

By recognizing "common citizenship," "commercial equality," and "common protection of all," the Alliance movement was on the road to racial justice and harmony. Humphrey predicted that Ocala would "be known in future ages as the burial of race conflict, and finally of race prejudice."[20]

It was not to be. Before the year was out conflict and prejudice scuttled further cooperation between the black and white Alliances. White tolerance of the Colored Alliance virtually evaporated in the heat of labor agitation among black cotton pickers in the late summer of 1891. Given the low price of cotton, plantation and farm owners pressed to reduce wages for picking cotton to below 50 cents per hundred pounds. Black field hands responded to the wage cuts by agitating for raising wages to 75 cents or $1 per hundred pounds. Superintendent Humphrey took up their cause. He spent the summer organizing in the cotton districts of the South for a cotton pickers' strike, predicting that a million farm laborers would refuse to go into the fields come the September strike date.

Members of the Colored Alliance expressed doubts about the strike. Some black farmers opposed raising wages because they employed black labor. Andrew Carothers warned a strike would "engender a race feeling, bitter and deep and lasting, and one which may result in riot and bloodshed!"[21] E. A. Richardson, the black superintendent of the Georgia Colored Alliance, swore that his members "will go into no such foolish so-called strike" that "would be fatal to our order." He also challenged Humphrey's leadership, questioning "why he did not belong to the white people's Alliance instead of the colored Alliance." Because of such dissension Humphrey and his colleagues set up a separate Cotton Pickers' League to organize the strike. Even so, in the public eye the strike was the work of the Colored Alliance and its general superintendent.[22]

The strike failed. On individual farms in east Texas and South Carolina, pickers refused to go into the fields only to be promptly fired and driven off by the owners. Order prevailed across the cotton states except in the Arkansas delta region near Memphis, where Ben Patterson and two dozen other field hands made a determined effort to organize an effective strike. Violence between strikers and nonstrikers made Patterson and his colleagues the target of a manhunt. Within two weeks a white posse lynched Patterson and fourteen other organizers. Blacks suspected that many more strikers were murdered than the number reported in the newspapers.[23]

The strike and the lynchings in Arkansas revealed the deep chasm between the Alliances. The "common protection of all" declared at Ocala was shattered by the clash between farmer entrepreneurs and the farm laborers who worked their fields and harvested their crops. "The negro Alliance can never succeed in its demands by fighting the white Alliance," observed a white Alliance newspaper. "The white farmers of the South are the best friends the colored people have," the *Progressive Farmer* reminded its readers. It also advised them to "leave their cotton in the fields rather than pay more than 50 cents per hundred to have it picked." The lesson was clear. When blacks discarded subordination, the friendship that white farmers offered turned to antagonism and lynch law.[24]

Only remnants of the Colored Alliance survived the aftermath of the cotton pickers' strike. But at least in name the Colored Alliance played a role in the original formation of the third party. Potentially representing over a million votes, its support would lend the new party political momentum. With that in mind the leaders of the Colored Alliance, including the white officers of the Georgia Colored Alliance who failed to consult with the black membership on the issue, endorsed the formation of the People's party. The endorsement carried at least symbolic importance. After the long nightmare of the Civil War and its bitter aftermath, where conflict over black freedom and black rights pitted white Americans against one another, the People's party offered a vision for reconciling North and South. The presence of the Colored Alliance gave symbolic meaning to the new party's efforts to span the sectional divide.[25]

In May of 1891, the Industrial Conference at Cincinnati provided a theatrical presentation of this symbolism. Two white Alliance members, a Union veteran and Confederate veteran, greeted each other at the front of the stage of the Cincinnati Music Hall. The delegates cheered wildly when the two old veterans clasped hands. Meanwhile, several paces behind the two embracing veterans stood a solitary member of the Colored Alliance. The presence of the Colored Alliance provided a welcome reassurance to those northern Populists whose hopes for national reunion often combined with sentiments that the former slaves should be afforded fair treatment. When Hamlin Garland's fictional Ida Wilbur demanded "justice for the negro," she spoke for the former abolitionists and other reformers within the ranks of Populism who clung to notions of black rights.[26] The *Kansas Farmer*, in its promotion of the Farmers' Alliance, enthused about a movement of "Southern inception" that made "no distinctions of race." It boasted that Leonidas Polk, a former Confederate officer, supposedly presided over the Colored Alliance with its million members, and that Polk and the other Farmers' Alliance leaders "have everywhere sensibly abated race friction." Claims of this nature had minimal connection with reality. Nonetheless, the simple presence of the Colored Alliance made it that much easier for northern reformers to embrace the Farmers' Alliance and its vision of national reconciliation.[27]

The stage in Cincinnati also provided assurance to white reformers from the South. Members of the Southern Alliance feared that the proposals for a new third party would dangerously weaken the Democrats and white supremacy.

Because of such concerns, members of the Southern Alliance, except for a small number of delegates from Texas, stayed away from the Cincinnati convention. But the staged embrace between white veterans served to allay fears that northern reformers looked to meddle in southern race relations. Indeed, staging ceremonies to bury the bloody shirt—appropriately stained with pokeberry juice—and emotional reunions of Civil War veterans became standbys of Populist gatherings. And, as with the broader veterans' culture, these reunions tended to reflect Henry Grady's New South outlook that white brotherhood could be reborn with the national recognition of the principles of white supremacy and segregation. In the Populist context, burying "sectional prejudice" was predicated on recognizing that blacks had their place in the commonwealth of reform—a separate place several paces to the rear.[28]

From its early Texas beginnings the National Farmers' Alliance and Industrial Union, or Southern Alliance, made national reunion a principle of the order, a principle affirmed by the *Southern Mercury* in an 1888 editorial: "This country is one, nothing can divide it. The northern warrior has wooed and won the southern bride. This is not the south and north of '63; it is the great United States of '88." The growing acceptance of the universality of white supremacy tied the knot of this newly found national harmony. Echoing Henry Grady's speech in Dallas, the *Southern Mercury* stressed that only northerners blinded by antisouthern prejudice could fail to accept "Anglo-Saxon domination [as] the unalterable decree of nature."[29]

The "Anglo-Saxon" ideal of national reunion spurred the organizational growth of the Southern Alliance on the Great Plains, in the Far West, and elsewhere outside of the former Confederate states. This happened despite the failure of the merger negotiations between the Southern and Northern Alliances in part because Milton George refused to accede to Charles Macune's insistence on the whites-only clause. But even in Illinois and the Prairie states, the Southern Alliance's organizational limitations only highlighted the success of its principles as farm reformers increasingly defined national reunion in terms acceptable to the white South.[30]

Leonidas Polk, the national president of the Farmers' Alliance, served as the farm reformers' ambassador of national reconciliation. "There shall be no Mason and Dixon line on the Alliance maps of the future," he told a roaring crowd of six thousand Kansas farmers on July 4, 1890. "It shall be one nation and one flag!"[31] The following year at the California People's party convention in Los Angeles, Polk declared that "our hearts, hands and arms are widespread to receive all, from any state or section." The delegates jumped on their chairs to shout their approval. From coast to coast the "beloved Polk" sought to "join the hands of the Blue and Gray" and "break down the barriers of prejudice and animosity."[32]

THE BLUE AND THE GRAY.

"LET US CLASP HANDS ACROSS THE BLOODY CHASM."—Horace Greeley anticipated the inevitable. The Farmers' Alliance takes up his burden twenty years after he laid it down.

Figure 6.1. "Let us clasp hands across the bloody chasm," in the *Dallas Southern Mercury*, September 3, 1891 (Dallas Public Library)

Polk's humanity, however, was for whites only. Throughout his adult life he adhered to the pledge he made in the *Progressive Farmer* "to be true to the instincts, traditions and history of the Anglo-Saxon race." A Union Whig at the time of the Civil War, he would later join the Democratic party in outraged response to the postwar federal policy of protecting black voting and civil rights, which he considered "the greatest crime of modern times." As a scientific farmer, he viewed antebellum slavery as a model "system" of labor control. He judged blacks to be "a race of strong animal passion, unchecked by any moral force." Only with the discipline of slavery were African Americans formed into "a perfect component part of an elaborate machine."

Emancipation, in Polk's opinion, had destroyed the profits and efficiency of that machine. He hoped that the work of the Colored Alliance might create a more reliable labor force. But he was skeptical. The notion of allowing blacks to work their own crops, even as tenants, was a travesty, as he considered blacks to be incapable of useful labor without direct white supervision. He believed that only white wage labor could sustain the profitable farming system of the future.[33]

A self-described progressive, modernizer, and "young man's man," Polk viewed African Americans as "an incubus—a solid, dead barrier to our progress." He believed that free blacks outside of white control had no place in a modern society. And he welcomed black emigration as a possible solution. In short, his nationalism was a white nationalism. It was a vision of national reunion that drew the color line firmly across the national polity.[34]

The Farmers' Alliance defined itself as an association of "white" persons and denied membership to persons identified as being of African ancestry. When it came to other groups of questionable whiteness or American pedigree, however, drawing the color line often proved more complicated. Most members of the Farmers' Alliance thought of themselves as of "Anglo-Saxon stock," had roots in the Protestant churches, spoke English, and were American born. They often treated Catholic and non–English-speaking farmers with indifference or even hostility. Despite cultural barriers, a number of immigrant farmers joined the Alliance movement. Robert Schilling of Milwaukee, for example, edited the *National Reformer*, a German-language newspaper that adhered to Alliance doctrine.[35]

Several communities of Bohemian farmers in central Texas similarly looked to the Alliance as "the savior of the rural workers." They published a reform newspaper, *Roinik*, and organized into a series of suballiances near Caldwell, Texas. Charles Macune credited a Bohemian suballiance with a pioneering boycott of merchants that became an important tactic in Alliance business efforts. Yet Texas farmers wrote to the *Southern Mercury* protesting that "we want neither Bohemians nor Chinamen" in the state. When the Bohemian suballiances criticized the *Mercury* for printing such inflammatory statements, the editors rebuked them with the advice that although they may be bona fide members of the Alliance, they needed to make themselves "less Bohemian and more American."[36]

In the West, communities of Mexican farmers also joined the Alliance. Several Mexican suballiances in New Mexico petitioned for membership. White Alliance members reported that, notwithstanding their Catholic "bondage," Mexican farmers could be "enlightened through the Alliance" to embrace "progress and reform." Despite white Populist rhetoric about "drunken and renegade Indians," farmers of the Chickasaw Nation in the

Indian Territory also joined the Alliance. The North Carolina Alliance enrolled Cherokee and Croatan Indians, but only if they were "of pure Indian blood and not less than half white." In other words, for a tribe member to be eligible for membership he had to have mainly white ancestry and, according to the one-drop rule, no black ancestry. Recognizing the complexity of such restrictions, the Farmers' Alliance allowed each state a degree of discretion as to the complexion of its members, with the proviso that "none but white men shall be elected as delegates to the Supreme Council."[37]

While the Alliance color line stretched and bent around the meanings of whiteness and Americanness, it pulled taut against the Chinese. In eastern Texas and Mississippi large plantation owners had experimented with the importation of Chinese field workers, inflaming anti-Chinese attitudes. White resentment against the Chinese ran especially deep on the West Coast where Chinese labor played a considerable role in the agricultural economy. White farmers viewed Chinese agricultural techniques as alien and primitive, and also felt threatened by the success of Chinese farmers in the vegetable business. White owners of small orchards resented the power of the big fruit growers who relied on Chinese labor. Alliance farmers believed that Chinese labor, as a tool of land monopoly, posed an obstacle to agricultural progress. Yet at harvest time many medium and small growers also relied on Chinese workers.[38]

In practical terms, farmers' dependency on Chinese workers tempered their enthusiasm for expulsion. When California voters sent the Farmers' Alliance leader Marion Cannon to the U.S. Congress, they did so with the hope that he would keep his promise to not just restrict immigration, but to expel the Chinese from the country. At least rhetorically he kept his word, while at the same time he reassured employers that talk of expulsion would not, in fact, disrupt their demands for Chinese labor. It turned out that practical measures to expel the Chinese were of less importance for the ethos of reform than the symbolic significance of a language of a social purging of the racially inferior Chinese.[39]

White solidarity vis-à-vis the Chinese extended beyond the West Coast. In his 1888 speech at the Texas State Fair, Henry Grady welcomed the "exclusion of the Chinese [as] the first step in the revolution" that would solidify white brotherhood. White supremacy was not a sectional issue, he explained to the Texas farmers. "It speaks wherever the Anglo-Saxon touches an alien race. It has just spoken in universally approved legislation in excluding the Chinamen from our gates." Grady's anti-Chinese appeal received praise from the editors of the *Southern Mercury*.[40] Tom Watson's *People's Party Paper* demanded strict enforcement of exclusion laws against Chinese "moral and social lepers," and Mary Lease similarly warned of a "tide of Mongols." A small number of reformers, especially those interested in Asian religions, accepted the idea that the Chinese were part of the human moral family. But from Illinois to Texas and Georgia to California, the farmers' movement largely embraced the vision of a "white man's country" purged of "Asiatic labor."[41]

Although the vision of racial purging or expulsion was mainly directed at the Chinese, it had other implications. White farmers attacked the Chinese as "a foreign class, who could not if they would, and would not if they could, become American citizens." African Americans, by contrast, had gained their citizenship in the national ordeal of the Civil War. As a solution to the "Chinese problem," a Populist newspaper promoted a scheme to move blacks from Georgia to southern California, thereby providing "first-class labor by people who will become good citizens."[42] Tom Watson held that, unlike "a few tribes of red men or a few sporadic Chinese," blacks "are a part of our system, and they are here to stay." Most Populists probably agreed. But this epoch of Chinese exclusion and Indian removal was a time of volatile change. And visions of a "purely white man's country" kept alive the possibility that African Americans could also be targets of exclusion and removal.[43]

This possibility became a reality in Comanche County, Texas. Located on the western edge of cotton and grain farm settlement, Comanche County experienced two extraordinary developments during the tumultuous summer of 1886. One string of events led the Farmers' Alliance to organize a local third party that drove the Democratic old guard from county offices. The combination of severe drought, hard times, and the assertive presence of Greenback activists proved the Democrats' undoing. On June 4, the leaders of the Farmers' Alliance called for a mass meeting at the courthouse to air political grievances, an act the Democrats viewed as an "utterly, scandalously, outrageous" act of political treason. The courthouse meeting resulted in a plan to organize farmers on the basis of school districts to prepare for a citizens' convention in August. In the ensuing elections the "Farmers' Ticket" or "People's Ticket" captured every county office—the first Populist victory in the "ten years' war" with the local Democrats.[44]

In the midst of this political trauma, violence against Comanche's black citizens also convulsed the county. On Saturday, July 24, the news spread that an eighteen-year-old black field hand named Tom had shot his white employer's wife. A crowd of five hundred local citizens hung Tom from a tree on Monday at noon. Souvenir hunters chopped up pieces of Tom's body before the men in charge ordered local blacks to dispense with the rest of the corpse in a shallow ditch. That evening armed white men rode to the homes of African Americans with the warning that all blacks must leave the county within ten days or face a similar fate. A group of white citizens, alarmed at the lawlessness of the expulsion order, called a meeting that passed a resolution against the mob. But the mob pressed its case by threatening white critics that they too "may pull on the tight end of a rope." The several dozen black residents of the county took no chances and packed up. By the ten-day deadline Comanche County became what its boosters would advertise for decades to come: "Strictly a White Man's Country."[45]

The challenge of "mobocracy," according to a commentator in the local Democratic newspaper, should be the "vital issue" for the upcoming elections. Comanche's elected officials, the commentator urged, should be made to pay for their "conspicuous silence" in face of the mob. The Farmers' Alliance joined the ranks of the conspicuously silent. It held its citizens' convention on Monday, August 2, one week after the lynching and three days before the deadline for the forced evacuation of the county's black citizens. Thomas Gaines, who would soon emerge as one of the key organizers of Texas Populism, drew up the convention's resolutions. The resolutions protested monetary inequities, tariff injustice, and corporate robbery. But Gaines and the farmers' convention fell silent about the expulsion order against their black neighbors. The only act of the convention that pertained, although indirectly, to the racial violence was a general resolution for "the rigid enforcement of the criminal laws" to secure life and property.[46]

The resolution carried multiple meanings given the exceptionally brutal assault then under way on black life and property. For some white citizens, it may have read as an endorsement of the swift punishment of a black criminal. For other white citizens, it may have read as a mild rebuke of the extralegal proceedings against the black community. Either way, it amounted to surrender before white violence. Few could doubt that Alliance members were themselves involved in the violence given the lynch mob's size and the breadth of the Alliance's influence in the district. The resolution showed that the Alliance leaders would not risk offending their own members or broader white solidarity with an explicit defense of black life and property. In that sense, the failure to confront this violence reflected the racial antipathies endemic to rural Texas.

But what about forced removal? Why did this extraordinary edict fail to provoke a response from the farmers' convention? Apparently, reform leaders such as Thomas Gaines could accept the notion that African Americans, no less than the Chinese and the Native peoples, were subject to exclusion and removal. Tom Watson may have believed that blacks were "here to stay." Other reformers, however, entertained the possibility of a territorial separation of the races. In an era of dynamic population shifts and rampant speculation about the biological incompatibility of the "Teuton" and the "Negro," Leonidas Polk stated that he would welcome "with delight and rejoicing" a black exodus out of North Carolina. Lon Livingston, president of the Georgia Farmers' Alliance, reputedly had a plan to remove Georgia's black population to a Texas reservation. The Alabama Populists endorsed the voluntary removal of blacks from the state.[47] As a solution to America's "race question," Mary Elizabeth Lease recommended that blacks be transferred to the tropics. And in 1894 James R. Sovereign, leader of the Knights of Labor and a prominent Populist, in a dramatic reversal of the organization's earlier commitment to biracial organizing, called for the deportation of American blacks to Africa. That blacks formed the loyal majority of the Knights' southern membership underscored the terrible irony of Sovereign's demand for their removal.[48]

When they discussed the possibility of a territorial separation, white reformers usually presented it as a progressive solution, a humane and beneficial step for both blacks and whites. Parallel ideas percolated within the African American community. Some southern blacks hoped for a more peaceful and autonomous life by migrating to Kansas, Indiana, Mexico, or Liberia. In Kansas, several hundred black members of the African Colonization Club pledged to vote the Populist ticket if the Populist administration would help obtain transportation to Liberia.[49] Modern race consciousness inspired a wide array of demographic experiments and innovations. However, when compelled by an organized and violent majority, as the black Populist leader John Rayner understood, such innovations threatened frightful consequences. Such was the case in Comanche County, Texas.[50]

The Comanche farmers' convention bent to mob rule with its failure to confront the removal order. Its resolution for the rigid enforcement of the law, however, was more than an empty gesture; it was also part of how Populism defined its mission. Populism conceived of itself as the party of law, order, and due process. Progress required clean government and replacing the Democratic old guard of "bulldozing," corruption, and violence. Populist and Democratic practice often proved dismally similar when it came to the treatment of black citizens. Even so, African Americans paid close attention to the smallest shades of difference given their lack of options and the perils they faced. As W. H. Warwick, the superintendent of the Virginia Colored Alliance, put it, blacks were "ready to act with any party that will go to work to remedy the evils" of ballot stuffing and lynch mobs.[51] This sentiment goes a long way to explain the motives of blacks who threw in their lot with the People's party in the face of considerable personal risks of white retribution. Black Populism represented the narrow hope that the new party might indeed deliver on its promise of law-based government and due process.

Such a hope brought John B. Rayner into the Populist fold. He joined the Texas People's party in 1892 and quickly gained a reputation as the "silver tongued orator of the colored race." The Texas party had other black officials, including Melvin Wade of Dallas, R. H. Hayes of Fort Worth, and

J. B. RAYNER

Figure 6.2. John Rayner, Populist organizer and orator (Doe Library, University
of California, Berkeley)

C. M. Ferguson of Houston. Rayner, however, was the most prominent. He
was also the least urban as he made his home and political base in the remote and desolate farm districts of east Texas. By profession—like so many
white Populists—he worked as a schoolteacher and occasionally as a Baptist
minister. Unlike many of his white counterparts, he had only a secondary
interest in the economic problems of agricultural reform. His commitments
were primarily political. He viewed Populism as a means to a political end
whereby a person such as himself might obtain the legal and political standing that he was denied for most of his adult life.[52]

As a young man Rayner looked forward to his prospects in post–Civil War
North Carolina. With the assistance of his white father, he received a classical education in Raleigh before he moved to rural Edgecombe County to seek

his fortune. The county offered an ambitious young black man political possibilities, for it had a Republican administration and a two-thirds black majority. For several years he held the appointed position of constable of the grand jury of the superior court. In 1875 he won election as a township magistrate. By this time, however, the Democrats busily prepared to drive out black officeholders and "redeem" the state for white supremacy. Toward this end the Redeemers rewrote the state constitution to restrict local self-government and make the office of magistrate an appointed rather than elected position. The Democrats viewed the presence of black judicial officials as a particular insult to the white race. The Redeemer government closed all doors to Rayner, despite his education, his experience, and his electoral support.[53]

The wrongs of Redemption proved a defining experience in Rayner's life. He never forgot or forgave. "The civilization that teaches me to think, and then limits my aspiration," he would later note, "will asphixicate itself with the mephitic breath of its own intolerance."[54] As his biographer Gregg Cantrell points out, Rayner and many blacks of his generation who experienced Reconstruction spent their adult lives trying to regain what they had lost. A first step was to leave the shattered expectations behind and join the black exodus out of North Carolina for a new start in Texas.[55]

Rayner settled in the east Texas county of Robertson, a county of large cotton plantations with black tenants, sharecroppers, and laborers accounting for almost half the population. He tended to stay out of the political fray as he grew increasingly disillusioned with the Republican party. The "lily-white" Republicans, he observed, appealed only to "complexional prejudices, blue veins, straight hair and business sentiments." Black Republicans, meanwhile, had been reduced to political impotence, what he contemptuously described as "hotel flunkies, barbers, dude school teachers, ignorant preachers, saloon waiters." Of course, Rayner himself was a schoolteacher and a preacher. Those were the professions open to an educated black man. But he was also the son of a U.S. congressman and had once held positions of authority. He believed in power, not sentiment. He ridiculed efforts to revive the "cadaverous carpetbagism" of the defeated biracial Republican coalition and he viewed challenges to white power as both futile and absurd. "The only rights we negroes will ever enjoy," he counseled, "will be rights the southern white man gives us."[56]

Rayner looked to powerful whites, especially those willing to recognize the worth of a man such as himself, as the best hope. "The superior man," he believed, "is he who makes a righteous use of power."[57] The Populists, in his calculations, were white people of that type. His fellow black Populist Melvin Wade, with his experience in the Knights of Labor, demanded and expected that the People's party would provide equal treatment, "work[ing] a black and white horse in the same field." Rayner, on the other hand, had few illusions about Populism as a vehicle for racial equality. He did, however, hope that the third party would have the power to overthrow Democratic rule. And toward this end he made common cause with wealthy and influential whites who otherwise shared little with their black neighbors. He made a working alliance with E. S. Peters, a Robertson County planter who owned several thousand acres of cotton lands and was the president of the Texas branch of the American Cotton Growers Association. Rayner and Peters, along with another wealthy planter, led the work of the county's Populists.[58]

White Populists in Texas knew that without the black vote the third party was lost. People's party meetings often included black men and they occasionally elected black delegates to party conventions. For a man of Rayner's ambition the People's party allowed him to tour the state speaking to black and white audiences, setting up new Populist clubs in his wake, and rising to the party's highest councils. Such biracial politics, however, did not translate into challenging the principles of segregation or white supremacy. The People's party in Texas rarely disrupted the white monopoly of officeholding and black Populists made no claims on statewide office. Even such an effective campaigner as Rayner did not run as a candidate.[59]

Rayner focused his political energies on electing Populist judges and sheriffs at the county level. The People's party, he believed, represented law and order—ideals to which he had been committed since his days as a magistrate in North Carolina. Before the public he stressed the importance of obedience to the law for the uplift of the black race. In part this was designed to placate white audiences. It also conformed to his notion that the cultivation of the law-abiding duties of citizenship was essential for racial progress. Moreover, as he saw it, the worst enemies of progress were lawless white mobs and corrupt and ignorant officers and jurors. Hence the imperative to put "the best white citizens" in the jurors' box. At the same time, blacks had to be part of the legal process. "The man who is not allowed to help enforce the law can not reverence the law," he reasoned. "Therefore all educated worthy tax paying Negroes, feel that they have a legal and moral right to serve as jurors and help enforce the law."[60]

Rayner considered the jury question essential. He hoped that seating black jurors in cases involving black defendants would provide a minimal safeguard against the widespread practice of convicting blacks on trumped-up charges and delivering them to the abuses of the convict-lease system. The People's party proposed reforms in the convict labor laws and made occasional promises to place blacks on juries. White Populists also voiced opposition to mob violence and lynching. But the practical distinction between white Populists and white Democrats often remained submerged under the politics of white supremacy. Take jury service, for example. In Nacogdoches County, Texas, Democratic leaders vehemently protested when the Populist sheriff summoned blacks to jury duty, accusing the sheriff of pandering to black voters to gain reelection. Meanwhile, in Cass County, Texas, Populists accused the Democrats of hugging black voters so closely "they smelled like a negro for a month after the election." The Democrats had crossed the line, according to the Populists, with their promise to put blacks on juries.[61]

Mutually contradictory charges were inevitable given that both Populists and Democrats pledged themselves to the principles of white supremacy and accused each other of political calculation with their promises of legal rights and due process for African Americans. Perhaps the Populists, as compared to the Democrats, showed less duplicity in making their promises. But any measure of comparable sincerity must take into account that the Democratic party was not a monolith. Democrats bribed, terrorized, and "bulldozed" black voters. But they also put up reform candidates like Texas attorney general James Hogg, who spoke out more forcefully against lynching and extralegal violence than any white political leader in the state. Reform Democrats such as Hogg appealed to black voters for much the same reason that the Populists did. Any distinction was a matter of shade. For Rayner and the black Populists, nonetheless, this shade was meaningful, especially in light of the possibilities of toppling Democratic power. [62]

In his private papers John Rayner criticized race prejudice as "the Devil's race track." He resented white claims of superiority and the obstacles to black political and economic opportunities. At the same time, he was wary of "utopian" challenges to the racial system. The failure of white Populists to challenge the "Negro" signs in the railroad cars troubled black Populists like Melvin Wade. Rayner, on the other hand, made peace with the separate but equal doctrine as it corresponded to his own understanding of racial difference. Like most late nineteenth-century Americans, he accepted the idea that race was an essential and natural marker of human characteristics. The separation of public facilities by race only reaffirmed this notion.[63]

Rayner also saw in the separate but equal doctrine possibilities for positive good as seen by his contribution to the platform of the Texas People's party. He helped shape two measures of particular interest to blacks when he served on the platform committee at the 1894 state convention in Waco. The first called for state accommodations for the insane "without discrimination in color." The second demanded more funds for both white and black schools, but with the significant proviso that the segregated schools would also have racially separate administrations, whereby "each race shall have its own trustees and control its own schools." Separate administrations for segregated institutions would provide careers for educated and talented blacks.

Rayner himself would later seek the post of superintendent of the state Colored Blind Asylum. But more broadly he believed that a more complete separation would open the way for the free progress of both blacks and whites.[64]

In this cause Rayner had an important ally in Thomas L. Nugent, the foremost political figure of Texas Populism. Born in 1841 to a slaveholding family in Opelousas, Louisiana, Nugent attended college and studied for the Methodist ministry before serving in the Confederate army. After the war, he taught school, passed the bar, and began legal practice on the Texas frontier. He made a name for himself as a "scientific and practical lawyer" and served several terms as a district judge before resuming private practice in Fort Worth in 1891. Although a religious person, Nugent, like Rayner, had little use for church or creed. Religion meant improving the "living present," and establishing "a government of law and order organized on the lasting foundations of political equality and justice."[65]

Nugent considered himself a scholar and philosopher. He entered the work of reform with aspirations to remake society in accordance with a humanitarian philosophy. He was especially concerned with the free development of the intellect. As a colleague explained, Nugent believed that "a government, or corporation, or individual that obstructs or quenches the intellectual life of another commits a crime and inflicts a grievous and irreparable wrong." He devoted his public work to alleviating such wrongs, and showed concern for the ill treatment of prisoners and the insane. He expressed sympathy toward the Farmers' Alliance, the Knights of Labor, and the trade unions. Yet, again much like Rayner, he never fully embraced the doctrines of these groups. This was so even when their doctrines were incorporated into the program of the party of which he was the standard-bearer. He evinced little political ambition, suffered failing health, and lacked the oratorical skills of an effective political campaigner. Nonetheless, Nugent obtained mythic status as the Populist candidate for Texas governor in 1892 and 1894. The more his foes attacked him for his heterodoxy, the more his reputation rose as a martyr for his principles.[66]

His unconventional attitudes toward African Americans contributed to Nugent's sainted reputation. He was troubled by slavery as a young man growing up in a slaveowner's home where he reportedly spent evenings reading the Bible to an invalid slave woman. During the war he came to believe that the abolitionists and Grant's armies were doing God's work. He later spoke ardently of the "humanity and unique greatness of Lincoln." He also toyed with the idea that the former slaves should be compensated for their unpaid labor. To those who argued that the slaveholders should have been paid for the loss of their slaves, Nugent replied that "having had the services of the slaves for several generations for nothing, justice rather demanded that the slaves, rather than their owners, ought to have been paid." Such unconventional opinions might have left another white politician vulnerable to charges of race treason. But Nugent used his southern pedigree and record of Confederate service to skillful advantage.[67]

Nugent carefully avoided public action that might challenge the methods of white supremacy. This, for example, explains his opposition to antilynching legislation. During the winter of 1892–93, white mobs in Paris, Texas, hung several innocent men and ritually tortured and burned Henry Smith to death. Such barbarism was an increasingly common feature of southern life as blacks suffered the most intense campaign of lynchings in American history. In response to the Paris events, then Democratic governor James Hogg called for trying the lynchers for murder and submitted legislation to compensate families of victims by penalizing members of lynch mobs with fines. Nugent objected that such "fearsome legal retributions" against lynchers were "extreme" and "essentially unwise and unjust." Although he said that he would not apologize for the lynchings, he argued that the white people of Paris acted in "a frenzy of grief and rage" and therefore could not be held responsible for their actions. From Hogg's perspective or, more pertinently, from that of the black community, this argument did amount to an apology for lynching. But such were the consequences of Nugent's quest to navigate America's racial dilemma without confronting the despotism of white power.[68]

Nugent believed that only strict segregation would eventually calm the racial waters and allow peaceful progress for both blacks and whites. "My idea is that separation, as far as possible, is best for the negro," he wrote. "Anything which helps to remove this controversy about so-called and impossible social equality is wise." Accordingly, he proposed a more complete segregation starting with the penitentiaries, asylums, and other state institutions. He also suggested that separate facilities should have segregated black and white administrations. In promoting racial separatism, Nugent did not consider himself a Negrophobe or race-baiter, but a freethinker, a humanitarian, and a disciple of progressive reform.[69]

John Rayner mainly shared Nugent's precepts about race and viewed him as a sympathetic friend. At the 1894 Texas People's party convention Rayner made an emotional speech seconding Nugent's nomination as the party's candidate for governor. "Nominate Nugent," Rayner assured the delegates assembled at Waco, "and the negro will be as faithful to your flag as he was to your wives and children when you were fighting the battles of your country." His invocation of the myth of the faithful slave suggests that he aimed to please his largely white audience. The ardor of his enthusiasm for Nugent's candidacy also reflected common visions for white and black progress, in-

cluding shared hopes in racial separatism. Nugent's dominant presence at
the Waco convention helps explain the easy success of Rayner's plank in the
platform for racially separate administrations of Texas schools.[70]

White Populists viewed racial separatism as a positive good and "social equality" as a definite evil. "We have no advocates of social equality with the
darkey," a North Carolina Populist explained. "There is not a cartload of
white men in the State that would tolerate such an idea a moment, and the
negroes don't want it."[71] At the same time, white Populists could and did
appeal for black and white unity based on common interests. As Henry Grady
told the farmers at Dallas, creating a new racial order meant that the white
man had to lead the black man "to confess that his interests and the interests of the [white] people of the South are identical."[72] On the same principles the Populists made experiments to win black votes by emphasizing a
shared economic interest. In Grimes County, Texas, blacks were a majority
of the population, and winning a portion of the black vote was essential to
Populist political strategy. John W. H. Davis, the white secretary of the county
People's party, appealed to black voters on the basis of a common resentment of supply merchants and cotton traders. Responding to a Republican
boast that black voters would remain loyal to the party of Lincoln, Davis
replied: "But sir we think the niggers will take sids with the labor class of
people, and in defence of his little children who sets under the persimmon
sprout while his wife chops cotton." The Populists would presumably gain
the black vote if they asked them questions about electing merchants to "represent you in the legislature and colect your tax." After all, the merchant
"prices your cotton . . . your corn peese and potatos—even your doz eggs."[73]
Davis's focus on the merchant, however, revealed how narrow and contradictory the Populist appeal to the black voter could be. True, both blacks and
whites suffered from the price fixing of merchants and cotton purchasers.
But blacks suffered as well at the hands of white farmers who, as landlords
and employers, short weighted their cotton, charged exorbitant interest, and
otherwise defrauded black tenants and field hands of their wages and income.
    Charles C. Post, the chairman of the Georgia Populist party, explained
the racial politics of cotton prices before an audience in Battle Creek, Michigan, where concerns about the plight of the former slaves were kept alive by
old abolitionist sentiments. According to Post, "The best thing they could
do for [blacks] was to turn in and help the People's party . . . bring cotton
up to where we could afford to pay a nigger more than fifty cents a day without ourselves coming out in debt to the merchant to do it." Better farm prices
would help white farmers to settle accounts with the merchants and thereby
improve the life of their black tenants and laborers. In political reality, the
logic that blacks should go to the ballot box to help white farmers to secure

higher prices implied a leap of faith, a leap that black voters were reluctant to take.[74]

The solution to the "race question," Tom Watson believed, lay in "the simple proposition that each race will be led by self-interest." Watson, one of Georgia's wealthiest landowners and the state's leading Populist politician, held that poor whites and blacks would march in step to the voting booths in pursuit of their "identical interests." To make his case he sounded nearly like a racial egalitarian, contending that "the accident of color can make no possible difference in the interest of farmers, croppers, and laborers." In the celebrated case of Seb Doyle, one of his black political supporters, Watson appeared to put color-blind principles on the line. Doyle, threatened by a Democratic mob, sought refuge on Watson's farm where hundreds of white farmers armed with Winchester rifles gathered to defend Doyle and the Populist leaders. Out of this event historians have portrayed Tom Watson as a racial rebel leading the Populist challenge to the southern racial order.[75]

The episode, however, must be understood in context. The mixture of race and politics in Georgia flared into violence, especially in Watson's "Terrible Tenth" district. The Democrats resorted to murder and beatings to drive blacks away from the Populists. At the same time, the Populists used terror and intimidation to prevent blacks from voting for Democrats. White Populists carried Winchester rifles to protect their black supporters, even while applying Ku Klux Klan methods against their black opponents. At times, blacks voted for Democrats because their offers of justice could be equal to or even more convincing than Populist ones. Georgia governor William Northen, for example, a reform Democrat and former Alliance member, gained considerable black support because he advocated funding black schools and spoke out strongly against lynching. Both white Populists and white Democrats, locked in a bitter political confrontation, issued promises and employed violence to influence the decisive black vote.[76]

When Watson spoke of the identity of interests between blacks and whites he also left no doubt about his commitments to segregation and white supremacy. "I want no mixing of races," he assured a July 4 crowd in 1893. "It is best that both should preserve the race integrity by staying apart." And he reiterated his pride in his Anglo-Saxon race, "stronger, in the glorious strength of conception and achievement, than any race of created men." Blacks had their place in Watson's party, a separate and inferior place as indicated by a report in Watson's newspaper of a Populist rally and picnic in Marion County. The white citizens "all ate until we could eat no more," according to the report, after which "the darkeys and dogs ate all they could." As one of Watson's followers put it, while the Populists promised blacks justice they also let them know that "it is the white man's country."[77]

No promises of better prices for cotton or eggs could overcome black reluc-tance to support the Populists. Populism, with its largely landowning mem-bership and its commitment to the ideals and practice of white supremacy, had at best mixed responses from black voters. Even when blacks did cast votes for the Populists, in three-way races they tended to split their votes among the competing parties. In Grimes County, Texas, for example, Afri-can Americans divided their votes among Democrats, Republicans, and Populists in the 1894 elections. Only when the Republicans refrained from fielding a candidate in the governor's race of 1896 did a majority of black voters in Grimes County support the Populist candidate. At the same time, the black Republicans in Grimes County had a history of successful inter-party collaboration with mainly white independents, including the Popu-lists. Democrats attacked such cooperation as "fusion" with "Republicans and Negroes." Most Populist leaders agreed. Although there were local and fleeting exceptions, Populist leaders in most southern states avoided system-atic cooperation with the Republicans.[78]

In North Carolina, however, Populist-Republican cooperation showed its power. More than elsewhere in the South, the state had a competitive party system into the 1880s and 1890s. The ruling Democrats faced a Republican opposition with strong support among whites in the western hill country and among blacks in the eastern plantation districts. North Carolina also had Marion Butler, who was a Populist leader willing to cooperate with the Re-publicans against the common Democratic foe. Unlike Watson in Georgia, Butler showed little enthusiasm for appealing directly to black voters. But his political ambition and daring led him to horse trade with the white lead-ers of the Republican party. Butler's vision of race relations contributed to the striking success of this policy, as well as to its bloody destruction.[79]

Born in rural Sampson County, North Carolina, in 1863, Butler came of age amid the postwar intellectual ferment. He attended the University of North Carolina, where he joined the Dialectic Society and assimilated the New South doctrines of education, progress, modernity, and white supremacy. As a stu-dent, he launched his career as a public speaker with an oration explaining why "unprogressive" blacks were better off in slavery. Returning to Sampson County to teach school, he found a hospitable environment for his reform ideas in the Farmers' Alliance and soon emerged as the president of the county Alliance. By 1888 he edited the Clinton *Caucasian*, one of the most influential Alliance newspapers in the state. Just to make sure the message in the name would be understood, the masthead also carried the motto: "Pure Democracy & White Supremacy." Referring to the motto, Butler pledged: "We will forever preach that this is a CAUCASIAN GOVERNMENT. . . . Therefore it is of right ought to be and must be, MANAGED BY WHITE MEN ONLY."[80]

Figure 6.3. Marion Butler, president of the North Carolina Farmers' Alliance, national chair of the People's party, and Populist U.S. senator (Southern Historical Collection, Wilson Library, University of North Carolina, Chapel Hill)

As for "Pure Democracy," by the summer of 1892 Butler had concluded that the corrupt leaders of the Democratic party had betrayed the Democratic heritage and the white race. Like many southern Populists, he held that the People's party was the home of true Democrats. At the same time, he recognized that no reform was possible in North Carolina as long as the old-guard Democrats exercised statewide control of elections and local government. Both Populists and Republicans, despite their ideological and political differences, chafed at these measures and collaborated at the grass roots for clean elections and local self-government. Butler understood the possibilities of such cooperation and made ballot reform "the rallying cry" of the 1894 state elections.[81]

The results surpassed his most optimistic expectations. The Populist-Republican candidates won, making North Carolina the first and only southern state since the overthrow of Reconstruction where Democratic rule was successfully challenged. The new state legislature sent Marion Butler to the U.S. Senate. Butler, then thirty-two years old, was the youngest member of the Senate and perhaps its most energetic as he worked relentlessly to put Populist reforms on the national agenda. He also took part in the work of the North Carolina legislature, which made sweeping democratic changes in the election laws and restored local self-government. Under the new rules, few blacks gained prominent office, with the notable exception of Republican George Henry White's election to the U.S. Congress (the last black person elected to Congress from the South until the 1970s). At the local level, however, blacks did gain minor positions as well as patronage jobs in post offices.[82]

But neither Butler nor his party budged from their racial convictions. Although it eventually dropped the "White Supremacy" motto from its masthead, the *Caucasian* continued to rage against the perceived outrages of "miscegenation" and "social equality." And Butler still cast the People's party as a white man's party of white rule, a reality that the African American community well understood. As one black Republican claimed, blacks might vote for the fusion candidates, "but no negro is a Populist or Democrat." Of course, there were black Populists and black Democrats, but this assessment indicates how many African Americans understood the white supremacist commitments of the two parties. Whites who voted for Populist-Republican fusion had the same understanding and were confident that a party led by a man like Marion Butler posed no threat to the racial order.[83]

"We are in favor of white supremacy, but we are not in favor of cheating and fraud to get it." This is how Butler explained reform tactics in Edgecombe County, John Rayner's old stomping ground where blacks outnumbered whites and "would elect their own to every office in the county" in a fair vote. The reformers wanted both an honest election and white rule. So they compromised with the black majority by allowing two blacks on the ticket. It was better to let "a few negroes to hold office," Butler reasoned, than to corrupt the political process or endanger white power. This struck a chord with white Republicans and disaffected Democrats who had also suffered from the cheating and fraud of the Democratic machine.[84]

The machine struck back. The Democrats launched a massive "white supremacy campaign" to purge North Carolina of black office holding. They reviled Populist-Republican fusion as a tool of "Negro domination." They attacked the presence of black postmasters as an insult to "white ladies" who would be forced to buy stamps from black men. They sponsored "Red Shirt Clubs" made up of "respectable and well-to-do" citizens who intimidated, defrauded, and murdered black voters and political opponents. The violence devastated the Populist-Republican coalition and the Democrats swept the 1898 elections. White Democrats celebrated the election results with a riot against the black citizens of Wilmington, burning the offices of an African American newspaper, killing twelve people, and driving others from their homes.[85]

The virulence of the Democratic assault stunned Marion Butler. He was a disciple of Henry Grady and a new type of modern leader for a New South. His public record, from his college days through his leadership of the Farmers' Alliance and the People's party, confirmed his commitment to the vision that segregation and white supremacy were essential to the nation's progress. Yet the Democrats demanded an unquestioned monopoly of power. They portrayed Butler as a tool of "niggers and coons." Angry citizens subjected their young United States senator to rotten eggs and death threats and effectively closed the door on a political career that once held such promise.[86]

To seal their victory the Democrats pushed for a constitutional amendment to disfranchise North Carolina's black voters by way of a poll tax and a literacy test. The Populists split on the amendment. Most Populist editors saw advantages in removing the black voter and with him the "negro scare crow" from politics. Marion Butler disagreed and fought the amendment as unconstitutional and a threat to the white franchise. In his view, colonization to remove blacks from the state was a better solution. As another Populist editor reasoned, encouraging a black exodus would better safeguard white women from the black rapist. Butler managed a compromise at the Populist state convention in April 1900. Rather than supporting disfranchisement, Butler and the Populists proposed to amend the constitution to prohibit any person of African American ancestry, "to the third degree inclusive," from holding public office. In elections that summer, Democratic fraud and Populist ambivalence combined to strip African Americans of their voting rights.[87]

Given North Carolina's unique opportunities for black politics, the adoption of poll taxes and literacy tests marked a critical step in the steady destruction of black suffrage across the South. From the outset, members of the Farmers' Alliance and the People's party had mixed opinions about disfranchisement. In 1890, Edward R. Cocke, leader of the Virginia Farmers' Alliance, petitioned to end black voting by repealing the Fifteenth Amendment. On the other side of the argument, that same year in Mississippi, Alliance leader Frank Burkitt protested the adoption of literacy tests and poll taxes, fearing that they would take voting rights from poor whites. In 1892, Alabama Populists took a similar stand against voting restrictions, but also proposed an exclusive white primary as a means to protect the white vote. In Georgia, blacks voted into the twentieth century. Tom Watson welcomed disfranchisement when it finally arrived, bitterly concluding that black voters "simply have no comprehension of virtue, honesty, truth, gratitude and principle."[88]

In Texas, Annea Yabrough, an Alliance woman from Bell County, wrote to the *Southern Mercury* in June 1888 to argue that "a great many men as well as women . . . should not vote." She proposed that female suffrage should accompany a competency test to strip the vote from "the most ignorant Negro." Macune's *National Economist* printed similar arguments from the women's suffrage movement.[89] But it was not until the mid-1890s that white Populists in Texas started to deliberate in earnest against black voting rights. The *Southern Mercury* warned: "If the negro does not qualify himself to be a freeman, and act like one, the American people will become so thoroughly disgusted . . . that they may rise in their might and take the ballot away from him."[90]

White Texans carried through on the threat with a poll tax in 1902 and with a whites-only primary the following year. The Populists saw the poll tax as a menace to the poor white voter, but the whites-only primary they welcomed as a better "solution of [the] long unsolved question" of the black vote. The whites-only primary had at least the appearance of *herrenvolk* democracy; that is, a democracy for whites that corresponded to the separate and unequal ethos diffused so broadly by the Farmers' Alliance in the 1880s. It removed African Americans from electoral politics with remarkable efficiency.[91]

Disfranchisement left John Rayner deeply disillusioned. He had come to distrust the capricious and dangerous white majority. His Populist dream of democratic progress evolved into the nightmare of democracy's power to effect harm. He expressed special bitterness and enmity toward poor whites and the "iconoclastism" and "agrarianism of white tenant farmers." In one sense, this anger was misplaced. After all, the well-educated and well-heeled "best citizens" of the New South elite bore much of the responsibility for the new racial order that gained institutional traction during the Populist years. This is especially the case with black disfranchisement, where those with the most wealth tended to align themselves with the Democratic party and its partisan efforts to strip the franchise from the potential voters of the Republican and Populist opposition.[92]

But as Rayner and other black Populists surely understood, poor whites did broadly support black disfranchisement. The records of the Farmers' Alliance and the People's party attest to the fact that Populism had at best a mixed record when it came to suffrage restriction. Removing blacks from the voter rolls, however, represented only one phase, usually the crowning act, in a process that systematized, rationalized, and codified segregation and racial social control in a modernizing society. In that regard, Rayner had good reason to implicate the white farmers' movement in that process.[93]

In terms of outlook, the white Populists of the South shared Henry Grady's vision of white supremacy and racial separatism as cornerstones of modern, scientific, and progressive race relations. In the old abolitionist strongholds of the North and West, individual Populists still clung to notions of racial equality. But their voices could scarcely be heard above the celebrations of national reunion on the basis of "Anglo-Saxon" solidarity. And such solidarity was more than rhetorical. It was given life by the Farmers' Alliance, a secular movement of unprecedented scope in American history that organized from coast to coast on the "Anglo-Saxon" principles of Chinese exclusion and further separation of black from white. When the Populists went into politics they found themselves entangled in the web of an innovative racial ideology, an ideological web that they had helped spin over rural America.

Even so, the Populist challenge to Democratic rule in the South held much significance for race relations. In translating the ideology of white supremacy into practice, the evidence suggests that both parties included more and less virulent white supremacists. Although the Populists occasionally showed a practical caution compared to the fanatical racial campaigns of the Democrats, the significance of Populism did not lie in possible shadings in a common master race ideology and practice. Rather it lay in the Populist role in reviving political competition. The Populists, no less than the Democrats, represented white supremacy, as did the "lily-white" Republicans. But when the Populists engaged in political combat with the Democrats—especially when this combat made for alliances with a Republican party that continued to have a significant African American constituency—cracks opened in the walls of racial oppression.

Party competition mattered. It gave black political activists opportunities to speak and organize. It also compelled all three parties to address issues of concern to potential black voters, including "an honest count," legal due process, and school funding. As long as blacks still had the franchise, party competition at times required negotiations with the black community. But in no case did these negotiations call into question the basic assumptions of the New South racial outlook. The Democrat James Hogg displayed personal courage when he sought murder charges for the ringleaders of the Paris, Texas, lynch mob that burned alive Henry Smith. The Populists Tom Watson and Marion Butler also showed bravery: Watson by protecting Seb Doyle from a Democratic mob, and Butler in his defense of black voting rights. But Hogg, Watson, Butler, and the other southern white members of their parties never articulated a challenge to white supremacy and segregation.[94]

Black Populism, on the other hand, contained a covert element of subversion. The public pronouncements of the Colored Alliance, and particularly those of its white superintendents, reassured the white South that its members acquiesced in the separate but equal doctrines of white supremacy.

But black members such as the Reverend J. L. Moore of Florida clearly understood this as a stratagem, as a means toward black progress and a new trial of strength out of which educated and prosperous African Americans "will come to the top" and "come to stay."[95] For his part, John Rayner embraced much of the New South racial creed, but rejected its permanence. He believed that even in the confines of segregation and white supremacy, by taking part in politics blacks could pursue racial uplift and transcend the system of "racial egoism."[96]

At great personal risk, Moore, Rayner, and other African Americans seized on the possibilities opened up by divisions within the white supremacist camp. In their hopes for schools and a better life they organized the Colored Alliance in the face of white neglect and hostility. In an expression of faith in the political process, they exploited interparty competition to press demands for education, legal justice, and political rights. Not only the black Populists but also a much larger number of black Republicans (and an overlooked number of black Democrats) bore the brunt of the white supremacist campaigns of intimidation, beatings, and murder. But by the turn of the century, Jim Crow statutes, disfranchisement amendments, and the powerful reassertion of nationalistic white solidarity largely dashed black hopes. It is impossible to separate the Populists from this brave new world of race relations; hence the depths of Rayner's bitterness.

7

CONFEDERATION

Urban, Labor, and Nonconformist Reform

On his arrival in Chicago in the fall of 1895, the Texas Populist John Flaherty found the reform movement in the big city mired in an ideological muddle. "To you Texas populists who have a fixed and sound idea of the political and monetary conditions," he wrote the *Southern Mercury* back in Dallas, "it is incomprehensible how people can be so blind to their own best interests." Chicago reformers "go and hear the single tax man and shout themselves hoarse over his panacea for the public ills. They shout the same acclaim to the international bi-metalic lunatic, and roar with delight at the 16 to 1 silver tongued orator." In a "wilderness of doubt and uncertainty," the clutter of innovations, schemes, and proposals competing for the attention of the city dweller contrasted sharply with the "keen kernels of truth, without husk or chaff," that the rural reform press provided its readers. "Thank God," Flaherty concluded, "that the rural population of the great state of Texas have the understanding of good government and pure politics as taught and expounded through that grand searchlight of liberty, the *Southern Mercury*!"[1]

The displaced Texan longed for the "bed-rock" certainties and "pure politics" of rural reform. The urban cacophony proved unsettling for a visitor accustomed to a tightly edited rural reform newspaper and an organized lecturing network. Rural conditions facilitated a degree of public "singleness of purpose" that did not translate into the tumult of city life. Nevertheless, the distinction between urban muddle and rural purity carried less substance than Flaherty's letter suggested. Despite appearances, rural reform harbored its own complex mixture of ideas. Moreover, Populism signified a melding of rural reform with working-class and urban constituencies.

The People's party rested on an untidy coalition—a "confederation of industrial orders"—that cut across the rural-urban divide. Denver, Butte, Dallas, Cleveland, Topeka, and San Francisco counted among the urban centers of the Populist movement. Chicago, America's second city and its most modern and dynamic commercial metropolis, played an influential role in Populist thought and activity. Populism had weaker connections with New York City, Boston, and Philadelphia, much as it had fewer ties with the farmers of New York State, Massachusetts, and Pennsylvania, where traditional political institutions were more deeply entrenched. Across the Populist territory to the south and west, however, nonfarm constituencies played a vital role in the movement. Populist-oriented workers active in the labor movement, together with an array of middle-class activists and nonconformists, gave life to the ideal of a "commonwealth of reform" built on a confederation of rural, labor, and urban organizations.

In cities across much of the Midwest and West, urban labor federations overcame their reservations about farmers to make political agreements with the rural Populists. Other sections of the labor movement came to Populism by deeper conviction. Labor Populism had especially strong roots among miners and railway employees, two of the largest and most dynamic contingents of the labor movement. Miners and railway workers gravitated toward rural reform in part because of their physical proximity to farmers. Often living in semirural environments, miners and railway workers made tangible connections between rural reform and urban labor. Familiarity allowed for the cross-pollination of ideas. Labor Populists shared the faith of their rural counterparts in large-scale organization and state building. Diggers of coal, like the growers of wheat and cotton, sought market regulation to rationalize the national market. Railway workers, abused by the centralized power of the railway corporations, joined farmers in seeking regulatory commissions, mandatory arbitration, and ultimately government ownership. Especially with the onset of the economic depression of 1893, the organized farmer appeared to the labor Populist as a promising force for political and economic reform.

Middle-class activists formed another constituency in the rural-urban Populist coalition. Derided by its enemies as the party of harebrained "cranks," the People's party served as a meeting ground for iconoclasts seeking unconventional paths to renovate the society's economic, political, and cultural life. It attracted sponsors of every type of innovation, from good roads enthusiasts to supporters of phonetic spelling and dietary reform. Most important, economic utopian and panacea movements—Bellamy Nationalist clubs, Single-Tax leagues, cooperative colonies, and Greenback and Free Silver societies—often held significant positions within the Populist "confederation of industrial orders."

The prominent place of such nonconformists within Populism begs for explanation. Historians have tended to ignore their presence. Or, similar to John Flaherty's observation about Chicago reform, they have rendered the nonconformists comic and of little consequence, part of an urban muddle, as opposed to the pure and true rural Populists. Other historians have provided more sympathetic treatments, portraying the nonconformists as utopian bearers of republican tradition and evangelical piety. The Single Taxers, Nationalists, and other seekers of social renovation have thus been likened to "neorepublican prophets" who joined rural reform in a crusade to recapture a lost arcadia, a "pastoral realm" overrun by the commercial, large-scale, and secular "armies of modernism."[2]

The nonconformist Populists emerged out of a diverse but decidedly modern milieu. Many of the activists of nonconformist reform lived in the emerging bohemias of San Francisco, Denver, Chicago, and other cities, where if there was a single notion that provided them with a common self-identity it was that they aspired to be on the cutting edge. They desired new types of relations between women and men, new ways to dress and eat, and new economic and political models. The urban nonconformists were drawn to rural Populism because of their commitment to alternative paths of development. This included shared visions that personal fulfillment required the benefits of a rational and modern economy, with large-scale cooperative enterprise and state-centered regulation.

The nonconformist groups lacked the size and cohesion of the farm and labor organizations. Yet they played an important role in connecting farmers and wage earners, as their intellectual and cultural impact on the "confederation of industrial orders" extended beyond the weight of their numbers. In her study of roots of "a truly modern America" in the bohemian subculture, historian Christine Stansell observes that elements of this culture also formed in Davenport, Iowa, and other provincial cities and towns "where middle-class and working-class people met each other," and "where socialism, populism, or syndicalism cohered into organizations." Nonconformists of the Populist persuasion lived in less self-consciously sophisticated bohemian environments than that of Greenwich Village. Nonetheless, Stansell's observation suggests the role that they played in building bridges between urban and rural reform and spreading a modern sensibility in the American heartland.[3]

The labor movement, if not a "wilderness of doubt and uncertainty," was at least a complex and faction-ridden terrain for Populist reform. On the eve of the 1892 elections, Samuel Gompers, the president of the American Federation of Labor (AFL), cautioned workers against reliance on the People's party. Populism, he warned, was sustained by employing farmers, whose interests were at odds with wage earners. Election returns seemed to confirm Gompers's analysis, as the People's party had mixed results in working-class districts. Urban mechanics and laborers at times found the Populist focus on reform at the federal and state levels less compelling than the local political issues addressed by the traditional parties. A cultural divide placed barriers to cooperation between Catholic and other non-Protestant immigrant workers and rural reformers, who were mainly raised in English-speaking and Protestant homes. Although in the Midwest the Populists succeeded in gaining significant support among non-Protestant immigrants in the 1894 elections, they failed to do so in the East. Employer intimidation in mill and mining towns also played a role in limiting labor votes for the third party.[4]

Despite the barriers, much of the organized labor movement ignored Gompers's warnings. By 1894 the groundswell of labor support for Populism briefly cost Gompers his presidency of the American Federation of Labor. The 1894 Denver convention of the AFL rebuked Gompers and elected as federation president John McBride, the leader of the United Mine Workers (UMW) union and a driving force of the People's party in the mining towns of the Midwest. At the time, the AFL was rife with ideological factions. These included "pure and simple" trade unionists led by Samuel Gompers of the cigar makers' union. Thomas Morgan, a Chicago machinist, led the socialist trade unionists, while John McBride led the unions most sympathetic to Populism. All of these groupings bore the hallmarks of modern trade unionism. They recognized the division of society by interests or class. They accepted the necessity of large-scale organizational combination to regulate markets and counter the combined power of employers and corporations. And, philosophically speaking, they understood the necessity of organization in the positivist framework of the evolutionary imagination— an imagination inspired as much by Spencer as Marx.[5]

At the Denver convention, Morgan and the socialists proposed that the AFL unions adopt political action along the lines of the British Labor party. Gompers believed that the unions should avoid the hazards of independent politics and, with the support of a section of the Populists, succeeded in defeating the proposal. Morgan then turned the tables on Gompers by joining with the Populists to elect McBride as the federation president, the first and last time Gompers would lose such a vote.

Morgan's support for the Populist McBride highlighted divisions within both the Socialist Labor party (SLP) and the AFL unions. Some socialists, including SLP leader Daniel DeLeon, disparaged Populism as representing bourgeois interests antithetical to those of the workers, a position matching that of Gompers. Morgan disagreed. Along with other SLP and trade union activists, he held that labor and its radically anti-capitalist agenda had much to gain from a tactical alliance with rural reform.[6]

John McBride, on the other hand, represented a contingent of labor activists who were Populist by conviction. Such labor activists spoke a common language and shared common concerns with their ideological and cultural cousins on the farm. The labor Populists moved comfortably within Populist circles. In Illinois, Ohio, Wisconsin, Colorado, and other states, miners and other labor Populists provided the core support of the People's party.[7]

Much of the impetus for labor Populism originated within the Knights of Labor. The Knights gathered into its assemblies a broad assortment of Americans. It organized workers—men as well as a significant number of women—of virtually every trade, skill, race, and ethnic group. It also attracted shopkeepers, artisans, and farmers. Its diversity of membership partly explains why scholars have described the Knights as representing the premodern and decentralized economy of small producers, as opposed to the trade unionism of the AFL that represented a modern counterbalance to corporate power.[8]

The Knights, however, also organized along trade union lines. By 1886, industrial unionism had transformed the Knights into a colossal organization, with some 700,000 members. Within five years, the destructive combination of red scares, employer blacklists, and court injunctions had broken the industrial organizations of the Knights. The AFL unions proved more durable. But the explanation for this lies mainly with the vulnerability of the semiskilled and unskilled workers organized by the Knights, rather than the triumph of modern over premodern organization.[9]

The labor Populists shared much in common with their rural counterparts. They tended to be drawn from the same demographic pool of the American-born or English-speaking immigrants. The labor Populists also shared the farmers' boosterism and enthusiasm for progress, and the economic and political traumas of the 1880s and 1890s brought them to similar conclusions about reform. Much like the farmers, they sought to build centralized interstate organizations to regulate regional and national markets and to match corporate organizational power. Unlike those workers whose political perspective tended toward the local, the labor Populists focused on corporate regulation, arbitration commissions, public ownership, and other reforms at the state and federal levels.[10]

In the spring and summer of 1894, the labor movement faced a crisis. The combined blows of unemployment, blacklists, and court injunctions left the trade unions in shambles. A growing number of workers looked to rural reform for answers. They had seen farmers set up organizations that appeared to be more powerful than what workers had been able to build. They had seen farmers experiment with cooperative business models that potentially offered greater equity and security than the corporate model. And they saw farmers press for state reforms with a sureness that many late nineteenth-century workers sought to emulate. "It is the advanced farmers," observed the labor editor John Swinton, who have risen against corporate despotism and "who have formed great organizations":

> In recent years the political ideas of the farmers of the West have been way ahead of those of the battered masses of the wage-workers in our cities. They have acted with more independence than the denizens of cities; . . . they have not shrunk from seeking redress for their wrongs through the ballot-box and the established agencies of the State.

"The main thing," Swinton concluded, "is that [the farmers] are on the right course, and if we of the cities ever catch up with them, woe-betide the plunderers who hold our country in their grip!" Swinton's estimates were widely shared within sectors of the labor movement, giving strength to the ideal of a Populist labor-farmer coalition.[11]

Coal miners, like farmers, felt the burdens of rural isolation and back-breaking toil. In the late nineteenth century, much of the labor of both miners and farmers still involved semiskilled hand work. Like many farmers, some miners were also proprietors who owned small mining operations. Farmers also occasionally owned mines. Miners kept vegetable gardens and raised livestock. Some farmers worked in the mines during the off-season. Furthermore, like their farming counterparts, miners were acutely aware of their place within the global maelstrom of commerce. As cotton provided the raw material of booming textile industries on both sides of the Atlantic, coal provided the fuel that fired the furnaces and boilers of iron works, railroads, and steamships. The *United Mine Workers' Journal* reported that a 20,000-horsepower ocean steamer burned four hundred tons of coal a day, the equivalent of a year's work for a coal miner. It took nearly 200,000 American miners, armed with picks and shovels, to pry enough coal out of the ground to power the nation's industrial revolution.[12]

Miners and farmers followed parallel paths to large-scale, centralized organization. In the 1860s, Daniel Weaver, a veteran of the Chartist movement in England and an Illinois miner, led the first efforts to establish a national organization of coal miners. They looked to organization as a means to overcome the isolation of their rural and scattered environment, and to gain the power of knowledge. "Our objects are not merely pecuniary," Weaver explained to his fellow Illinois miners, "but to mutually instruct and improve each other in knowledge, which is power; to study the laws of life; the relation of Labor to Capital; politics, municipal affairs, literature, science, or any other subject relating to the general welfare of our class."[13]

Self-education fueled discontent. As William Wallace, a contributor to the *United Mine Workers' Journal*, explained, Herbert Spencer was quite mistaken to find irony in "the way in which the more things improve the louder become the exclamations about their badness." Indeed, it was with the advance of the miners' own enlightenment that the "besetting evils" appeared more appalling. "The louder the cry against the badness of things," Wallace noted, "the greater the evidence of social progress."[14]

In the 1880s, thousands of coal miners joined the Knights of Labor, attracted to its ranks by its system of industrial unionism. The order's District Assembly 135 enrolled miners across the industry from Pennsylvania to Texas. This form of industry-wide organization offered the type of centralized and uniform system the miners sought to stabilize coal prices and control the national labor market. When Texas miners went on strike against the giant Texas and Pacific Coal Company in November 1888, for example, the Knights prevented the company from recruiting replacement miners in Pennsylvania and Illinois. The center of Texas mining was in remote Erath County. As a stronghold of the UMW and of the Farmers' Alliance, it is not surprising that Erath County was also one of the first counties in Texas to elect a People's party slate.[15]

In 1890, the AFL's miners' union, the National Progressive Union, merged with District Assembly 135 of the Knights. The new organization, the United Mine Workers of America, was led by John McBride of Ohio, a founding member of the AFL who had been a member of the Knights and understood its system of industrial organization. He served as the commissioner of the Ohio Bureau of Labor Statistics and was dedicated to the state regulation of the coal industry, advocating for compulsory arbitration boards, marketing laws, and health and safety commissions. He sympathized with plans to nationalize the railroads, which would provide a more ordered environment for the coal industry. He was a committed Greenbacker, believing that an expanded currency would stimulate investments and markets. McBride embraced businesslike politics and moved toward the Populist party with sure but careful steps.[16]

In McBride's Ohio and in Illinois, Indiana, and other big coal-producing states, the UMW often wielded controlling influence within the state labor councils. Even in a rural state like Texas, the UMW was one of the two strongest trade unions in the state labor federation. Although it only enrolled a fraction of the nation's miners, its influence extended well beyond its membership. In the spring of 1894 the UMW called for a work stoppage in the hopes of bringing order to the coal industry. Nearly 90 percent of the nation's soft coal miners, or 180,000 workers, took part. Although governors, judges, and soldiers succeeded in breaking the strike,

Figure 7.1. John McBride, United Mine Workers leader and Populist president of the American Federation of Labor (UMWA Archives)

its scope indicated the commitment of UMW members to organizing the industry on a national basis.[17]

Miners experimented with cooperative enterprise. At the local level, they attempted to organize small cooperative mines and set up cooperative stores to put pressure on local merchants and other middlemen. Miners also tried various innovations in large-scale cooperation, which the union championed as "one of the most modern ideas for the advancement of labor." One such cooperative plan entailed a commercial understanding with an Ohio wholesale distributor to market coffee under the UMW label throughout the nation's mining districts. As the *United Mine Workers Journal* told its readers: "Remember you are directly interested in the profits of the 'United Mine Workers' Gold Medal Coffee.'" The union made similar marketing agreements for

"U. M. W. Soap" and other products. The *Journal* also promoted a "wholesale mining" proposal floated by William Pomeroy, the scheming leader of the Illinois State Federation of Labor. Pomeroy's plan involved a cooperative investment company to finance the boring of a five-mile-long tunnel under the Rocky Mountains to extract ores and minerals. The project promised to be "a guaranteed money maker as a railroad tunnel."[18]

John McBride and the mine workers toiled to bring centralized organization and structure to an unorganized and unregulated coal market. The coal industry, with its hundreds of mining operations spread between Pennsylvania and Iowa, suffered from intense competition. Price cutting became endemic in the 1880s as the transportation revolution had made all coal districts competitors in a single market. "Railroads and telegraphs had annihilated space and time," John McBride explained, "until the East was no longer the market of Eastern coal-fields, nor the West of those in its section. The same was true of the North and South." The pressure on coal prices intensified further with the introduction of natural gas, electricity, and more fuel-efficient machinery. In the five years from 1882 to 1887, the price of a ton of coal in Illinois dropped from $1.52 to $1.08, bringing the miners' compensation down with it. "The inexorable law of supply and demand," McBride told his fellow miners, "determine[s] the point where our interests unite" with those of the mine owners.[19]

The miners sought a solution in industrial rationalization, or what labor historian David Brody aptly describes as "market unionism." The late nineteenth-century labor movement is usually portrayed as a protest against capitalist centralization and combination. With "market unionism," however, workers pushed to centralize competing capitalists. In 1885, John McBride facilitated a joint conference in Chicago with labor leaders and the big coal operators to forge an interstate agreement to impose order onto the national coal industry. In Chicago, and at subsequent conferences, the miners combined with the coal capitalists to establish a stable, industry-wide scale of prices to be paid for a bushel or ton of coal, and thereby "give each party an increased profit."[20]

The coal miners' "market unionism" mirrored undertakings among farmers. The rationalization and order that John McBride worked so tirelessly for in the coal industry, Charles Macune and farm reformers strove for in the cotton, wheat, and other unorganized and competitive markets. Some mine owners, however, viewed "market unionism" as a potential challenge to their managerial prerogatives. Fragile interstate agreements periodically broke down as class warfare descended on the coalfields. Republican politicians like Ohio Governor William McKinley dispatched troops to suppress the miners. President Cleveland and the Democrats did the same. Federal judges delivered the most telling lessons. By their close collaboration with the coal capitalists in issuing injunctions for the suppression of the miners, federal judges made it clear to John McBride and other labor Populists that the old legal framework was no longer suitable to modern conditions.[21]

The problem, McBride explained to the AFL national convention in 1895, lay with an antiquated constitution. The existing federal and state laws, he told the delegates, "were made and adopted for the purpose of protecting men and methods now dead." The law needed to protect labor, and not only property. And the government needed the prerogatives to bring rational order to industry. The "changed industrial conditions," the "improved mental status," and the "modern environments of labor" required a modern legal structure "in keeping with the progress of our people along commercial and industrial lines." The coal miners looked to Populism as the vehicle for such a change.[22]

Like the miners, railroad workers often had rural roots, and many lived in small towns and villages. They, too, worked in a competitive national labor market. But more than the miners—and more than any other sector of American labor—railroad workers faced corporate power in its most centralized and organized form. Railroad corporations set the pace in the development of the professional, bureaucratic, and hierarchical methods of modern business organization. Railroad managers directed the work of thousands of employees spread along thousands of miles of road. Railroad workers looked to organize accordingly, and made their own experiments in large-scale and uniform methods of industrial organization.[23]

The employees of the Southwest Railway System created one of the first such organizations in the mid-1880s. It took the form of the Knights of Labor District Assembly 101, which briefly succeeded in organizing nearly ten thousand workers across the Southwest. The early successes of District Assembly 101 stirred the popular imagination with the possibility of building a modern labor organization as a counterbalance to modern business organization. Farmers recognized a parallel with their own efforts at large-scale organization and the potential for a combination of "industrial orders." Although the railroad workers failed to defend their organization on the Southwest System, their efforts to do so provided ideas and energy for the Populist movement in Texas and across the region.[24]

Texas was the epicenter of the American railroad boom of the 1880s. Between 1879 and 1889, railroad construction crews laid down over six thousand miles of track, more than tripling the state's total railway mileage. New urban centers arose to serve the new railroads. In the same decade, the number of towns in Texas with over four thousand inhabitants expanded from eleven to twenty, and those with ten thousand or more doubled from five to

ten. With its six railroads, the population of Dallas nearly quadrupled, growing from ten thousand to nearly forty thousand residents during the 1880s.[25]

Railroad machinists, trainmen, and track workers formed critical constituencies of the new towns. Most railroad workers were American born and
shared much in common with other Texas settlers. Black and Mexican workers performed unskilled labor for the roads, which, compared to fieldwork,
was a relatively desirable position. Besides the color line, the railroad labor
force was sharply divided by skill and trade. Engineers or mechanics whose
skills were much in demand received better terms of labor than unskilled
hands. Nonetheless, as a group, the men who built and manned the railroads
felt a considerable collective pride as instruments of progressive change. They
also enjoyed considerable civic prestige as members of fraternal orders, voting citizens, and civic boosters.[26]

The social position of railroad workers rose further with their incorporation into the Knights of Labor. By the mid-1880s, the Knights had set up
assemblies at virtually every railroad depot in Texas, and successfully organized Jay Gould's railroads. The New York financier owned the Missouri
Pacific, the Texas & Pacific, and other railways that formed the Southwest
System, making Gould the largest employer in Texas. Over four thousand
workers were on the Gould payroll in Dallas alone. Gould had a reputation
for unscrupulous and ruthless business practices, and many Texans welcomed the Knights as a means to check his power. In 1883, telegraphers
struck Gould's Southwest telegraph system and affiliated to the Knights. In
1885, railroad workers conducted two successful strikes on the Gould lines
and gained recognition of their organization.[27]

The railroad workers' success, however, proved short-lived. On March 1,
1886, nearly ten thousand workers initiated what was soon known as the
Great Southwest Strike by stopping trains to enforce union recognition. Two
months later the workers' organization was crushed. Court injunctions,
martial law, citizen vigilantism, and arrests destroyed District Assembly 101.
With the red scare simultaneously unfolding in the wake of the Haymarket
events in Chicago, strikers and organizers on the Southwest System were
blacklisted, jailed, driven into hiding, or chased out of town.[28]

Much of the antilabor hysteria focused on Martin Irons, the chairman of
the executive board of District Assembly 101. The severity of the persecution impressed the future Populist and socialist leader Eugene Victor Debs,
who at the time of the strike served as the secretary of the Firemen's Brotherhood and helped to keep the trains running. "In the popular mind," Debs
noted, "Martin Irons was the blackest hearted villain that ever went unhung."
In the ghoulish fantasies of antilabor agitators, Irons was a murdering and
adulterous communist. The *Nation* magazine described him as "one of the

worst criminals now at large in the United States." In reality Irons was a typical labor Populist whose life transcended the urban-rural and labor-farmer divide.[29]

Irons's life wanderings resembled that of other restless men who came to work in the railroad boomtowns of late nineteenth-century America. Born in Dundee, Scotland, Irons arrived with his parents in New York City when he was fourteen years old. There he apprenticed in a machine shop and witnessed the humiliation of his shopmates. He also learned of the appalling conditions women experienced in the city's needle trades. Seeking "more tolerant employers and more independent men," Irons boarded a ship for New Orleans. He soon took charge of a machine shop and made a comfortable living. Although he resided in a community where blacks were held as chattel slaves, their dependent condition was of little concern to the master mechanic. He was, however, deeply troubled by the hard life of his white colleagues. "I felt a deep desire within me," Irons later recounted, "to emancipate my fellow-workingmen from their wage-bondage, more intolerable, it seemed to me, than the involuntary bondage of the Southern black."[30]

Irons tried his hand at a variety of professions, prospected for lead, went into business as a storekeeper, and repeatedly ended up back in a machine shop. He continued to agitate for labor reform, including for the protection of children and women in factories. In the 1870s, he became an officer in the Grange and helped set up a Grange wagon factory in Lexington, Missouri. He also rose as a leader of the Odd Fellows.[31]

Irons enrolled in the Knights of Labor in 1885 when he came to work in the railroad shops in Sedalia, Missouri, a central depot of the Southwest System. In the Knights' organizational system Irons believed that he had finally found the means to "counterbalance the power of aggregated and incorporated wealth." As a well-qualified mechanic known for his personal courage and integrity, Irons quickly rose to the leadership of the railroad workers' organization. Elected as the chairman of the executive board of District Assembly 101, he soon found himself in a desperate, and losing, contest with incorporated wealth.[32]

In the midst of the Great Strike, Jay Gould sent Irons a telegraph requesting a meeting. The strike leader purportedly replied: "I am in Kansas City." This was understood as an extraordinary answer for a mechanic to give to one of the most powerful men in America. That, however, was precisely the point. Irons did not subscribe to radical notions of transforming property relations. But he and the strikers he represented were committed to the idea of organizational equity. The often isolated and mistreated railroad worker needed the power of systematic, uniform, and centrally directed organization.[33]

Corporate leaders such as Jay Gould had little tolerance for any challenge to their organizational monopoly. As one manager explained to a congres-

MARTIN IRONS IN 1870
From picture loaned the Union Banner by Eaton Williams, Waco

Figure 7.2. Martin Irons, leader of the Great Southwest Railroad Strike (Institute for Labor Studies at the University of Missouri at Kansas City)

sional committee: "I said to [Martin Irons] that we knew nothing of the Knights of Labor . . . we should employ individuals directly and not treat with organizations in any case of any kind." The managers responded to the Great Strike by purging Knights from the payrolls. The blacklist was so complete that Martin Irons could not find employment in a machine shop anywhere in the Southwest. The blacklist emptied the railroad towns of eastern Texas of former strikers, forcing them to either leave the region or seek a liveli-hood in farming or other occupations. The Knights of Labor on the South-west System—briefly a model labor organization for "counterbalancing" corporate power—ceased to exist.[34]

In the immediate aftermath of the Great Strike, fired workers had time on their hands for political canvassing. "Missionaries [were] on every corner and in every bar-room," talking up the Knights' political agenda.[35] The first priority was legislation recognizing labor's right to incorporate into trade unions and other associations. "The laws recognize thousands of combinations of capitalists, but no combination of laborers," noted a Knights official. "This must end." The workers also demanded compulsory arbitration laws placing disputes between labor and capital under the authority of a state commission.[36]

The Knights' political agitation roiled the political waters of the railroad towns across Texas, as antimonopoly tickets challenged the Democratic party establishment during the summer and fall of 1886. In Tarrant County, a coalition of Fort Worth railroad employees and black voters elected an independent mayor and sent an independent to the state legislature. In Dallas, Jerome Kearby, a lawyer who gained renown in labor circles for defending indicted Knights, and a future leader of Texas Populism, ran a strong independent congressional race. A laborers' convention in Parker County passed a resolution against both of the traditional political parties. In Comanche County political independents subscribing to the labor agenda made a clean sweep of the local elections.[37]

Given the early successes of the antimonopoly candidates in the Texas railroad towns, a political coalition between farm and labor reform held much promise. "Unless some eruption occurs between the Knights of Labor and the Farmers' Alliance," warned the nervous editors of the *Austin Statesman*, "the affairs of Texas stand a good chance of falling into the hands of those organizations at the state election next fall."[38] It turned out, however, that the Farmers' Alliance was ambivalent about such a political coalition, and members were sharply divided in their attitudes toward the labor movement. At the time of the Great Strike, it was common practice for an Alliance member to also belong to the Knights, and some local alliances provided strikers with food and solidarity. Other alliances joined the cries of the antilabor vigilantes and demanded an end to dual memberships with the Knights and the severance of all ties with the labor organization.[39]

The supporters of the Knights appeared to have the upper hand when the Texas State Farmers' Alliance met at Cleburne in early August 1886. The much-publicized "Cleburne Demands" endorsed the legal incorporation of labor organizations, a national bureau of labor statistics, railway regulation, and other concerns of labor reformers. The influence of the Knights at Cleburne indicated the extent to which the farmers had looked to the railroad union as a model of large-scale organization. It reflected concerns for the Alliance's own organizational legitimacy under an increasingly intolerant political regime. Yet, even at Cleburne, forces were at work striving for an alternative to a political alliance with labor. This was the meeting where Charles Macune first appeared as a delegate. Placing the Alliance on a business footing, Macune adroitly steered the Alliance movement away from independent political action and labor reform.[40]

Alliance leaders recognized the symmetry of the "business unionism" of Samuel Gompers with their own efforts at business organization. The *Southern Mercury* reported on the "sensible" and "moderate" principles of the AFL trade unions—evidence "that organized labor in itself is not necessarily a bad thing."[41] Meanwhile, attitudes hardened toward the Knights of Labor. The Farmers' Alliance ended dual membership with the Knights, and for the next three years avoided practical cooperation with the labor organization. When cooperation resumed in the Populist coalition of the early 1890s, it was with a different Knights of Labor. In the wake of the destruction of District Assembly 101, the Texas Knights evolved into a type of fraternal society. William E. Farmer, a prominent planter in Van Zandt County, emerged as the leading Knight in the state. Like many farmers, he joined the Knights at the height of its power in 1885 and joined the Farmers' Alliance the following year. Farmer helped keep the Knights alive as a respectable fraternal order largely stripped of its trade union functions.[42]

The national officers of the Knights followed a similar shift in orientation. As the Knights continued to lose members and strength, the leadership downplayed demands to shorten the work day and other strictly wage-earner concerns. At the same time, the Knights increasingly looked to the business politics of the farmer as the path to reform. "To-day the crops seem to be the business barometer of our nation," as Symmes Jelley, a national officer of the Knights, observed. "Upon them the railroad is dependent for freight, the banker for exchange, the country for exports, and the whole world for bread." And toward the farmer the Knights' leadership looked for labor's future.[43]

In December 1889, Terence Powderly, the general master workman of the Knights of Labor, addressed the Farmers' Alliance convention in St. Louis. Hoping to win the confidence of the assembled delegates, he reassured them that the Knights had no interest in reducing the working day for agricultural laborers. But it was on the "race question" that Powderly gave the St. Louis audience the most significant concession. "We believe that the Southern people are capable of managing the negro," he explained, to the applause and cheers of the delegates. By accepting the southern white "management" of African Americans, Powderly endorsed the new associational order of racial exclusion and white supremacy laid down by the Farmers' Alliance. Such an endorsement was especially tragic given that in much of the South black laborers constituted the Knights' most dedicated constituency.[44]

In Populist pageantry, the Knights of Labor played a key role in the "confederation of industrial orders." Officers of the Knights held positions in the new party. Significantly, in Texas this included Melvyn Wade of Dallas, one of the foremost black Populists in the state. But as an "industrial order" in the Lone Star State the Knights of Labor was more of a hope than a viable organization. The hope was kept alive in part by blacklisted railway workers such as Martin Irons. Hounded by railroad agents and an unrelenting press, Irons wandered the Southwest under a series of assumed names. He tried his luck at farming, organized a rural lodge of the Knights, and gave speeches for the People's party. Because railroad agents refused to sell a ticket to the once powerful chairman of District Assembly 101, Irons drove the rural roads in a horse-drawn buggy, spreading the message of Populist reform.[45]

The principles of industrial organization that Martin Irons and the Knights of Labor had fought for continued to agitate America's railroad workers long after the destruction of District Assembly 101. Eugene Victor Debs emerged as the standard-bearer of this agitation. This was the same Debs who had helped keep the trains running during the Great Southwest Strike. In the following years, however, he grew disillusioned with the craft orientation of the railroad brotherhoods and the self-defeating internecine warfare it generated. He attempted to create a centralized federation of brotherhoods under a supreme council, while he slowly arrived at the conclusion that workers needed modern industrial organization—like that attempted by the Knights on the Southwest System—as a counterbalance to corporate power.[46]

In the winter of 1893 Debs presided over the founding of the American Railway Union (ARU), a union open to all railroad workers without regard to skill or craft. Within a year the Chicago-based union enrolled 150,000 members, making it by far the largest and potentially most powerful labor organization ever organized on the nation's railroads. The ARU confronted a menacing corporate combination. The two dozen railroad lines with terminals in Chicago united into the General Managers' Association for the purpose of suppressing unions and enforcing wage reductions on their employees. In explaining the aims of the ARU, the Populist editor Henry Vincent noted that the order "embraces all forms of organized labor, as perfectly as the railway managers' combine represents the monopolists of the country." The unification of "twenty-three giant corporations," the editor observed, "gave to labor an example that could only be operated upon in return."[47]

The corporate managers and the railroad workers clashed in a decisive trial of strength when the ARU launched a boycott of Pullman passenger cars. In the spring of 1894 the employees of the Pullman Passenger Car Company went on strike to resist deep pay cuts and the high cost of living in George Pullman's company town outside of Chicago. The Pullman employees belonged to the ARU and their mistreatment and the company's refusal to arbitrate their grievances was viewed as a threat to railway workers across the industry. The new union would be rendered powerless if it failed to protect the isolated employees of the Pullman Company. On June 26, Debs and the ARU leadership directed the members to refuse to handle trains that had Pullman cars attached. The tactic proved effective when tens of thousands of workers from Detroit to San Diego and from Duluth to Dallas joined the boycott. The workers' action crippled the nation's rail traffic, sparing only the eastern seaboard.[48]

The General Managers' Association responded by firing union members and recruiting replacement workers. The concerted and repressive measures of the railroad corporations had been expected. The equally concerted and repressive measures of the federal administration and judiciary, however, shocked the railway workers and much of the country. Grover Cleveland dispatched federal troops to break the boycott in Chicago, Los Angeles, Sacramento, and other union strongholds. Federal prosecutors requested indictments against the ARU leaders under the Sherman Antitrust Act, while federal judges imposed far-reaching injunctions against the boycotters. On July 10 a special grand jury indicted Debs and three other union leaders on conspiracy charges.[49]

The federal charges against Eugene Debs resulted in a prison sentence. But unlike Martin Irons, who was hounded into a lonely obscurity, the persecution of Debs raised his prestige among both farmers and workers and created for the reform movement a celebrated martyr. Explanations for such different outcomes include the reputation Debs had earned as an officer of the Firemen's Brotherhood. Although Samuel Gompers of the AFL failed to take action in support of the Pullman boycott, Debs was a known quantity within the craft unions and had broad sympathy within the AFL membership. Debs and the ARU also did a far better job of publicity. This had little effect on the rabidly antilabor daily press. But it was reflected in the weekly reform newspapers, including important Chicago-based publications, which painted a heroic picture of Debs and his union.

The support expressed in the rural press for Debs and the railroad workers reflected anxieties that farmers' combinations could fall victim to the courts, just as workers' combinations had. Henry Vincent, having moved from Kansas to Chicago to edit the *Chicago Searchlight*, warned his rural readers that judges would next impose injunctions on farmers for withholding their stock or grain. Although farm reformers mainly escaped the wholesale legal assault suffered by the labor movement, they had reason for concern. At the time, farmers' organizations faced mounting legal threats to their existence under the antimonopoly statutes. In a case settled the following year, the Illinois Supreme Court ruled that a dairy cooperative represented an illegal restraint on trade. If Debs was indicted under the Sherman Anti-Trust Act, farmers naturally feared that they could be next.[50]

Farmers' anxieties were compounded by the shocking levels of repressive force that the federal government unleashed against the Pullman boycotters. The jailing of Debs appeared as part of a larger pattern of lawlessness by government leaders, prosecutors, judges, and federal troops. In the wake of the Pullman boycott, corporate power loomed as an immediate threat to individual liberty. Although elements within the Populist movement had long warned of such a threat, the danger became palpable with the Pullman boycott.

Rural Populists in Illinois, despite the damage of the boycott to fruit shipments, appealed to farmers to support the railroad workers. "Their battle is our battle, because it is a struggle for liberty and the right to exist," declared a special committee of the Cook County People's party that included such rural reformers as David M. Fulwiler of the Farmer' Alliance. The Cook County Populists pointed to the danger of a corporate-controlled judiciary jeopardizing the "right of free speech, the right of trial by jury, and the sanctity of habeas corpus." They passed a resolution calling for the formation of "leagues of defense for the preservation of the rights of American citizens and protection against lawlessness in any of its forms."[51]

The scope and force of federal action against the railroad workers aroused concerns throughout the reform movement. In a speech at the Farmers' Alliance encampment in Grandview, Texas, Populist leader Thomas Nugent warned that, although strikes and boycotts were harmful and self-destructive, oppressing discontented laborers with "Gatling gun and rifle, with bayonet and revolver" threatened to destroy American liberty. As a jurist, Nugent was troubled by the "constructive criminality" applied in the Supreme Court decision upholding the Debs conspiracy conviction. In a paper on the subject, he compared it with the Dred Scott decision, observing that "labor has few rights to-day which organized capital is bound to respect." Chicago reformers reprinted Nugent's Grandview speech and distributed it widely to the city's beleaguered workers. The sympathy expressed by rural Populists for the Pullman boycotters was especially striking given the hostility of the big-city newspapers and much of middle-class opinion. The contrast was not lost on the leaders of the ARU, who increasingly looked to make common cause with rural reform.[52]

Eugene Debs had shown little interest in farm questions during his career as an officer of the railway brotherhoods. He had distrusted Populist agitation that blurred the distinctions between farmer and worker. His attitude started to evolve along with his disillusionment with craft unionism. As he embraced the industrial unionism of the Knights of Labor he also welcomed practical cooperation with the Farmers' Alliance. The ARU removed a potential obstacle to such ties with a sharply contested vote to deny membership to black workers. Although Debs was personally opposed to excluding blacks from the union, he was unreservedly enthusiastic about a "triple alliance" that would politically fuse the ARU with the Farmers' Alliance and the Knights of Labor. "When this scheme is consummated," Debs predicted, "it will be the greatest step ever taken in the interest of the laboring people of the country."[53]

The storm unleashed by the Pullman boycott swept away the hopes for such a "triple alliance." Injunctions, jail sentences, and blacklists largely dismantled the ARU, and Debs devoted most of his energies to salvaging the remains. He hoped to rebuild the union with better-trained and disciplined members. In the next confrontation with the organized power of the railway corporations, he saw the necessity of more "thoroughly organized and systematized" lines of operation, allowing the central leadership to "be able to harmonize, control and direct the entire membership from headquarters."[54]

At the same time, Debs attached special urgency to political reform. A lifelong Democrat, by the spring of 1894 he had already proclaimed himself "an out and out People's party man."[55] In the aftermath of the Pullman boycott, the ARU leadership proposed new legal protections including compulsory arbitration laws and legislation to bring labor conflicts within the jurisdiction of the regular courts, and thereby curtail rule by injunction and the lawlessness of the corporations. "Hit the ballot box," Debs urged his followers.[56] "While working for the A.R.U.," Debs wrote a friend in the fall of 1894, "we are all united upon the People's party question."[57]

Debs, meanwhile, received scores of invitations from farmers eager to hear his message. Whether discussing industrial organization, political reform, or making lodge rooms into schoolhouses, he spoke a language that rural reformers understood, and they claimed him as one of their own. Farmers lent the hard-pressed railroad workers much-needed moral and political support. The warm reception that Debs received on extensive western tours stirred his expectation that the rural hinterland would blaze the way to the nation's progress. In the historical moment, it seemed to many American workers that the country's "advanced farmers," as Swinton described them, might lead the way to a better future.[58]

The Omaha Platform of the People's party declared in favor of the permanent "union of the labor forces of the United States."[59] The historian Richard Hofstadter dismissed the rhetoric of united labor as a symptom of the irrational side of agrarian protest. Why else would the farmer as a rural capitalist throw in his lot with the class politics of the hired man? Why would the farmer, whose "commercial position pointed to the usual strategies of the business world," embrace the goals of labor? For Hofstadter the answer lay with self-delusion rather than the quite businesslike and specific issues that brought farmers, railway employees, and coal miners into a "confederation of industrial orders."

Moreover, Hofstadter fixed the concepts of class and labor in a manner that would not have made sense to many participants in late nineteenth-century reform movements. [60] The principle enshrined in the People's party platform that "if any will not work, neither shall he eat," and similar Populist rhetoric, may have corresponded to a Marxist concept of work and labor that focused on the wage-earning and propertyless proletariat. But most Populists were versed in a reform language that rendered work and labor as broadly signifying "producers" who contributed to creating wealth. The "union of labor forces" in the Omaha Platform therefore also appears as the "class" of "plain people."[61] Similarly, Tom Watson gave the term "the people" virtually the same significance as "the laborer," who works with "brawn or brain, with thought or speech." For such Populists, a broad spectrum of trades, professions, and occupations—farmers, mechanics, miners, craftsmen, doctors, editors, and manufacturers—might be included in the expansive and fluid category of labor.[62]

Tom Watson equated "the people" and "the laborer" with "the great Middle Class." Indeed, as they saw society increasingly divided between "the two great classes—tramps and millionaires," the Populists tended to view themselves as belonging in the middle. Such a middle identity would bear out the argument of the historian Robert Johnston, who contends that Populism represented a middle-class radicalism that corresponded to middling socioeconomic groups of small proprietors or the lower petite bourgeoisie. However, describing the Populists of the 1880s and 1890s as "middle class" raises a number of conceptual issues. Among other things, it contains the paradox that the Farmers' Alliance at the foundations of Populism was born of deep antipathy toward the store owners and other small proprietors of village and town. Further, even if most farmers might be viewed as small proprietors, the influential presence of railway workers, miners, and other wage earners within the Populist coalition complicates any simple "middle-class" designation.[63]

Significantly, the Populists themselves usually used the term "class" as a synonym for "interest," rather than as a socioeconomic category as implied by the concept of middle class or petite bourgeoisie. Populists often used *class* as a term of derision. *Class legislation* meant injustice because it favored the interests of one group over another. The Conger Lard Bill, for example, was perceived as "class legislation" because it would have protected the meat-packing industry at the expense of cotton producers by placing a tax on lard mixed with cottonseed oil. In the Populist lexicon, however, *class* could also serve as a descriptive term for a profession, a trade, an occupation, or an industry. In that sense, class was usually another way of affirming the legitimacy of a business or commercial interest.[64]

The People's party was conceived as a coalition of such interests. The Farmers' Alliance had defined itself as a business organization of the "whole class" of cotton growers or, more expansively, of the various "agricultural classes." However, as the Alliance took steps to create a third party, it became readily apparent that the success of the new party would depend on its ability to forge an all-class confederation. As Charles Macune explained in the fall of 1891, the new party "could not be a class party and succeed. It would have to be a people's party in fact and represent alike all classes of citizens."[65] Marion Butler made a similar appeal for a coalition that would combine every interest of both town and country, which, despite their "different lines" of commercial activity, shared "identical" or at least "complementary" aims.[66]

The Populists viewed their new People's party as a fusion of interests, or a "confederation of industrial orders." Labor Populism, as organized contingents of modern American industry, fit nicely into the schema. But where did the professional and other middling urban interests belong in this confederation? The Populists attempted to solve this problem by setting up Industrial Legions and Citizens' Alliances that would parallel the "industrial orders" of farm and labor Populism. The nonconformist movements—the Single Taxers, the Nationalists, the Cooperative Commonwealers, and other seekers of social renovation—filled the ranks of these Legions and Alliances. The nonconformist activists usually did not associate as members of any particular trade, business, or otherwise identifiable "industry." And their multifarious clubs and societies tended toward disarray rather than order. Nonetheless, these clubs and societies formed an integral part of the "industrial orders" of the Populist confederation. Although often mistakenly characterized as narrowly middle class, the nonconformist movements mobilized a wide range of men and women, from businesspersons seeking civic reform to labor radicals pursuing anticapitalist agendas. The nonconformists supplied Populism with committed activists, stimulated urban Populist coalitions, built bridges between farm and labor Populists, and shaped ideas for a modern future.

The San Francisco boardinghouse of Anna Fader Haskell and Burnette Haskell offers an entry point for examining the somewhat mysterious world of nonconformist reform. Their home lodged sailors and other seminomadic laborers and provided a central meeting place for reform activities. German-speaking anarchists, Irish trade unionists, and other labor activists from across the country and across the political spectrum frequented the Haskell home. So, too, did the traveling lecturers of the Farmers' Alliance. The executive committee of the city's Nationalist club, guided by the ideas of Edward Bellamy's utopian novel *Looking Backward*, held its weekly meetings in the parlor. The house also served as the headquarters of the Kaweah colony, a cooperative experiment in the Sierra foothills inspired by Laurence Gronlund's visions of a "Cooperative Commonwealth."[67]

Burnette Haskell described the colony's membership as "old and young, rich and poor, wise and foolish, educated and ignorant, worker and professional man. . . . There were temperance men and their opposites, churchmen and agnostics, free-thinkers, Darwinists, and spiritualists, bad poets and good, musicians, artists, prophets, and priests. There were dress-reform cranks and phonetic spelling fanatics, word-purists and vegetarians. It was a mad, mad world." The same eclectic madness characterized much of the "Industrial Legions" of urban and nonconformist reform.[68]

The San Francisco Nationalist club, one of the movement's largest, with over five hundred members, presented a public image of Victorian respectability. The club boasted that "the most perfect harmony reigns" in its meetings, and that its members included "twenty-six physicians, several lawyers, authors, artists, teachers and professors of music." In light of such claims, historians have stressed the cultural gap separating the "genteel" middle-class Nationalist and the mud-spattered and gritty Populist. Yet, claims of "perfect harmony" to the contrary, an especially vitriolic and brawling form of factional warfare was just one of the many ways in which the Haskells and the San Francisco Nationalists bent social norms. And beneath the boasts of professional membership lay a multiclass bohemian subculture that reached across the spectrum of the Populist coalition.[69]

Anna Fader Haskell had a reputation as a hardworking and talented reform activist. She was also a hard-living contrarian and iconoclast. She held in contempt religion and its moralistic trappings. She ridiculed sentimental notions of spirituality and argued with Burnette "about whether there is an intelligence behind the creation—he understanding that there is and I understanding contrary." She considered marriage a failed institution—an attitude that her husband understood as evidence of women's "polygamous nature" and inability "to understand monogamic love." Her personal discontent focused on a woman's alienation in married life. "I am so unsatisfied. I am sick of playing second fiddle all the time," she reported in her diary. "I am sick of it and I aint going to live my life out in this senseless clam like way."[70]

The routines of daily life tormented Anna. She occasionally had Burnette do the housework while she set type in the movement's printing office. Otherwise, she sought solace in smoking her cigarillos, reading "beautiful but indecent" French novels, and bathing in the public baths. Only night brought her relief. In one of her first meetings with Burnette, the two of them stayed up until three in the morning "discussing the theory of evolution until we were wild." Late-night chess games or debates about science, politics, and literature provided moments of calm in their stormy marriage. She occasionally held boxing matches in her home. One such match left her "awfully lame," she told her diary, but "I felt a good deal better after boxing and singing than I have for a long time."[71]

Evenings also meant political gatherings. Although nominated as president of the San Francisco Nationalist club, Anna declined in favor of the position of secretary, which put her in the center of the political action. She "kicked" at the woman's job of serving refreshments, but enjoyed the stormy executive meetings that filled her house with people and "every one speak[ing] as loud as they can." After meetings she and a "big gang" went out to the coffeehouses, or sought the excitement of watching a house fire.[72] Years later she would write her sister-in-law of the "stupendous" 1906 earthquake, explaining that "the hell of fire—the deafening reverberations of dynamite—constitute an experience that is wonderful. I am glad not to have missed it." Like flames of the urban inferno in Ignatius Donnelly's *Caesar's Column*, an enthusiasm for destruction accompanied Anna's singular belief in evolutionary progress.[73]

The Haskells' world was not as genteel as Nationalist publications suggested, nor was it as middle class or as urban. Burnette Haskell came from a once-wealthy family, briefly attended college, and joined the California bar. He was intimately connected with the labor movement. In the mid-1880s, during a sojourn to Denver, he gained renown as a labor organizer and was at the center of the radical and reformist circles that would later contribute to the triumph of the Populist coalition in Colorado. His years of organizing on the San Francisco waterfront contributed to the success of the Coastal Seamen's Union, which had over four thousand members and represented the most powerful trade union on the Pacific Coast. Sailors lodged in the Haskells' house, took part in their reform projects, and were Anna's companions. Anna also organized among unemployed workers in the city's Golden Gate Park.[74]

Although urbanites in the 1880s, both Haskells maintained extensive connections to the rural world from which they came. Born in 1857 on a ranch and orchard in Sierra County, California, Burnette's parents brought him to San Francisco for an education. While his brother returned to farming, Burnette lectured extensively in farm communities and later attempted his own return to fruit growing. For her part, Anna Fader was born on a small farm in Trinity County, and at the age of twenty-three left home on her own to find employment in San Francisco. Her brother, meanwhile, earned $1.50 a day cutting hay as an agricultural laborer. After the collapse of her marriage to Burnette, Anna returned to rural California to teach in a one-room school. The personal lives of the Haskells straddled the divisions separating

Figure 7.3. Burnette Haskell, nonconformist activist and founder of Kaweah colony (Bancroft Library, University of California, Berkeley)

the urban and rural, the middle class and laboring class, the de-classed and the deeply rooted—an experience shared by many nonconformist activists in the Populist coalition.[75]

Populism arose from a rare mixture of farm and labor agitation, stirred with visions of future possibilities that, to a remarkable degree, transcended traditional social barriers. One of the most influential such visions was Henry George's Single Tax. Mistakenly characterized in Populist history as "little more than political flotsam," the Single-Tax movement had the striking capacity to appeal across class and cultural divisions, enjoying a significant following within all the constituencies of the Populist coalition.[76]

In its simplest form, George's plan would abolish the existing property taxes and tariffs, and replace them with a "single tax" on the unimproved value of the land. Taxes on buildings and other improvements, George argued, were strangling productive investment, encouraging land speculation, and protecting monopoly. The Single Tax offered a way out of stagnation and poverty by stimulating "improvement and production." For the urban entrepreneur, it offered tax relief for investing in new buildings or industrial facilities. For the urban worker, it offered jobs, better housing, and the possibility of home ownership on suburban parcels liberated from the grasp of real estate speculators. For the farmer proprietor, it offered incentive to build barns and drain and irrigate fields. For the land-poor or tenant farmer, it offered the hope of opening new lands to settlement and the chance of ownership. For each of these interests, the Single Tax pointed to unfettered development and progress. "The more houses, the more crops, the more building in the country," George wrote, "the better for us all."[77]

Although Burnette Haskell never fully subscribed to the Single Tax, he was closely linked to those who did. This included Edward W. Thurman, a leader of the Typographical Union. Thurman and other Single Taxers held prominent positions in the San Francisco labor movement and sought an alliance with Haskell and his labor friends on the waterfront as part of a labor-business coalition for municipal reform. In 1888 the Haskells launched a "Common Sense Party" to effect such a coalition and overthrow "municipal abuse." Six years later, a labor-business coalition facilitated by Single-Tax and Nationalist reformers won a striking victory against urban bossism and the influence of the Southern Pacific Railroad in municipal affairs. In November 1894, the mining engineer and real estate magnate Adolph Sutro won the mayor's office on the Populist platform of municipal ownership of Southern Pacific's streetcars and professional administration of city government.[78]

The Single Taxers in California also looked to reform at the state level. They made agreements with the Farmers' Alliance to push for the secret ballot and they worked to win farmers to the Single Tax. Although some farmers feared that the land tax would be a burden, other farmers were dedicated followers of Henry George. When California Populists at their 1894 state convention wrote a Single-Tax plank into their platform, the *San Pedro Times* observed that the third party had "scored a big point in gaining support for their ticket" among rural voters seeking land.[79]

In Illinois, the Single-Tax movement played a particularly influential role in the Populist coalition. The weekly meetings of the Chicago Single-Tax club attracted some of the city's most promising professionals, including the

Figure 7.4. Adolph Sutro, Populist mayor of San Francisco (California Historical Society, San Francisco)

young lawyer Clarence Darrow. His rapid rise to prominence as a star of reform politics suggests that the Single-Tax movement had room for freethinkers, agnostics, and iconoclasts. Having read *Progress and Poverty* as a young man in Ashtabula, Ohio, Darrow arrived in Chicago a "pronounced disciple" of Henry George. He quickly gained a reputation for his bohemian ways—what he described as his contempt for "ordinary rules of ethics or conduct." Influenced by his friend Morrison Swift, Darrow contemplated "modern thoughts about the rights of labor, and the wrongs of the world," and concluded that "business is legal fraud" and that "society is legal injustice." Such radical ideas led Swift to "social anarchism" and a life of poverty as an organizer of workers and tramps. Darrow chose to spread his "heresy" through a career in law and an effort to "destroy the system" from within.[80]

Populism caught the attention of Darrow and his Single-Tax colleague John Z. White, a Chicago print-shop owner and former officer of the Typographical Union. White served as the president of the city's Single-Tax club and was a leading spokesperson for the national movement. By the political campaign of 1894, both men had emerged as key figures in the Illinois People's party: Darrow, the fiery and tireless campaigner, who rallied both urban and rural crowds, and White, the Populist congressional candidate for the second district, with support among reformers in Chicago's working-class and middle-class neighborhoods.[81]

Not all Single Taxers shared the enthusiasm for Populism. Henry George himself expressed "indifference, or even hostility" to a Populist platform that failed to focus exclusively on his taxing remedy. George's inflexibility strained the reform coalition. In Chicago, it heightened friction within the workers' movement, already divided among Thomas Morgan's socialist-oriented workers, craft-oriented unionists, and Single-Tax adherents. The latter two groups combined with downstate Single Taxers, whose ranks included a sizable number of farmers, in a contest between "the Georgites and the Morganites" for the direction of Illinois Populism. At the same time, many of the state's farmers had reservations about both socialism and the Single Tax. The resulting compromises produced "crazy quilt" platforms for the People's party, reflecting the multiple influences of labor radicalism, farmers' organizations, and the Single Tax.[82]

The Chicago Single Taxers played a major part in the Populist campaign for urban reform. In the 1895 city elections, White and Darrow helped forge a reform alliance against Charles Yerkes's cable car monopoly and its corrupting influence. Although failing to gain the political successes of similar coalitions in San Francisco, Detroit, and elsewhere, the Populist campaign laid the foundation for a progressive cross-class alliance that would soon place public ownership of the street cars at the center of Chicago politics.[83]

In more rural states, the Populists tended to downplay the influence of the Single Tax, at least in their newspapers and political campaigns. Although the lack of publicity for the Single Tax makes it difficult to measure its influence, even in Populism's rural strongholds too many prominent Populists were animated by George's doctrines to discount their significance. The novelist Hamlin Garland, a self-described "Henry George apostle," lectured for the Farmers' Alliance and the People's party across much of the rural West.[84] Jerry "Sockless" Simpson, a Populist congressman from Kansas, was similarly committed to the Single Tax. As a successful farmer and stock raiser,

Simpson saw the Single Tax as a means to combat the railroad monopoly, and he built his career as a Farmers' Alliance lecturer and Populist politician on the railroad issue.[85]

In Texas, copies of George's *Progress and Poverty* sold for 30 cents and were distributed widely. Letters appeared in the *Southern Mercury* recommending the Single Tax to members of the Farmers' Alliance as a means "to put a stop to the further alienation of the land."[86] Moreover, the Colored Alliance showed strong support for the Single-Tax remedy. Black farmers and laborers rarely owned the dilapidated cabins they lived in or the land they worked, and among all the Populist constituencies they were the ones who suffered acute land hunger. Even a generation after emancipation, observed Richard Humphrey, the superintendent of the Colored Alliance, the former slaves were "still a multitude of homeless renters." Seven-eighths of black families, by his count, rented their homes and farms. When they did acquire property it was often of marginal value. In Texas, black-owned farms averaged one-eighth the acreage and one-quarter the value of white-owned farms. Poverty and white opposition made the black quest for land slow and treacherous.[87]

The Colored Alliance made no claims based on past servitude, nor did it propose land reform to divide properties of the plantation owners. Rather, Humphrey and the Colored Alliance championed Henry George's taxing system. The San Francisco–born reformer had designed his tax proposal as a means to break the grip of urban real estate moguls and the great western land speculators. The leaders of the Colored Alliance found it equally promising as a means to break the white land monopoly by reducing the tax barrier to property ownership and by compelling large owners to sell off unimproved land. "There are already millions of our people, colored and white, who favor this single tax plan," Humphrey argued, and "its enactment into law would place homes within reach of all the people."[88] A black minister in Alabama observed that the members of the Colored Alliance in his district "adopted the single-tax platform as the only means of political salvation for our race." He predicted that the Single Tax would bring "the consummation of freedom," although the minister noted that it would increase his own taxes as a landowner.[89]

Here the Colored Alliance had a potential ally in Thomas Nugent, the "sage" of Texas Populism. If elected governor, Nugent promised to seek relief from the "inherent viciousness of our present system of taxation" by means of a better system "outlined in the works of Henry George." The revenue realized would support state modernization: construction of schools, libraries, asylums, public utilities, and transit systems. The Single Tax could "diffuse the blessings of a glorious civilization," bringing the advantages of "closely associated life within reach of farmer, stockman, miner, [and] factory operative." Nugent believed that such was man's "resistless movements to a higher plane." Apparently, Nugent's vision was widely shared. The 1888 convention of the Texas Farmers' Alliance adopted a Single-Tax plank, and the Texas People's party in 1891 and 1892 included in its platforms demands for both a graduated income tax and the Single-Tax principle of taxing property "without any reference to the improvements."[90]

For Nugent and other Single-Tax Populists, George's tax plan offered a nuts-and-bolts fiscal remedy: practical legislation with immediate beneficial results. The collectivist scheme of Edward Bellamy's Nationalism, by contrast, seemed distant and intangible. "To me [Bellamy] was a poet," Hamlin Garland recalled, "a dreamer with a very vague emotional plan." Garland considered himself too much of a "Herbert Spencer individualist" to place much stock in Bellamy's collectivist vision.[91] Thomas Nugent expressed similar reservations about the practicality of Nationalism. As a political candidate he reassured voters that he had no intention of introducing Bellamyism into Texas politics and would safeguard the "undisturbed freedom" of the individual. What the future might bring, however, was another matter. For Nugent and many other reformers who shared his evolutionary imagination, *Looking Backward* provided a rough sketch of that future.[92]

First appearing in 1888, *Looking Backward* tells the story of Julian West, a Boston gentleman who awakened after more than a century of sleep to a collectivist utopia. There he discovered the new social order of Nationalism, where justice, prosperity, equality, and harmony prevailed. The peaceful workings of evolution brought about a planned and rational state capitalism. The process of incorporation and monopolization produced a single "Great Trust," making the nation "the sole capitalist and land-owner." Labor peace was achieved by placing the entire labor force under the central control of the "industrial army." Farms and workshops "combined as one" into "great bodies of men." The merchant houses and shops were replaced by vast state-run warehouses, where citizens paid for their orders with credit cards. The cost efficiency of large-scale educational systems made college degrees available to all. Centralized administration combined with technology—electric sound systems, pneumatic tubes, and other marvels—made for a healthful, cultured, modern life.[93]

Bellamy painted a future of uniform centralization, technologically driven organization, and statist control. Given that private farm enterprise was to disappear in this collectivist future, some farm reformers naturally viewed the Bellamyists with suspicion. In the labor movement, too, trade unionists like Arthur Dodge of the San Francisco Typographical Union denounced Nationalism as a form of state tyranny. Despite such criticisms, *Looking Backward* enjoyed fantastic popularity and sold 400,000 copies in the United States alone. It was the book of the decade, whose influence spread well beyond middle-class circles to a broad urban and rural readership.[94]

Rural reformers joined Nationalism's most dedicated enthusiasts. These included the Vincent brothers in Cowley County, Kansas. Their *Nonconformist* newspaper, arguably the most influential voice of midwestern Populism, serialized the saga of Julian West on its front pages.[95] In Georgia, the response to Nationalism, with its distinctly Yankee origins, was more subdued. Seeking to hang the Yankee collar on their Populist opponents, Georgia Democrats noted that "if the author of *Looking Backward* had lived in the forest country of Georgia among the men who guide the plow he would have been a leader in the Farmer's Alliance." In response, James King, a People's party candidate for the Georgia legislature penned a private salutation to Bellamy, in which he predicted that Populism would bury sectional division and praised *Looking Backward* as "little short of prophesy."[96]

Nationalism and the Farmers' Alliance intertwined to provide the impetus for the People's party in California. Nationalists like Burnette Haskell and Thomas Cator were on close terms with Farmers' Alliance leaders like John Gilbert of Fresno and Henry Dillon of Los Angeles. The Haskells also maintained a personal friendship with Anna Ferry Smith, a Civil War nurse and veteran labor organizer who personified the fusion of Bellamyism and Macunism in the Golden State. As the Nationalists' statewide organizer, Smith built Bellamy clubs in dozens of California towns and villages. When the Farmers' Alliance started work in the state, she joined its ranks and used her skills to spread its organization as well. In the process, a number of rural Nationalist clubs reorganized themselves as suballiances of the Farmers' Alliance.[97]

California led the way in this extraordinary melding of a collectivist movement inspired by a utopian novel with a practical farmers' movement based on business principles. Such a union can be explained, in part, by political expediency. Nationalists like Burnette Haskell and Thomas Cator viewed the Farmers' Alliance as a mass base for their reform projects and political ambitions. In turn, farm reformers like Marion Cannon saw the articulate and dedicated Nationalist cadre as essential for launching a third party and his political career. But the proximity of the two movements must also be explained by certain shared ideological commitments. The ideas of state-centered economics brought the futuristic world of Julian West into connection with the everyday strivings of labor and rural reform. And many readers of *Looking Backward* believed that the Populist vision paralleled the evolutionary trajectory set forth in Bellamy's fiction.

The parallels particularly impressed women. The Single Tax enjoyed a masculine following and was a choice topic—along with the tariff and currency questions—in men's clubs and other places where voters met. Bellamyism was different. The public world of Bellamy's utopia—impersonal, centralized, hierarchical—minimized the political role of both women and men. With "no parties or politicians," it suggested a decidedly nonpolitical future. But the private world of Nationalism offered a fulfilling and modern life. In it women were free to enjoy music and literature in the comfort of their homes, liberated from the burdens of housework by electrical appliances and by public laundries and kitchens. Women gained economic independence as the "feminine army of industry" provided them with suitably feminine careers. The nation rendered support for mothers in gratitude for "bearing and nursing the nation's children." Economic necessity was thus removed from marital decisions. Marriages of "pure love" meant not only domestic happiness, but also eugenic purification, as the unhindered operation of "sexual selection" would transmit "the better types of the race" and let the "inferior types drop out."[98]

The feminist author Charlotte Perkins Gilman observed that *Looking Backward* had "put in popular form the truth of the ages, and done it at a time when the whole world was aching for such help."[99] Frances Willard, then serving as the president of the National Council of Women, suspected that the real author was not Edward Bellamy but "Edw*ina*"—"we believe a great hearted, big-brained *woman* wrote this book." She had a point in that Bellamy's portrayal of the future was surely influenced by the women's movement of urban Boston. In its essentials, it also corresponded to strains of thought articulated in the ranks of rural Populism by hundreds of women lecturers, journalists, and educators.[100]

The economic visions of Nationalism and rural reform converged in significant ways. In 1888 Bellamy predicted that in the future a single gigantic warehouse would supply all of the needs of the entire city of Boston. That same year, Charles Macune and the Farmers' Alliance built a massive warehouse in Dallas with plans to supply the entire rural population of Texas. For the Vincent brothers and other Populists, the parallels between rural reform and Nationalism were unmistakable. The Bellamyists recognized the connections as well. When California Nationalists followed Anna Ferry Smith into the rural districts to organize the Farmers' Alliance, large-scale cooperative marketing was her primary selling point. Although some urban-based Nationalists lacked enthusiasm for farmers' cooperatives, the schemes to build centralized farmers' exchanges epitomized the type of undertaking that attracted the Nationalists to the farmers' cause.[101]

In *Looking Backward*, the corporations led the way to the collectivist future. "The popular sentiment toward the great corporations," Bellamy explained, "ceased to be one of bitterness" as people realized the role they played in social evolution. "The most violent foes of the great private monopolies were now forced to recognize how invaluable and indispensable had been their office in educating the people."[102] When he wrote this, Bellamy may not have been aware of similar views expressed by Charles Macune, or the admonitions in Farmers' Alliance publications for farmers to "organize as intelligently and solidly as Standard Oil Company has."[103] But these ideas were commonplace within the Populist coalition. "The Standard Oil Company is denounced more vigorously than almost any other one monopoly," noted an editorial in the *Journal of the Knights of Labor*. "Yet, on behalf of the Standard, it can be said with truth that the public get a better article of coal oil at less than half the price." "Let the monopolies, the trusts, and the syndicates grow," the labor Populists advised, as monopoly will give way to "further steps in the direction of Nationalism."[104]

For Thomas Nugent, the Nationalist utopia remained—"as the millennium" —in the distant future. The weight of human selfishness meant that society still had a long distance to evolve before realizing Bellamy's dream. At the same time, he recognized that the incorporation of American society—as the individual "merge[d] into the corporation" and the common associated life—was leading toward a collectivist future. Nugent shed no tears for the passing of a bygone individualism. "Already Jeffersonian simplicity is transcended," he observed with anticipation, as a "composite age is dawning upon the world with its quickening and uplifting power."[105]

Modern society, the "composite age" of the present, carried within itself the complex, integrated, and centralized society of the future. Reformers understood this process as a hard fact of social evolution. The Danish-born reformer and social theorist Laurence Gronlund, more than anyone else, provided the American reform movement with an understanding of the practical workings of this process. His celebrated work, *The Co-operative Commonwealth*, popularized the ideas of a "scientific" and "evolutionary" socialism. Published in 1884, his book anticipated the ideas in Bellamy's *Looking Backward*, and Gronlund would later join the Nationalist movement. *The Co-operative Commonwealth* sold fewer copies than Bellamy's more famous work. Yet it had a profound impact on reform circles precisely because it was not a romantic novel about a beautiful dream, but a functional treatise on modern conditions.[106]

For Gronlund the future was everywhere. The Jordan Marsh department store in downtown Boston provided a "miniature model" of the giant warehouses that would trade all human wants from coal to cotton goods and thereby eliminate middlemen and merchants. The bonanza farms spreading on the Great Plains proved the advantages of "cultivation on a grand scale." The associated creameries in the Midwest "showed that butter and cheese can be made much better and more cheaply in one dairy than on a hundred farms." The future would extend "to *all* human pursuits" the principles of the economy of scale and centralized direction. "Imagine," Gronlund encouraged his readers, "manufactures, traffic and commerce, conducted on the grandest possible scale . . . add that central regulative system which Spencer says distinguishes all highly organized structures . . . and—behold the CO-OPERATIVE COMMONWEALTH!"[107]

The "cooperative commonwealth" slogan gained popularity among diverse constituencies of the Populist coalition. It gave a broader meaning to the practical strivings of farm reformers and their large-scale cooperative enterprises, as well as to the coal miners and railroad employees and their industrial organizations. It also provided a line of action for nonconformist reform. The evolutionary process could not be left to happenstance; it required conscious effort. The commonwealth of the future, Gronlund argued, "must also be incarnated—made alive—in men and women." This idea inspired efforts in California, Colorado, Tennessee, Mexico, and elsewhere to build cooperative colonies in line with Gronlund's vision.[108]

Soon after the publication of the *Cooperative Commonwealth*, Burnette Haskell launched the Kaweah Cooperative Colony in the Tulare County foothills of the Sierra Nevada. Gronlund, with whom the Haskells shared "sympathy and friendship," served as the colony's titular secretary. The colony adopted a centralized scheme of organization, rejecting the "town-meeting" idea of democracy as "not up for dealing with complex industrial administration." Instead, it stressed "administration by the competent." Taking the federal post office as a model, the colony appointed officers with wide authority comparable to a postal superintendent, with the distinction that the colony's superintendents were to be elected from below. At the same time, the Kaweah leaders also emphasized that this did not imply the right of removal from below, or other tendencies toward "mob-ocracy."[109]

The colony was to provide a prototype for the coming commonwealth. It attracted a considerable number of women artists, musicians, writers, and other reformers looking for innovation in cultural, moral, and social norms. Women's health and physical fitness bore special importance, as one colonist argued, since it determined "whether the children of that glorious future which is ahead of us will be more beautiful, symmetrical and strong than the children of to-day." But the high expectations for the colony were largely dashed by internal dissent typically associated with living in close quarters and primitive conditions. Men shirked work, and women ended up shouldering more than their share to keep their families fed and sheltered.[110]

The principal business of the Kaweah Colony Company was business. Whereas the transcendentalists at Brook Farm and similar communities envisioned philosophically utopian islands in the ocean of commercial degradation, the Gronlundists at Kaweah were boosters in search of commercial success. In the Haskells' notion of reform, efforts to establish a more just and rational social order were expected to also yield financial reward. "Dear me," Anna Fader lamented to her diary of the family's money problems, "if we only had a few hundred thousand dollars—how comfortable we could be." News that Burnette had "struck a bonanza in the shape of an asbestos mine" turned out to be one of the "many schemes" that failed to materialize. The colony at Kaweah was the Haskells' most ambitious investment.[111]

Organized as a joint-stock company, the colony's business plan called for the construction of a mountain road to harvest the timber in Kaweah's giant redwood groves. In turn, lumber profits would finance the construction of an industrial, agricultural, and transportation empire. The colonists planned to build their own railroads and canals to transport wood veneers, marble, fruit, wine, and other products to the world market. With their own shipping line, they would ply the European, Latin American, and Far Eastern trade.[112]

In 1890, after successfully completing the mountain access road but before the logging operation realized profits, the colony ran into opposition from the authorities. The federal land office refused to recognize the colony's claims to the land. Prosecutors charged Haskell and his partners with mail fraud for soliciting investments in the enterprise. Congress delivered the fatal blow by declaring the Kaweah redwood groves part of a newly created national park. As federal troops evicted the colonists from the forest, Haskell faced new charges for allegedly cutting trees on federal property.[113]

Haskell struggled to turn his remaining Kaweah holdings into a profitable fruit-growing enterprise. He hoped to raise money for capital improvements on the land by writing scientific articles for William Randolph Hearst's newspapers. But his legal troubles cost him his newspaper job. While he watched his Nationalist colleague and rival Tom Cator rise to the leadership of California Populism, Haskell—blacklisted and poverty stricken—slid into a lonely alcoholic despair. Other Kaweah colonists, meanwhile, proved more successful with their orchards and joined the growing ranks of Tulare County's cooperative fruit growers.[114]

Even as Kaweah failed, reformers launched similar colonies in Colorado, Oregon, Texas, Mississippi, and several other western and southern states. The Ruskin colony in central Tennessee attracted Populist activists from across the country. The colony was planned and financed by Julius Wayland, one of Populism's most successful publishers. Born in Indiana and a printer by trade, Wayland made his way to Colorado, where he earned a small fortune in real estate speculation. In the early 1890s, he published a Populist newspaper and helped the Colorado People's party sweep the polls. In 1894 he moved the publication of his nationally popular newspaper, *The Coming Nation*, to Tennessee, where he launched the Ruskin colony. With the printing press as its main industry, he hoped to turn the colony into what he called "a propaganda center" for the cooperative commonwealth.[115]

Wayland designed a model community for the employees in Ruskin's industries. The original scheme included "scientifically constructed" homes, as well as "good schools, free libraries, natatoriums, gymnasiums, lecture halls, parks and pleasure grounds." The colony planned "a large building centrally located . . . for housework on a large scale" to liberate women from the burdens of washing and cooking. The community would be organized on modern business lines. The key to success, according to Wayland, was to adopt corporate systems for the collective good. "All you need is an organizer like these capitalists and keep the profits yourselves."[116]

The Ruskin colony accepted only white members. Most of the colonists came to Tennessee from the North or West, and shared a common vision of racial separation with their white southern colleagues. Wayland would later explain that it was the capitalists who "mix up the races, reducing blacks, whites and yellows to a common level," and that the coming of majority rule would "separate the races and lift them all to the highest level of which each were capable." Segregation was an integral part of the modern experiment.[117]

The Topolobampo colony on the Pacific Coast of Mexico represented the most ambitious enterprise of all the cooperative colonies. With some five hundred settlers, it drew more attention and investments than any other Populist colonization scheme. The plan for the project originated with Albert K. Owen, a railroad promoter who wanted to construct a rail line between Austin, Texas, and the Sea of Cortez in the Mexican state of Sinaloa. At the end of the line on lands adjacent to Topolobampo Bay, Owen hoped to build the model "Pacific City," an agricultural, industrial, and transportation complex planned in accord with the ideas of Henry George, Edward Bellamy, Burnette Haskell, and other nonconformist reformers.[118]

The first settlers at Topolobampo arrived in the late 1880s from Kansas, California, and Colorado. For Kansas farmers, a new rail line to Mexico's West Coast represented a Pacific port five hundred miles closer than San Francisco or San Diego. It also offered a significant investment opportunity. "The plan suggested is strictly one of business," Owen assured investors. "We incorporate to do what other companies are doing in all commercial countries." He predicted that within ten years Topolobampo would emerge as a "great commercial haven," with a bustling harbor, electric streetcars, railroads, and steamship lines. It would realize "Bellamy's future in the present" with tracts of model housing, miles of irrigation pipes, bonanza farming, cooperative retailing, and centralized wholesaling and shipping. The "Pacific City" would rival any metropolis on the West Coast.[119]

To attract capital and settlers, the colony set up the Kansas-Sinaloa Investment Company with its main office in Enterprise, Kansas. Real estate booster John Breidenthal served as the secretary of the investment company prior to serving as the Kansas state banking commissioner under the Populist administration and as the chairman of the Kansas People's party. Other leading Populists also lent support to the Topolobampo project. The Vincent brothers, by way of their *Nonconformist* publishing operations, printed and distributed the *Integral Co-Operator*, the newspaper of the Kansas-Sinaloa Company. The company solicited investments from midwestern farmers by offering $20 shares in exchange for livestock and land. Farmers of "limited means" could "secure for themselves a permanent and beautiful home" in Sinaloa, and doing so would assure that the value of the land "will rise as rapidly as did the most favored localities of Southern California."[120]

Boosters, investors, and settlers paid little heed to the fact that this American Populist enterprise lay within the territory of Mexico. Perhaps some of them shared the broader Populist concerns about international trade. The Northern Alliance aspired to improved access to Central and South American markets. Marion Cannon was obsessed with the need for a deep-water port in Los Angeles and a Nicaraguan Canal to better link southern California with Asian and European commerce. The Chicago Populist and bimetalist George S. Bowen drew plans for a "Pan American Bank" for "securing the South American trade."[121]

American farmers had expressed interest in securing international markets since before the founding of the republic. In the 1880s and 1890s, at least some Populists understood the quest for agricultural markets within the framework of the new and modern doctrines of an imperialist division of the globe. A farmer from Miltonvale, Kansas, for example, who, as a partisan of greenbacks and "progress and advanced ideas," dreamed of driving England and Spain from the Americas and to extend the borders of the United States to all of Central America and the Caribbean—"from the Artic to the isthmus," as he put it. He predicted that Mexico, "knowing her insignificance," would soon be gladly absorbed.[122]

A better-known Kansas Populist, Mary Elizabeth Lease, in her 1895 treatise, *The Problem of Civilization Solved*, declared that "our war cry is the Americas for the Americans." To gain control of markets as part of a "world partition," she urged that "we should at once proceed to assert a protectorate over the Latin nations of America." The northern white nations, in Lease's vision, could only thrive with "tropical markets," and the "colonization of the tropics."[123]

Few Populists may have read, much less agreed with, Lease's treatise. Yet it indicates that the Populists enjoyed no special immunity from the imperialist virus circulating through late nineteenth-century America and Europe. Contrary to Richard Hofstadter's claims, however, Populism was hardly an imperialist vanguard. Most Populists paid little heed to foreign affairs. Those Populists that did tended to have a dim view of the plans for an American naval empire, which they saw as antithetical to efficient and popular government. "Strengthening of our Navy; building Forts, Arsenals, and Dock

Yards," Tom Watson warned in 1892, "has a deep meaning lurking underneath." Six years later, when the United States went to war with Spain in 1898, the Populists, like most Americans, tended to embrace the cause of Cuban independence and to support the war effort. However, as the imperial nature of the American intervention grew more apparent, the Populists grew increasingly disenchanted.[124]

By this time, however, the People's party had suffered years of sharp decline. On the Sea of Cortez, the Topolobampo colony had collapsed. The colony had suffered chronic shortages of food and fresh water, and lacked capital to realize its railroad and irrigation schemes. The colony's land passed into the hands of the American-owned United Sugar Company. The major role that such giant corporations played in U.S. foreign policy made it quite evident that when it came to imperialism the Populists were at the most merely dabblers, and the sugar, banking, and other corporate interests were the true vanguard.[125]

Eugene Debs and the Populist labor leaders of the American Railway Union drew up their own plans for a cooperative colony. In 1895, Debs served a six-month sentence for his part in the Pullman boycott. Sitting in federal prison, Debs and his colleagues read Karl Kautsky and other socialist writers. They also studied Henry George and Edward Bellamy, as well as Laurence Gronlund, who Debs considered "one of the brainiest men of our times." In prison they received Wayland's *The Coming Nation*, which celebrated the release of the ARU leaders with a special issue that sold nearly 150,000 copies. At the time, the reputation of Eugene Debs within reform circles soared, and many within the Populist coalition hoped that he would lead the national People's party ticket in 1896.[126]

Debs, meanwhile, focused on a plan to colonize an unspecified western state with unemployed workers and land-hungry farmers. The fate of the thousands of blacklisted ARU members weighed heavily on Debs, and he hoped that colonization would provide them a secure place to make a fresh start. His guiding idea was that if enough displaced railway workers settled in a sparsely populated state it would be possible to forge a farmer-labor Populist majority that would take control of the elected offices and thereby create a model of the cooperative commonwealth for the rest of the nation to follow. Although nothing came of this plan, it was a step in the process of his radicalization and eventual adoption of socialism.[127]

On lecture tours for his newfound socialism, Debs met some of his most attentive audiences in the former strongholds of the rural movement. In April of 1899, Martin Irons stood in a crowd pressing to hear Debs speak at Waco, Texas. The leaders of the two once-mighty railroad workers' organizations were introduced to each other at the end of the lecture. An observer noted that the chat with Debs provided "some happy moments for the battered little 'down and outer.'"[128] In the previous years Irons had crisscrossed Texas spreading the Debsian vision of Populist socialism among cotton farmers and tenants. The meeting with Debs gave Irons a rare moment of recognition in his otherwise anonymous toils. For his part, Debs saw in the traces of poverty and broken health on the face of the former Knight the scars of sacrifice common to martyrs in the struggle for a more just world—"from Jesus Christ to Martin Irons."[129]

The explanation for why Debs could draw crowds for his socialist lectures in the rural districts of Texas, Kansas, and other formerly Populist territory lies in part with the Populist roots of his message. The name of Debs was inseparable from labor Populism. The efforts of Debs and the ARU to establish industrial organization captured the imagination of broad sections of the labor movement that formed essential constituencies of the Populist coalition. At the same time, Debs was intellectually connected to nonconformist reform. During his Populist days, he never held tight to any particular reform scheme or panacea being peddled in the clubs and on the sidewalks of Chicago. The ideas of George, Bellamy, Gronlund, and the other nonconformists, nonetheless, shaped Debs's thinking, ideas that frayed the borders between middle class and working class, urban and rural reform, and inspired a generation of activists with visions of a rational, scientific, and just future forged of the modern present.

8

SHRINE OF SCIENCE

Innovation in Populist Faith

As a leader of the Populist movement in Georgia, Charles C. Post stirred controversies with his investigations of "mental science" and the fallacies of religion. Post believed that the Christianity in which he was raised failed to comply with modern demands. He searched for a belief system more suitable to an era of discovery and progress, and he found "mental science" especially persuasive. Its scientific ethos marked an improvement over worn-out Christian dogmas, placing the human spirit in the same framework of empirical exploration as electricity and similar natural phenomena.

"Mental science," as Post understood it, exposed the very notion of a supreme being as contrary to reason and logic. "The evolution of man had scarcely proceeded beyond the ape," Post explained, when the idea originated "that some great, big man made us." However, "in the light of a more scientific day," the concept of a god was "idiotic" and irrational. "Dependence upon 'God' or any one else," he concluded, "weakens the individuality; destroys the will; obliterates the Ego."[1]

Post's unorthodox religious opinions emerged as a political liability when he served as managing editor of Tom Watson's *People's Party Paper* and as the chair of the Georgia People's party. The Democratic press attacked Post's "atheistic, anarchistic, communistic" views, which only confirmed the dangerous nature of the Populist threat. Even within Populist ranks, Post's views on religion may have pushed the limits of acceptable heterodoxy. It would be a mistake, however, to dismiss his views as an anomaly, an odd deviation from the Populist norm, because it would be difficult to define a norm within a spectrum of religious belief that was so diverse, adaptive, and iconoclastic. From Georgia to California, and Texas to Illinois, Populism attracted into

its ranks free religionists, Christian socialists, agnostics, spiritualists, Theosophists, Swedenborgians, occultists, and mental scientists. The enemies of
Populism were quick to attack the "heretics" and "infidels" who played a
prominent part in the third-party movement. They did so unfairly as Populists were just as likely to be members in good standing of the established
churches, and many religious iconoclasts had a presence in the traditional
parties as well. But a kernel of truth lay in the attacks on the Populist "infidels": the People's party provided a wide tent for religious innovators who
sought explanations consistent with a modern and "more scientific day."[2]

Post published his views about God, apes, and science nearly three decades before this same mix of ideas gripped the nation in the famous "Monkey Trial" of 1925, when John T. Scopes faced criminal charges in Dayton,
Tennessee, for teaching evolution in his high school biology class. The climate of the Scopes trial, with its sharply drawn lines between science and
religion, provides an important contrast with the more expansive notions
of faith that influenced the Populist movement in the 1880s and 1890s. Populism remained remarkably free of dividing lines or strife on religious matters despite the wide range of belief and nonbelief that coexisted within its
ranks. For the religious outsiders and heterodox, the Populist quest for social and economic improvement coincided with their own search for bet-
tering the human social and mental condition. For those remaining within
the Christian denominations, coexistence with alternative belief systems
indicated the extent to which their own worldview adapted to the progressive and modern ethos of the times.

Among believers and nonbelievers alike, the Populists freely combined
political and economic reform with moral principles. In so doing they formed
what historian Peter Argersinger describes as a "religio-political movement."
Many Populists were raised in homes where the Bible was the most read book
or was the only book. Farmers' Alliance and People's party lecturers made
extensive use of biblical metaphors, citing scripture with greater ease than
they quoted Jefferson, Lincoln, or Shakespeare. A number of Baptist and
Methodist ministers and lay clergy joined the movement to preach the gospel of political and economic reform. And rural reformers organized out-
door meetings that, with their big tents, picnics, and passionate oratory,
resembled camp meetings of the evangelical churches.[3]

Their evangelical style, use of biblical metaphor, and moral frameworks
have led some historians to characterize the farm and labor movements of
this era as expressions of a traditional piety resisting the encroachments of a
secular and modern culture. However, to portray Populism as an example
of pietistic resistance is to overlook the most salient features of its religious
configuration. Populist gatherings—whether addressed by a lay preacher in
Texas or by an avowed agnostic in Chicago—had little to do with the evan-

gelical objectives of saving souls or winning converts to Jesus. In content, if not style, Populist "religio-politics" tended to be decidedly nontraditional, as they were shaped by the new, innovative, modern ideas that swept across America's religious and intellectual landscape in the 1870s, 1880s, and 1890s.[4]

The post–Civil War decades posed sharp challenges to the ways Americans had discussed and understood both the natural and spiritual worlds. The dramatic combination of scientific discovery and technological innovation —most critically the Darwinian theory of evolution and the harnessing of electric power—produced a "scientific age." Demonstrations of empirical evidence and rational inquiry gained authority as the ultimate validations of truth and right. Scholars subjected the Bible to the same standard, as Americans grew increasingly aware of the historical rather than sacred origins of scripture, and as Jesus evolved in the imagination from the son of God to a model of human conduct. Moreover, global interconnections spread knowledge of non-Christian belief systems and posed questions about the universal nature of spiritual life.[5]

Theological conservatives worked to renew old commitments in a climate of ideological turmoil. Evangelicals of the Holiness movement, for example, focused on emotional conversion and biblical literalism. The conservative groups also showed concern for social problems, but remained preoccupied with saving souls and personal piety. Despite the emergence of such movements, it was not until after the First World War that sharp dividing lines would separate "fundamentalism" from "modernism" within evangelical Protestantism. In the 1880s and 1890s, the lines of separation proved porous, as the evangelical forerunners of what later emerged as fundamentalism readily absorbed modern ideas and methods, and theological conservatives could and did embrace social reform. Even so, the Populists and the more conservative evangelical groups such as the Holiness movement tended to remain apart. Although they campaigned across many of the same rural districts, most theologically conservative evangelicals clung to different ideas than those of most Populists about the ills besetting organized religion, and they were motivated by what were mainly distinct intellectual and political concerns.[6]

Populist ideas about religion corresponded to schools of religious thinking that more or less consciously sought to adapt to the modern and scientific age. The religious historian Grant Wacker uses the phrase "innovative thinkers" to describe those who searched for new and adaptive beliefs. He divides these innovators into three descriptive groupings: the religious liberals who remained within the traditional denominations—including the Baptist, Methodist, and other evangelical churches—but wanted to liberalize and modernize church doctrine and practice; the free religionists who still considered themselves Christians of some type but desired freedom from the constraints of the established churches and creeds; and the agnostics, or those who might also be described as the religiously heterodox who searched for explanations for natural and spiritual phenomena outside of the framework of Christianity or any religion. The Populist movement provided a meeting ground for such innovators, and the movement's religiosity mainly circulated around groupings of Christian liberals, Christian free religionists, and various schools of non-Christian thought.[7]

The "Monkey Trial" of 1925 provides a historical vantage point for examining the Populist world of faith of the 1880s and 1890s. The trial took place in the rural county seat of Dayton, Tennessee, where John Scopes, a high school science teacher, was charged with violating the newly adopted state law against teaching Darwinian science in the public schools. Broadcast live on radio, the trial provoked a national sensation. The defining moment came when Clarence Darrow, a defense attorney representing Scopes, put on the stand William Jennings Bryan, a member of the prosecution. The confrontation between Darrow and Bryan defined the cultural and political significance of the trial. On the one side, Darrow, the urbane Chicago lawyer, advocated the modern, secularist, worldly, and scientific values of the urban elite. On the other side, Bryan, the Great Commoner from Nebraska, stood guard for evangelical religion, ordinary folk, and the traditional values of rural America. Or so it was understood by millions of Americans at the time.[8]

The fist-shaking confrontation between Darrow and Bryan continues to shade interpretations of America's cultural and political fault lines and has cast a long shadow across the legacy of Populism. Bryan's Populist endorsement in 1896 combined with his performance at the Scopes trial has fused Populism with fundamentalist Christianity in historical commentary. Richard Hofstadter observed that Bryan's fundamentalism was a product of the decay of rural Populism and "the shabbiness of the evangelical mind." More recent analysis focuses on continuity, stressing that Bryan at Dayton reflected an "unflagging" Populist faith. Or, as Kevin Phillips puts it, Bryan epitomized a Populism propelled by the Third Great Awakening of evangelical revivalism. In the standard interpretation, the high drama of the Scopes trial represented the climax of the long resistance of a traditional pietistic culture to the onslaught of secular modernism, a resistance reaching back across the decades to the barricades of the Populist revolt.[9]

But this rendering muddles the historical record. Among other things, it was the agnostic Clarence Darrow, not the Democrat Bryan, who was a Populist stump speaker in the heyday of the People's party. Darrow had the ability to whip up crowds at Populist election rallies so that, as one contemporary observed, they resembled "regular old fashioned revival meetings." This observation contains a cautionary note that just because something resembles a revival meeting does not mean that it was one. It reaffirms that history does not run backward and that the religious configuration of Populism cannot be readily extrapolated from the Scopes trial that took place almost thirty years after the Populist movement's demise. To attempt this extrapolation risks turning the protagonists at Dayton into caricatures and failing to take into account the dynamic intellectual and religious climate of the 1880s and 1890s that shaped the outlook of both Bryan and Darrow as well as of the Populist movement itself.[10]

At the Scopes trial, under questioning from Darrow, Bryan conceded that the "seven days" referred to in Genesis could be interpreted as seven "periods." This and similar failures to defend a literal interpretation of the Bible shocked and dismayed Bryan's fundamentalist supporters. But anyone acquainted with Bryan's background should not have been surprised. As a young man, Bryan had been exposed to the winds of liberal theology and religious innovation. Born in 1860, as a boy he studied the Bible and the McGuffey Reader within the secure surroundings of a prosperous home in the small town of Salem, Illinois. Although his father was a committed Baptist, Bryan, at age thirteen, joined the Cumberland Presbyterians, who embodied a more expansive and hopeful vision of salvation. Soon thereafter he left home to attend Whipple Academy and Illinois College, where his studies included chemistry, physics, and evolutionary biology. Shaken in his religious convictions, he struggled to find a cosmology that made sense in a scientific age. In his search he looked into free thought and exchanged letters with Robert Ingersoll, the famous agnostic orator and critic of religion. But he never left the church, and after his youthful explorations he remained comfortably within the Presbyterian creed for the rest of this life.[11]

Settling in the church, however, did not mean settling in secure tradition as the Presbyterian church and other evangelical denominations were in the throes of change. In 1874 a well-known Presbyterian preacher in Chicago, David Swing, faced a heresy trial within his church for challenging literal interpretations of the Bible. This sensational case marked a watershed event in the wide acceptance of the New Theology that was spreading throughout the established churches. Religious historians have described the new thinking as a secular, progressive, and modernizing impulse within evangelical Protestantism. The controversies provoked by the New Theology continued to shake the church establishment during the Populist decade. Reflecting on the "battle of the creeds," the Presbyterian minister Thomas Dewitt Talmage observed in 1891 that "this is a time of resounding ecclesiastical quarrel. Never within your memory or mine has the air been so full of missiles" and explosive controversy within the church.[12]

Bryan experienced the religious explosions close at hand. In the early 1880s he lived and studied law in Chicago, which was a center of religious innovation.

He associated with a theologically moderate wing of the Presbyterians and at one point he helped block a conservative takeover of the church's general assembly. In line with the adaptive philosophy of his church, for many years Bryan considered evolutionary theory to be compatible with his religion. In the early twentieth century, with its violent social and global conflicts, he grew increasingly skeptical of the Darwinist outlook. He became a pacifist and befriended Leo Tolstoy, with whom he spent some time during a diplomatic mission to Russia. Bryan came to understand social Darwinism as a violent doctrine legitimizing social conflict—"a merciless law by which the strong crowd out and kill off the weak." In light of the carnage of the First World War, he came to reject Darwinist theory in any form.[13]

Although Bryan remained a Democrat, his commitment to reform won him respect among many Populists. Clarence Darrow was such a Populist. Darrow won celebrity in Populist ranks with his spirited legal defense of Eugene Debs after the Pullman boycott, and found both ideological kinship and an audience for his oratory in the third-party movement. The 1894 elections proved the high-water mark for Illinois Populism, when Darrow's speeches before enthusiastic crowds of laborers and farmers in Cook County, Joliet, and elsewhere across the state provided a catalyst for the People's party campaign. When the third party later fused with the Democrats, Darrow returned to the Democrats and supported the Bryan campaign. Years afterward, he grew increasingly cynical about politics, embracing the antidemocratic skepticism of Friedrich Nietzsche. This is why Garry Wills, for example, stresses that "Darrow was no populist." Hence the irony of historical memory as refracted through the Scopes trial.[14]

In the course of their lives Bryan and Darrow confronted strikingly similar moral and religious choices. Darrow, three years older than Bryan, grew up in rural Ohio, where he, too, studied his McGuffey Reader. He regularly attended Presbyterian service and Sunday school, although he was influenced by his father's religious skepticism as well. Like Bryan, Darrow looked to the agnosticism of Robert Ingersoll for answers to the spiritual problems posed by the modern world. But unlike Bryan, Darrow made Ingersoll's convictions his own. As a young man he studied Darwin and Henry George. During the 1890s he considered himself a "devoted admirer" of Tolstoy and would later join with his fellow Tolstoyan, Bryan, in opposing the American war in the Philippines and criticizing imperialism. Darrow also found significance in the economic doctrines of Marx, and later in Nietzsche's criticism of Christian belief and other accepted truths. Toward the end of his life he looked into spiritualism, but the ideas of rational enlightenment that he first learned from Ingersoll always asserted themselves.[15]

Their cultural backgrounds attest to the fact that Darrow and Bryan had more in common than their legacies suggest. The heat and drama of their confrontation at the Scopes trial might be better explained by cultural proximity than distance. Both men had common beginnings in a rural evangelical environment. Both men made similar commitments to economic and political reform. And both men's belief systems were shaped by the scientific and modernizing ideological currents coursing through late nineteenth-century American life. During the 1890s they shared these points with each other, as well as with many of the farmers, laborers, and other activists who gathered under the tents of Populist reform.[16]

When the Populists combined their reform message with religion, it most often took the shape of an innovative and liberal theology. Many Populists pursued a restless social Christianity devoted to progress among the living and adapted to a developmental outlook. Through political and economic reform they labored to advance "God's evolutionary law for the progress of humanity."[17] Often expressed in the vernacular of rural America, the Populists' social Christianity corresponded to the same currents of thought that produced the New Theology and the evolving social gospel within the Protestant churches of Chicago, New York, and Boston. Historians have noted the similarities between the social gospel and the religious ideas of labor and farm reformers. Despite the overlapping nature of these ideas, however, scholars have attributed strikingly dissimilar significance to the stirrings in the religious world of elite and nonelite Americans.

On the one hand, religious historians have stressed the modernizing, scientific, and adaptive nature of the urban and middle-class social gospel. Social Christians like Washington Gladden, Richard Ely, and other leading clergy and academics are widely recognized as innovators of new, liberal, and progressive ideas suitable to a modern society. On the other hand, social historians have described equivalent ideas articulated by workers and farmers as restorative expressions of a preindustrial and pre–Civil War evangelical tradition. This discrepancy is explained by the prevailing tendency to regard progress and modernity as the domain of the urban elites, whereas the lower classes, presumably steeped in hidebound tradition, reacted to progress and modernity with the cultural weapons bestowed by their ancestors. Remove this presumption, and the social Christianity expounded at open-air camp meetings and in rustic meeting halls appears similarly innovative, modern, and adaptive to science as that espoused from the high pulpits and professors' lecterns.[18]

Of course, there were important distinctions. The urban upper- and middle-class reformers embraced a social Christianity directed toward alleviating the sufferings of others and harmonizing social interests. In contrast, farm and labor reformers preached a social Christianity based on self-activation, and they mixed their message of "brotherhood" with a spirit of class grievance.

Attitudes toward the Protestant churches also diverged. Unlike the largely church-based social gospel, the social Christianity associated with Populism often reflected discontent with, and distance from, the existing religious institutions, with no particular commitment to organize alternative ones.

The rural churches faced a widely perceived crisis that influenced the social Christianity associated with rural reform. Rural ministries languished during the hard economic years of the 1880s and 1890s. Tight church budgets in Kansas meant cutbacks in the delivery of religious services in remote country districts. In the vastness of Texas, less than 30 percent of the population counted themselves as part of an organized church. Across the South, rural churches suffered in disrepair. Church membership was below the national average, with fewer rural southerners belonging to churches than their urban counterparts. The Populist *Coming Nation* quoted the figures of a Baptist minister who estimated that of the thirty million Americans who nominally belonged to churches, less than half had any practical church ties, while thirty-two million Americans "attend no church at all" and were "bitter in their hostility to all churches." Discontent with organized religion, according to the minister, explained why "church after church in our rural districts die."[19]

The crisis of the rural churches was probably not as dire as portrayed. Nonetheless, for many farmers Sunday sermons about saving souls seemed distant from their pressing worldly concerns, and ministries bemoaned empty benches in the churches and the dearth of religiosity among the people. One minister seeking rural converts lamented that it required making a balloon ascent for him to persuade Texans to look toward heaven. Farm reformers viewed the failings of the churches as of one piece with the political and economic ills affecting American life.[20]

Officially, membership in the Farmers' Alliance required no religious test beyond belief in a supreme being "by whatever name he may be known."[21] At the same time, many Alliance members expressed a commitment to a Christian-inspired "moral law." The Reverend Isom P. Langley lectured for the Agricultural Wheel before joining Charles Macune in the Farmers' Alliance. His essay "Religion in the Alliance" provided a concise expression of the moral concerns that brought Protestant evangelicals into the Alliance movement. In his view, organized religion was being rejected by the people because of its failure to modernize its mission. In the conviction that "science is what we know, and not what we suppose," farmers increasingly subjected the churches to a more exacting standard.[22]

The religious establishment's focus on doctrine and conversion, Langley explained, had led it astray from concerns about the human condition and improving life in the here and now. "One of the main reasons why we have so many empty seats in our churches," he noted, "is the abundance of empty stomachs and unclad limbs." For the churches to expand their reach, they needed to "study the physical needs of their people more, and give them less theology." If the "religious world" wanted to put itself in line with the "great principles of humanity," it needed to follow the "true religion" found in the Farmers' Alliance and similar reform movements. Alliance meetings barred discussion of biblical interpretation, creed, or sectarian denomination. All such matters were subordinated to "the one great question," as Langley posed it: "How can we better the condition of those who earn their bread by the sweat of their faces?"[23]

Farm reformers articulated true religion as a response to the religion of avarice. Selfishness, argued Western Reader, a woman correspondent with the *Southern Mercury*, stood in the way of human progress. Selfishness ridiculed government regulation, poor relief, and farmer and labor organizations "as the offspring of vile heresy." It derided as cranks and fanatics those who, like "Count Leo Tolstoe," devised methods to uplift and dignify those who worked in fields and workshops. "To love others more and better than we love our own Deity-stamped corpus," she bitterly noted, was "considered impossible by these mole-visioned self-worshippers." Not a punishing God, but greedy men were responsible for wrongs and abuses. Therefore, only "human agencies," like the Farmers' Alliance, could overcome society's ills and "harmoniz[e] the forces of evolution."[24]

The "one great question" of earthly improvement formed the most striking feature of Populist religiosity. Farmers trained in scripture pointed to the "sulphurous region" below as the source of economic inequities. They closed arguments about the need for business cooperation with a nod to the teachings of Christ. Rarely, however, did public discussion of religion veer from the tracks of economic and political reform. The debates about women's rights, more than other controversies, touched on biblical interpretation and piety. A Texas farmwoman opposed women's suffrage, for example, on the grounds that, as the heirs of a sinful Eve, women could only be redeemed at the Resurrection. Other women raised questions about the ability to devote the required time to Bible reading if they took part in farmers' meetings. But these were isolated opinions. As for Bible reading, as one Louisiana woman explained, it was "a daily duty as much as sweeping our rooms," which must not interfere with the pressing task of reading newspapers and keeping abreast of events in the reform movement and the world.[25]

In North Carolina, with its relatively stable religious structures, the Populist movement had closer connections to the Protestant denominations than perhaps in any other state. Leonidas Polk, although not personally reflective on religious matters, lent his organizational talents to building church institutions, served as the lay president of the state Baptist convention in 1889 and 1890, and helped to establish the Baptist Female Seminary (now Meredith College) in Raleigh. Polk's *Progressive Farmer* and Marion Butler's *Caucasian* reprinted extensively from the sermons of prominent Protestant clergy. And in North Carolina, as in much of the South, that meant first and foremost the Reverend Thomas Dixon Jr. His weekly talks appeared in the pages of the *Caucasian*, the *Progressive Farmer*, and other Populist newspapers. Farmers listened to Dixon's lectures read aloud at meetings of local suballiances. "Would that the Christian pulpit had ten thousand Tom Dixons," wrote Marion Butler.[26] "Truly [Dixon] is another Patrick Henry," observed the *Progressive Farmer*. "Long live Dixon!"[27]

In the twentieth century, Thomas Dixon found fame and fortune as the author of *The Leopard's Spots* and *The Clansman*, the white supremacist novels on which D. W. Griffith based his film *The Birth of a Nation*. Part of a prominent North Carolina family, Dixon's older brother Clarence became one of America's leading evangelical ministers. His brother Frank gained prominence in the national Chautauqua Society and his sister Delia Dixon Carroll won renown as a physician. As a young man, Thomas was in the center of North Carolina's reform-minded political, business, and religious circles. Serving in the state legislature, Dixon introduced the bill that financed Leonidas Polk's proposal for an agricultural college. In 1886 Dixon joined the Baptist ministry and quickly gained national attention for his speaking skills and fresh ideas. He ministered the Dudley Street Church in Boston and the 23rd Street Baptist Church in Manhattan, and it was his Boston and New York sermons that filled the pages of the southern Populist press.[28]

As a minister, Dixon gained celebrity as a liberal innovator and self-styled progressive. He sought to recast religious faith in what he perceived as "the language of modern life, grateful for all of the light of science, philosophy, and criticism." As historian W. Fitzhugh Brundage explains, Dixon rejected traditional formulas, rituals, and creeds as "unsuited to the modern world." Dixon viewed the "maxim of progress" as the first principle of an "aggressive Christianity" untrammeled by tradition. "Progress," he pointed out, "has always been made by a life and death struggle with tradition and bigotry." In this regard, his white supremacist outlook should not be viewed as anomalous; he was a scientific racist, whose views reflected how much of the southern (and American) progressive and scientific culture embraced racialized notions of development and modernity.[29]

Dixon spoke at length on the "religious wars" over whether the Bible was of supernatural provenance or should be seen as an ancient text of human authorship. When Charles A. Briggs, a professor at Union Theological Seminary in New York City, was charged with heresy by the Presbyterian Church, the Populist *Caucasian* defended Briggs under the headline "Our Heretic," and carried extensive commentary from Dixon on the nature of the Bible and science. For Dixon, the "distinction drawn between the church and the world" was artificial. Both the religious conservatives and the agnostics of the likes of Robert Ingersoll, he argued, missed the essential "sacredness of the secular" and the "work of God" in the advance of scientific understanding.[30]

Dixon had studied Darwinian biology as a student at Wake Forest College and attempted to adapt what he had learned to religious principles. He recognized that the "creative process" took place across "countless ages" and that God made man as the "magnificent product" of the process. The "preponderance of evidence," he explained, may "confirm the theory of an evolutionary process of creation, but man is not a brute because he grew out of this underworld any more than a flower is dirt because it grew out of the soil." Along with printing Dixon's sermons, the *Caucasian* occasionally carried the sermons that Thomas Dewitt Talmage delivered to his congregation in Brooklyn, New York. Unlike Dixon, Talmage preached moderation in the "battle of the creeds" over evolution and related questions. At the same time, Talmage considered the question of human origins unimportant to his beliefs. "I am not so interested in who were my ancestors ten million years ago," he noted, "as what I am to be ten million years from now."[31]

Thomas Dixon attended the Cincinnati "Industrial Conference" in May of 1891. He saw in the emergence of the new People's party the realization of his own hopes for a "new Christian socialism." Populism, he explained to his New York congregation, stood on "the platform of the modern social democrat." Founded on "a great moral idea," it "implied the breaking up of the traditions of a generation," and would replace the old sectional conflict with attention to "truly national issues." He also interpreted the Populist vision as a religious vision. His phrase "Jesus the socialist" broadly explained his political outlook. To those who raised fears of government paternalism, he argued, "I believe in a *strong* government." In 1892 he launched his own urban reform party to bring his vision of Christian socialism to New York City.[32]

Dixon eventually left the Baptists and in 1895 he founded a "People's Church" or "People's Temple." His new church combined liberal religious principles with social reform, and on at least one occasion Dixon shared his pulpit with the Kansas Populist Mary Elizabeth Lease. The *Caucasian* and other reform newspapers provided detailed coverage of Dixon's religious career. The ministers in the great churches of New York and other big cities may have fired most of the "missiles" in the religious wars shaking the established dominations. Nonetheless, in the Populist backcountry a reader of the reform press was fully aware of the contending forces in conflict and of the theologically liberal sympathies of the Populist editors.[33]

In Texas, the Populist gubernatorial candidate Thomas Nugent drew relentless attacks from his Democratic opponents for his heterodox religious views. Nugent did not shy from the conflict and vigorously defended his religious principles. Raised in a Methodist household, he studied for the ministry and had a lifelong interest in theology. He gave up the ministry, however, because he enjoyed playing the violin, a pleasure frowned on by the properly pious. He was attracted to the ideas of Emanuel Swedenborg. The cultural scholar Louis Menand points out that Swedenborgianism was "a religion for liberals" as it "appealed particularly to rational and scientific minds." Like Albert Francisco, Thomas King, and other prominent Texas Populists, Nugent was drawn to Swedenborg's philosophy because of its emphasis on the present life rather than on future salvation, and its reliance on reasoned inquiry and empirical evidence rather than emotional experience or doctrinal faith. Nugent, however, remained aloof from the Swedenborgian church and pursued a social Christianity as a free religionist outside of creed or denomination.[34]

In July of 1893, while addressing a large gathering on Chautauqua Hill on the outskirts of San Marcos, Texas, Nugent sharply attacked Protestantism for its "tyranny of opinion." He drew a parallel between Protestantism and the Catholic Inquisition. Although no longer as in the case of Galileo forcing "a recantation on bended knees of obnoxious scientific opinions," the Protestant churches no less effectively applied the "thumb screws" of public opinion to enslave independent thought. To make his point, he cited the ongoing heresy trial of Charles A. Briggs in New York. Closer to home, Nugent might have noted earlier controversies swirling around the Baptist and Methodist churches of central Texas. This included the expulsion of James D. Shaw of Waco's First Street Methodist Church, and the heresy trial of the Cross Timbers farmer and Baptist minister, Henry Renfro.[35]

It did not matter, Nugent argued, whether one viewed Jesus Christ as a "God-man" or a "man only." In either case, Christ's efforts at human betterment had inspired the ideals of a Christian socialism to which Nugent subscribed. In a letter to a Swedenborgian minister in Galveston, he explained that he had not done church work for years because he predicted that the ecclesiastical era was ending. It would soon be replaced by a glorified social state, in which the Lord, "as the man of the people," directed the world's organized industries. Nugent, who read across a range of social and religious theory, had arrived at a Christian socialism that reflected both the religiosity of Edward Bellamy's Nationalism, and the secularism of Washington Gladden's evolving social gospel. His highly publicized views on these matters provided ammunition for his Democratic enemies to label him a "crank" and accuse him of heresy. Nevertheless, his beliefs, or at least his refusal to hide them, only raised Nugent's esteem in the eyes of Texas Populists. The reform movement adopted the so-called "Nugent

tradition" as its moral banner, elevating his life to a symbol of commitment to high ideals.[36]

In style, if not substance, Nugent belonged in the deliberating environment of the Chautauqua lecture rather than the stormy gatherings of the Populist camp meeting. Populist stump speakers fired audiences with passionate
oratory, gripping anecdotes, and biting satire against political opponents.
Nugent's speeches were free of such methods. He articulated his message in
an analytical language similar to that spoken in the urban North by the scholarly advocates of the social gospel. Yet the message reverberated across the
dusty plains and piney forests of rural Texas, often translated into the vernacular by former preachers like Harrison "Stump" Ashby, S. O. Daws, and
James Madison Perdue, who left the traditional gospel to preach "the gospel
of universal emancipation."[37]

The black Populist leader John B. Rayner counted among Populism's
former ministers who left the church to become a free religionist outside of
denomination or creed. Rayner could stir black and white audiences like no
one else in the remote backcountry of eastern Texas. His success as a speaker
stemmed largely from oratorical skills learned from previous years in politics and the Baptist ministry. For Rayner, like other Populist preachers, or-
dination as a minister provided a means to supplement his meager earnings
from teaching and politics. But he never found a home in the church, and he
became a lifelong critic of preachers and their religious denominations. He
especially attacked "emotionalism in the pews." "Emotional religion," he
observed, "makes more noise than it does a Christlike character." Black
churchgoers, Rayner warned, were working their racial ruin by their "absurd
faith in the exorcising power" of religion, the "talismanic influence" of the
churches, and "belief that prayer can eliminate reaping after sowing." The
teaching of theology would become superfluous, he later predicted, when
the people learned social hygiene and "obedience to the laws of eugenics."[38]

Criticized by his political enemies for such heterodox views, Rayner remained unapologetic. "I have no creedal theology," he explained. "I do not
believe in creeds; I see no necessity for different denominations." He did
believe, however, in living a moral life and was deeply concerned with ethi-
cal problems. According to his own social Christianity, he understood that
true religion lay in service for the good of the people. The extent to which he
did good service, Rayner challenged his critics, provided "an exact measure
of the God force in my character." It was the churches and their preachers
who violated the true religion of social improvement.[39]

A young woman from Fair View, Texas, wrote to the *Southern Mercury* expressing her concerns about the eating habits of itinerant preachers. The local
alliance had yet to hold its summer picnic. "If we do not hurry up," she

warned, the "preachers will come along" and eat all the chickens in the district, leaving none for the picnic—"for you know how they like chicken." Complaints about preachers' appetites corresponded to a broader distrust of the churches and their ministers. The Populists watched with dismay as the churches, with their "spiritual" religion, catered to their wealthy benefactors and defended the status quo.[40]

Cyrus Thompson, a leader of the North Carolina Farmers' Alliance and People's party, excoriated the churches for standing on "the side of human slavery." Thompson served as a Methodist lay worker, and his disaffection from the church reflected sentiments that had taken hold among reformers across much of the Populist territory.[41] Bettie Gay was one of the few Texas Populists with standing in the Baptist church. Even so, her gender barred her from the ministry, and she, too, sharply criticized the churches and their silencing of women's voices.[42] In Chicago, Lester Hubbard, an avowed Christian socialist and editor of the widely circulated *Farmer's Voice*, aimed some of his sharpest words at the church. He accused the clergy of standing "on the side of gold and power." The nation's ministers, Hubbard observed, "deal out still more deadly soporifics" than the lawyers, "for they speak *ex cathedra* as regularly constituted religious oracles." There were exceptions to this rule. But, the "pity and marvel of it is that only here and there can a minister be picked out from among tens of thousands of professed teachers of holy things, who preaches the gospel of charity and justice."[43]

The Populist critique of the churches took an especially biting tone in Kansas, where reformers regularly attacked the "churchianity" of a religious establishment that fed the people "the dry husks of worn-out creeds" and twisted Christianity "to aid in the robbery of the poor." Mary Elizabeth Lease condemned a "hypocritical Church," an "avaricious Ecclesiasticism," and a religion that "remains blind and mute" in the face of individual suffering. "Hygiene," Lease stressed, "is more valuable and not less sacred than the Lord's supper." Another Kansas Populist noted how the "minions of greed and class legislation" controlled the church press, which "is either silent or in actual sympathy with the cruel measures used to grind the spirit . . . out of the people."[44]

The criticisms of the churches pointed to the gap between the Populist movement and organized religion. In part, the rift reflected class prejudice. Church institutions tended to rely on upper- and middle-class parishioners for financial support, constituencies that perceived the self-organization of the lower classes as a dangerous threat to the social order. The labor strife in the spring and summer of 1894 made the threat palpable. In response to the Pullman strike and boycott, the Protestant press supported the use of federal troops to put down "this Debs carnival of lawlessness and violence." Although the Catholic *New World* expressed a more sympathetic attitude toward the railroad workers, even the Protestant denominations at the heart of the emerging social gospel almost uniformly distanced themselves from the workers' cause. Upper- and middle-class patrons embraced a social Christianity that did not include Debs and his labor-Populists.[45]

The Protestant churches adopted a similar attitude toward Coxey's Army, or the so-called "Industrial Armies," that marched on Washington to demand a "good roads" bill and federal spending to relieve the plight of the unemployed. Jacob Coxey, the most prominent figure in the march, was a businessman and People's party leader from Ohio. As the marchers made their way across the continent during the spring of 1894, newspapers warned of a "tramp menace." A dangerous horde threatened the homes and villages of the American heartland. But the heartland welcomed the invaders as heroes. When the California "Industrials" arrived in the railroad towns of the upper Midwest, huge crowds came out to greet them. Farmers drove in on wagons laden with supplies. Railroad workers went on holiday. As Jack London, an eighteen-year-old unemployed sailor at the time, wrote in his diary, the receptions for the tramp army turned into "general rejoicing" that was "like the Fourth of July."[46]

The leaders of the churches, however, were noticeably absent from such "general rejoicing." As one Iowa minister explained, church charity did not extend to the unemployed because they "would not work if given an opportunity."[47] When a band of California marchers arrived in Topeka, Kansas, the Populist *Chicago Searchlight* remarked caustically about the clergy's cold indifference toward the unemployed camping on the banks of the Kansas River. At a civic rally held in honor of the marchers, a self-described Christian socialist pointedly criticized the churches as obstacles to peaceful reform. "IF CHRIST CAME TO TOPEKA," read the *Searchlight* headline, "He Would be Cheered by the Commonwealers and Hobos. NOT BY THE CHURCHES."[48]

The fear and hostility that the clergy displayed toward the unemployed fit the larger pattern of distrust separating organized religion from Populist reform. Notable exceptions, however, provide further evidence of the general rule. Myron Reed, the pastor of Denver's largest Congregational church, was forced to resign after giving a sermon sympathetic to the Industrial Armies. Edward McGlynn, the Catholic pastor of St. Stephen's Church in New York City, shared the podium with Jacob Coxey at a Long Island rally for the unemployed and the People's party. McGlynn later joined Clarence Darrow as a featured stump speaker in the Populist campaign in Illinois. A rebellious social Christian, McGlynn suffered years of excommunication for his reform efforts.[49]

The African American church provided another exception to the clerical hostility toward Coxey's Army. The Coxey movement represented one contingent of reform that openly challenged the color line, as several African

Americans marched and camped with the mainly white marchers. Although a symbolic gesture, this act of defiance attracted much attention from the black churches. In Topeka, the local black Baptist press welcomed the arrival of the same California "Industrials" that had been shunned by Topeka's white clergy. The black Baptists expressed sympathy for the plight of the unemployed and protested their persecution at the hands of the "impudent and autocratic railroad companies." When Coxey's Army arrived in Washington, D.C., on May 1, 1894, tens of thousands of mainly black residents lined Pennsylvania Avenue to greet the marchers. They included George W. Lee, the minister of the Vermont Avenue Baptist Church, one of the largest churches in the country. A neighboring black church, the African Methodist Mount Pisgah Negro Chapel, served as the Washington headquarters of an Industrial Army from New England that was led by Clarence Darrow's "social-anarchist" friend Morrison Swift.[50]

The warm welcome the African American churches offered the Coxey marchers suggests that the black clergy adopted a more open attitude toward the reform movement than the white clergy did. In a Jim Crow world where blacks had restricted access to the public square, the black churches played a critical role in the Colored Farmers' Alliance and other reform efforts. White Populists, on the other hand, showed little inclination or desire to expand their role within the existing churches or to create or build new ones. Many Populists adopted a social gospel resembling the religiosity of church-based movements that emerged later in the twentieth century. But Populism, or at least its white variant, in most places lacked a church base. In that sense, Populist social Christianity seemed a practical confirmation of Thomas Nugent's prediction of a post-ecclesiastical era.[51]

The Populists enlisted a significant complement of men and women whose beliefs ranged outside of a Protestant or Christian framework. This group included advocates of free thought or agnosticism, who believed that the existing empirical evidence could not sustain a belief in God. In the decades after the Civil War, agnostics articulated what historian James Turner describes as a "distinctly modern unbelief," and carved out a significant place in American intellectual and cultural life. Andrew Carnegie, Elizabeth Cady Stanton, Samuel Clemens (Mark Twain), Samuel J. Tilden, Oliver Wendell Holmes Jr., Thomas Edison, and a host of other prominent Americans aligned themselves with the cause of free thought.[52]

The cause was inseparable from the name of Robert Ingersoll. The son of an evangelical minister, Ingersoll came of age in a devoutly evangelical household in southern Illinois. He later rebelled against his upbringing, discovered Voltaire and European rationalism, and waged a lifelong campaign to expose the failings of Christianity and religious belief. In the 1880s and 1890s, "the Great Agnostic," as he was known, spoke to overflow audiences in meeting halls and opera houses across the country. He thrilled crowds in hundreds of towns and villages of rural America with his fiery attacks on "superstitious religion" and his defense of the "religion of science." When he made a whirlwind tour of Texas, women and men traveled from farms a hundred miles distant to hear his message. Ingersoll's views were broadly debated in the nation's newspapers. This included the rural press, which reprinted refutations of his religious "mistakes," as well as his insights on such matters as patriotism, romantic love, and the rural home.[53]

Many Americans perceived men or women who publicly questioned the existence of God as an especially dangerous type. They were part of the godless breed of "infidels" who threatened to destroy a Christian America with dynamite and anarchy. To voice sympathy for agnosticism therefore came with risks, which makes it all the more striking that the Populist movement included a significant contingent of outspoken freethinkers. In Illinois, Clarence Darrow was a prominent agnostic in the Populist campaign. In Kansas, the Vincent brothers—Henry, Cuthbert, and Leo—also drew attacks as dangerous "infidels." The Vincents' *Nonconformist* newspaper regularly carried irreverent barbs, including a popular rendition of "Gould's Prayer," that caused political enemies to decry their blasphemous "denunciations of Christianity." In the Republican press at least, the Vincents' agnosticism proved their proclivity to anarchy and violence. Yet their unbelief and relentless attacks on the churches hardly diminished the instrumental role the Vincents played in the Populist movement.[54]

Eugene V. Debs was Populism's most celebrated agnostic. In the wake of the Pullman boycott, the conservative press charged Debs with the crimes of anarchy, violence, and destruction. The evidence that he was a "pronounced infidel" proved the case. Indeed, labor Populism seemed a special haven for the godless. In an expression of defiance, the anthem of the American Railway Union (ARU) made a point that the movement welcomed nonbelievers. The anthem appealed to "get aboard the Union train" where there was room "For women, men, and children, too—For Christian, Infidel, and Jew." The reference to Christians applied to a considerable number of ARU members who ascribed to a social Christianity. They looked to their union to represent "the rapidly-evolving God-men," and to bring to life Christian principles of social justice. The mention of Jews in the list of included groups provided a rhyme for the verse and expressed religious tolerance. And the sarcastic reference to the "Infidel" voiced pride in Debs and other reformers who embraced free thought.[55]

For Debs, free thought was a moral doctrine that he had imbibed from childhood. He grew up in Terre Haute, Indiana, where he studied the McGuffy Reader like most American schoolchildren. At home, however, on Sunday evenings his French-born father read aloud the works of Voltaire, Rousseau, and others from the French Enlightenment. When as a young man Debs met Robert Ingersoll, they became close, lifelong friends. In Ingersoll's labors Debs saw the Voltaire of his youth translated into a sensational oratorical campaign for free thought and moral truth. The famous infidel, Debs observed, was "the most talked about man in America," as his enemies were driven into a frenzy by "his merciless attacks upon their ancient Jehovah, their orthodox hell, and their pious traditions." But his friends "fairly worshiped him as a savior of humanity."[56]

Ingersoll's "sound money" Republican politics notwithstanding, Debs had profound respect for his determined struggle to rid the world of religious superstition. On Ingersoll's death in 1899, Debs wrote that Ingersoll had done more to improve the human condition than any man in any age. Debs's entire extended family loved Ingersoll, he explained, because of his defense of right and "unceasing denunciation of the wrong." "In our household as in many thousands of others," Debs later wrote to Ingersoll's widow, "the name Ingersoll is held in reverential love and adoration." The "great agnostic" represented "the essence of true religion," and practiced "the religion of love and service and consecration of humanity."[57]

To its critics, agnosticism spawned depravity and wickedness. To its adherents in the reform movement, however, it provided the test of truth and spurred strivings for high morals, goodness, and justice. Such were the convictions that fed Debs's own preoccupations with Christ-like self-sacrifice. Late nineteenth-century agnostics could and did match the moral fervor of their religious counterparts. As James Turner notes, "Moralism was the peak that still stood, prominent in its isolation, after other beliefs had eroded." For agnostic Populists the same was true, as unbelief formed one of the supporting structures of their Populist faith.[58]

As the secretary of the People's party in Grimes County, Texas, John W. H. Davis devoted his public energies to enacting the Populist agenda of economic, financial, and political reform. In his private contemplations, however, these reforms were closely intertwined with questions of faith. He understood that religion as practiced was "dead." Christianity ignored the here and now with its misplaced focus on "your dead carcass after death." Yes, Davis conceded, a "pure undefiled Christianity," combined with an honest ballot, would bring the necessary improvements. But he was troubled by the question of whether such a secular brotherhood could still be called Christianity at all. In search for answers he turned to non-Christian beliefs. He read across a range of spiritualist and other metaphysical literature, and carefully clipped and filed in his personal papers Charles C. Post's article about the evolution of man, apes, and the irrationality of belief in God. For

Davis, it made no sense to have "a political hell on earth" and a "religious heaven by the same person." He searched for a unified vision of spiritual and material progress. The study of "mental science" was of a piece with his investigations into census data and national legislation, inseparable parts of a single quest for human improvement.[59]

Davis understood the controversial nature of his religious views and kept his studies of "mental science" to himself. Because of efforts to avoid public discord, it is difficult to quantify the number of Populists who believed in spiritualism, "mental science," or similar metaphysical systems. The task is even more complex given that many other Americans—from faithful Christians to skeptical agnostics—entertained curiosity about communicating with the spirits of the dead and other metaphysical practices. In Texas, among the signs that the Populists showed interest in their movement, the *Southern Mercury* extended sympathy toward the spiritualists in the face of ostracism by "religious fanatics." Texas spiritualist associations, although small in number, only organized in districts that also happened to be Populist strongholds. The impoverished cotton farmers of Davis's Grimes County, for example, sustained a spiritualist organization with twenty-nine official members.[60]

The most prominent spiritualist in Texas, Eben LaFayette Dohoney, ran as the People's party candidate for a state judgeship. Dohoney was also one of the leading prohibitionists in the state. Although most Populists sympathized with the temperance movement, the Texas People's party preferred "local option" restrictions on alcohol sales rather than alienating German and other voters. This tolerant gesture was largely undone in the public mind by placing Dohoney on the Populist ticket as he was well-known for his strident prohibitionist views. The spiritualists did not view alcohol abuse as a sin, the work of the devil, or a ticket to eternal damnation. But it did threaten public health. And the spiritualists' commitment to health and fitness made them uncompromising foes of the liquor industry.[61]

The tangible connections between spiritual reform, health reform, and social reform brought spiritualists into the Populist ranks. The spiritualists did not confine their attention to the séance. Their belief in progress—the "continuous progressive unfoldment" of the human condition—translated into social activism. A number of spiritualists embraced an "evolutionary revolution" toward the cooperative commonwealth. The spiritualist newspaper *Carrier Dove* popularized legislation making the federal government responsible for financing and regulating cooperative corporations "under comprehensive and uniform laws." Although less specific than Charles Macune's subtreasury plan, the proposal was premised on the same state-centered and cooperativist assumptions.[62]

The spiritualists rejected the framework of Christianity in favor of what they understood as a scientific outlook. Like the Swedenborgians, the spiritualists used the language of modern science and based their claims on empirical evidence rather than emotion or doctrine. They viewed the discovery of the ability to communicate with the spirits of the dead as a confirmation of reason and science in the struggle against the mysterious and supernatural, just as the harnessing of electricity confirmed the scientific age. Although spiritualism bore the brunt of intense hostility from the churches and the pious, it had a considerable public presence in late nineteenth-century life. Like other cultural movements of the era, the spiritualists made extensive use of the camp meeting. Crowds five thousand to ten thousand strong gathered under spiritualist tents to hear the speeches of famous mediums. Although some of the participants were city people enjoying a rural retreat, the movement had a broad rural following. The annual camp meetings of the Mississippi Valley Spiritualists Association lasted for a month and drew thousands of participants from Texas, Minnesota, and everywhere in between.[63]

Spiritualism provided an attractive alternative for women. The Christian churches, with their ordained clergy and scriptural proscriptions, placed obstacles to women's expression and equality. "Spiritualism," its practitioners stressed, "has no oracles, no priests, no leaders. The truth, wherever found, is all it seeks." Women thus found opportunities as trance mediums and truth seekers. Victoria Woodhull, the best-known spiritualist of the 1870s, connected spiritualism in the public mind with free love and challenges to traditional gender roles. Although most spiritualists distanced themselves from Woodhull's free love ideas, they campaigned for women's progress, advocating dress and dietary reform, job protection, career opportunities, and the right to vote. The spiritualists played a prominent role in the national suffrage movement, and in California the trance medium Laura de Force Gordon led the state suffrage association.[64]

Given their ideas about reform, spiritualists often made good Populists. The editor Annie Diggs, the silver crusader George Bowen, and the novelist Hamlin Garland were among other prominent midwestern Populists involved with spiritualism. James Vincent Sr., father of the Vincent brothers, popularized spiritualist ideas in the pages of the *Nonconformist*. His wife had been a spiritualist, and after her death he grew dissatisfied with religious interpretations of the afterlife. "While for myself I have no faith in the teachings of the bible," he conceded, "I cannot deny the doctrine of immortality." He found the solution to otherwise unexplainable phenomena in spiritualism, which provided empirical proof that "the mind is active everywhere." Only the scientific methods of the séance allowed for the perception of this electricity-like force.[65]

Spiritualism played a large role in California Populism. Marion Cannon, exercising his authority as president of the state Farmer's Alliance, pointedly ruled against a candidate for membership who did not believe in a supreme being. This ruling, however, served to allay public fears, as both the Farmers' Alliance and the People's party in California owed a great deal to spiritualism and related movements that flourished in the state's climate of religious tolerance and experimentation. Here it should be kept in mind that much of the California movement had a nonreligious character, marked more by a casual drift from religious concerns than commitment to alternative beliefs. Cannon himself showed disinterest in spiritual matters, and although his wife was a committed church member, the church was one of the few organizations in which he did not take part. At the same time, a section of the reform movement in California embraced non-Christian beliefs in which a supreme being played an ambiguous part or no part at all.[66]

The spiritualist colony at Summerland, south of Santa Barbara, served as an organizing center for Populism. James S. Barbee, a Confederate veteran authorized by the national Farmers' Alliance to organize on the West Coast, was closely tied to Summerland and, with the assistance of Alliance organizer Anna Ferry Smith, made it a base of statewide organizing. Burdette Cornell, a recent arrival from the Midwest known by the Populists as "our Nebraska Farm Boy," served as the secretary of the Summerland Spiritualist Association. He traveled extensively throughout the state as a Farmers' Alliance organizer, setting up suballiances in remote rural districts. A spiritualist cadre, which included prominent women activists such as Mary A. White and Addie Ballou, similarly helped build the Nationalist clubs and the People's party in California.[67]

Besides the spiritualists, adherents of the related belief system known as Theosophy were similarly attracted to Populism. Theosophists also approached spirituality from the modern standpoint of rational inquiry and scientific validation. However, instead of focusing on communication with the dead, they studied what they viewed as the advanced ideas of Buddhism, Hinduism, and other Asian belief systems. They also explored magic and the mystical, not out of belief in the supernatural, but in pursuit of "occult science," that is, rational and scientific explanations for unexplained psychic phenomena. Founded by the Russian émigré Helena Petrovna Blavatsky, the Theosophist movement, with headquarters in Madras, India, established branches in forty-two countries, with more than one hundred American chapters. Its followers tended to be in self-conscious revolt against the confines of traditional belief, and saw themselves as innovators on the cutting edge of a new, modern, and scientific world outlook. Their British counterparts, historian Alex Owen writes, pursued "a thoroughly modern project" with "distinctively avant-garde themes and preoccupations." The same pursuit brought American Theosophists to Populist reform.[68]

Inspired by Buddhist and related ideas about the unity of life, Theosophists came to similar conclusions as the social Christians about human solidarity and social reform. They found the doctrines of Bellamy's Nationalism especially attractive. Although Edward Bellamy himself was a social Christian, several of his closest associates, including Cyrus Field Willard, Sylvester Baxter, and other founders of Nationalism were Theosophists. In California, the Theosophists played a major role in organizing Nationalist clubs up and down the state. The influence of "occult science" spread well beyond the organized Theosophist societies, as occult lecturers and practitioners formed part of the bohemian subculture of reform. The caustically skeptical and atheistic Anna Fader Haskell found their ideas "rather absurd." Yet, much to her chagrin, her husband Burnette had a long-standing interest in magic and named their son after the mystical Chaldaic god Astoroth.[69]

Mystical religion remained in the shadows of the Populist movement. It had its moment of national attention, however, with Coxey's Army and the prominent role played by Jacob Coxey's coleader of the march, Carl Browne. During the 1870s, Browne had served as secretary to Denis Kearney in the California Workingmen's party agitation for Chinese exclusion. He later joined the Theosophists, who, ironically, provided some of the clearest voices on the West Coast in favor of racial tolerance. In 1893 he met Jacob Coxey, the Ohio Populist. The Californian introduced the Ohioan to both Theosophy and to the idea of organizing "Industrial Armies" as a means to bring the plight of the unemployed to public attention. The result was the famous march on Washington. Along the way, they mixed their campaign for a "good roads bill" with Theosophist teachings about Jesus, Buddha, Krishna, and immortality.

Coxey and Browne dubbed their march "The Commonweal of Christ," and announced to crowds of spectators that their march was a manifestation of the reincarnation of Jesus and other spiritual masters. This left many observers perplexed. The official chronicler of the march, Henry Vincent, received an inquiry as to what precisely was the nature of Coxey's religious views. To this he replied that, as far as he understood it, Coxey's religion "was to uplift humanity, relieve the oppressed and 'let my people go free.'" As for Coxey's church, Vincent described it as "the big one," which "takes in all humanity irrespective of sect divisions." Such an explanation made sense given the liberal and inclusive environment of Populist religiosity.[70]

Adherents of Theosophy saw themselves as the vanguard of a global unification of religious beliefs. They represented a small part of a much broader late nineteenth-century enthusiasm in America to learn from non-Christian belief systems. The wave of interest culminated in the 1893 World Parliament of Religions held in conjunction with the Chicago World's Fair. The organizer of the event, John Henry Barrows, a liberal theologian and minister of Chicago's First Presbyterian Church, promoted the Parliament as "the most phenomenal fact of the Columbian Exposition." The Parliament drew over 150,000 people from across the nation and the globe to its sessions. Reform-minded participants welcomed the opportunity to learn "what God has wrought through Buddha and Zoroaster." They saw the event as a turning point in the quest for understanding the universal "religion of humanity" and "science of religion." The nation's newspapers carried detailed reports. In North Carolina, the front-page headline of the Populist *Caucasian* saluted the "Unique Assembly" and provided its rural readers with an account of how the followers of Christianity, Buddhism, Confucianism, Islam, Hinduism, Zoroastrianism, and "all religions" sought unity on the basis of "the golden rule."[71]

Such liberal religious sentiments expressed in rural Populist newspapers help explain the clash over comparative religion in Dayton, Tennessee, so many years later. At the Scopes trial, Darrow queried Bryan about what he knew of Buddha and Zoroaster, of which Bryan claimed to have little familiarity. Darrow's purpose in this line of questioning was not to ridicule Bryan for his ignorance of obscure subjects. Rather, he grilled Bryan about the existence of other belief systems for the same reason he pressed him on the relationship between the earth and the sun. Darrow sought to expose the closed-mindedness of a new fundamentalist doctrine that was predicated on rejecting once widely popularized and accepted knowledge—knowledge that had once shaped the intellectual environment of reform.[72]

Byran's stand at the Scopes trial, historians have noted, reflected popular anxieties during the interwar years about the antidemocratic implications of science. It would be anachronistic, however, to place such anxieties as a source of the Populist agitation of the 1880s and early 1890s. Even reformers dedicated to their Bibles shared a common faith in scientific progress. The "Principles of the Alabama Farmers' Alliance," for example, in a somewhat unique affirmation for an Alliance declaration, endorsed the Bible as "the book of truth," while at the same time pledging to the common "belie[f] in the acquirement of scientific agriculture." Far from fearing its power, science gave the Populists faith and shaped their religious understanding. The reform movement rode a wave of self-confidence that farmers, laborers, and the ordinary folk could assimilate the new physical and biological principles. Once absorbed, they could harness these principles to resolve the new economic, political, and spiritual problems of modern society. This faith was shared across the religious spectrum, from evangelical preachers to occultists and agnostics. In that sense, science served as the modernizing glue of Populist belief.[73]

Science was the hope of the reform movement. As countless reform lecturers and editorials stressed, the poverty and inequities faced by farmers and laborers were the result of unscientific methods of governance, business, finance, and education in a scientific age. The Populists shared their deference to science with late nineteenth-century Americans of other political persuasions. This deference had precedents in the American experience, as it resembled the scientific beliefs of Jefferson and his contemporaries. Like Jefferson, the Populists looked to validate their ideas in science and Enlightenment thought. They, too, believed that the "science of government" was analogous to the laws of physics and biology governing the natural world. At the same time, the Populists expressed a passion and urgency in their scientific convictions that was mainly absent from the contemplative explorations conducted at Monticello, for the Populists saw science as a practical and immediate instrument of self-liberation.[74]

Only "by the light of science" could the people find the way to their own salvation. This idea formed the central theme of Thomas Cator's address before a packed house in San Francisco's Metropolitan Temple on July 4, 1890. A veteran of the Knights of Labor and the rising political star of Populism in California, Cator gave the Independence Day audience what they had come for—a scathing indictment of the injustices of corporate power. He titled his address "Millionaires or Morals: Which Shall Rule?" And he covered the familiar litany of abuses that allowed bankers and corporate executives to accumulate obscene wealth at the expense of the people. Corporate wealth accretion was an economic and social problem. It was a moral problem because it violated scientific principles. Given that "science, morality and truth are one," Cator explained, "all science is moral, all that is unscientific will produce immorality." Therefore, if society was to regain its moral bearings, the people needed to follow "the morning star of science."[75]

Cator exhorted the crowd to fight for the scientific outlook in public affairs. The public schools needed to adopt a more "thoroughly scientific" curriculum, emphasizing investigation, statistics, and the spirit of inquiry. "The minds of the masses," Cator stressed, "must be trained to solve by reason the questions before us, and to follow scientific truth [wherever] it may lead."[76] Wherever science might lead, it gave the people cause for confidence in the future:

> Science invents machines which leave no room to doubt any prophecy. Machines to talk, to write, to fly. Science opens the heavens and the earth, levels the mountains, fills the valleys, connects the oceans, photographs the heavens, weighs the worlds, and shows to the most simple the relation of man to man, and of men to all created things.
>
> Above all, by [science's] persistent, steady advance, by its sure progress, its eternal never-ending scope, it breaks down all pessimism; it baffles despair; it cheers the faint heart . . . it calls freedom from her grave . . . it dethrones the wrong; it raises up the right; it ushers in the inheritance of the children of toil.[77]

Cator's florid language might have been especially overblown. The basic theme, however, echoed throughout the Populist movement. The same certainties about scientific virtue were shared by other Americans including those in academia and government service. In the 1880s and 1890s, such certainties swelled unchecked by the lessons of poison gas, nuclear warfare, or other horrors wrought by later advances in chemistry and physics. The "creed of science" may have had its critics. Doubts and criticism, however, failed to contain Populist faith. An editorial in the Stafford, Kansas, *People's Paper* about the global advances in combating disease reflected the Populist mood. "Notwithstanding that there are occasional protests" against vaccination, science was marking one success after the next against smallpox, rabies, diphtheria, and cholera. "Wonderful is the rule of science," enthused the Populist editors.[78]

Equipped with a "scientific manner," Miss Inez Hughey lectured her colleagues in the Texas Farmers' Alliance, the people themselves could solve "the problems of life." From desperate rural poverty to urban slums, no social evil could withstand the assaults of modern science in the hands of the people.[79] "Science and art," John Rayner believed, were the "twin children of Christianity." Only the science of social hygiene could raise the impoverished African American farmers of east Texas from their degradation.[80] Similarly, Lester Hubbard, in his jeremiad about the "revolting evils" of the big city, held that only science offered hope for the wretched inhabitants of Chicago's tenements. "A scientific system of rapid transit," he argued, would dismantle "the noisome dives and dens, where poverty and crime now swelter and breed corruption." Planning could ensure urban growth on "enlightened, scientific and human lines."[81]

Farmers needed to master the relevant branches of the natural sciences if they were to solve the everyday problems of growing crops and raising stock. But farmers were more than crop growers and stock handlers. They were citizens and thinkers who needed to have a scientific understanding of their place in nature and society. Charles Macune, a loyal Baptist and medical doctor, was one of the leaders of rural reform most involved in spreading the gospel of science. The pages of his *National Economist* kept farmers "properly informed as to the progress of modern science." It also advertised inexpensive scientific literature, including works by Edward Clodd, who popularized the ideas of Darwin, Spencer, and Huxley. Clodd's *The Story of Creation: A Plain Account of Evolution* started with nebular theory and the origin of the solar system, and ended with the social evolution of modern man. "No farmhouse in America should be without it," the *National Economist* urged its readers. At 30 cents a copy, such publications "will make a nation of scholars of our people."[82]

For the Populists, science offered more than a means to solve social and political problems. It also represented the highest ideals of truth, morality, and progress. Within the ranks of Populist reform, the faith in science transcended region, race, gender, and religious affiliation. It formed a cornerstone of the movement's moral and intellectual edifice, functioning as the modern creed of the reform coalition. Mrs. J. Morton Smith gave voice to this creed in an essay she read to the men and women gathered in a meeting of the Bell County, Texas, Farmers' Alliance in the spring of 1888. "The marble column may monument the statesmen and the barristers of other days,"[83] Mrs. Smith assured her fellow farmers of the central Texas plain:

> but Agassiz and Lavoisier, Humboldt and Cuvier, will live in history when those barristers will be forgotten, and the monumental shafts shall have crumbled into dust. Poets may sing in measured verse of the victories of conquering heroes, but the triumphs of Arkwright and Crompton and Cartwright will be sounded down the ages, as long as a factory runs its looms or steam propels its machinery. Orators may extol in studied eloquence the fame of Fox and Pitt and Clay and Webster, but the starry spheres will hymn forever the names of Galileo and Kepler.[84]

For the people's progress the lesson was clear. The new generation, Mrs. Smith concluded, must "bow at the shrine of science, and treasure up unfading jewels from the balmy fields of thought."[85]

Conclusion

Populist Defeat and Its Meaning

"You shall not crucify mankind upon a cross of gold." With this indictment of the financial establishment, William Jennings Bryan, a young congressman from Nebraska, electrified the delegates to the Democratic Convention gathered under the hot roof of the Chicago Coliseum in July of 1896. On the fifth ballot, Bryan won a surprise nomination as the presidential candidate. The nomination marked a historic shift in party alignment, with the Democratic party embracing a platform of minting silver, a federal income tax, and other reforms demanded by rural and labor constituencies. Two weeks later, at its convention in St. Louis, the People's party also endorsed Bryan for president.[1]

For Republicans, and a considerable number of "sound money" Democrats, the Populist endorsement confirmed their worst fears about the Bryan campaign. They viewed the Populists and their reckless currency doctrines as instruments of "anarchy" and "lawlessness." Theodore Roosevelt, the police commissioner of New York City at the time, believed that the Populists were "plotting a social revolution," and to check their efforts at "subversion" he proposed lining up twelve Populist leaders against a wall and "shooting them dead." Similarly apocalyptic and fearful language characterized the hard-fought election campaign that pitted the Democratic-Populist Bryan against the "goldbug" Republican William McKinley.[2]

Bryan's loss that November inflicted wounds on the People's party from which it never recovered. Populism failed in presidential politics. It failed to sustain a viable presence at the polls. And it failed to maintain any semblance of cohesion, as the movement slid into rancorous discord over who was to blame. "Middle-of-the-road" Populists accused the architects of "fusion" with the Democrats of betraying principles. The "fusionists" accused their critics of failing to recognize political realities. The faithful of both camps continued to keep the People's party name alive into the twentieth century. But their small numbers only confirmed that what had once been a powerful social and political movement was no longer so. Populism failed, leaving in its wake the question of why.

Lawrence Goodwyn has provided the most stirring explanation: the "democratic promise" of Populism fell victim to an insidious and Judas-like "shadow movement" ("fusionists") that betrayed honest and straight "middle-of-the-road" Populism to the tender mercies of corporate power. Such a rendering makes for gripping tragedy. However, it has little to do with the interior fault lines of Populist politics and ideology. It also fails to take into account the external obstacles that the movement faced. Among other things, the Populists had to break the formidable grip in which the two established parties held the political system. This presented a challenge that the People's party came as close to meeting as any third party had since prior to the Civil War. That the Populists realized the electoral strength that they did is at least partly attributable to their innovative melding of "middle-of-the-road" and "fusionist" tactics. Such flexibility was facilitated by the Populists' distrust of partyism, a distrust that also contributed to the Populists' undoing.[3]

Goodwyn's tragedy fits within the larger narrative of the defeat of traditional society by modernity: Populism failed because the wheels of history rolled over it. When social and cultural historians portray late nineteenth-century social movements as expressions of resistance to the market and modernity, it is difficult to avoid the conclusion that such movements, despite the heroism and humanity they may have revealed, were doomed from the outset by an inexorable historical process. In a provocative dissent, James Livingston recognizes comedy where others see tragedy. For Livingston, as much as for Lasch, Hahn, McMath, Thomas, and other scholars, Populism represented the premodern and republican past. But, unlike the others, he rejects the notion that the destruction of that past frames the tragic narrative of the twentieth century. Modernity offered democratic and progressive possibilities, Livingston contends, and farm and labor movements—with their soft-money doctrines and fear of "concentrated market power"— opposed the advent of the modern market society. The demands of modernity, Livingston implies, required the "eradication of Populism."[4]

The setbacks suffered by the People's party at the polls, however, must not be read as extended referenda on the historical rights or wrongs of the Populist program. Populist electoral setbacks said little about the historic necessity, much less inevitability, of gold or silver, greenbacks or subtreasury loans. Summing up the defeat of the Populists and other late nineteenth-century reform movements, Gretchen Ritter writes that their loss was not determined by either destiny or nature. Their defeat "was not dictated by the anonymous forces of historical progress and economic modernity." Rather, she concludes, "political choice, structural constraints, and historical contingency shaped the fate of the antimonopolists."[5]

Nor did the Populists lose because their views were unrealistic. True, their rhetoric could be far-fetched. Their discussion of the currency, for example, although grounded in plausible assumptions about the benefits of inflation, could also be utopian, paranoid, or apocalyptic. This, however, cannot explain the movement's failures, because the movement had no monopoly on delusional thinking. If anything, the Populists were outdone in this respect by academic and corporate elites who convinced themselves of numerous absurdities. Gold standard advocates, for example, could match any contenders when it came to absurd and paranoid arguments, as they dogmatically insisted that any deviation from a gold-based currency would immediately dispatch civilization to the hell fires of anarchy. Such flights of fancy— "superstition" as the Populists rightly called it—circulated as profound wisdom among American scholars and business leaders. As C. Vann Woodward noted, "The political crisis of the nineties evoked hysterical responses and apocalyptic delusions in more than one quarter." The Populist electoral failure therefore provides for a poor measure of the fanciful or overwrought. But it does say a great deal about which quarter had what political resources in terms of political machinery, mass media, bribery, and fraud—and the will to energetically use such resources.[6]

Populism's failure must also be viewed in light of what came after. In the wake of the defeat of the People's party, a wave of reform soon swept the country. Progressive Era legislation in the first years of the new century expanded the role of government in American life and laid the foundations of modern political development. Populism provided an impetus for this modernizing process, with many of their demands co-opted and refashioned by progressive Democrats and Republicans. By a turn of fate, Populism proved far more successful dead than alive. At the same time, the process of co-optation and refashioning produced a reconfiguration of the social dynamics of reform. The Populist vision for a modern America was increasingly eclipsed by a corporate vision. Before examining what that meant, it is first necessary to provide a framework for Populism's political defeat.

The endorsement of Bryan at the People's party convention provoked a bitter dissent from "middle-of-the-road" Populists. They rightly feared that the movement's principles would be co-opted by the Democrats only to scuttle the full Populist program. At the same time, their accusations of heresy against the "fusionists" obscured the reality that fusion had always been part of Populist politics. Although the 1896 presidential ticket had important symbolic meaning, from its inception the People's party had entered into compromising fusion agreements with Democrats and Republicans at the state and local levels. In that sense, cries against "fusion" merely reflected the harsh realities that a third party confronted when it challenged the two-party monopoly in a winner-take-all political system.[7]

The rise and fall of the People's party in California put these realities in sharp relief. At the new party's 1891 founding convention in Los Angeles, state Farmers' Alliance president Marion Cannon led the delegates in renouncing forever the Republican and Democratic parties and pledging to the People's party "our lives, our fortunes and our sacred honor." The following year, Cannon was elected to the U.S. House of Representatives and his reputation soared as a Populist hero. Meanwhile, eight Populist representatives held the balance of power in the state assembly in Sacramento. Expectations ran high that if the Populist "Big Eight" held firm they would force the legislature to send People's party leader Thomas Cator to the U.S. Senate. With their focus on national legislation, the Populists were willing to horse trade in local and state affairs to gain a Senate seat. However, one member of the bloc defected and Cator lost the seat to reform Democrat Stephen Mallory White. The scandal deepened as Marion Cannon was implicated in negotiating the deal with White, a treasonable act for which he was indignantly expelled from the Populists' ranks.

The high drama surrounding Cannon's treachery tended to cloud an essential fact: the state People's party owed virtually every success it had at the polls to fusion agreements with the two old parties. All but one of the eight Populists in the California legislature were elected with Democratic or Republican support. Cannon himself owed his 1892 election victory to a Democratic endorsement that was orchestrated by Stephen Mallory White. Yet, Cannon's betrayal demonstrated the dangers and limits of such agreements. Defending the purity of the Populist platform, the California People's party rejected further entangling compromises and adopted a "straight" or "middle-of-the-road" policy. The new policy proved disastrous.

The 1894 elections taught the California Populists a harsh lesson. At the local level, they scored encouraging victories. In San Francisco, Adolph Sutro gained the mayor's office on a People's party ticket. At the state level, too, the Populists ran a strong campaign, doubling their votes from two years before. But more votes translated into severe losses. The People's party only sent one representative to the state assembly, despite winning 26 percent of the vote outside of San Francisco. The Democrats, running on a reform platform of railroad nationalization and free silver, were also nearly frozen out of the legislature, sending only seven representatives to the assembly. The lesson was clear. The previous policy of Populist-Democratic fusion would have given the two reform parties an overwhelming majority in the state assembly. But the "middle-of-the-road" policy delivered fifty-three of the sixty-one seats in the assembly to the pro-railroad Republicans. For the next election cycle, the Populist Thomas Cator, in an ironic twist, negotiated a new fusion pact with Democrat Stephen Mallory White that allowed the Populists to capture eleven seats in the state legislature and two seats in the U.S. Congress.[8]

Similar arithmetic was at work elsewhere. In Kansas, Nebraska, and Colorado, Populist electoral success required fusion with reform Democrats to overcome Republican dominance. In North Carolina, and to a lesser extent in Texas and Alabama, Populists fused with Republicans to challenge Democratic power. The configuration of parties and their relative strengths varied from state to state. But everywhere "middle-of-the-road" policies were the rare exception. Most Populist voters understood how the winner-take-all electoral system worked, and willingly cast their votes for the joint tickets required by fusion pacts with other parties. Because fusion was often negotiated by party managers behind closed doors, the negotiations at times provoked unease and distrust among the rank-and-file membership. In public, meanwhile, the Populists kept up a steady attack against the traditional parties in order to justify the third party's very existence.[9]

Not surprisingly, the dual requirements of party solidarity and fusion stirred heated debates within Populist ranks. The Bryan campaign of 1896 brought the controversies to a head, and rent the party into warring camps. The patterns of division, however, tended to be both unpredictable and nonideological. Among fusionists, there was a hope that the silver question would facilitate broad electoral agreements with reform Democrats and pro-silver Republicans. This hope was shared by both dedicated free-silver enthusiasts, as well as silver skeptics and Greenbackers who believed that the silver issue, despite its limitations, could be used as an opening to realize other Populist demands, including the subtreasury, the income tax, and railroad regulation. Populists who had been veterans of the Knights of Labor and the Greenback movement had extensive experience with fusion politics, and many of them viewed political parties as an inherent evil and bridled at the constraints of party loyalty. The nonparty ideal of "putting principle above party" led reformers of all ideological stripes to embrace fusion.[10]

"Middle-of-the-road" Populists countered that fusion would rob the People's party of its purpose. Free silver or some other watered-down electoral agreement was no substitute for the principles embodied in the full Populist platform. A vocal and active minority rejected the fusion policy. Herman Taubeneck, the national chair of the People's party from 1892 to 1896, bore much of their wrath. Montana Populists considered Taubeneck and other national officers as "traitors to the principles which have raised them from obscurity."[11] Gasper Clemens, a leader of the Kansas "midroaders," warned that the fusionists were "plotting the destruction of the last political hope of the common people of this land." Like other critics of fusion, Clemens placed the blame on a failure of leadership by Taubeneck. "The whole truth is," Clemens concluded, "our national chairman has lacked a whole Napoleon of being a great leader or any leader at all."[12]

Although "midroaders" were present in every state organization, their numbers ran especially strong in the South, where fusion touched on explosive issues of race, section, and party loyalty. At the state level, fusion agreements with Republicans posed a dilemma for white southern Populists. As demonstrated by Populist success in North Carolina, they had little chance of unseating Democratic power without the help of black Republican votes. With such votes, however, they faced the charge of racial and sectional treason, a charge that ultimately destroyed North Carolina's Populist-Republican administration. Fusion with Democrats posed an equally severe dilemma for southern Populists. Their original break with the Democratic party had provoked intense acrimony amid charges and countercharges of betraying the party of Redemption and white supremacy. For many Populists, the wounds proved too deep for amicable collaboration at the polls. In Georgia, Texas, and elsewhere in the former Confederacy, putting a Democrat at the head of the national People's party ticket involved a concession to sworn party enemies that large numbers of Populists were not prepared to make. In a complex way, the antiparty vision was weaker and party loyalties more intractable in the South, keeping many southern Populists "in the middle of the road."[13]

Black Populists registered bitter protests against the endorsement of Bryan. John Rayner grasped immediately that the endorsement threatened to end his role and that of other black Populists in reform politics. The black vote would no longer be a contested vote if Populist-Democratic fusion cemented white solidarity at the polls. At the 1896 Texas Populist convention, Rayner convened a conference of black delegates to decide between "Republican oppressive conservatism and Democratic rashness." They chose the former and campaigned for McKinley. The white Populists also attempted cooperation with Texas Republicans as some "midroad" Texans voted for McKinley that year. But the weakness of Populist-Republican fusion in Texas meant, as Rayner knew it would, the effective closing of the possibilities for black political participation once opened by the conflict between Populists and Democrats.[14]

The two old parties, meanwhile, mobilized to destroy the Populist challenge. They employed their control of the electoral machinery to "count out" Populist votes. Southern Democrats showed special enthusiasm for robbing Populists at the polls, and for good measure resorted to shotguns and murder to terrorize opponents and suppress the Populist vote. Bribery and fraud contributed to the dissension within Populist ranks. In Kansas, "midroaders" accused the "fusionists" of using "every tactic known to the ballot-box-stuffers" in the South, while the "fusionists" believed that the Republicans used bribes to convince Populists to vote the "midroad" ticket. In railroad, mining, and mill towns across the country, company blacklists effectively restrained potential Populist votes. The two established parties also employed their overwhelming advantage in terms of the mass media. The weekly periodicals of rural reform, with their shoestring budgets, were no match for the highly capitalized daily newspapers. Whether editorially aligned with Republicans or Democrats, the mainstream press systematically played on racial, sectional, and class fears to alert readers to the Populist menace.[15]

In those states where the two-party system was strong, where both Democrats and Republicans mobilized competitive political machinery, the Populists scored few political successes. The Populists never gained an electoral foothold in the vote-rich Northeast, where the old parties were most deeply entrenched. Nonetheless, despite their advantages, the managers of the two established parties grew to understand that they faced great risk if they failed to put Populist reform into their political calculations. They recognized that co-opting Populist demands often proved the most effective means to meet the third-party challenge and to gain on the political competition. In the West and the South, Democrats and a considerable number of Republicans championed free silver, the income tax, labor protection, railroad regulation, and other Populist causes. This process of co-optation squeezed the life out of the People's party and ushered in a wave of reform that, from a Populist point of view, had a decidedly mixed result.[16]

Charles Macune, after leaving the Farmers' Alliance in 1892, spent the next thirty years in the small towns of rural Texas practicing law and medicine and serving as a Methodist preacher. In 1920 he wrote down his reflections on the rise and fall of the Farmers' Alliance. He expressed no regrets. "No movement can survive when there is no necessity for its existence," he observed, "and its very success from a business point of view obviated the necessity of its existence, as did its success as a national organization in the field of economics." Given the poor showing of Alliance business ventures—ventures for which Macune bore considerable responsibility—it might have appeared disingenuous for him to judge the Alliance's demise as a result of its success. Yet his judgment contained important, if partial, truths.[17]

Macune had reason to be pleased when he surveyed the rural scene in 1920. What he could not have known was that in the autumn of that same year farm prices would plunge and the agricultural economy would fall into two decades of depression. Millions of poor farmers lacked the capital to survive slack global markets or the demands of mechanization, and the ensuing cycles of state intervention failed to stem the demographic collapse of the farm population. But before that cascade of events, Macune witnessed what he believed was remarkable progress toward a modern and prosperous rural life. From 1896 through the end of the First World War, global demand produced a "golden era" in American agriculture. The market prices for cotton, wheat, and other export crops rose steadily. The dollar value of the average farm tripled. Farmers invested accordingly by adding 120 million acres to the nation's farmlands. The prosperity bypassed many farmers, especially black farmers in the South, where the combination of white hostility and intense poverty meant that black farm ownership was already in decline. Nevertheless, decline remained in the future for most American farmers. The century began well for those staple crop producers in a position to take advantage of high demand for fiber and grain.[18]

Good prices on the world market sent an influx of global cash into the rural economy. Farmers invested in improvements, purchasing the latest in modern conveniences advertised by Sears, Roebuck and Company, Montgomery Ward, and other mass-marketing systems. They acquired water pumps, washing machines, and new kitchen appliances to modernize their homes and relieve the burdens of women's chores. An automobile was the most expensive and significant new purchase made by farmers during the boom years. The Model T connected farmers to town and to one another as never before. In 1920, a third of all American farmers owned at least one car or truck. Telephones also transformed rural communication. Improvements came more slowly to the South. By 1920, less than 15 percent of southern farmers owned a telephone, although many more farmers used the telephone of a neighbor. Even in the remoteness of Macune's rural Texas, more prosperous cotton farmers lit their houses with gas or electric lights. Electricity remained an unaffordable luxury for most Texas farmers. Yet electricity's introduction into rural life was a sign of future possibilities.[19]

Macune must have been especially gratified to witness improvements in rural education. As Farmers' Alliance members had once so vigorously advocated, farmers in the new century approved taxes necessary to build schools, modernize facilities, and hire professional teachers. Federal legislation expanded the opportunities of farmers' sons and daughters to attend high schools and colleges, providing funds for rural vocational training and other rural educational projects. Federal funding for rural roads, combined with the postal system's expanded rural delivery, brought education and information that much closer to rural homes.[20]

Even as the Farmers' Alliance passed from the scene, its message of scientific farming and improved technique gained an ever-broader following among the nation's farmers. The practical outcome of the Populist revolt, according to educational historian Rush Welter, "was better technical training and a greater interest among farmers in learning about technical advances in agriculture." Enrollments grew dramatically in Farmers' Institutes. As a hybrid educational system that the Farmers' Alliances helped to build, the Farmers' Institutes combined the efforts of state agricultural agencies, college extension services, and farm organizations. In 1901–02, over eight hundred thousand farmers took part in Farmers' Institutes. Twelve years later, in 1913–14, over three million farmers participated. As historian Gilbert Fite observes of the cotton South, the doctrine of scientific agriculture was "little short of a religion." The *Progressive Farmer*, formerly Leonidas Polk's voice of the Farmers' Alliance and the People's party, emerged in the new century as the South's most widely read and influential agricultural periodical, spreading the word of scientific farming and business methods. Farmers' organizations such as the Farmers' Union, the Farmers' Educational and Cooperative Union in Texas, the American Society of Equity in the Midwest, and a revitalized Grange worked to spread the doctrines of scientific and systematic farming. Although taken together these organizations lacked the size or strength of the Farmers' Alliance, their presence indicated that such organizations were not as obsolete as Macune suggested.[21]

From a "business point of view," Macune had reason to boast of the success of Farmers' Alliance principles. By the end of his second presidential term, Theodore Roosevelt's vision of progressive reform included instituting "effective cooperation among farmers." Echoing the old Populist message, Roosevelt stressed that "under modern economic conditions," the "cooperative system [was] exactly the form of business combination" farmers needed to put themselves "on a level with the organized interests with which they do business." In line with this vision, the ideal of centralized cooperative enterprise gained legal and institutional strength. The Clayton Anti-Trust Act of 1914 and subsequent Progressive legislation provided exemptions from antitrust laws for farm cooperatives.[22]

With the turn of the century, farmers formed successful monopolies in the California fruit and specialty crop industries. After reorganizing to conform to the Clayton Act standards, by 1920 the California Fruit Growers Exchange claimed ten thousand members and shipped $59 million worth of fruit under the Sunkist brand name. Raisin, prune, and walnut growers, under the Sun-Maid, Sunsweet, and Diamond labels, established similarly effective cooperative enterprises. Meanwhile, in the upper Midwest, the success of the Land O'Lakes brand marked the power of cooperative creameries in national marketing.[23]

In 1920, the president of the California raisin association replied to the charge that the raisin growers had formed a monopoly: "Call us a trust, if you will, but we're a benevolent one." This response reflected the dual realities of the cooperative impulse. On the one hand, much like industrial trusts, the agricultural cooperatives built centralized and hierarchical structures, laying the foundations for much of what became the modern agribusinesses we know today. On the other hand—despite similar systems of management, marketing techniques, and business practices—a farmers' trust held a distinct claim to "benevolence." Whereas industrial monopolies required the combination of a relative handful of industrialists, the small start-up costs in agriculture meant a farmers' monopoly required the participation of many thousands of individual farmers. The adherence of a large number of farmers with small and medium-sized holdings made a Sunkist or a Land O'Lakes possible. At times when smaller producers proved ideologically resistant to the centralized regime of cooperative monopoly, such monopolies tended to crack. In the 1880s and 1890s, however, the ideological commitment to regulated marketing ran strong, providing a powerful impetus for the modern system of centralized and large-scale cooperation.[24]

The nation's grain and cotton farmers hoped that in the new century they, too, would reap the benefits of modern systems of agricultural rationalization. Under the Wilson administration, Congress passed regulatory legislation, including the Warehouse, Grain Standards, Cotton Futures, and Land Bank Acts, which facilitated the organization and standardization of agricultural credits and markets. Congress and the U.S. Department of Agriculture also gave support to marketing cooperatives. The Smith-Lever Act of 1914 authorized educational extension services to provide expertise in cooperative business methods. The USDA set up agencies to facilitate cooperative enterprises, and its Bureau of Markets gave aid to cooperatives by providing them with systematic information about yields and markets. It also facilitated the growth and power of the American Farm Bureau Federation, including its cooperative experiments in the marketing of grain, cotton, fruit, dairy, and other products.[25]

As compared to Macune's designs for a subtreasury system, federal intervention in the farm economy remained halting and incomplete. Nonetheless, as a path-breaking architect of federal marketing and credit systems, Macune must have been impressed by the progress made. The budget of the U.S. Department of Agriculture grew by more than 700 percent between 1900 and 1915. In 1917, it had a budget of $280 million. Its staff of almost 19,000 men and women made the USDA one of the largest departments in the federal bureaucracy. America's entry into the First World War—and the political decision that a strong farm economy was essential to national security and the war effort—only intensified the pace and accentuated the centralizing and bureaucratic features of federal involvement in rural life. By 1920, doubts in Congress about federally centralized systems of marketing and credit meant that the U.S. Department of Agriculture devolved some of its responsibilities to the states. By this time, however, federal and state bureaucracies were well on the way to making the farming business a highly regulated, organized, and subsidized sector of the American economy.[26]

Progressive Era reforms addressed other goals of the Farmers' Alliance and People's party. In 1913, the Federal Reserve Act partially met earlier reform demands for a more flexible and expansive currency. The same year, a constitutional amendment realized Populist demands for a federal income tax. Railroads and telecommunications remained in private hands, but they were subject to closer federal regulation, while local municipalities formed public utility and transit systems. Women's suffrage and Prohibition amendments fulfilled the hopes of many rural reformers of the previous generation. The adoption of the secret ballot, the direct election of senators, and the initiative and the referendum in a number of states—all Farmers' Alliance and People's party demands—indicate the extent to which rural reform, with its hostility to partyism and legislative deal making, both shaped and conformed to Progressive Era political developments.

Macune had helped pioneer the professional farm lobby when he opened the national office of the Farmers' Alliance in Washington, D.C. With access to the national legislature and bureaucracy, he lobbied to elevate farming to the level of a business interest on a par with the other commercial interests making up the modern economy. Thirty years later, farming did indeed represent a powerfully organized business interest. The farm lobby, with the backing of allied politicians, emerged as one of the most effective lobbies in Washington. Marketing associations, the Grange, the American Farm Bureau Federation, and other farm organizations, as Elisabeth Clemens points out, "emerged as central components of a project of bureaucratic state building." At the same time, both Democrats and Republicans ignored the rural vote at their peril. From 1915 to 1920, the North Dakota Nonpartisan League, with its program of state-owned banks and grain elevators, scored a series of political victories and gained influence in a dozen other midwestern and western states. If nothing else, the Nonpartisan League reminded political managers of the power of the farm vote. By the 1920s, the "agricultural bloc" formed one of the country's most politically potent interest groups.[27]

In the South, the white rural voter found new strength with black disfranchisement. In the name of progress and clean government, electoral reforms eliminated the African American vote in the states of the former Confederacy and consolidated the Democratic regime of white supremacy. Within the more secure framework of white primaries and "whites only" politics, rural reformers often successfully competed with the old guard of Democratic rule. Their ranks included former Populists like James (Cyclone) Davis of Texas and Georgia's Tom Watson. Both men gained notoriety in their later careers as arch-Negrophobes and friends of the Ku Klux Klan. They also continued to advocate reforms reflecting earlier Populist commitments. In 1916, Davis won a U.S. congressional seat, and four years later Watson was elected to the U.S. Senate. The late political successes of the likes of Watson and Davis reflect the extent to which the Democratic power structure of white supremacy co-opted and adapted to the impulse of rural reform. This, too, it could be argued, marked a success for the "business principles" of racial exclusion that Macune had articulated for the Farmers' Alliance so many years before.[28]

In short, Charles Macune was right: modernizing agriculture and the modernizing state marched in step—vindicating the principles of the Farmers' Alliance. In the process, however, much had changed. The social base of reform shifted and narrowed. Urban and academic elites claimed the mantle of leadership in rural modernization. The farmer-labor coalition weakened. And broad visions of social reorganization gave way to increasingly limited considerations of agricultural efficiency and social integration. The Populist impulse was spent, giving rise to something else.

The passage of the Federal Reserve Act of 1913 pointed to the direction of the shifting nexus of reform. Aroused to action by the financial panic of 1907, a wide range of banking, industrial, farming, and other business leaders sought to modernize America's archaic and patchwork monetary and financial systems. The banking establishment sought to protect the prerogatives of corporate managers and their control over the new system. The farm lobby and reform Democrats from the West and the South sought to ensure that rural constituencies would be given equitable access. The final product reflected concessions to all parties. Provisions long sought by rural reform included a more elastic currency to facilitate circulation and economic expansion. Later in the twentieth century, the need for such elasticity was well established in financial orthodoxy, although in 1913 some members of the financial establishment continued to denounce the notion as Populist financial heresy. The Federal Reserve Act also provided for a regulated and standardized system of rural lending, making a reality of farmers' demands for access to reliable lines of credit.[29]

In significant ways, however, the Federal Reserve Act represented the eclipse of Populist ideals. The money question, as the Farmers' Alliance Committee on the Monetary System had explained, was ultimately about the "levers of power" and who controlled them.[30] People's party leader Herman Taubeneck had expressed the same idea: "Who shall issue the necessary paper money and control its volume? This is the pivot upon which the money question revolves. It is the pith, the marrow, the alpha and omega of this great subject."[31] To put the levers of control in the hands of the public, the Populists believed, required centralization. It meant replacing the federally chartered and corporately owned banks of the National Banking System with a federal subtreasury system and other institutions centered in the Treasury and Post Office departments in Washington. Alternative proposals circulated within the Farmers' Alliance, including a scheme for regional centralization with a "Cotton States Bank" and a "Grain States Bank" under the direction of regional "Mother Banks." The People's party, however, insisted on centralizing the power to issue money and credit in the national bureaucracy in Washington.[32]

In this regard, the Populists were no less "centralizers" than their corporate opponents. James Livingston argues that only the corporate elite and their intellectual allies favored monetary centralization because they alone represented modernity, whereas the Populist coalition of farmers and laborers stood for premodern "dispersed assets." But simply because the corporate elite claimed that their views were the only ones that conformed to the requirements of modernity did not necessarily make it so. The Populists were equally committed, if not more committed, to centralization as a means to rationalize and modernize the nation's monetary and credit systems. They looked to the Bank of France as a model, a system that was centralized, rationalized, bureaucratic, and modern, and that formed quite independently of corporate industry. If monetary centralization provides a test of modernity, then the Populists were at least a step ahead of most of their adversaries.[33]

In terms of the levers of power, however, the Federal Reserve System bore little resemblance to the Populist ideal. The problem lay not with centralization, but in the structural distribution of control. If anything, the devolution of responsibilities to regional reserve banks only weakened the possibility of public accountability. The requirement that gave bankers and their business allies a majority on the regional boards of directors did the same. Most strikingly, the enormous power conferred on an unelected Federal Board of Directors epitomized how far monetary "science" had evolved toward an exclusive enterprise. Populists believed that the regulation of the money supply could and must be understood by the people whose business interests and livelihoods were affected by it. Expert statisticians and economists provided an essential service. But when properly compiled and presented, "any mechanic" could understand the essential rules governing currency volume, production, and demand. Gathered in their meeting lodges, farmers and laborers could master the "science of money" and thereby wrest the levers of monetary power from the corporate elite. Such was the Populist vision that faded into memory as a handful of financial wizards took the reins at the Federal Reserve.[34]

The Country Life Movement reflected a change in the social dynamics of rural reform. In the 1880s and 1890s, rural modernization was largely driven by rural people. In the first years of the new century, urban people—

government officials, academics, ministers, business leaders—grew alarmed at what they perceived as rural backwardness. The Roosevelt administration set up a Commission on Country Life to explore paths to "better farming, better business, and better living on the farm." The Commission's 1909 report warned that the "incubus of ignorance and inertia is so heavy and widespread" in rural America "as to constitute a national danger." The report pointed to stagnant farm productivity, crude business methods, appalling sanitation and hygiene, overworked women, poor schools, and primitive churches. Country Life reformers looked for remedies. They exuded a sublime self-confidence that through education and regulation, social ills could be healed and those deemed dangerously on the margins could be safely integrated into the progressive society. Much as upper- and middle-class Progressives had set their sights on "cleaning up" the urban slums, now they would also bring modernity to the rural districts.[35]

The recommendations of the Country Life Commission translated into policy that, for the most part, enjoyed support among rural constituencies. The Smith-Lever Act of 1914 formalized a national system of agricultural extension services to help farmers apply scientific and business methods. Federal and state agencies committed resources to fact-finding surveys and to a broad campaign to improve rural homes, schools, and churches. Progressive Era urban reformers focused on many of the goals of rural modernization that rural Populism had articulated a generation before—a fact that was both the greatest strength and the most glaring weakness of the Country Life Movement.[36]

A number of farm reformers resented what they perceived as an act of usurpation. They pointed out that for years farm organizations had pointed to the same rural deficiencies and the same needs for reform the Country Life Commission presented as new discoveries. Nahum J. Bachelder of the national Grange caustically noted that the Grange itself was a "country life commission," and one with greater knowledge of rural conditions. Bachelder suggested that perhaps the Grange should set up a "commission on city life" to study deficiencies in urban life. Farm reformers who had spent their lives toiling in the traces of rural modernization often resented the paternalistic assumptions that inspired the Country Life Movement.[37]

Country Life reformers paid special attention to improving the lot of rural women. Their proposals closely resembled those heard in the Farmer's Alliance in the 1880s and 1890s to modernize women's lives. They sought to place women's work in the home and garden on systematic and business lines, to boost efficiency by equipping kitchens and laundries with the latest appliances, and to improve women's cultural, social, and economic opportunities. However, when rural women and men discussed these issues among themselves in their suballiance meetings, it carried a different meaning from the concerted campaign of university professors, trained ministers, and other perceived outsiders. Despite their best efforts to reassure their rural subjects of their good intentions, the urban-based reformers often appeared as zealous missionaries seeking, as the Country Life Commission put it, "to teach persons how to live."[38] Farmwomen at times responded coolly to expert lectures on hygiene and health. After wearing themselves out scrubbing and cleaning, they had reason to resent the exhortations from learned professors about clean homes and the civilizing effects of "combating dirt."[39]

Urban reformers expressed similarly paternalistic and condescending attitudes toward the rural church. Again, the agrarian reformers of the previous generation had addressed the same deficiencies of the country churches that the Country Life reformers did. They, too, had criticized the "intense sectarian consciousness" that tended to put doctrine and creed above the social needs of the farmers. As the Country Life Commission put it, the country church failed as "effective agents in the social evolution of their communities." The Populists had felt similarly, and many of them had abandoned the church in search of other avenues of spiritual expression. The Country Life Movement, however, looked to reorganize the country church on the urban model, as urban professors and ministers tried to replace the small rural church with a new, modern, and consolidated church.[40]

Predictably, the urban-based campaign for rural modernization opened fissures of distrust. Although rural people tended to support Progressive Era reforms, they also questioned the intentions of academics, urban ministers, and state and federal government agents seeking to refashion their homes, schools, and churches. Skepticism occasionally led to resistance. Historians have noted that the 1925 Tennessee law against teaching evolution in the public schools, for example, was driven less by ideological objections to Darwin than by an effort to reassert majority will over matters of education and religion in the face of intervention by perceived outsiders.[41]

Meanwhile, academics, church officials, and government experts undertook extensive surveys of "rural problems." Among the problems they sought to resolve was why farmers responded with such ambivalence to urban efforts at rural uplift. Part of the explanation lay with farmers' skepticism about the intentions of their self-appointed urban benefactors. At the same time, a working assumption of the burgeoning field of rural sociology was the need to look deeper into the peculiar features of the rural environment and rural mind that led farmers to resist innovation, science, and progress. For modernity to come to the American countryside, it would take the concerted efforts of scientific experts and state agencies to convince the farmers to go along.[42]

As the influence of urban-based elites in rural reform grew, the reform impulse was channeled along a narrower and more exclusive path. The Farmers' Alliance had originally promised to organize cotton, wheat, and other producers as a class. Rich and poor farmers alike would find strength in business organization. Alliance enterprises quickly demonstrated, however, that such organization was far more accessible to prosperous and land-owning farmers than cash-poor and debt-strapped small farmers and tenants. The Progressive Era system of business organization tilted even more sharply in favor of the former, and largely excluded the latter. The broad Populist "confederation of industrial orders" gave way to a narrower coalition of the propertied and the exclusively white.

The Populist coalition placed African Americans in a subordinate and marginalized position. In Populism's wake, however, racial exclusion grew yet more pronounced and menacing. Black farmers and farm laborers were effectively removed from the farm reform agenda with the destruction of the black franchise. In 1908, W. E. B. DuBois, then a sociologist at Atlanta University, wrote to the Country Life Commission to convince the commissioners to investigate the conditions of rural blacks, noting that "the very center of the farmer problem in the South is the Negro Problem."[43] DuBois was ignored. The only mention of the Southern "race problem" in the Country Life Commission was a recommendation to ban the sale of alcohol in rural districts. As DuBois had predicted, the reform agenda in the South was dictated by white scholars, business leaders, and landowners who favored the system of racial caste. The black farmer, representing the most impoverished and distressed section of rural America, was omitted from the deliberations of the commissioners.[44]

In the 1880s and 1890s, the Colored Farmers' Alliance had gained a nominal place within the Populist confederation. In pursuit of black votes, the People's party had made promises of equitable treatment. However, it may be an overstatement to speak of a failure to deliver in this regard, as white Populists never offered much to their black counterparts in the first place. By the turn of the century, white rural reformers, including erstwhile Populists, counted among the worst antiblack demagogues. Meanwhile, the separate and unequal pattern of rural association, reinforced in the previous decades by the Farmers' Alliance, would leave black farmers and tenants especially vulnerable, as farm organizations and federal and state farm agencies systematically denied protections to African Americans.

Deprived of his constituency by the poll tax and white primary, the former black Populist John Rayner abandoned hope in the political process and devoted himself to black education and uplift. He worked as the financial agent of the Farmers' Improvement Society, an organization devoted to improved farming methods, purchasing homes, and fostering cooperative stores. Rayner also turned to Social Darwinist race theory to make sense of the African American predicament. The scientific ordering of society, as he understood it, produced deep inequalities. "The inequality of man," he observed, "is the axle upon which the restless wheel of evolution turns man continually toward the perfect and sublime." What the race needed was a mechanism to ensure that the superior blacks would supplant the inferior ones. He found that mechanism in eugenics, otherwise known as social hygiene. Where eugenics education failed, he proposed state intervention "to sterilize all physical and mental derelicts."[45]

Rayner's newfound enthusiasm for social hygiene corresponded to similar ideas expressed in the 1880s and 1890s by Mary Elizabeth Lease, Bettie Gay, George Bowen, and other white Populists. They shared common interests in racial betterment through the selective improvement of the racial stock. But the context in which these ideas were pursued underscored the gulf separating the black experience from that of white reformers. White Populists had embraced notions of social hygiene with a confidence in unlimited possibilities and an abiding faith that their superior offspring would represent an ever-powerful majority within the "cooperative commonwealth" of the future. In contrast, Rayner grasped at eugenics within the claustrophobia of frustrated dreams. At the dawn of the new century, as the tyranny of white supremacy shut off other avenues of reform, or made them overly dangerous, he found in eugenics what appeared to be a biologically certain and a relatively safe, if narrow, channel for black uplift.[46]

Populism had promised considerably more to the labor movement. But for the labor Populists, employer blacklists and court injunctions destroyed their organizations and their hopes. The corporate and business elite displayed an obsessive hostility to broad-based labor organization, an attitude that carried deep into the twentieth century. The First World War brought signs of change, with war administrators granting the railway brotherhoods and the American Federation of Labor a degree of legitimacy as a labor interest, but within much the same narrow business frameworks as the farmers' interest. The fierce suppression of the postwar industrial union drives, however, reinforced that much remained the same.

The presence of coal miners, railroad employees, and other workers within the Populist coalition partly explains why so many upper- and middle-class Americans responded to the reform movement of the 1890s with such apocalyptic dread. The Populists may have embraced Eugene Debs of the American Railway Union as an upstanding citizen and advocate of progressive reform, but many urban and wealthy observers viewed this embrace as proof that Populism would deliver the country into the hands of anarchistic train wreckers and dynamite bombers. Although such unreasoned anxieties about the Populist threat focused on the labor movement, they were not restricted to it. It was one thing for the well educated and well born to advocate rural modernization and market regulation. But when ordinary farmers and laborers advanced their own demands on these questions, no matter how similar in content, it provoked deep apprehension among urban elites.

The demise of Populism constricted the social base of reform. Instead of farmers, coal miners, and other poorly educated women and men gathering in lodges and meeting halls for self-education and self-mobilization, the initiative passed to expert women and men, with professional training and administrative posts. Instead of relatively inclusive and expansive social visions that attracted a wide spectrum of nonconformist activists, the goals of reform also narrowed. This left some former Populists searching for alternatives. Bettie Gay, Anna Ferry Smith, Eugene Debs, Henry Vincent, Clarence Nugent (Thomas Nugent's son), Julius Wayland, and other Populists looked to socialism. In the early twentieth century, former Populist strongholds in Texas, Kansas, Oklahoma, California, and elsewhere provided fertile recruiting grounds for the new Socialist party.[47]

These veterans of the Farmers' Alliance and the People's party looked to radical solutions because Charles Macune was partly mistaken. Populism had indeed failed to the extent that it had encompassed an alternative vision of the future society. The two visions clashed. The one embraced by the corporate and urban elites largely triumphed by the turn of the century. The elites won because they controlled the political process, the pulpits, and the press. They had the labor spies, blacklists, access to the courts, and other means of repression against their opponents. They also had the power to incorporate much of Populist reform into their own more constricted agenda. The twentieth-century social order was never a given. Instead, it was made, shaped by competing visions of what the modern should be.

The Progressive reformers of the early twentieth century saw themselves uplifting the human condition, shaping popular modes of thought, and engineering the society of the future. The efforts of the Country Life Movement to remake rural life reflected a vision that agrarian scholar James C. Scott describes in a broader context as "high modernism." The concept of "high modernism," Scott writes, is "best conceived as a strong (one might even say muscle-bound) version of the beliefs in scientific and technical progress that were associated with industrialization in Western Europe and in North America from roughly 1830 until World War I." It displayed "a supreme self-confidence about continued lineal progress" and "increasing control over nature." "High modernism," Scott concludes, was a "sweeping vision of how the benefits of technical and scientific progress might be applied—usually through the state—in every field of human activity."[48]

Bringing Scott's concept to bear on American rural history, Deborah Fitzgerald writes that "high modernist" urban leaders of the 1920s and 1930s persuaded reluctant farmers to "become modern." By her account agricultural college professors, government agents, bankers, and other business leaders sought "to bring agriculture kicking and screaming into the modern world." In other words, modernity was imposed from the outside on a largely static rural environment.[49]

Fitzgerald's narrative poses a number of outstanding questions, especially about earlier developments. What does it say about late nineteenth-century social conflict and the historic role of Populism and similar movements? Would the term "high modernism" apply to the Populist vision, at least as Scott defines it? No less than their industrial counterparts, Leonidas Polk, Charles Macune, Mary Elizabeth Lease, Marion Cannon, Reuben Kolb, Herman Taubeneck, Marion Butler, Thomas Nugent, Marion Todd, William Peffer, and a host of other Populist leaders displayed a "muscle-bound" belief in progress, science, and technology. Their "evolutionary imagination" gave them enormous self-confidence that the course of progress was both lineal and knowable. They believed in the human capacity, through government action and otherwise, to harness nature and cure a broad range of society's ills. And they acted accordingly as agricultural commissioners, politicians, state appointees, and executives of powerful farm organizations.

Yet, if the Populist leaders counted among the "high modernists" of their day, they were of a special type. Unlike the Country Life Movement of the early twentieth century, rural Populism grew from rural roots. These roots were evident in the network of men and women—Populism's "organic intellectuals"—that sustained the movement's systems of lectures and rural newspapers and brought a modernizing vision to farmers' homes and meeting lodges. Where the Country Life Movement looked to improve the lot of others, the Populists were modernizers from within. They spoke in the language of self-help and sought improvements on the principle of self-activation.

The Populists incorporated into their modernizing vision mass organizations enrolling millions of common working people. In late nineteenth- and twentieth-century Europe, Asia, Latin America, and Africa "high modernists" of various types—socialists, radicals, nationalists, populists—built their modern systems on labor, peasant, and other mass organizations. In the United States, the Populists took extraordinary strides toward making mass organizations of farmers and laborers the mainspring of their vision of social reconstruction. The Farmers' Alliance and associated "industrial orders" gave flesh to the majoritarian, if not entirely democratic, principles that Populism pursued.

Where the Country Life leaders may have felt most comfortable in the university laboratory or business board meeting, the Macunes and Polks of Populism were at home in gatherings of people with callused hands and sunburned necks. Manual labor was part of the ethos that shaped the possibilities for a broad and inclusive coalition. Many rural Populists disapproved of strikes and labor boycotts and erected walls of hostility against immigrant and Chinese workers in particular. Yet the emergence of labor Populism within the ranks of railway employees, miners, and other sections of the working class revealed that Populism had the potential of an expansive organizational alliance.

As social engineers, the Populists were second to none in terms of earnest commitment and scope of vision. The Populist movement contained too many diverse and contradictory elements to speak of a single Populist social blueprint. Some of these elements, such as Bellamy's Nationalism, represented influential mental constructs more than a practical system of reform. Other elements were not unique to the Populists at all but were broadly pursued by modernizers among business, academic, and political leaders. This was especially true in regard to race, with all of the ominous implications that entailed.

Nonetheless, the sum of Populist strivings leaves a distinct outline of what their "cooperative commonwealth" might have looked like. In regard to the nation's business, the Populists hoped to take the materials at hand—the latest technologies and organizational systems—and use them to rationalize markets and regulate and centralize the channels of commerce and finance. Their vision involved a complex and dynamic combination of public and private, cooperative and corporate, municipal and nationalized property relations. Progressive Era models contained elements of this complexity. However, the Populist version was more flexible in terms of encroachments on private and corporate prerogatives. This included a major role for the self-organization of labor within the management and structure of the economy, a role that American corporate managers would fiercely—and successfully—resist.

The Populists wanted an active government to ensure fair access to the benefits of modernity. By way of the referendum and the initiative and other political reforms, Populists sought to reshape government as an agency of the majority rather than of the corporate and wealthy minority. A federal income tax on high incomes was part of the Populist goal of checking the concentration of wealth and spreading the abundance of farm and factory to those who produced it. But there was a reason why so much of the Populist imagination focused on publicly owned and subsidized systems of postal delivery, telecommunications, railways, and the perfection of the public system of education. The Populist republic would squarely and equitably place even the rural "clodhopper" on the national and international grid of modern culture and knowledge.

For the 1892 electoral canvass, Thomas Watson published a campaign book under the title *Not a Revolt; It Is a Revolution*. Populism would usher in "a new order of things," "re-mark the lines of life," and bring a complete "revolution in the old systems."[50] In the fever of electoral warfare, both friends and foes of the third-party movement tended to accept similar terms: for better or for worse, a Populist victory at the polls meant a momentous transformation of American society. Through the prism of time, it is apparent that a Populist triumph would have been less of a revolution than advertised. A Populist United States would have taken evolutionary steps to reform and rationalize the capitalist system. Perhaps it would have placed American institutions on paths akin to those of Canada or even Denmark— significant changes but hardly the overthrow of existing conditions. Yet, Populism did indeed represent something momentous. It mobilized millions of ordinary men and women in an effort to steer the political and economic institutions of an increasingly modern, technologically sophisticated, and globally connected society. The significance of this movement lay in the act of trying.

NOTES

INTRODUCTION

1. *Chicago Times*, July 14, 1894.

2. Woodward, *Agrarian Rebel*, 138.

3. *St. Louis Globe-Democrat*, cited in *Caucasian*, December 1, 1892.

4. Turner, "The Significance of the Frontier in American History," 32.

5. Hicks, *The Populist Revolt*; Parrington, *Main Currents*; Woodward, *Agrarian Rebel*, and *Origins of the New South*.

6. Hofstadter, *The Age of Reform*, 12–22, 46–47; Ferkiss, "Populist Influences on American Fascism"; Lipset and Raab, *The Politics of Unreason*, 90–99. Peter Novick writes: "No interpretative tendency of the 1950s was more typical of the general movement of intellectual opinion, or reverberated more widely throughout the culture, than the sharp downward turn in the historical reputation of the Populists." See Novick, *That Noble Dream*, 337–41.

7. Woodward, "Populist Heritage and the Intellectual," in *The Burden of Southern History*, 141–66; Rogin, *The Intellectuals and McCarthy*; Pollack, *The Populist Response*; Nugent, *The Tolerant Populists*.

8. Goodwyn, *Democratic Promise*, 612–14, and *Populist Moment*, ix and xxi.

9. Thompson, *The Making of the English Working Class*; Calhoun, *The Question of Class Struggle*; Hahn, *The Roots of Southern Populism*; Palmer, *"Man over Money"*; Thomas, *Alternative America*. The analytical treatment of Populism rests on a wider literature about the nineteenth-century market revolution, including Sellers, *The Market Revolution*; Stokes and Conway, *The Market Revolution in America*; Hahn and Prude, *Countryside in the Age of Capitalist Transformation*; Clark, *The Roots of Rural Capitalism*; Merrill, "Cash Is Good to Eat"; Henretta, "Families and Farms." For limitations of the market revolution as an interpretative construct, see Bushman, "Markets and Composite Farms." For a treatment of how the concept of republicanism has influenced recent historical thinking about American history, see Daniel T. Rogers, "Republicanism."

10. Mattson, "The Historian as a Social Critic," par 6; Lasch, "The Populist Campaign against 'Improvement,'" in *The True and Only Heaven*, 168–225; and, "Communitarianism or Populism," in *The Revolt of the Elites*, 92–114; and, "Populism." Lasch's critiques of the culture of development and materialism influenced President Jimmy Carter, and Lasch visited the White House prior to Carter's famous "Crisis of Confidence" or "Malaise" speech of July 15, 1979. See Horowitz, *Jimmy Carter and the Energy Crisis of the 1970s*, 17, 24, 67–72, 157–61. Louis Menand discusses Lasch's conception of populism as the antidote to modernity and progress in "Christopher Lasch's Quarrel with Liberalism," in Menand, *American Studies*, 210–15.

11. Lasch, *The True and Only Heaven*, 213; Turner, "Understanding the Populists," 371; Thelen, *Paths of Resistance*, 4, 7. Leon Fink, referring to the Knights of Labor in the 1880s, makes two relevant observations. First, he takes issue with views that subordinate "the creative political dimension of social movements to cultural resistance," thereby exaggerating "the purely defensive aspects of movement building." Second, he warns of the failure in recent social history "to distinguish between the traditions upon which a movement draws and traditionalism itself." See Leon Fink, *Workingmen's Democracy*, 220.

12. Norman Pollack registers a significant dissent to the view of the Populists as antimoderns. "The shift from modernization from above to modernization from below," Pollack writes, "was the main paradigmatic contribution of Populists to capitalist development." See Pollack, *The Humane Economy*, 66. However, Pollack's analytical focus is on other questions, especially on the humane and democratic features of Populism. For another intriguing dissent, see Lustig, "Populism and the Corporation," in *Corporate Liberalism*, 39–46.

13. Cronon, *Nature's Metropolis*, xv–xix; Rebecca Edwards, *New Spirits*; Danbom, *Born in the Country*, 64–85. The term *modern* is being used here in a different sense than the term *modernist* or *modernism*. Although the distinctions are often ambiguous, *modernist* is frequently associated with a twentieth-century cultural movement that challenged epistemological and moral certainties, whereas *modern* refers to the process of modernization from the traditional society of peasant agriculture to the capitalist society of social differentiation, mobility, commerce, industry, and innovative science and technology. For perspectives on modernism in American life, see Cotkin, *Reluctant Modernism*; Singal, *Modernist Culture in America*.

14. Berman, *All That Is Solid*, 90–91; *National Economist*, May 3, 1890. See also Keith, *Country People*; Stromquist, *A Generation of Boomers*. Wilma Dunaway's research indicates that southern Appalachia, often portrayed as one of the last holdouts of a self-sufficient society isolated from the market, was well integrated with the market and the Atlantic economy even prior to the Civil War. See Dunaway, *The First American Frontier*, 1–13.

15. Cronon, *Nature's Metropolis*; Danbom, *Born in the Country*, 83. Deborah Fitzgerald points to the widespread use of tractors in the mid-twentieth century as the marker at which American farmers "become modern." See Fitzgerald, "Accounting for Change," in Stock and Johnston, *The Countryside in the Age of the Modern State*, 189–212. Tractor

power was surely an important step in the modernization of farming, but it was a step in a long historical process.

16. Berman, *All That Is Solid*, 95–96. Eric Foner writes that modernity "involves such basic changes in the structure of a society as rapid economic development, urbanization, industrialization, the creation of an integrated national economic and political structure, and generally, the spread of market-oriented capitalist economic relations and of mental attitudes viewing continuous social change as natural and desirable." See Eric Foner, *Politics and Ideology in the Age of the Civil War*, 20. The last of these, the Populist mental attitudes toward change and innovation, are the principal subjects of this study.

17. Tracy, "Rise and Doom of the Populist Party."

18. In emphasizing the movement's moral culture, Bruce Palmer writes that the Populists "rarely used the words 'economic' or 'economy.'" See Palmer, *"Man over Money,"* 14. This claim is mistaken, as the Populists often made economics and the economy (in those and equivalent terms) their primary topics of discussion, and titled one of their flagship publications *The National Economist*. Although only a small passage in Palmer's valuable book, the failure to address Populist ideas on their own stated terms is a weakness of the recent scholarship. For a concise discussion of the "cultural turn," see Sewell, "The Concept(s) of Culture."

19. Kammen, *Mystic Chords of Memory*, 46–48; Norris, *The Octopus*. In his study of the views of Kansas Populists toward the railroads, Thomas Frank notes: "Many Populist leaders perceived their efforts as part of an international and inexorable movement of social progress." See Frank, "The Leviathan with Tentacles of Steel," 52. In his 1932 work, *The Idea of Progress*, John B. Bury explained that the idea required "an act of faith," just as belief in Providence or immortality, and counted with other acts of faith in shaping human conduct (see pp. 1–4). In his introduction to Bury's work, Charles Beard noted that "those who imagine that the idea of progress was lately discovered by the promoters of business enterprise" would do well to study the profound influence that the idea exerted on the social and political history of eighteenth- and nineteenth-century Europe and America (see prefatory note, ix–xi).

20. Henry George, *Progress and Poverty*; Garland, *A Spoil of Office*, 249.

21. In her study of "Agricultural Innovation and Modernity in the Lower South, 1730–1815," Joyce Chaplin argues that notions of innovation and progress were shared by both the plantation elite of the tidewater and white farm settlers of the interior. See Chaplin, *An Anxious Pursuit*, 165–84. See also May, *The Enlightenment in America*; Cohen, *Science and the Founding Fathers*; Brown, "Modernization and the Modern Personality in Early America, 1600–1865"; Craven, "The Agricultural Reformers in the Ante-Bellum South"; Palmer, *"Man over Money,"* 199–221. In this work, Palmer examines the Jeffersonian and Jacksonian influence on Populist expression.

22. Bloch, *Historian's Craft*, 35.

23. For the Populist critique of applying the doctrine of "struggle for existence" to justify oppression and inequality, see Clanton, *Kansas Populism*, 67–68. The phrase "evolutionary imagination" is taken from Mark Pittenger's excellent study of the influence

of evolutionary theory on American Socialism. See Pittenger, *American Socialists and Evolutionary Thought*, 64. See also Hofstadter, *Social Darwinism in American Thought*; Bannister, *Social Darwinism*; Numbers, *Darwinism Comes to America*.

24. At the St. Louis Conference, each of the "Confederated Organizations" received twenty-five votes plus an additional vote for every ten thousand members. See the *Advocate* (Topeka), December 23, 1891; Hicks, *The Populist Revolt*, 211–12, 225–26; McMath, *American Populism*, 160.

25. Ostler, *Prairie Populism*. This work provides convincing evidence that practical considerations of party alignments and prospects for electoral success were the key variables in the proportion of the Populist vote in Kansas, Nebraska, and Iowa.

26. Lasch, *The True and Only Heaven*, 218.

27. For an excellent regional study that documents the complexity of Populism, see Ayers, *The Promise of the New South*, 214–82.

28. Hicks, *The Populist Revolt*, 337. See also Robert W. Larson, *Populism in the Mountain West*, 3–16, 147–59. Larson demonstrates that the Populists in the mountain states were part of the "mainstream movement," and were not mainly driven by the silver issue. For a classic study of urban and labor Populism, see Destler, *American Radicalism*; Clinch, *Urban Populism*. Robert McMath's *American Populism* provides a good overview of Populism's extension, although it leaves the "shadow movement" concept partly intact.

29. Brown, *Knowledge Is Power*, 2; *National Economist*, November 11, 1890.

30. The educational historian Rush Welter contends the ideal of progressive education proved a solvent of Populist protest, bringing farmers into the progressive consensus. See Welter, *Popular Education*, 166–68.

31. Scholars have argued that the concerns of Populist women were separate from the issues associated with the middle-class women's movement. Christopher Lasch wrote that feminism—with its focus on women's autonomy, economic independence, the egalitarian family, voting rights, and modern science—constituted a class program directed against ordinary women and men like the Populists. See *Women and the Common Life*, 166–68. Michael Goldberg's fine study of reform women in Kansas draws more careful distinctions between rural and middle-class women. See Goldberg, *An Army of Women*, 163, 182, 207–9. In 1975, Julie Roy Jeffrey wrote an article in *Feminist Studies*, "Women in the Southern Farmers' Alliance," that linked women's participation in the movement with their strivings for a more modern life. Recently, Laura Lovett has explored this theme in her study of women, reform, and eugenics. See Lovett, "Conceiving the Future"; see also Buhle, *Women and American Socialism, 1780–1920*, 82–90; Wagner, "Farms, Families, and Reform"; Watkins, *Rural Democracy*; Marti, *Women of the Grange*; Paula C. Baker, *The Moral Frameworks of Public Life*; Osterud, *Bonds of Community*; Barthelme, *Women in the Texas Populist Movement*. For important works on Populism that have little discussion of the role of women, see Hicks, *The Populist Revolt*; Hofstadter, *The Age of Reform*; Goodwyn, *Democratic Promise*; Palmer, *"Man over Money"*; Hahn, *The Roots of Southern Populism*.

32. Dunning, *Farmers' Alliance History*, 183. The Populist critique of monopoly is often mistakenly identified with such works as Lloyd's *Wealth against Commonwealth*, an exposé of the Standard Oil Company that generated little public attention when it was published in 1894 only to be rediscovered by later generations of muckrakers and trust busters. For the public's response to *Wealth Against Commonwealth*, see Jernigan, *Henry Demarest Lloyd*, 63. It should be noted that Populists often expressed skepticism about trust busting (as opposed to public ownership). The Populist editor Julius Wayland, for example, opposed laws that "would compel a great trust" to break up its operations. "Make no laws against the present monopolies," he urged, but "every monopoly will have to be met by a counter monopoly of the people." See "Good Monopolies," in *Coming Nation*, January 27, 1894.

33. Robert McMath contends that the "movement culture" of the Farmers' Alliance emerged out of the premodern traditions of rural self-sufficiency, not the later cooperatives. See McMath, "Sandy Land and Hogs," in Hahn and Prude, *Countryside in the Age of Capitalist Transformation*; Parsons et al., "The Role of Cooperatives."

34. Woeste makes a strong case for interpreting agricultural cooperation as an effort to adapt corporate principles to farmers' needs, although she inexplicably separates the Farmers' Alliance and the Populists from this effort. See Woeste, *The Farmers' Benevolent Trust*, 1–12, 31, 35.

35. Sanders, *Roots of Reform*, 6, 387–88, 410.

36. *Journal of the Knights of Labor*, February 6, 1890; John, "Governmental Institutions as Agents of Change"; Crenson, *The Federal Machine*; Carpenter, "State Building"; Kernell, "Rural Free Delivery." The frequently repeated misconception that Populist protest took the form of mass actions analogous to the labor, civil rights, or antiwar movements of other eras, with their celebrated sit-ins and street demonstrations, belies the Populist focus on education, lobbying, and the ballot. An exception, for example, was Jacob Coxey's march on Washington, in which unemployed marchers demanded passage of a federal "Good Roads" bill and specific currency reforms. The Coxey march, however, was criticized for its "irregular methods" by Tom Watson, Ignatius Donnelly, John Davis, and other leading Populists who believed the ballot was the exclusive means of redress. See *Chicago Searchlight*, June 29, 1894; Ridge, *Ignatius Donnelly*, 329; "Government by Multitude," in John Davis Scrapbooks; *Nonconformist* (Indianapolis), May 31, 1894.

37. The business historian Kenneth Lipartito notes how nineteenth-century reform movements sought to recast society in line with "science, efficiency, and reason," and in the process developed the institutional hierarchies and "bureaucratic values and structures" that would be shared by modern corporate capitalism. Although he does not focus on Populism, it fits the pattern that Lipartito describes. See Lipartito, "The Utopian Corporation," 94–97, 107.

38. Nugent, *The Tolerant Populists*; Woodward, *Agrarian Rebel*, 219–22, 239–40; Woodward, *Origins of the New South*, 254–58; Goodwyn, *Democratic Promise*, 299; Goodwyn, "Populist Dreams and Negro Rights." For less optimistic views of Populist racial attitudes

and practices, see Shaw, *The Wool Hat Boys*, 3, 54, 87; Litwack, *Trouble in Mind*, 372; Hahn, *A Nation under Our Feet*, 425, 432; Saxton, *The Indispensable Enemy*, 237.

39. Barbara Fields makes the important clarification that popular dissent from the ruling Democratic planter elite in the South did not necessarily mean dissent from white supremacy. She notes that the distinction between "ruling class" and "redneck" racial ideologies bore its practical significance for African Americans. "But practical choice and historical explanation are not the same," since "historical analysis cannot distinguish these positions as 'more' and 'less' racist." See Fields, "Ideology and Race in American History," 160.

40. McBride, "Coal Miners"; Brody, "Market Unionism in America: The Case of Coal," in *In Labor's Cause*, 131–74.

41. Woodward, *Agrarian Rebel*, 138; Thompson, "The Transforming Power of the Cross," in *The Making of the English Working Class*, 350–400; Gutman, "Protestantism and the American Labor Movement," in *Work, Culture, and Society*, 79–117; Thomas, *Alternative America*, 364–65.

42. Cator, "Millionaires or Morals?" 11.

43. Kazin, *The Populist Persuasion*, 3; Nunberg, "The Curious Fate of Populism"; Raines, "Winning the Populism PR War"; Wilentz, "Populism Redux." Robert Johnston also treats populism with a small *p* as a constant of American political life, from the anti-Federalists of the late eighteenth century down to the present. In his insightful study of middle-class politics during the Progressive Era, Johnston identifies populist democracy with a type of middle-class anticapitalism and radicalism whose political influence is still felt in the first years of the twenty-first century. See Johnston, *The Radical Middle Class*, xiv, 87–89; 258, 266–77.

The following pages may shed light on the historical complexities of middle-class politics. However, the late nineteenth-century Populists with a capital *P* are mainly described as reformers rather than as radicals because of their broad commitment to evolutionary reform.

44. Berk, *Alternative Tracks*; Sklar, *The Corporate Reconstruction of American Capitalism*; Livingston, *Origins of the Federal Reserve System*.

CHAPTER 1

1. Dunning, "Unrecorded History of the Alliance," in *Farmers' Alliance History*, 10–19; Garvin and Daws, *History of the National Farmers' Alliance*, 14. Several related organizations used the name Farmers' Alliance, including the Colored Farmers' Alliance and the Chicago-based National Farmers' Alliance or Northern Alliance. In this work, the term *Farmers' Alliance*, unless indicated otherwise, refers to the National Farmers' Alliance and Industrial Union or Southern Alliance, which was the largest and most influential organization within the Populist coalition.

2. Dunning, *Farmers' Alliance History*, 13.

3. Turner, "The Significance of the Frontier"; Hofstadter, *The Progressive Historians*, 76.

4. Shannon, *The Farmer's Last Frontier*, 51; Danbom, *Born in the Country*, 132–33; Fite, *Cotton Fields No More*, 15; Chaplin, *An Anxious Pursuit*, 25.

5. Dunning, *Farmers' Alliance History*, 7–8, 13.

6. Macune, "Farmers' Alliance," 3–4; Dunning, *Farmers' Alliance History*, 11; Morgan, *History of the Wheel and Alliance*, 93; McMath, *Populist Vanguard*, 8; Garvin and Daws, *History of the National Farmers' Alliance*, 16, 27.

7. Robert McMath, "Sandy Land and Hogs in the Timber," in Hahn and Prude, *The Countryside in the Age of Capitalist Transformation*, 205–29; see also McMath, *American Populism*, 44–46.

8. William Norton and Leonard Guelke point out that along agricultural frontiers, primitive and subsistence methods, rather than perpetuating a "noneconomic" way of life, reflected a brief interlude, "for good economic reasons," before farmers succeeded in forging closer ties to markets. This observation bears on farmers' strivings in the Cross Timbers. See Norton and Guelke, "Frontier Agriculture?" See also Conzen, *Frontier Farming in an Urban Shadow*. The term *booster* often carries the pejorative connotation of the shrewd speculator. Here it is used only to connote the culture and practice of promotion as an essential part of the late nineteenth-century world of settlement and development. See Jocelyn Wills, *Boosters, Hustlers, and Speculators*, 3–10; Simpson, "Boosterism in the West." Robert McMath describes the Populist movement in California and Florida as "a mix of boosterism and social criticism," yet portrays the movement elsewhere as "fundamentally at odds" with boosters. See McMath, *American Populism*, 46, 48–49, 82, 98, 139.

9. Campbell, *Gone to Texas*, 311; population statistics for Jack, Parker, and Wise counties, in U.S. Department of the Interior, *Report on Population at the Eleventh Census*, Part I, 41–42; Witherspoon, "Populism in Jack County, Texas," 69; Fite, *The Farmers' Frontier*, 200; Danbom, *Born in the Country*, 147.

10. R. D. Holt, "The Fence Cutting War," 71–75, 79; *Rural Citizen*, February 14, 1884.

11. Texas People's Party Platform, August 1891, in Winkler, *Platforms of Political Parties in Texas*, 296; "St. Louis Demands, December 1889," "Ocala Demands, December 1890," "Platform of the Northern Alliance," "Cincinnati Platform, May 1891," "Omaha Platform, July 1892," in Hicks, *The Populist Revolt*, appendixes A, B, D, and F, 428, 431, 433, 438, 445; *Kansas Farmer*, February 9, 1887; Shannon, *The Farmers' Last Frontier*, 203–6, 217; Cochrane, *The Development of American Agriculture*, 87–91; *Junction City Union*, April 26, 1884, in Malin, *Winter Wheat*, 119–20, also 29–31.

12. *Caucasian*, April 25, 1889.

13. Miller, *Oklahoma Populism*, 38–39, 62; Wickett, *Contested Territory*, 140; *Kansas Farmer*, November 29, 1888.

14. *National Economist*, April 13, 1889; "The Agricultural Wheel," in Dunning, *Farmers' Alliance History*, 197–218.

15. Benjamin Heber Johnson, "Red Populism?" in Stock and Johnston, *The Countryside in the Age of the Modern State*, 15–37; Garland, "Glimpses of the Navajo Indians," "A Typical Indian Scare: The Cheyenne Trouble," in *Observations on the American Indian*, 83–87, 145–57 and, "Drifting Crane"; McGerr, *A Fierce Discontent*, 204–5; *Kansas Farmer*, November 29, 1888.

16. Robert W. Larson, *New Mexico Populism*, 35–47, and *Populism in the Mountain West*, 103–15.

17. Witherspoon, "Populism in Jack County, Texas," 58, 72–83, 169–77; *Rural Citizen*, March 6, 1884, April 10, 1884.

18. *Rural Citizen*, May 4, 13, 20, 1886. Robert McMath, describes the arrival of the railroad in Cross Timbers as a "distressing development," part of the intrusion of the market on the self-sufficiency of the yeoman farmer. However, farmers at the time understood that the success of their farming operations depended on proximity to the railroad. Farmers made their decisions of where to settle accordingly, and in districts without railroads, such as Cross Timbers, campaigned to attract them. See McMath "Sandy Land and Hogs in the Timber," in Hahn and Prude, *Countryside in the Age of Capitalist Transformation*, 219.

19. *Southern Mercury*, May 31, 1888; *Rural Californian*, January 21, 1887; Noblin, *Agrarian Crusader*, 91–95, 114–15, 155; Fite, *The Farmers' Frontier*, 24–27, 142–43, 164, 199; Rogin and Stover, *Political Change in California*, 15–16; Danbom, *Born in the Country*, 145.

20. Kellie, "Personal" and "Political Memoir" in *A Prairie Populist*, 8–10, 148–50.

21. Frank, "The Leviathan with Tentacles of Steel," 41, 47; *Kansas Farmer*, January 5, 12, February 9, May 26, 1887. Gene Clanton explains that Kansans "in all walks of life" recognized the centrality of railroads to the success of industry and agriculture, "and practically everybody became, in one way or another, railroad promoters." See Clanton, *Kansas Populism*, 18–19, 38–39.

22. Noblin, *Agrarian Crusader*, 76–80; see also Beckel, "Roots of Reform," 183–97; Ayers, *The Promise of the New South*, 223–24.

23. Mayo, *Southern Women*, 26; see also McMath, *Populist Vanguard*, 66–67; Ayers, *The Promise of the New South*, 220.

24. Hofstadter, *The Progressive Historians*, 125.

25. Dunning, *Farmers' Alliance History*, 8.

26. Greene, *Pure and Simple Politics*, 19, 29–36; Gompers, *Seventy Years*, 104–6.

27. Macune Jr., "Biographical Sketch of C. W. Macune"; Garvin and Daws, *History of the National Farmers Alliance*, 146–47; Morgan, *History of the Wheel and Alliance*, 298–300.

28. *Burnett Bulletin*, November 7, 1874, in Macune Jr., "Biographical Sketch of C. W. Macune."

29. Garvin and Daws, *History of the National Farmers Alliance*, 45–47.

30. McMath, "Alliance Membership in Perspective," in *Populist Vanguard*, appendix B, 164–66.

31. Schwartz, "An Estimate of the Size of the Southern Farmers' Alliance, 1884–1890"; Morgan, *History of the Wheel and Alliance*, 72–73, 134; Noblin, *Agrarian Crusader*, 205–6.

32. McMath, *Populist Vanguard*, 77–89; Argersinger, *The Limits of Agrarian Radicalism*, 40–43, and *Populism and Politics*, 22–23; McNall, *The Road to Rebellion*, 238–43; Robert W. Larson, *Populism in the Mountain West*, 27–28; *National Economist*, October 11, 1890; Walters, "The Period of the Populist Party," 102–4. Jeffrey Ostler notes that the state Farmers' Alliances often inflated their membership figures. For example, the claim of one hundred thousand members of the Kansas Alliance in the spring of 1890 was probably closer to ninety thousand members. See "Farmers' Alliance Membership," in Ostler, *Prairie Populism*, appendix A, 181–83.

33. *Western Rural*, January 10, 31, February 16, May 2, 1891; see also Roy V. Scott, *The Agrarian Movement in Illinois*, 3.

34. *National Economist*, April 27, 1889; Garvin and Daws, *History of the National Farmers Alliance*, 45–47.

35. McMath, *Populist Vanguard*, appendix A, 161–63; Steelman, *The North Carolina Farmers' Alliance*, 18. The term *local intellectuals* comes from Mallon, *Peasant and Nation*, 12, 294–95.

36. McCabe, *History of the Grange Movement*, 431; *National Economist*, March 30, 1889.

37. Message of Acting President, C. W. Macune, Proceedings of Farmers' State Alliance of Texas, Waco, January 1887, in Dunning, *Farmers' Alliance History*, 49.

38. President Macune's message at National Farmers' Alliance at Shreveport, October 12, 1887, in Dunning, *Farmers' Alliance History*, 70.

39. Noblin, *Agrarian Crusader*, 208; *Caucasian*, April 11, 1889.

40. *Southern Mercury*, July 24, 1888.

41. Ayers, *The Promise of the New South*, 234.

42. Knights of Labor, Proceedings of the General Assembly (1886), in Kremm and Neal, "Challenges to Subordination," 254; *Galveston Daily News*, January 7, 1886.

43. *Austin Statesmen*, April 7, July 31, 1886; *Dallas Morning News*, July 1, 2, 4, 16, 18, 19, 1886; *Town and Country*, June 26, 1886; *Times-Democrat*, March 26, 1886, in Ruth A. Allen Labor Movement in Texas Collection.

44. *Journal of United Labor*, June 11, 1887, in Ali, "Black Populism," 53.

45. Morgan, *History of the Wheel and Alliance*, 72–73; Hahn, *A Nation under Our Feet*, 414–15.

46. *Rural Citizen*, April 29, 1886.

47. Morgan, *History of the Wheel and Alliance*, 72–73, 134; Ali, "Black Populism," 71–73.

48. In his discussion of urban associations, Jason Kaufman observes that the spread of fraternal orders in the late nineteenth century "promoted a system of social differentiation in America in which voluntarism, brotherhood, and mutual aid became bywords for segregation, not integration." See Kaufman, *For the Common Good?* 6. Although

Kaufman's work focuses on urban segregation by religion, language, and gender, the point bears special relevance to rural race relations.

49. Centennial Alliance Minute Book, March 16, 1894; William F. Holmes, "The Arkansas Cotton Pickers' Strike," 194.

50. *Progressive Farmer*, February 5, 1889, January 21, 1890.

51. McLaurin, *The Knights of Labor in the South*, 141–42; see also McMath, "Southern White Farmers." Northern and western blacks also looked at the Farmers' Alliance with suspicion. Commenting on the Alliance's whites-only clause, a black editor in Topeka, Kansas, noted that it made plain "to every colored man that his Alliance intends to plot the oppression of colored Farmers." See *American Citizen*, August 11, 1888, in Thomas C. Cox, *Blacks in Topeka*, 126.

52. McMath, *Populist Vanguard*, 44–45; Ayers, *The Promise of the New South*, 235; Richard Manning Humphrey, "History of the Colored Farmers' National Alliance," in Dunning, *Farmers' Alliance History*, 288–92.

53. *National Economist*, January 25, 1890.

54. *Progressive Farmer*, August 26, 1890.

55. *Southern Mercury*, April 19, 1888.

56. *National Economist*, March 14, 1889.

57. Hahn, *A Nation under Our Feet*, 417.

58. Gaither, *Blacks and the Populist Revolt*, 63.

59. Cantrell, *Limits of Southern Dissent*, 207; *National Economist*, December 30, 1890.

60. Dunning, *Farmers' Alliance History*, 8.

61. Fite, *Cotton Fields No More*, 25.

62. Drache, *The Day of the Bonanza*, 204–9, 219.

63. Wyckoff, *The Workers*, 167–74.

64. *People's Party Paper*, May 27, 1892; *Caucasian*, August 10, 1893.

CHAPTER 2

1. *Caucasian*, February 4, 1892.

2. Gillespie County Alliance Minutes, January 9, 1892.

3. *Western Rural*, June 20, 1891.

4. Hamlin Garland, *A Son of the Middle Border*, 458–59.

5. *Western Rural*, June 20, 1891; see also Cronon, *Nature's Metropolis*, 343.

6. *Prairie Farmer*, February 10, 1894.

7. *Prairie Farmer*, February 10, 1894.

8. Richard R. John, "Recasting the Information Infrastructure," in Chandler and Cortada, *A Nation Transformed*, 56, 68, 82–84; *Chicago Times*, April 4, 1894.

9. Lease, *The Problem of Civilization Solved*, 310; see also Fuller, "The Populists and the Post Office."

10. Roy V. Scott, *The Reluctant Farmer*, x; see also Rosenberg, "Science, Technology, and Economic Growth," 3.

11. Kirkendall, "The Agricultural Colleges," 3–7.

12. Orsi, *Sunset Limited*, 280–81. The historical understanding of farmer-academic conflict is also shaped by farmers' resentments toward the Country Life Movement in the early twentieth century. Not surprisingly, farm organizations committed to modernizing rural life at times resented the paternalism of the urban missionaries of the Country Life Movement. See Bowers, *The Country Life Movement*, 102–27.

13. Alan Marcus writes: "Little of the tension between college personnel and their agricultural opponents stemmed from a disagreement over school mission. . . . Nor was the tension a manifestation of a clash between the forces of modernity and those of tradition. Both sets of participants demanded a new farmer." See Marcus, "The Ivory Silo," 24. See also Marcus, *Agricultural Science and the Quest for Legitimacy*.

14. Welter, *Popular Education*, 161–75.

15. Gillespie County Alliance Minutes, April 14, 1888.

16. *Southern Mercury*, April 19, 1888.

17. *Southern Mercury*, February 14, 1889, in Barthelme, *Women in the Texas Populist Movement*, 190; see also Bury, *The Idea of Progress*, 50–53; Macune, "Farmers' Alliance"; Morgan, *History of the Wheel and Alliance*, 93.

18. Garvin and Daws, *History of the National Farmers' Alliance*, 17, 27.

19. *Southern Mercury*, June 6, 1889, in Barthelme, *Women in the Texas Populist Movement*, 209–10.

20. Mitchell, *Political Education*, 93–100.

21. *Advocate* (Topeka), January 30, 1890; see also Mitchell, *Political Education*, 95–96, 112. The frequency of local suballiance meetings varied. The approximately sixty members of the Centennial Alliance in Bell County, Texas, met every two weeks, while the much smaller Lone Tree Alliance in Jewell County, Kansas, met one evening every week. See Centennial Alliance Minute Book; Lone Tree Farmers' Alliance Minute Book.

22. Lone Tree Farmers' Alliance Minute Book, November 20, 1890.

23. *National Economist*, November 11, 1890.

24. Deborah Beckel explains that historians have tended to portray Polk as simply a farmer without examining Polk as also a merchant, booster, white supremacist, and progressive member of the New South elite. Although his enthusiasm for industrial promotion dimmed with the growing agricultural distress, she notes that Polk "continued to believe that with the right information and methods, farmers could succeed. He kept his promotional skills. He was loathe to let go of white supremacist . . . convictions. And always, he advocated PROGRESS." See Beckel, "Roots of Reform," 192. Along with Polk, Reuben Kolb was another apostle of scientific farming in the rural South. Leader of the Alabama Farmers' Alliance and People's party, Kolb served as the state commissioner of agriculture, the president of the National Farmers Congress at Chicago, and successfully marketed his own "Kolb Gem" strain of watermelon seeds. See Hackney, *Populism to Progressivism in Alabama*, 6–7.

25. Noblin, *Agrarian Crusader*, 22, 27, 29, 31, 34, 37; Chaplin, *An Anxious Pursuit*; Beckel, "Roots of Reform," 167–69.

26. Noblin, *Agrarian Crusader*, 76–80, 109; Beckel, "Roots of Reform,"183, 185–87, 196–97; Ayers, *The Promise of the New South*, 223–24; Polk, *Report of L. L. Polk, Commissioner of Agriculture*, 8–12, 26–27, and, *Handbook of North Carolina*, 160–65, 267–69, and, *Report on the General Condition of the Agricultural Interests*.

27. *Farmer and Mechanic*, February 21, 1878; see also *Farmer and Mechanic*, March 21, 1878; Polk, *Report of L. L. Polk, Commissioner of Agriculture*, 23–26; Noblin, *Agrarian Crusader*, 105–14; Hunt, *Marion Butler*, 24; Beckel, "Roots of Reform," 204, 325–28, 355n. Polk predicted that farmers would calculate the benefits of changing the fence laws based on their own conditions, and therefore proposed that such changes should be decided at the county level. For example, local Alliances in Newton Grove, North Carolina, and Bright Star, Arkansas, both reported an abundance of timber for fencing and local opposition to fencing stock. See *Caucasian*, January 1, 1891, April 7, 1892; *Southern Mercury*, July 31, 1888. Besides the availability of timber for fences, in his study of the fence law debates in the South, J. Crawford King Jr. notes that the division tended to not be between "haves" and "have-nots," but between livestock raisers and crop farmers. He also points to a racial dimension. See King, "The Closing of the Southern Range"; Fite, *Cotton Fields No More*, 8. Steven Hahn locates the origins of Populism in the context of changes in rural life as expressed in the resistance of yeoman farmers and tenants to the new fencing laws. Populism arose in the Georgia up-country, according to Hahn, from the resistance of yeoman farmers with their precommercial mentality to the new fence laws and the rising "agrarian bourgeoisie," who "believed in the moral and economic superiority of commercial society and sought to hasten its advance." However, Shawn Everett Kantor and J. Morgan Kousser contend that Hahn's evidence fails to substantiate the link between fence laws and Populism. See Hahn, *The Roots of Southern Populism*; Hahn, "A Response"; Kantor and Kousser, "Common Sense or Commonwealth?"; Kantor and Kousser, "A Rejoinder"; Kantor, "Supplanting the Roots of Southern Populism." Leading Populists such as Leonidas L. Polk were a precise fit for Hahn's characterization of the "agrarian bourgeoisie." As to the Farmers' Alliance in North Carolina, its genesis is inseparable from its core constituency: landholding farmers organized by Polk for the purpose of advancing commercial society. Polk's message of rural modernization and scientific farming formed an essential part of the educational campaign of the Farmers' Alliance, a national campaign that spread much wider and deeper than the elite groupings of the "agrarian bourgeoisie."

28. Noblin, *Agrarian Crusader*, 91–95, 114–15, 155; Beckel, "Roots of Reform," 311–13, 330; Steelman, *The North Carolina Farmers' Alliance*, 6–7.

29. Noblin, *Agrarian Crusader*, 142–46; Wiebe, *The Search for Order*, 114.

30. *Progressive Farmer*, February 10, 1886, in Beckel, "Roots of Reform," 436, 443–45. Poe, *Col. Leonidas Lafayette Polk*; Ayers, *The Promise of the New South*, 225; Steelman, *The North Carolina Farmers' Alliance*, 10–12; Noblin, *Agrarian Crusader* 156–61, 170–78.

31. Robert McMath uses the term *agricultural-political complex* in *Populist Vanguard*, 37–38; see also Morgan, *History of the Wheel and Alliance*, 287; Noblin, *Agrarian Crusader*, 202; Steelman, *The North Carolina Farmers' Alliance*, 14. Historians have attempted to find a breach between elite and nonelite notions of progressive and scientific education within the Farmers' Alliance and Populist movement, but such a breach is difficult to document. See Mitchell, *Political Education*, 132, 174; Goldberg, *An Army of Women*, 149–50.

32. *National Economist*, August 10, 1889, in Mitchell, *Political Education*, 97; *Rural Californian*, January 1987; *Western Rural*, January 3, 1891; *Kansas Farmer*, June 9, 16, 1887. Discussing the benefits of technological innovation, Milton George wrote: "In everything we must recognize the fact that we are in the midst of progress. The slowness with which mankind accepts innovation leads to a vast waste of energy and a great loss of advantage." See Milton George, "Progress," in *The Industrial Struggle*, 89.

33. *Western Rural*, May 31, 1891.

34. "University of California," *San Francisco Overland Monthly*, October 1892; Cleburne meeting of Texas Farmers Alliance, August 6, 1886, in Garvin and Daws, *History of the National Farmers Alliance*, 41–42; see also Roy V. Scott, *The Reluctant Farmer*, 29–32, 37, 52, 57.

35. *National Economist*, March 14, 1889; see also Poe, *Col. Leonidas Lafayette Polk*, 7.

36. Rosenberg, "Science, Technology, and Economic Growth"; *People's Party Paper*, May 27, 1892; see also Roy V. Scott, *The Reluctant Farmer*, 58.

37. *Pacific Rural Press*, January 3, 1891; Roy V. Scott, *The Reluctant Farmer*, 58–59, 64–103; Vernon Carstensen, "Overview of American Agricultural History," in Peterson, *Farmers, Bureaucrats, and Middlemen*, 18; Hackney, *Populism to Progressivism in Alabama*, 7; Sharrer, *A Kind of Fate*, 103: Marcus, "The Ivory Silo," 34.

38. *Prairie Farmer*, October 6, 20, 1894; Goldberg, *An Army of Women*, 149–50; Janet G. Humphrey, *A Texas Suffragist*, 88; *Kansas Farmer*, January 26, February 2, 1887, December 6, 1888; Beckel, "Roots of Reform," 431n, 539–41, 551; *Caucasian*, May 23, 1889, March 27, 1890; Noblin, *Agrarian Crusader*, 161. David Vaught writes that California growers spurned the Farmers' Institutes and university scientists in favor of "home-mixed solutions." Such attitudes, however, were precisely those that the Farmers' Alliance sought to overcome, as the farmers and growers at the head of the Farmers' Alliance were also in the forefront of the Farmers' Institutes and other forms of collaboration with university experts in California. See Vaught, *Cultivating California*, 49; *Pacific Rural Press*, January 3, March 28, October 17, 1891, January 2, 1892; Walters, "Populism in California," 90, 168–69; Hall, "California Populism at the Grass-Roots," 196; McGreevy, "Farmers, Nationalists, and the Origins of California Populism," 484.

39. *National Economist*, December 13, 1890, in Mitchell, *Political Education*, 136.

40. Goldberg, *An Army of Women*, 148–51.

41. *Southern Mercury*, May 10, 1888.

42. "To the Alliance People of Bell County," Centennial Alliance Minute Book, undated.

43. *Southern Mercury*, August 14, 1888.

44. *Southern Mercury*, September 11, 1888.

45. *Southern Mercury*, November 13, 1888. The concern for improving literary culture registered at the grass roots, with local Farmers' Alliances sponsoring a wide array of literary programs. The small Lone Tree suballiance in Jewell County, Kansas, for example, purchased two dollars' worth of books of plays for its literary exercises and lending library. See Lone Tree Farmers' Alliance Minute Book, November 13, 1890, December 6, 1890, April 9, 1891.

46. *Southern Mercury*, October 16, 1888.

47. *National Economist*, May 18, 1889.

48. Lecture notes from 1894 campaign, in "Notes of J. W. H. Davis," in Rushing Collection.

49. *Southern Mercury*, July 7, 1888.

50. *Progressive Farmer*, January 22, 1889.

51. *Southern Mercury*, May 10, 1888.

52. *Webster Signal*, in *National Economist*, November 11, 1890; see also Centennial Alliance Minute Book; Mitchell, *Political Education*, 139.

53. Lon Livingston, "The Needs of the South," in Dunning, *Farmers Alliance History*, 284–85; see also Mayo, *Southern Women*, 32; U.S. Department of the Interior, Abstract of the *Eleventh Census*, 46; Ayers, *The Promise of the New South*, 418; Fine, *Cotton Fields No More*, 40–42.

54. Texas Superintendent of Education, Sixth Biennial Report, 1888, in Rice, *The Negro in Texas*, 219.

55. Woodward, *Origins of the New South*, 63–64.

56. *Caucasian*, March 14, 1895.

57. *Progressive Farmer*, January 21, 1890.

58. *Dallas Morning News*, July 6, 1886.

59. R. D. Holt, "Fence Cutting War," 72.

60. Texas Superintendent of Education, in Rice, *The Negro in Texas*, 218.

61. *Progressive Farmer*, May 13, 1890.

62. Mayo, *Southern Women*, 131–32; see also Gaston, *The New South Creed*, 101–2.

63. Richard Manning Humphrey, "Colored Farmers' National Alliance," in Dunning, *Farmers' Alliance History*, 288–92; see also *National Economist*, April 4, 1891.

64. *National Economist*, March 7, 1891.

65. *National Economist*, December 30, 1890.

66. *National Economist*, November 11, 1890; see also McMath, *Populist Vanguard*, 111–12.

67. *National Economist*, March 30, 1889; see also *National Economist*, April 6, May 18, 1889.

68. *National Economist*, April 26, 1890.

69. Penciled note written "around 1895," in "Notes of J. W. H. Davis," in Rushing

Collection. In North Carolina, Marion Butler briefly published his Populist *Caucasian* as a daily in 1895. See *Caucasian*, February 7, 1895. In California such attempts failed to materialize. See John S. Dore to Thomas Cator, December 14, 1892, in Cator Papers; see also Hicks, *The Populist Revolt*, 131; Noblin, *Agrarian Crusader*, 150.

70. Penciled note written "around 1895," in "Notes of J. W. H. Davis," in Rushing Collection; see also Lutsky, "The Reform Editors and Their Press."

71. Gillespie County Alliance Minutes, October 4, 1889.

72. *National Economist*, May 18, 1889, March 15, 1890; *People's Party Paper*, December 3, 1891.

73. *National Economist*, January 16, 1892; see also *National Economist*, January 23, 30, February 6, 20, 1892.

74. Dunning, *Farmers' Alliance History*, 371, 411, 461, 463.

75. Morgan, *History of the Wheel and Alliance*, 391–96.

76. *Southern Mercury*, July 24, 1888.

77. Centennial Alliance Minute Book; Gillespie County Alliance Minutes; Lone Tree Farmers' Alliance Minute Book; Gove County Farmers' Alliance Minute Books.

78. Centennial Alliance Minute Book.

79. Vincent Brothers, *Populist Hand-Book for Kansas*, 1891, in Welter, *Popular Education*, 172–73.

80. *Southern Mercury*, May 10, 1888.

81. *Southern Mercury*, May 9, 1889.

82. Mayo, *Southern Women*, 131–32, 274.

83. *Southern Mercury*, August 14, 1888; see also *National Economist*, March 4, 1889; *Prairie Farmer*, February 10, 1894.

CHAPTER 3

1. *Southern Mercury*, August 28, 1888.

2. *Southern Mercury*, May 31, 1888; Barthelme, *Women in the Texas Populist Movement*, 48.

3. *Southern Mercury*, May 31, 1888. For a similar discussion see the debate "Advancement of Women" in *Kansas Farmer*, January 19, 26, February 2, 1887.

4. Garland, *A Spoil of Office*, 352. See also Degler, *At Odds*, 338.

5. *Advocate* (Topeka), July 22, 1891; see also Barthelme, *Women in the Texas Populist Movement*, 48.

6. Watkins, *Rural Democracy*, 66; Wagner, "Farms, Families, and Reform," 200; Marti, *Women of the Grange*, 89–91; "Women in the Alliance," in Garvin and Daws, *History of the National Farmers' Alliance*, 94–100.

7. McMath, *Populist Vanguard*, 67; see also *Advocate*, Meriden (KS), September 21, 1889, January 16, 1890; Watkins, *Rural Democracy*, 58–59; Steelman, *The North Carolina Farmers' Alliance*, 19; Centennial Alliance Minute Book, March 19, 1892.

8. Cott, *The Bonds of Womanhood*, 3, 69, 201; Friedman, *The Enclosed Garden*, 110, 130; Ryan, *Womanhood in America*, 143.

9. Historians have placed a similar emphasis on women's voting rights, locating suffrage at the center of nineteenth-century strivings for women's progress. See DuBois, *Feminism and Suffrage*, 15; Edwards, *Angels in the Machinery*, 104–10; Barthelme, *Women in the Texas Populist Movement*, 48; Buhle, *Women and American Socialism*, 84.

10. *Southern Mercury*, July 5, 1888. Laura Lovett applies the concept of "nostalgic modernism" in her thoughtful study of how Populist women and subsequent reformers mixed nostalgia about the home and motherhood with modernizing change, which also leads to her exploration of the pronatalist currents in Populist thought. See Lovett, "Conceiving the Future," 1–16, 26–62. Julie Roy Jeffrey emphasizes that on the farmers' frontier the women's domestic roles as mothers and wives served to reaffirm their "civilizing mission," see Jeffrey, *Frontier Women*, 130.

11. Diggs, "The Women in the Alliance Movement"; *Marion Record*, September 4, 1891, in Farmers' Alliance Clippings; Willard and Livermore, *A Woman of the Century*, 718–19.

12. Diggs, "The Women in the Alliance Movement"; *Advocate* (Topeka), July 29, 1891. Michael Goldberg writes that Lease and Diggs adopted the urban cultural worldview and were alienated from the rural culture of women on the farm. See Goldberg, *An Army of Women*, 163, 182, 207–9. Rebecca Edwards makes a similar case. See Edwards, *Angels in the Machinery*, 102. The same argument could be applied to the male professionals at the head of the rural movement. Hence the task of explaining why the worldview of Alliance leaders such as Todd, Diggs, Polk, and Macune resonated so broadly among rural women and men.

13. Schwantes, *An American Odyssey*, 131; Todd, *Professor Goldwin Smith*, 97.

14. Barthelme, *Women in the Texas Populist Movement*, 45–46; Diggs, "The Women in the Alliance Movement."

15. Diggs, "The Women in the Alliance Movement"; Bettie Gay, "Influence of Women in the Alliance," in Dunning, *Farmers' Alliance History*, 308–12.

16. Ayers, *The Promise of the New South*, 221; McMath, *Populist Vanguard*, 66.

17. Bettie Gay, "Influence of Women in the Alliance," in Dunning, *Farmers' Alliance History*, 308–12.

18. *National Economist*, May 18, 1889.

19. Centennial Alliance Minute Book, August 17, September 21, 1894, April 6, 1895.

20. *Southern Mercury*, June 7, 1888.

21. Steelman, *The North Carolina Farmers' Alliance*, 19.

22. *Advocate*, Meriden (KS), September 21, 1889, January 16, 1890.

23. Gillespie County Alliance Minutes, September 30, 1893.

24. McMath, *Populist Vanguard*, 67, and *American Populism*, 126; Goldberg, *An Army of Women*, 139–42; Wagner, "Farm, Families, and Reform," 1; Jeffrey, "Women in the Southern Farmers' Alliance."

25. *Southern Mercury*, July 5, 1888; see also Morgan, *History of the Wheel and Alliance*, 247–57. The notion that women faced severe hardships due to rural isolation was a consistent theme in Farmers' Alliance literature and formed an essential part of the movement's vision for women's progress. Scholars, however, have debated the extent to which rural women actually experienced such isolation. Deborah Fink's study of women in rural Nebraska tends to confirm the extraordinary desolation and loneliness of farm life and also contains a concise treatment of the scholarly debate. See Fink, *Agrarian Women*, 54–55, 72–74. Dorothy Schwieder argues that women's isolation has been overstated. See her chapter, "Iowa Farm Wives, 1840–80," in Peterson, *Farmers, Bureaucrats, and Middlemen*, 152–68. A study of the records of the North Dakota Hospital for the Insane indicates that, contrary to widely held beliefs, a disproportionate number of women on remote farms did not go insane. See Handy-Marchello, *Women of the Northern Plains*, 80–81.

26. Wiebe, *The Search for Order*, 44, 111–32; McMath, *American Populism*, 40–42.

27. Morgan, *History of the Wheel and Alliance*, 250–51.

28. Martin, *The People's Party in Texas*, 102–12; Goldberg, *An Army of Women*, 29–32; Shannon, *The Farmer's Last Frontier*, 47–50; Garland, *A Son of the Middle Border*.

29. Goldberg, *An Army of Women*, 128; Faragher, *Sugar Creek*, 145, 154–55; see also Doyle, *The Social Order of a Frontier Community*.

30. Garland, *A Spoil of Office*, 149, 228, 231.

31. Garvin and Daws, "Woman in the Alliance," in *History of the National Farmers' Alliance*, 94–100; see also Deborah Fink, *Agrarian Women*, 72–73.

32. Wagner, "Farm, Families, and Reform," 147; Goldberg, *An Army of Women*, 208–9; see also Jane Adams, *The Transformation of Rural Life*, 84–85; Baker, *The Moral Frameworks*, 59. From the early days of the Grange in the 1870s, rural reformers insisted that the mindless drudgery of farm work took an extraordinary toll on women's health and sanity. See Marti, *Women of the Grange*, 73–75.

33. *Nonconformist* (Winfield, KS), July 4, 1889; see also Goldberg, *An Army of Women*, 209.

34. Garland, *A Spoil of Office*, 15, 351, 375.

35. Kellie, "Personal" and "Political Memoir," in *A Prairie Populist*, 8–10, 147–50.

36. Kellie, "Personal Memoir," in *A Prairie Populist*, 8, 32–33. Deborah Fink, describing the severity of Nebraska's environment and the horrors of its sod houses, notes that "women encountered a bleakness that they had not known before." See Deborah Fink, *Agrarian Women*, 32.

37. Kellie, "Personal Memoir," in *A Prairie Populist*, 8, 32, 54, 79, 83, 99, 106, 123.

38. Kellie, "Personal Memoir," in *A Prairie Populist*, 55–56, 65–66, 110.

39. *Nonconformist* (Winfield, KS), August 29, 1889; see also Marti, *Women of the Grange*, 77; Deborah Fink, *Agrarian Women*, 5, 43, 52. Julie Roy Jeffrey notes that even where wives and husbands were "co-partners in the frontier adventure," husbands tended to have the final say on major decisions, see Jeffrey, *Frontier Women: The Trans-Mississippi West*, 81.

40. Kellie, "Personal Memoir," in *A Prairie Populist*, 46, 83, 93–94, 100, 104, 111.

41. Kellie, "Stand Up for Nebraska," in Kellie, *A Prairie Populist*, 127–32.

42. *Nonconformist* (Winfield, KS), August 29, 1889.

43. *Southern Mercury*, July 12, 1888.

44. Bettie Gay, "Influence of Women in the Alliance," in Dunning, *Farmers' Alliance History*, 308–12.

45. Danbom, *Born in the Country*, 87; Nancy Grey Osterud, "'She Helped Me Hay It as Good as a Man': Relations among Women and Men in an Agricultural Community," in Groneman and Norton, *"To Toil the Livelong Day,"* 87–97; Wagner, "Farms, Families, and Reform," 142–44.

46. Garvin and Daws, *History of the National Farmers' Alliance*, 97–100; *Southern Mercury*, July 5, 1888.

47. Todd, *Professor Goldwin Smith*, 78–79; *Pacific Rural Press*, January 30, 1892.

48. *Kansas Farmer*, February 9, 1887; *Farmers' Voice*, December 28, 1888, January 5, 1889; *Southern Mercury*, May 31, 1888.

49. *Southern Mercury*, May 10, 1888.

50. *National Economist*, May 18, 1889.

51. Paula C. Baker, *The Moral Frameworks*, 128–29; Marylin Irvin Holt, *Linoleum, Better Babies, and the Modern Farm Woman*, 8, 30.

52. Bettie Gay, "Influence of Women in the Alliance," in Dunning, *Farmers' Alliance History*, 308–12; *Pacific Rural Press*, August 1, 1891.

53. *Farmers' Voice*, January 5, 1889; see also *National Economist*, October 25, 1890; *Southern Mercury*, August 28, 1888.

54. *Farmers' Voice*, January 5, 1889.

55. *National Economist*, July 26, 1890; see also Sharpless, *Fertile Ground*, 160–61.

56. "Women in the Alliance," in Garvin and Daws, *History of the National Farmers' Alliance*, 94–100.

57. Bettie Gay, "Influence of Women in the Alliance," in Dunning, *Farmers' Alliance History*, 308–12.

58. *Progressive Farmer*, May 13, 1890.

59. *Southern Mercury*, April 11, 1889.

60. *Southern Mercury*, July 31, 1888.

61. *Southern Mercury*, April 4, 1889, in Barthelme, *Women in the Texas Populist Movement*, 201–2; see also Diggs, "The Women in the Alliance Movement."

62. *Southern Mercury*, January 24, 1889; see also Litwack, *Been in the Storm So Long*, 244.

63. *Dallas Morning News*, July 31, 1892, in Gaither, *Blacks and the Populist Revolt*, 70.

64. *Progressive Farmer*, March 26, 1889, in Jeffrey, "Women in the Southern Farmers' Alliance," 82–83.

65. Sue Huffman Brady, "Changing Ideals in Southern Womanhood," in Eagle, *The Congress of Women*, 308; see also Sharpless, *Fertile Ground*, 160; Jeffrey, "Women in the Southern Farmers' Alliance"; Mayo, *Southern Women*.

66. *Southern Mercury*, February 14, 1888, in Barthelme, *Women in the Texas Populist Movement*, 191; *Southern Mercury*, April 19, 1888.

67. *Caucasian*, June 11, 1891.

68. *Caucasian*, March 23, 1893; Polk, *Inter-State Convention*, 7; *Prairie Farmer*, February 10, 1894; see also Marti, *Women of the Grange*, 81–85; Roy V. Scott, *The Reluctant Farmer*, 57.

69. Kellie, "Personal Memoir," in *A Prairie Populist*, 94.

70. *Kansas Farmer*, January 26, 1887.

71. *National Economist*, May 18, 1889.

72. *Pacific Rural Press*, October 17, 1891.

73. *People's Advocate*, February 15, 1894.

74. *National Bulletin*, May 1894, in John Davis Scrapbooks; see also *Southern Mercury*, April 19, May 31, June 7, August 28, September 25, 1888.

75. *Kansas Farmer*, February 2, 1887.

76. Todd, *Professor Goldwin Smith*, 28, 148; see also Todd, *Rachel's Pitiful History*; Jeffrey, "Women in the Southern Farmers' Alliance."

77. *Kansas Farmer*, February 9, 1887.

78. Lipartito, "When Women Were Switches," 1084–85; Gabler, *The American Telegrapher*, 107–44.

79. Mayo, *Southern Women*, xx–xxi, 167–68; Beckel, "Roots of Reform," 581; Ayers, *The Promise of the New South*, 74, 212; Campbell, *Gone to Texas*, 308.

80. *Southern Mercury*, September 25, October 9, 1890.

81. *Pacific Rural Press*, January 23, March 12, 1892.

82. *Southern Mercury*, August 14, 1888.

83. *Farmers' Voice*, December 28, 1888.

84. *Southern Mercury*, May 31, June 14, September 25, 1888.

85. "Kansas Needs Manufactures," in *Kansas Farmer*, June 30, 1887; *Caucasian*, April 4, 1889, March 20, 1890. Discussing the need to overcome "fear of venture" in setting up furniture mills, the *Caucasian* noted that "half a dozen such enterprises [would] double our population, double the value of real estate and put into circulation double the money now in the county." See *Caucasian*, March 21, 1889; see also *Southern Mercury*, June 28, 1888, March 14, 1889.

86. *Caucasian*, March 20, 1890.

87. *Progressive Farmer*, January 22, 1889; see also *Progressive Farmer*, February 5, 12, 1889; Ayers, *The Promise of the New South*, 112–14; Gilmore, *Gender and Jim Crow*, 23.

88. Beckel, "Roots of Reform," 186, 189–91, 638.

89. *Southern Mercury*, July 5, 1888.

90. *Kansas Farmer*, January 26, 1887.

91. *Kansas Farmer*, January 26, 1887.

92. Steelman, *The North Carolina Farmers' Alliance*, 160.

93. Kellie, "Personal Memoir," in *A Prairie Populist*, 110; see also *Southern Mercury*, July 5, 1888; Goldberg, *An Army of Women*, 79–85, 189–91.

94. *Western Rural*, January 3, 1891.

95. *The Voice*, February 6, 1890, in Blocker, "The Politics of Reform."

96. *People's Party Paper*, December 8, 1893. See also Wagner, "Farms, Families, and Reform," 275; Lovett, "Conceiving the Future," 55–56; Lorenzo Lewelling to Norton and Annie Hocket, December 8, 1893, in Lewelling, Governor's Office, Letter Press Books; Joseph Dana Miller, "The New Woman in Office"; Koven and Michel, "Womanly Duties." Walter Trattner draws a connection between the centralization of charity organizations and the "monopolization and trustification of big business." Although he stresses the role of urban middle-class reformers, the women and men of rural reform were also involved in this process. See Trattner, *From Poor Law to Welfare State*, 87, 94.

97. *Progressive Farmer*, May 13, 1890.

98. Kellie, "Personal Memoir," and "Political Memoir," in *A Prairie Populist*, 109–10, 144; *Kansas Farmer*, December 8, 1886; Wagner, "Farms, Families, and Reform," 275. Fannie McCormick was the Populist nominee in 1890 for the Kansas state superintendent of public instruction. See Clanton, *Kansas Populism*, 60.

99. *Southern Mercury*, August 21, 28, 1888; see also Wagner, "Farms, Families, and Reform," 281–83; Barthelme, *Women in the Texas Populist Movement*, 47–59, 111, 128. Bettie Gay was a founding member of the Texas Equal Rights Association in 1893. See Taylor, *Citizens at Last*, 89.

100. *Pacific Rural Press*, March 26, 1892; see also Blocker, "The Politics of Reform"; Willard, "The Coming Brotherhood"; Wagner, "Farm, Families, and Reform," 258–59.

101. Reprinted in *Advocate* (Topeka), June 17, 1891.

102. *Pacific Rural Press*, May 7, 1892. See also Burkholder, "Kansas Populism, Woman Suffrage, and the Agrarian Myth," 298–302.

103. Kellie, "Political Memoir" in *A Prairie Populist*, 163–64; Wagner, "Farms, Families, and Reform," 262–63; Clanton, *Kansas Populism*, 283n57.

104. Gilman, "What the People's Party Means," speech delivered June 9, 1893, in Gilman, *Charlotte Perkins Gilman*, 75; see also Gilman, *The Living of Charlotte Perkins Gilman*, 186–87, and *Women and Economics*, 5–12; Gronlund, *The Co-Operative Commonwealth, an Exposition of Modern Socialism*, 145–52; *Southern Mercury*, September 25, 1888.

105. *Southern Mercury*, May 3, 1888.

106. Ward, "Our Better Halves"; see also Gilman, *The Living of Charlotte Perkins Gilman*, 127; Bederman, *Manliness and Civilization*, 127–28, 135–36; Carl N. Degler, "Introduction," in Gilman, *Women and Economics*, xxxii–xxxv. Ward critiqued the "pre-Darwinian premises" of articles in *Popular Science Monthly* and other journals that attributed women's inferiority to natural selection.

107. Todd, *Professor Goldwin Smith*, 17–20, 148, 151–52. In North Carolina, a Farmers' Alliance newspaper carried an article defending Goldwin Smith, consenting to educating women and building them a university "if it shall be necessary," but opposed to "mixing of sexes" and breaking down the sexual division of labor. See *Caucasian*, January 23, 1890.

108. Waugh, *Woman's Wages*, 16–19, 42–45; *Farmers' Voice*, December 28, 1888.

109. *Southern Mercury*, August 28, 1888; see also Kerber, *Women of the Republic*, 200; Bannister, *Social Darwinism*, 14, 59.

110. *Pacific Rural Press*, March 12, 1892. As James Gilbert, the state lecturer of the California Farmers' Alliance, explained: "Their [women's] advancement is the keynote to American civilization. The mothers of children should hold their heads as high as man, and if she does not, her offspring cannot be what it should." See *Los Angeles Times*, July 8, 1891.

111. Todd, *Professor Goldwin Smith*, 146; see also Gilman, *The Living of Charlotte Perkins Gilman*, 127; Ward, "Our Better Halves."

112. Bettie Gay, "Influence of Women in the Alliance," in Dunning, *Farmers' Alliance History*, 308–12.

113. Jenny Beauchamp, "Ballot an Educator," in Taylor, *Citizens at Last*, 72–75; see also Bannister, *Social Darwinism*, 171.

114. Lovett, "Conceiving the Future," 29–30.

115. *Caucasian*, August 10, 1893.

116. Lease, *Problem of Civilization Solved*, 17, 31, 143, 151, 158, 169, 178, 180–82, 199, 220, 226, 250–55, 349.

117. *Southern Mercury*, January 31, 1889.

118. Berman, *All That Is Solid*, 95–96.

Chapter 4

1. *National Economist*, March 30, 1889.

2. Klepper, "The Economic Bases for Agrarian Protest," 103, 250; Roy V. Scott, *The Agrarian Movement in Illinois*, 20.

3. "National Alliance at Shreveport, Oct. 12, 1887," in Garvin and Daws, *History of the National Farmers' Alliance*, 63–83. In 1889, the California State Grange called on its members "to study well the lesson which these great corporations that dominate the country are teaching. . . . That in unity, in intelligent co-operation, there is strength, there is power. . . . We must do as the corporations are doing—meet combinations of capital and brains with like combinations." See Clemens, *The People's Lobby*, 170.

4. Macune, "Farmers Alliance," 22–24, 33; Goodwyn, *Democratic Promise*, 90; Destler, "Agricultural Readjustment," 106; *Prairie Farmer*, January 27, 1894; Barron, *Mixed Harvest*, 156; Chandler, *The Visible Hand*, 122–44.

5. *Southern Mercury*, September 25, 1888.

6. *Southern Mercury*, September 25, 1888.

7. Cross, "Co-operation in California," 544.

8. "National Alliance at Shreveport, Oct. 12, 1887," in Garvin and Daws, *History of the National Farmers' Alliance*, 63–83.

9. Wagner, "Farms, Families, and Reform," 316–17.

10. Dunning, *Farmers' Alliance History*, 138–39; McMath, *Populist Vanguard*, 51–52, 107–9, and *American Populism*, 139–40.

11. Polk, 5; *Progressive Farmer*, June 4, 1889.

12. Hunt, *Marion Butler*, 29; *Caucasian*, March 21, April 18, 1889, February 20, 1890; see also Fite, *Cotton Fields No More*, 13.

13. *Caucasian*, February 20, 1890; McMath, *American Populism*, 128–29; Shaw, *The Wool Hat Boys*, 97; *Los Angeles Times*, December 25, 1896.

14. Destler, "Agricultural Readjustment"; Roy V. Scott, *Reluctant Farmer*, 47; *Prairie Farmer*, January 6, 27, 1894; Knapp, *Great American Cooperators*, 13–14, 316–17; Grant, *Self-Help in the 1890s Depression*, 60; Keillor, *Cooperative Commonwealth*, 144–45.

15. Terry and Smith, "Mechanization of Lima Bean Threshing"; Donald Walker, e-mail message to author, February 3, 1999; *Los Angeles Times*, January 15, 1892. Marion Cannon was the paramount leader of the California Farmers' Alliance and People's party, at the national level helped steer the Farmers' Alliance into the third party, and served as a Populist representative in the U.S. Congress. Yet very little has been written about him apart from a dissertation by Philip W. Walker, who makes the intriguing characterization that "Cannon appeared as a sort of hybrid between the yeoman and the businessman, which constituted one of the characteristics of the beginning of agro-business in California." See Walker, "Un Populiste Californien," 116 (translated from the French).

16. *Pacific Rural Press*, November 29, 1890; *Ventura County (CA) Star*, July 1, 1983, in Cannon/Walker Family Papers; Walters, "Populism in California," 63, 68.

17. Walters, "Populism in California," 175; *Los Angeles Times*, October 30, November 1, December 5, 1891.

18. *Alliance Farmer*, November 5, 1891, in McGreevy, "Farmers, Nationalists, and the Origins of California Populism"; Magliari, "California Populism, " 117; Worster, *Rivers of Empire*, 214–15; Cross, "Co-operation in California"; Vaught, *Cultivating California*, 48.

19. Marion Cannon, letter to the editor, *Los Angeles Times*, October 3, 1892. In North Carolina, Leonidas Polk foretold that cotton mills would turn Charlotte into the "future London." See Beckel, "Roots of Reform," 186.

20. Magliari, "California Populism," 76–77; see also Couchman, *The Sunsweet Story*, 18.

21. Sunkist Growers, Inc., *Heritage of Gold*; Donald Walker, e-mail message to author, February 3, 1999; McBane, "The Role of Gender in Citrus Employment"; Teague, *Fifty Years a Rancher*, 45.

22. Erdman, *The California Fruit Growers Exchange*; MacCurdy, *The History of the California Fruit Growers Exchange*; Rust and Gardner, *Sunkist Growers, Inc.*; Teague, *Fifty Years a Rancher*, 76.

23. *Pacific Rural Press*, May 3, 1890, June 11, 1891, May 21, 1892; Couchman, *The Sunsweet Story*.

24. *Pacific Rural Press*, August 22, October 17, 1891; Walters, "Populism in California," 57; Magliari, "California Populism," 77; Hall, "California Populism at the Grass-Roots"; McGreevy, "Farmers, Nationalists, and the Origins of California Populism," 483–84.

25. John S. Dore to Thomas V. Cator, September 23, 1892, May 7, 1895, in Cator Papers; see also *People's Press*, October 20, 1894, in Cross California Labor Notes, carton 5; Walters, "Populism in California" 91, 169; Vaught, *Cultivating California*, 73–80.

26. *Pacific Rural Press*, February 25, 1890, July 25, 1891; Woeste, *The Farmer's Benevolent Trust*, 8–9. The Rochdale system allowed for considerable variation in practice. In the cooperative creameries in Minnesota, for example, the Rochdale rules required "one person, one vote." But such a rule would not have worked among citrus growers, where a far greater disparity existed between the large and small farmers. See Keillor, *Cooperative Commonwealth*, 6.

27. McCabe, *History of the Grange Movement*, 489–502; Cross, *Co-operative Stores* [Wisconsin], 7.

28. *Pacific Rural Press*, July 25, 1891; see also *Pacific Rural Press*, June 11, 1891; *Rural Californian*, February 1890; Cross, "Co-operation in California"; Woeste, *The Farmer's Benevolent Trust*, 65.

29. Carey McWilliams, "The Citrus Belt," in *Southern California*, 205–6; "Organization and Marketing Plan Adopted by the Southern California Fruit Exchanges," Los Angeles, August 29, 1893, in Rust and Gardner, *Sunkist Growers, Inc.*; Belknap, "The Era of the Lemon"; Teague, *Fifty Years a Rancher*, 76; McBane, "The Role of Gender in Citrus Employment."

30. *Pacific Rural Press*, October 25, 1890.

31. Altenberg, "Beyond Capitalism"; Orsi, "*The Octopus* Reconsidered," and Orsi, *Sunset Limited*, 319–22.

32. *Advocate*, Meriden (KS), November 22, 1889; see also Lone Tree Farmers' Alliance Minute Book, May 1, June 5, 1890, February 19, April 2, May 4, December 1, 1891.

33. *Advocate*, Meriden (KS), August 17, 1889; see also *Advocate*, Meriden (KS), September 14, 1889; *Kansas Farmer*, April 15, 1888.

34. *Kansas Farmer*, May 10, 1888; *Advocate*, Meriden (KS), August 17, September 7, November 9, 15, 1889.

35. *Kansas Farmer*, April 26, May 3, 10, 1888; *Advocate*, Meriden (KS), September 7, 1889. To avoid controversy over the word *trust*, the movement later called itself the Farmers' Federation of the Mississippi Valley, although Allen continued to use the original Farmers' Trust name in his businesses.

36. *Kansas Farmer*, April 5, May 3, 10, 1888; *Advocate*, Meriden (KS), September 21, 1889; August 12, 1891.

37. *National Economist*, August 3, 1889; Dunning, *Farmers' Alliance History*, 226–28; Destler, "The People's Party in Illinois," 33–34, 40.

38. *Southern Mercury*, October 9, 1888.

39. Garvin and Daws, *History of the National Farmers' Alliance*, 40.

40. "Circular Letter," in Archibald Johnson Rose Papers; see also Buck, *The Granger Movement*, 265; Parsons, "The Role of Cooperatives," 874–76; Fite, *Cotton Fields No More*, 52.

41. Gillespie County Alliance Minutes, August 20, October 7, 8, 1887, April 19, 1889.

314 NOTES TO PAGES 120–126

42. Gillespie County Alliance Minutes, October 7, 1887; Chereno Alliance Ledger, 1887.

43. *Southern Mercury*, October 30, 1888; *Advocate*, Meriden (KS), November 9, 1889.

44. *Southern Mercury*, March 14, 1889, June 6, 1880, June 20, June 27, July 4, 1889, in Barthelme, *Women in the Texas Populist Movement*, 198, 210–11, 212–15.

45. "By Laws of the Buda Cooperative Milling Ginning and Mercantile Association of [the] Farmers' Alliance," and "No. of Shares, 1890" in Buda Alliance Gin Records, 1890.

46. "No. of Shares, 1897," in Buda Alliance Gin Records.

47. "Plan for Co-operative Stores: By-Laws," in Garvin and Daws, *History of the National Farmers' Alliance*, 153–57; see also Dunning, *Farmers' Alliance History*, 8.

48. *Southern Mercury*, October 2, November 6, 22, December 6, 1888.

49. *National Economist*, April 6, 1889.

50. *National Economist*, April 6, 27, 1889.

51. *Southern Mercury*, June 28, July 21, August 14, 1888, March 14, 1889: *Caucasian*, April 4, 1889, March 20, 1890; Hackney, *Populism to Progressivism in Alabama*, 8.

52. Garvin and Daws, "Co-operation and Exchange," in *History of the National Farmers' Alliance*, 84–88.

53. Macune, "Farmers Alliance," 18–19, 25–26; Smith, "'Farmers of Texas in Business,'" 229n32.

54. Ousley, "A Lesson in Co-operation," 821.

55. Macune, "Farmers Alliance," 22–24.

56. *Southern Mercury*, November 6, 1888.

57. *Southern Mercury*, April 11, 1889; see also Macune, "Farmers Alliance," 32; Smith, "'Farmers of Texas in Business,'" 229–30.

58. Macune, "Farmers Alliance," 24; Smith, "'Farmers of Texas in Business,'" 233.

59. *National Economist*, December 14, 1889.

60. *Southern Mercury*, August 14, 1888.

61. *Southern Mercury*, August 14, 1888.

62. *Southern Mercury*, December 27, 1888. The Farmers' Alliance in North Carolina also viewed the local cooperatives as detrimental to centralized systems of marketing, and appealed to its members to avoid establishing cooperative stores because they undermined the Alliance's central purchasing system. See *Caucasian*, January 28, 1892.

63. *Southern Mercury*, August 21, 1888.

64. *Southern Mercury*, October 2, 1888; see also Barnes, *Farmers in Rebellion*, 86.

65. *Southern Mercury*, April 19, 1888.

66. Hahn, *A Nation under Our Feet*, 416–17; McMath, *Populist Vanguard*, 52; Rice, *The Negro in Texas*, 165–78.

67. Richard Manning Humphrey, "Colored Farmers' National Alliance," in Dunning, *Farmers' Alliance History*, 288–92.

68. William F. Holmes, "The Arkansas Cotton Pickers' Strike," 194–96.

69. Gillespie County Alliance Minutes, July 1888, April 1890; see also Barnes, *Farmers in Rebellion*, 86, 97; Ousley, "A Lesson in Cooperation," 828.

70. McMath, *Populist Vanguard*, 54–57; Macune, "Farmers Alliance," 27–28; Bancroft, *History of California*, vii, 738.

71. Dunning, *Farmers' Alliance History*, 7; see also Destler, "Agricultural Readjustment," 116; Roy V. Scott, *The Agrarian Movement in Illinois*, 41.

72. *Advocate*, Meriden (KS), January 30, 1890.

73. McMath, *Populist Vanguard*, 120–22; see also Goodwyn, *Democratic Promise*, 122; Macune, "Farmers Alliance," 33.

74. *Advocate* (Topeka), December 30, 1891.

75. Dewing, *A History of the National Cordage Company*, 4–12.

76. *New York Times*, July 12, October 24, 1891, February 7, 13, 20, 1892.

77. Roy V. Scott, *The Agrarian Movement in Illinois*, 76–77. Robert McMath provides a different interpretation of the National Union Company, which he describes as a betrayal of the original cooperative ideals of the Alliance and as being supported by conservative opponents of the People's party. See McMath, *Populist Vanguard*, 120–22.

78. *Advocate* (Topeka), December 30, 1891, January 6, 1892.

79. *Advocate* (Topeka), December 30, 1891.

80. Ayers, *The Promise of the New South*, 87; see also Danbom, *Born in the Country*, 133, 149.

81. *Progressive Farmer*, January 28, 1890; *Advocate* (Topeka), July 29, August 12, November 11, 1891.

82. Laird, *Advertising Progress*, 28–29; Buck, *The Granger Movement*, 246; Barron, *Mixed Harvest*, 164–71; *Farmers' Voice*, December 31, 1888; Destler, "The People's Party in Illinois, 1888–1896," 75, 80–81.

83. *Caucasian*, December 1, 1892.

84. Dewing, *A History of the National Cordage Company*, 12; Grant, *Self-Help in the 1890s Depression*, 6–7; *New York Times*, May 5, 8, June 3, 1893.

85. Luna Kellie, "Stand Up for Nebraska," in *A Prairie Populist*, 130.

86. *Kansas Farmer*, June 9, 1887; Lorenzo Lewelling to Richard Harrison, August 25, 1893, in Lewelling, Governor's Office, Letter Press Books; Frank, "Leviathan with Tentacles of Steel," 46–47; Grant, *Self-Help in the 1890s Depression*, 74–81. The Texas Populists proposed using prison labor for improving access to a Gulf port. At its 1892 convention, the Texas People's party demanded that all convict labor in the state be employed to construct double-track railroads from "the deepest water on the Gulf" across northern Texas. See Winkler, *Platforms of Political Parties in Texas*, 299.

87. The phrase "alternative tracks" is from Gerald Berk's *Alternative Tracks*, a study of the alternative possibilities of industrial regulation and development in late nineteenth-century America. Despite a misplaced emphasis on what he considers the "relatively decentralized" and regionalist vision of Midwestern farmers, his work provides an analytical framework for understanding alternative models of development.

88. *National Economist*, April 6, December 14, 1889.

89. Hofstadter, *The Age of Reform*, 46–47.

90. Kellie, "Stand Up for Nebraska," in *A Prairie Populist*, 130.

CHAPTER 5

1. Lecture notes from 1894 campaign, in "Notes of J. W. H. Davis," in Rushing Collection.

2. Marcus Mallard of Grimes County, Texas, generously provided information about Davis's life; lecture notes from 1894 campaign, and unlabeled ms., in "Notes of J. W. H. Davis," in Rushing Collection. Reflecting the importance Alliance members placed on national politics, the Lone Tree suballiance in Jewell County, Kansas, authorized the considerable sum of five dollars for a subscription to the *Congressional Record* for the suballiance library. See Lone Tree Farmers' Alliance Minute Book, December 6, 1890.

3. Summers, *The Gilded Age*, 207–9.

4. Summers, *Party Games*, 141–75, and *The Gilded Age*, 216–18; Jensen, *The Winning of the Midwest*, 34–153; Kleppner, *The Cross of Culture*; Keller, *Affairs of State*; Jean Baker, *Affairs of Party*.

5. Summers, *The Gilded Age*, 180–84.

6. Peffer, *Populism, Its Rise and Fall*, 31.

7. Penciled note written "around 1895," in "Notes of J. W. H. Davis," in Rushing Collection.

8. *Advocate*, Meriden (KS), September 21, 1889.

9. *Los Angeles Times*, October 22, 1891.

10. *People's Party Paper*, December 3, 1891. Similar conceptions of nonpartisan and scientific governance dominated the imagination among urban and academic reformers of the late nineteenth and early twentieth centuries. See Monroe, *Democratic Wish*, 97–119.

11. *National Economist*, December 14, 1889.

12. *Advocate*, Meriden (KS), October 5, 1889.

13. *Los Angeles Times*, September 2, 1892.

14. *People's Party Paper*, December 3, 1891.

15. Peffer, *The Farmer's Side*, 131–32, 170.

16. Argersinger, *The Limits of Agrarian Radicalism*, 12.

17. Clemens, *The People's Lobby*, 2, 17, 146, 177; see also Voss-Hubbard, "The 'Third Party Tradition' Reconsidered."

18. Hicks, *The Populist Revolt*, appendixes D, E, and F, 433–44.

19. Eric Foner, *The Story of American Freedom*, xviii.

20. Lecture notes from the 1894 campaign, in "Notes of J. W. H. Davis," in Rushing Collection; see also "Omaha Platform, July 1892," in Hicks, *The Populist Revolt*, appendix F, 441.

21. *Nonconformist* (Indianapolis), June 16, 1892.

22. *Caucasian*, June 6, 1889.

23. *Farmers' Voice*, December 29, 1888; Fuller, *American Mail: Enlarger of the Common Life*, 75.

24. *Pioneer Exponent*, July 7, 1888; see also Lyman B. Russell, "Comanche Newspaper History," in *Comanche Vanguard*, July 12–September 13, 1913; *Comanche Chief*, September 21, 1895; Fuller, "The Populists and the Post Office." James Turner has noted a correlation between the distance from railroad depots and the strength of Populist voting in Texas. The Comanche example suggests that patterns of newspaper circulation may have been an important variable. See James Turner, "Understanding the Populists," 365.

25. *People's Advocate*, May 24, 1894; see also *Pacific Rural Press*, January 23, March 12, 1892.

26. *National Economist*, May 11, 1889. Although the Department of Agriculture was yet a small bureaucracy compared to the postal service, farm reformers demanded its expansion. The 1887 Shreveport meeting of the National Farmers' Alliance adopted the resolution: "We demand that the Department of Agriculture be made one of the Departments of State; that it shall be increased in scope and efficiency, and in connection therewith there shall be established a bureau of labor statistics." See Garvin and Daws, *History of the National Farmers' Alliance*, 81.

27. *People's Party Paper*, January 21, 1892.

28. *Nonconformist* (Indianapolis), January 26, 1893; see also *National Economist*, April 26, 1890; Skocpol, *Protecting Soldiers and Mothers*, 102–51.

29. *People's Party Paper*, June 3, 1892, March 17, November 24, 1893; see also Hunt, *Marion Butler*, 89, 134–35.

30. For a discussion of rural free delivery and the centralization and modernization of the mail service, see Kernell and McDonald, "Congress and America's Political Development"; Kernell, "Rural Free Delivery"; Carpenter, "State Building through Reputation Building," and "The Political Foundations of Bureaucratic Autonomy."

31. *Nonconformist* (Indianapolis), January 26, February 16, 1893; see also *Kosse (TX) Cyclone* in *Pacific Rural Press*, March 12, 1892.

32. *Pacific Rural Press*, March 12, 1892.

33. *National Economist*, April 20, 1889; see also Frank, "The Leviathan with Tentacles of Steel," 41; Magliari, "Populism, Steamboats, and the Octopus," 450. Frank Norris's 1901 novel *The Octopus* contained elements of the Populist critique of the railroad. However, Norris's naturalist portrayal of the railroad as a machine disrupting nature diverged from typical Populist themes.

34. *National Economist*, April 6, 20, 1889; see also Higgs, "Railroad Rates"; Aldrich, "A Note on Railroad Rates."

35. Frank, "The Leviathan with Tentacles of Steel," 40.

36. *Kansas Farmer*, January 19, 1887; see also Martin, *The People's Party in Texas*, 26; *Progressive Farmer*, February 18, 1890; *Caucasian*, September 4, 1890. At the time of

railway labor conflict in the spring of 1886, Kansas farm reformers held a dimmer view, asking, "Who *owns* the railroad commissioners of the state of Kansas?" See *Tribune*, April 28, 1886, in John Davis Scrapbooks.

37. *Pioneer Exponent* in *National Economist*, September 13, 1890; see also *Caucasian*, August 11, 1892; Martin, *The People's Party in Texas*, 48; *Pioneer Exponent*, July 7, 1888; "Ocala Demands," in Hicks, *The Populist Revolt*, appendix B, 431. Elizabeth Sanders draws the distinction that late nineteenth-century farm reformers favored a *statutory* expansion of government but opposed the development of *discretionary* bureaucratic power. She attributes this to farmers' intrinsic preference for "local, decentralized, ad hoc arrangements." But farm reformers themselves did not draw such general distinctions at the time. They mainly showed confidence that the work of government could and would be undertaken by businesslike public agents, and therefore supported a variety of national and state government agencies with extensive discretionary power, including railroad commissions, agricultural price commissions, dairy and food commissions, and labor arbitration boards. The shift to demands for government ownership reflected practical realities of corporate power rather than an ideological rejection of discretionary bureaucracy. See Sanders, *Roots of Reform*, 387–89.

38. *Pacific Rural Press*, October 31, 1891; see also *Pacific Rural Press*, December 6, 1890, November 7, 1891, January 23, 1891, January 30, 1893, April 23, 1892; Nash, "The California Railroad Commission, 1876–1911"; Walters, "Populism in California," 123–24.

39. *Pacific Rural Press*, November 7, 1891; see also *Riverside Enterprise*, 1893 clipping, in Cannon/Walker Family Papers; *Los Angeles Times*, October 18, 1892; Walters, "Populism in California," 175.

40. *Nonconformist* (Indianapolis), April 6, 1893, April 26, 1894; "Omaha Platform, July 1892," in Hicks, in *The Populist Revolt*, appendix F, 442.

41. Percy Daniels, *A Crisis for the Husbandman*, 14, quoted in Frank, "The Leviathan with Tentacles of Steel," 50–51. The *Alliance Herald* also pointed to Australia's government-owned railways as "the kind of centralization we need in this country." See *Pacific Rural Press*, June 11, 1891.

42. Tom Watson, speech, Atlanta, May 19, 1894, cited in Watson, *The Life and Speeches of Thos. E. Watson*, 136–37.

43. Todd, *Railways of Europe*, v, 12, 57, 68.

44. *People's Party Paper*, July 22, October 21, 1892.

45. As Harry Tracy, a Populist authority on the money question, put it: "There has been less progress and improvement in monetary methods and systems than in any other function of government. Yet there exists no other human agency with equal power to mar or make a nation, community or individual interest." See Harry Tracy, "A Valuable Appendix, Treating of the Sub-Treasury Plan," in James H. Davis, *A Political Revelation*, 293. For background to the post–Civil War politics of money, see Ritter, *Goldbugs and Greenbacks*; Unger, *The Greenback Era*; Friedman and Schwartz, *A Monetary History of the United States*, 15–128.

46. Norton, *Ten Men of Money Island*. For an examination of Kellogg's influence on Norton and the Populist editors of his day, see Destler, "The Influence of Edward Kellogg upon American Radicalism, 1865–1896," in *American Radicalism*, 50–77.

47. Emery, *Seven Financial Conspiracies*, 12–13, 25, 33, 42, 55, 95–96. Emery used the term *Shylock* interchangeably with bankers and bondholders. The term was widely used in American literature, reflecting a pervasive anti-Semitic stereotype that associated Jews with greedy bankers and gold hoarding. Ignatius Donnelly, for example, who tended to advocate tolerance toward Jews, blacks, and other religious and racial groups (with the notable exception of the Chinese), nonetheless used the term *Shylock* in describing Jews as the "money-getters of the world." See Saxton, " '*Caesar's Column*,' " 32; Ridge, *Ignatius Donnelly*, 263–64, 325, 336–37. For different views of the significance of such language, see Hofstadter, *The Age of Reform*, 61, 77–82, 91; Woodward, "The Populist Heritage and the Intellectual," in *The Burden of Southern History*, 154–56.

48. Thomas Cator to Burnette Connell, December 21, 1893, in Cator Papers; see also Harvey, *Coin's Financial School*, including Richard Hofstadter, "Introduction," 1–80; Charles L. Macune, et al., "Report of the Committee on the Monetary System," in Dunning, *Farmers' Alliance History*, 124–30; Garvin and Daws, *History of the National Farmers' Alliance*, 81; Hicks, *The Populist Revolt*, appendixes A–F, 427–44; Ridge, *Ignatius Donnelly*, 328–29. For a different view, Lawrence Goodwyn's analysis of the movement centers on the division between the "greenback apostles," who represented the true Populists, and the supporters of the "utter delusion" of silver inflation, who represented a "shadow movement" alien to Populist culture. See Goodwyn, *Democratic Promise*, 18–21. As David Montgomery noted, "Goodwyn is not simply a historian who understands Greenback doctrine. . . . He *is* a Greenbacker." See Montgomery, "On Goodwyn's Populists."

49. *National Economist*, November 29, 1890.

50. *Ventura (CA) Weekly Democrat*, March 3, 1893; *People's Press*, October 20, 1894, in Cross California Labor Notes, Carton 5.

51. Charles W. Macune, et al., "Report of the Committee on the Monetary System," in Dunning, *Farmers' Alliance History*, 124–30.

52. Harry Tracy, "A Valuable Appendix, Treating of the Sub-Treasury Plan," in James H. Davis, *A Political Revelation*, 295, 298.

53. Ostler, "The Rhetoric of Conspiracy"; *People's Press*, October 20, 1894, in Cross California Labor Notes, Carton 5.

54. Hicks, *The Populist Revolt*, 186–204; Macune, "Farmers Alliance," 49–51. Although the subtreasury proposal is associated with Charles Macune, similar ideas percolated within farm movement circles. William Peffer, for example, proposed a related plan to create a loan bureau within the Treasury Department that would issue low-interest loans on receipts for stored crops. See Harrington, "The Populist Party in Kansas," 406; McMath, *American Populism*, 134.

55. Harry Tracy, "A Valuable Appendix, Treating of the Sub-Treasury Plan" in James H. Davis, *A Political Revelation*, 365, 378. The Populists proposed a number of variations of the subtreasury. Tom Watson, for example, proposed to place its credit functions in

the Post Office Department and to deputize private elevator and warehouse operators as federal agents. He also sought to replace a subtreasury bureau with an appointed "National Inspector" in the Agriculture Department whose office would centrally regulate the national markets in grain and cotton. See *People's Party Paper*, January 20, 1893, May 12, 1893.

56. Harry Tracy, "A Valuable Appendix, Treating of the Sub-Treasury Plan," in James H. Davis, *A Political Revelation*, 362, 365, 368; *Caucasian*, May 1, 1890.

57. *Advocate* (Topeka), May 6, 1891.

58. Roy V. Scott, *The Agrarian Movement in Illinois*, 128; *People's Party Paper*, March 10, 1892; *Alliance Farmer*, June 18, 1891; Altenberg, "Beyond Capitalism"; *Los Angeles Times*, February 23, 1892; McMath, *American Populism*, 141; Harry Tracy, "A Valuable Appendix: Treating of the Sub-Treasury Plan," in James H. Davis, *A Political Revelation*, 362, 368.

59. "In Congress, April 1889," in Watson, *The Life and Speeches of Thos. E. Watson*, 81; Malin, "The Farmers' Alliance Subtreasury Plan"; *Caucasian*, April 21, 1892.

60. Charles W. Macune, et al., "Report of the Committee on the Monetary System," in Dunning, *Farmers' Alliance History*, 124–30.

61. *Caucasian*, January 14, 1892; see also Hicks, *The Populist Revolt*, 187.

62. *Caucasian*, May 5, 1892; see also Shaw, *Wool Hat Boys*, 22–44.

63. *People's Party Paper*, April 28, 1892; *Nonconformist* (Indianapolis), February 15, 1894; Hackney, *Populism to Progressivism in Alabama*, 21.

64. *Nonconformist* (Winfield, KS), July 4, October 10, November 28, December 5, 1889.

65. *Advocate* (Topeka), July 29, 1891; see also Argersinger, *Populism and Politics*, 35.

66. *Garden City Alliance*, in the *Advocate* (Topeka), November 11, 1891.

67. Penciled note written "around 1895," in "Notes of J. W. H. Davis," in Rushing Collection.

68. Ridge, *Ignatius Donnelly*, 2–13, 288; Hicks, *The Populist Revolt*, 162–64; Goodwyn, *Democratic Promise*, 157–58.

69. Ridge, *Ignatius Donnelly*, 47, 93, 136, 174–75; Jocelyn Wills, *Boosters, Hustlers, and Speculators*, 87, 109.

70. Ridge, *Ignatius Donnelly*, 41, 77, 95, 124, 129–31, 247, 268–69.

71. Ridge, *Ignatius Donnelly*, 133, 145, 154, 172, 177, 260.

72. Ridge, *Ignatius Donnelly*, 196–210, 227–44, 262–78.

73. *People's Party Paper*, April 1, 1892; *Caucasian*, January 7, 1892.

74. "Omaha Platform, July 1892," in Hicks, *The Populist Revolt*, appendix F, 440.

75. "Omaha Platform, July 1892," in Hicks, *The Populist Revolt*, appendix F, 440.

76. "Omaha Platform, July 1892," in Hicks, *The Populist Revolt*, appendix F, 441.

77. James H. Davis, *Memoir*, 21, 59; Williams, "The Political Career of Cyclone Davis," 16–18, 22, 27, 34, 37, 52.

78. James H. Davis, *A Political Revelation*, 3, 133, 267–68. Thomas Watson also framed the Populist platform within the Jeffersonian heritage. See Watson, "The Creed

of Jefferson, the Founder of Democracy," in *The Life and Speeches of Thos. E. Watson*, 99–130, and *The People's Party Campaign Book*, 7–12.

79. Bruce Palmer provides a thoughtful discussion of southern Populism and the Jeffersonian tradition. His premise is that the Populists inherited the Jeffersonian hostility to government centralization, and were deeply committed to the traditional ideals of limited government, states' rights, and strict constitutionalism. Therefore, the Populists were conflicted by economic pressures that required a more active central government. See Palmer, *"Man over Money,"* 39–49. The premise in these pages is that this conflict was more rhetorical than substantive. Apart from opposition to the "Force Bill" on racial matters, southern and northern Populists alike showed little interest in states' rights or strict constitutionalism. They vigorously pursued a national and centralizing vision, and mainly referred to the Jeffersonian tradition as a source of political legitimacy and as a means to deflect attacks from their political opponents.

80. Kellie, "Stand Up for Nebraska," in *A Prairie Populist*, 127–32.

81. *People's Party Paper*, February 18, 1892.

82. *Nonconformist* (Indianapolis), March 16, 1893. In another expression of favoring federal power over the state legislatures, the Farmers' Alliance sponsored a plank in the Morrill Education Act of 1890 requiring state agricultural colleges to report directly to the secretaries of the federal Treasury and Interior departments. Distrusting local administrators and state legislatures, the farm reformers sought to establish direct federal oversight over the state colleges. See Marcus, "The Ivory Silo," 36.

83. James H. Davis, *A Political Revelation*, 285.

84. Kellie, "Stand Up for Nebraska," in *A Prairie Populist*, 130.

85. *Coming Nation*, September 23, 1893; see also "Omaha Platform, July 1892," in Hicks, *The Populist Revolt*, appendix F, 444.

86. Among their many differences, the Jacksonians and the Populists also held different notions of individual freedom. See Ellis, *American Political Cultures*, 53–56.

87. Hicks, *The Populist Revolt*, 406–7, 430; Texas People's Party State Conventions, 1891, 1892, and 1894, in Winkler, *Platforms of Political Parties in Texas*, 297, 299, 333. Few Populists would have predicted that the secret "Australian" ballot, far from weakening the grip of the Democratic and Republican organizations, when put into practice during the 1890s tended to strengthen the two major parties and restrict the prospects for a third-party challenge. The secret ballot also served to disenfranchise black and illiterate voters. See Summers, *Party Games*, 240–49, 253, 264, 268; McGerr, *Decline of Popular Politics*, 64; Kousser, *The Shaping of Southern Politics*, 51–60; Argersinger, "'A Place on the Ballot.'"

88. *People's Advocate*, June 21, 1894.

89. Michael E. McGerr, *Decline of Popular Politics*, 85, 98, 103–4, 216. In the early 1890s, the state of Georgia perhaps led the nation in electoral fraud and political violence and intimidation. According to Barton Shaw, "The Populists used the same methods as their [Democratic] opponents, if not with the same aplomb." See *The Wool Hat Boys*, 76, 93–94, 120.

322 NOTES TO PAGES 163–166

90. In his *The Just Polity* and *The Humane Economy*, Norman Pollack examines the writings of Nugent, Doster, Henry Demarest Lloyd, and similarly democratic-minded reform thinkers to emphasize Populism's democratic and humane nature.

91. "Judge Nugent at San Marcos," July 21, 1893, in Nugent, *Life Work of Thomas L. Nugent*, 170–77.

92. *Pacific Rural Press*, January 23, 1892; James H. Davis, *A Political Revelation*, 285; Carl S. Vrooman, "Taming the Trusts," in Frank, "Leviathan with Tentacles of Steel," 50. Vrooman, "Twentieth Century Democracy," 293; Watson, *The Life and Speeches of Thos. E. Watson*, 81–82, 136–37.

93. *Century*, April 1894, in Malin, *Confounded Rot about Napoleon*, 186–96; *Harper's Weekly*, October 29, 1892, August 26, 1893. Citing the protections the "Code Napoleon" offered to farm property, a January 21, 1890, editorial of the *Rural Californian* described the French emperor as "a great statesman as well as a great soldier."

94. Watson, *Napoleon*, 43, 258, 294, 302, 682.

95. Watson, *The Story of France*, 1046, 1049–50; Watson, *Napoleon*, 266, 268–69, 302, 310, 332, 682, 693, 704.

96. "Story of My Life," in Watson, *The Life and Speeches of Thos. E. Watson*, 19.

97. Woodward made this observation in 1938. More recent historians who identify southern Populism as a uniquely democratic movement have ignored Tom Watson's books on France and Napoleon, although these works represent systematic expositions of the political philosophy of an influential southern Populist. See Woodward, *Agrarian Rebel*, 335–42.

98. *Ventura (CA) Weekly Democrat*, March 3, 1893.

99. Lease, *The Problem of Civilization Solved*, 7, 75.

100. John Davis, "Napoleon Bonaparte," October 1895, 290–301; December 1895, 124–35; April 1896, 765–83. See also John Davis, "On the Money Question," in *Knights of Labor Journal*, August 27, 1891, in John Davis Scrapbooks; "The French Assignats," in the *Junction City (KS) Tribune*, November 23, 1893, in John Davis Scrapbooks; "John Davis on Napoleon," in the *Nonconformist* (Indianapolis), June 13, 1895, in John Davis Scrapbooks. Discerning Kansas Populists also noted Napoleon's "boorishness" when it came to women's rights. See *People's Paper* (Stafford, KS), August 30, 1894.

101. According to Lawrence Goodwyn, experiments with democratic forms within the Farmers' Alliance gave rise to Populism's democratic challenge to the "centralized environment of modern America." For Goodwyn, these democratic forms were largely matters of interior human reality, registered in the realm of "ethos," "élan," and "cultural license." See Goodwyn, *Democratic Promise*, xi–xiii, xxiii. As a result, a reader might readily draw a picture of the Populist movement culture of the 1890s as the movement culture of the 1960s writ large. A different picture emerges from an examination of how the Farmers' Alliance actually worked in terms of the methods and culture of its organizational system.

102. *Progressive Farmer*, February 5, 1889. County officers were also frequently required to give bonds to limit financial abuses of authority. In drought-stricken and

impoverished western Kansas, officers of the Gove County Alliance gave bonds of between one hundred and five hundred dollars. See Gove County Farmers' Alliance Minute Books, August 23, 1890.

103. Shaw, *The Wool Hat Boys*; "The Alliance Moses," 22–44; Garvin and Daws, *History of the National Farmers' Alliance*, 45–47; *Southern Mercury*, September 25, 1888; *Advocate* (Topeka), November 4, 1891; *Alliance Farmer*, June 11, 25, July 2, 1891; *Pacific Rural Press*, January 23, 1892.

104. *Pacific Rural Press*, March 26, 1892; Marion Butler, "Keynote Speech," July 22, 1896, in Bryan, *The First Battle*, 259–64.

105. *Advocate* (Topeka), July 15, November 4, 1891.

106. *Pacific Rural Press*, April 23, 1892.

107. *Alliance Farmer* (Los Angeles), July 25, 1891.

108. *Advocate* (Topeka), May 13, 1891.

109. *Caucasian*, May 28.

110. *Caucasian*, September 3, 1891.

111. *Nonconformist* (Indianapolis), November 15, 1894, in Argersinger, *The Limits of Agrarian Radicalism*, 1–36.

112. Elisabeth Clemens, "From Agrarian Protest to Business Politics," in *The People's Lobby*, 145–83.

113. Lecture notes from 1894 campaign, in "Notes of J. W. H. Davis," in Rushing Collection.

CHAPTER 6

1. *Galveston Daily News*, September 28, 1894; Perry, "The Negro in the People's Party" 36–39; Cantrell, *Limits of Southern Dissent*, 282–83; Rice, *The Negro in Texas*, 79–80; "The Negro's Opportunity in the South," undated letter from John B. Rayner to the *Houston Post*; Rayner, "The Spirit of Abraham Lincoln Calling His Colored Children Whom He Emancipated," undated ms.; "Some of J. B. Rayner's Wise Sayings," undated ms., in Rayner Papers.

2. As the *Southern Mercury* put it: "This is a white man's country, and it must remain so just so long as Caucasian superiority is permitted to assert itself." See *Southern Mercury*, September 26, 1889, in McMath, *Populist Vanguard*, 46; *People's Party Paper*, July 15, 1892; Robert Allen, *Reluctant Reformers*, 71.

3. "The Negro's Heart," undated letter from John B. Rayner to the *Christian Register*, in Rayner Papers; see also Gilmore, *Gender and Jim Crow*, 3, 61–63, 71, 255n10; Cell, *The Highest Stage of White Supremacy*, x, 20, 181–83; Perman, *Struggle for Mastery*, 6–7; Hale, *Making Whiteness*, 6–10; Woodward, *The Strange Career of Jim Crow*, 91.

4. "Mr. Grady in Dallas," in Grady, *Life and Labors*, 186–95.

5. "Mr. Grady in Dallas," in Grady, *Life and Labors*, 163–64.

6. *Progressive Farmer*, January 7, 1890; *Caucasian*, January 9, 1890; see also Noblin,

Agrarian Crusader, 212; Woodward, *Origins of the New South*, 146–47; Hunt, *Marion Butler*, 29; Ayers, *The Promise of the New South*, 87. For a different view that stresses the differences between rural reformers and the New South leaders, see Woodward, *Agrarian Rebel*, 165–66; Gaston, *The New South Creed*, 148–50, 219–21.

7. Grady, *Life and Labors*, 404–6.

8. Gaston, *The New South Creed*, 208–12.

9. Woodward, *Origins of the New South*, 254–58; Pollack, *The Humane Economy*, 78–83; Palmer, "*Man over Money*," 50–66; Goodwyn, *Democratic Promise*, 299.

10. *Southern Mercury*, April 19, 1888.

11. *National Economist*, June 28, August 16, 1890. Although unnamed by Elzey, the Johns Hopkins professor could well have been Herbert Baxter Adams, who taught young southern progressives such as Thomas Dixon Jr. the "latest in evolutionary science" combined with the "Teutonic germ theory" of racial history. See Gilmore, *Gender and Jim Crow*, 67–68.

12. Rabinowitz, "Epilogue," *Race Relations*, 329–39; Litwack, *Trouble in Mind*, 229–37.

13. Jeffrey, "Women in the Southern Farmers' Alliance," 82–83; Gilmore, *Gender and Jim Crow*, 23; Ayers, *The Promise of the New South*, 112–14; Gaither, *Blacks and the Populist Revolt*, 70; *Caucasian*, April 18, 1889, May 11, 1893; Hale, *Making Whiteness*, 128–38. John Cell focuses on the urban phenomena that provided the modern impulse toward segregation. See Cell, *The Highest Stage of White Supremacy*, x, 131–35. A parallel process unfolded in rural settings, with factories, railroads, and other modernizing forces at work in the rural districts.

14. Litwack, *Trouble in Mind*, 231–33; Ayers, *The Promise of the New South*, 145.

15. *Caucasian*, February 20, 1890; see also Woodward, *Origins of the New* South, 211–12; Crowe, "Tom Watson," 109; McMath, *Populist Vanguard*, 126; Palmer, "*Man over Money*," 56; Saunders, "Southern Populists and the Negro," 249–50; Robert Allen, *Reluctant Reformers*, 62; Gaither, *Blacks and the Populist Revolt*, 70–72.

16. *Southern Mercury*, July 5, 1888, in Barthelme, *Women in the Texas Populist Movement*, 46–47; see also Hackney, *Populism to Progressivism in Alabama*, 45–46.

17. *National Economist*, March 7, 1891, December 14, 1889, January 17, 1891; *Progressive Farmer*, January 27, 1891; Abramowitz, "The Negro in the Agrarian Revolt."

18. Steelman, *The North Carolina Farmers' Alliance*, 178–79; Ali, "Black Populism," 100; see also McMath, *Populist Vanguard*, 46, 125; Roy V. Scott, "Milton George and the Farmers' Alliance Movement," 11, 107–8.

19. *National Economist*, January 17, 1891; see also Richard Manning Humphrey, "Colored Farmers' National Alliance," in Dunning, *Farmers' Alliance History*, 153, 288–92; Abramowitz, "The Negro in the Agrarian Revolt," 93.

20. Richard Manning Humphrey, "Colored Farmers' National Alliance," in Dunning, *Farmers' Alliance History*, 288–92.

21. William F. Holmes, "The Arkansas Cotton Pickers' Strike"; see also Kremm and Neal, "Challenges to Subordination."

22. *Caucasian*, September 17, 1891.

23. William F. Holmes, "The Arkansas Cotton Pickers' Strike."

24. *Progressive Farmer* reprinted in *Caucasian*, September 17, 1891.

25. Shaw, *The Wool Hat Boys*, 54.

26. Garland, *A Spoil of Office*, 345.

27. *Kansas Farmer*, November 19, 1890; *Nonconformist* (Winfield, KS), September 12, 1889; Abramowitz, "The Negro in the Agrarian Revolt," 94–95; Gaither, *Blacks and the Populist Revolt*, 34; Williams, "The Political Career of Cyclone Davis," 35. Milton George of the Northern Alliance remained more skeptical about Southern Alliance claims of racial justice. Yet he hoped that the paternalistic efforts of the two alliances could provide the proper instruction to fit the former slaves "for a self reliant citizenship." As for the Colored Alliance, George saw it as the willing pupil in this educational work of national reconciliation. See *Western Rural*, January 31, 1891.

28. McMath, *American Populism*, 145–46; Davis, *Memoir*, 55; "Mr. Grady in Boston," in Grady, *Life and Labors*, 243–74; "Mr. Grady in Dallas," in Grady, *Life and Labors*, 188; Blight, *Race and Reunion*, 198–201, 265.

29. *Southern Mercury*, December 6, 1888; see also Garvin and Daws, *History of the National Farmers' Alliance*, 17.

30. Charles Macune, "On the Northern Alliance," in Dunning, *Farmers' Alliance History*, 109. In 1891, in a gesture of reconciliation and friendship with the white South, the new Populist majority in the Kansas legislature voted unanimously to reject the so-called "Force Bill" to provide federal protection for southern black voters. See clipping "Old Party Mendacity," August 16, 1894, in John Davis Scrapbooks.

31. Noblin, *Agrarian Crusader*, 20–21, 297.

32. *Topeka Advocate*, November 11, 1891; *Progressive Farmer*, January 7, 1890; *People's Party Paper*, August 4, 1893; *Caucasian*, June 16, 1892.

33. Beckel, "Roots of Reform," 198, 334, 438, 486; Noblin, *Agrarian Crusader*, 40–49, 83; Gilmore, *Gender and Jim* Crow, 77; *Farmer and Mechanic*, February 7, 1878; Polk, *Handbook of North Carolina*, 147; Polk, *Report on the General Condition of the Agricultural Interests of North Carolina*, 6–7; Polk, *Inter-State Convention*, 6.

34. *Progressive Farmer*, April 30, 1889, May 21, 1889, in Noblin, *Agrarian Crusader*, 199; see also Beckel, "Roots of Reform," 438. Polk's views about race and reunion corresponded to a narrative widely popularized by Thomas Dixon Jr. in his white supremacist novel *The Clansman* (1905) that was turned into the feature film *The Birth of a Nation* (1915). In the 1880s, Polk collaborated with Dixon and the other young self-consciously modern reformers of Raleigh's Watauga Club to establish North Carolina's state agricultural college. See Blight, *Race and Reunion*, 111–12, 394–96; Gilmore, *Gender and Jim Crow*, 66–67; Noblin, *Agrarian Crusader*, 165–66.

35. McMath, *Populist Vanguard*, appendix A, 161–62; *National Economist*, September 6, 1890.

36. *Southern Mercury*, December 6, 1888; see also Macune, "Farmers' Alliance," 13.

37. *Progressive Farmer*, January 7, 1890; see also *People's Party Paper*, May 26, 1893; *Southern Mercury*, June 28, July 12, August 14, 1888; Beckel, "Roots of Reform," 536.

38. Rice, *The Negro in Texas*, 161; Wharton, *The Negro in Mississippi*, 97–99; Saxton, *The Indispensable Enemy*, 210; *Alliance Farmer*, June 11, 1891; *Rural Californian*, January 21, February [?], 1890; *People's Advocate*, May 31, 1894.

39. Walker, "Populiste Californien," 321–24; Marion Cannon, "Diary of Trip East," in Cannon/Walker Family Papers.

40. "Mr. Grady in Dallas," in Grady, *Life and Labors*, 188–89; *Southern Mercury*, November 13, 1888.

41. *People's Party Paper*, June 2, June 16, 1893; Lease, *The Problem of Civilization Solved*, 35, 220. See chapter 8 for discussion of the role of comparative and Eastern religions in Populist belief.

42. *People's Advocate*, January 4, May 31, 1894.

43. Watson, "The Negro Question in the South."

44. *Comanche Vanguard*, July 19, 26, 1913; Lightfoot, "The Human Party."

45. *Town and Country*, July 29, 1886; Lightfoot, "The Negro Exodus from Comanche County, Texas," 410–12; *Comanche Chief*, September 21, 1895.

46. *Town and Country*, August 4, August 12, 1886; *Comanche Vanguard*, August 23, 1913; Martin, *The People's Party in Texas*, 129n20.

47. *Progressive Farmer*, April 20, May 21, 1889, in Noblin, *Agrarian Crusader*, 199. Tom Watson claimed that Leonidas "Lon" Livingston, the "Moses" of the Georgia Farmers' Alliance, not Leonidas Polk, authored the plan for a black reservation in Texas, as in Gaither, *Blacks and the Populist Revolt*, 43. See *People's Party Paper*, September 30, 1892.

48. Lease, *The Problem of Civilization Solved*, 361; see also *Savannah Tribune*, June 2, 1894; Phillip Foner, *Organized Labor and the Black Worker*, 62–63; McLaurin, *The Knights of Labor in the South*, 148; Fredrickson, *The Black Image in the White Mind*, 246–48.

49. John Wright to Lorenzo Lewelling, April 30, 1893, July 2, 1894, in Lewelling, Correspondence Files, Box 1; see also Gaither, *Blacks and the Populist Revolt*, 208n91; Reynolds, "The Alabama Negro Colony in Mexico, 1894–1896."

50. "The Negro's Heart," undated letter from John B. Rayner to the *Christian Register*, in Rayner Papers. For an excellent treatment of African American emigration strategies in this era, see Hahn, *A Nation under Our Feet*, 317–63. The magazine of Edward Bellamy's social reformist movement carried an anonymous article advocating the creation of a separate black state in the American South as the best means to achieve black equality and progress. See Anonymous, "The Negro's Part."

51. *People's Party Paper*, July 15, 1892.

52. Cantrell and Barton, "Texas Populists," 664–72; Perry, "The Negro in the People's Party," 35–37; Pitre, *Through Many Dangers, Toils and Snares*, 124–26.

53. Cantrell, *Limits of Southern Dissent*, 183–88.

54. "Some of J. B. Rayner's Wise Sayings," undated ms., in Rayner Papers.

55. Cantrell, *Limits of Southern Dissent*, 188.

56. *Southern Mercury*, December 12, 1895.

57. "Some of J. B. Rayner's Wise Sayings," undated ms., in Rayner Papers.

58. Goodwyn, *Democratic Promise*, 288; *Southern Mercury*, December 12, 1895; Cantrell, *Limits of Southern Dissent*, 207; Hyman, *The Anti-Redeemers*, 172–73.

59. Perry, "The Negro in the People's Party," 35–38. In Kansas, where the Populists promised to put blacks on the ticket and "treat the colored boys fair," they made the gesture of nominating a black man for state auditor. See *People's Advocate* (Hill City, Kans.), July 20, 1894; Chafe, "The Negro and Populism," 409.

60. "The Negro's Heart," undated letter from John B. Rayner to the *Christian Register*, in Rayner Papers; see also Abramowitz, "John B. Rayner—A Grass-Roots Leader," 161, 165; Cantrell, *Limits of Southern Dissent*, 217.

61. *People's Party Paper*, July 14, 1893; see also Cantrell, *Limits of Southern Dissent*, 211; *Houston Daily Post*, October 19, 1894, in Perry, "The Negro in the People's Party," appendix E, 65–66. The Populists and Democrats exchanged similar mutual accusations about placing blacks on juries in Georgia, where Tom Watson accused his Democratic opponent James Black of "promising to put the negroes in the jury boxes." Summing up this debate, Robert Saunders points out "the available evidence fails to show a discernible distinction between Populist and Democratic attitudes concerning Negro jury service. If anything, [Democrat] James C. C. Black put forth a more positive stand than any Populist." See Saunders, "Southern Populists and the Negro," 247–48.

62. Cantrell and Barton, "Texas Populists," 662–63. Prior to disfranchisement, the Democrats frequently competed with the Populists and Republicans for the black vote. In Alabama, for example, the Democratic leadership sponsored prominent black lecturers, and black Democrats organized an Afro-American Democratic League. See Hackney, *Populism to Progressivism in Alabama*, 35.

63. "Some of J. B. Rayner's Wise Sayings," undated ms.; "The Negro's Opportunity in the South," undated letter from John B. Rayner to the *Houston Post*, in Rayner Papers; Goodwyn, *Democratic Promise*, 288.

64. The 1896 platform of the Texas People's party further specified that "each race shall have its own pro rata portion of the school fund, and its own trustees, to be elected by the respective races, and control its own schools." See Winkler, *Platforms of Political Parties in Texas*, 333, 382–83; Cantrell and Barton, "Texas Populists," 684; Cantrell, *Limits of Southern Dissent*, 273.

65. Nugent, *Life Work of Thomas L. Nugent*, 13, 33, 73; Martin, *The People's Party in Texas*, 115–18.

66. Nugent, *Life Work of Thomas L. Nugent*, 57, 117; see also Martin, *The People's Party in Texas*, 115–18.

67. Nugent, *Life Work of Thomas L. Nugent*, 67–68.

68. "On the Subject of Lynch Law," February 6, 1893, in Hogg, *Speeches and State Papers*; "Judge Nugent on the Burning," in Nugent, *Life Work of Thomas L. Nugent*, 249–50. Nugent's attitude toward lynching was similar to the stand of the Populist press elsewhere. The Vincent brothers' *Nonconformist* (Indianapolis) reflected sentiments in favor of black equality, but reported on plans to burn alive Henry Smith without criticism and with lurid details. See *Nonconformist* (Indianapolis), "A Negro Brute's Crime,"

February 2, 1893. In North Carolina, the Farmers' Alliance newspaper, the *Caucasian*, opposed the principle of lynching as a "remedy of the uncivilized society," while endorsing specific lynchings as "justified by public sentiment, if not by law." See *Caucasian*, January 16, 1890, September 10, 1891.

69. Nugent, *Life Work of Thomas L. Nugent*, 339; see also Perry, "The Negro in the People's Party," 17.

70. Cantrell, *Limits of Southern Dissent*, 213.

71. *Caucasian*, April 4, 1895.

72. "Mr. Grady in Dallas," in *Life and Labors of Henry W. Grady*, 186.

73. Lecture notes from 1894 campaign, in "Notes of J. W. H. Davis," in Rushing Collection.

74. *People's Party Paper*, August 12, 1892.

75. *People's Party Paper*, August 12, September 16, October 28, 1892; see also Woodward, *Agrarian Rebel*, 238–42; Goodwyn, *Democratic Promise*, 296–97, 300. For a less sanguine assessment of Watson and the Doyle episode, see Shaw, *The Wool Hat Boys*, 88–89; Crowe, "Tom Watson, Blacks and Populists Reconsidered," 106–8.

76. Shaw, "The Populists after Dark," in *The Wool Hat Boys*, 78–90; Ayers, *The Promise of the New South*, 273.

77. *People's Party Paper*, July 15, 1892, April 14, July 7, November 13, 1893.

78. Cantrell and Barton, "Texas Populists," 663; Martin, *The People's Party in Texas*, 97–98; Hahn, *A Nation under Our Feet*, 398–400, 439–40; Gaither, *Blacks and the Populist Revolt*, 97. The Populist-Republican coalition that controlled local government in Grimes County, Texas, was driven from office in 1900 in a wave of Democratic intimidation, violence, and murder. See Goodwyn, "Populist Dreams and Negro Rights."

79. Kousser, *The Shaping of Southern Politics*, 182–95. Marion Butler was one of the most significant leaders of the Populist movement. After the death of Leonidas Polk, Butler led the Alliance and the People's party in North Carolina, served as the national president of the Farmers' Alliance and the national chairman of the People's party, and was the only Populist elected to the U.S. Senate from the South. Yet, because his experience does not fit well within previous ideological assumptions about Populism, little has been written about him. James L. Hunt's excellent political biography, *Marion Butler*, fills an important omission.

80. *Caucasian*, March 14, 1889; see also Hunt, *Marion Butler*, 15–30. Norman Pollack writes that Marion Butler's efforts to diffuse the race-baiting by the Democrats showed that he was arriving at the conclusion "that racism was incompatible with reform." See Pollack, *The Humane Economy*, 79–80. This assessment, however, fails to take into account the degree to which Butler and his colleagues viewed segregation and white supremacy as intrinsic to the reform agenda.

81. Hunt, *Marion Butler*, 51–67; Beeby, "'Equal Rights to All and Special Privileges to None'," 170–72. A Populist newspaper in Louisiana, for example, explained: "The People's Party in this state is a white man's party. . . . If you want white supremacy join the Populists [;] if you want to go into a party that acknowledges its failure to even exist

without uniting with the negro, then follow the modern so-called Democracy." See *Louisiana Populist*, August 24, 1894, in Gaither, *Blacks and the Populist Revolt*, 69.

82. Hunt, *Marion Butler*, 77–86; Kousser, *The Shaping of Southern Politics*, 186–87; Anderson, *Race and Politics in North Carolina*, 242–51, 280–95; Ali, "Black Populism," 200.

83. Beeby, "'Equal Rights to All and Special Privileges to None,'" 172; see also Hunt, *Marion Butler*, 65, 152; Gaither, *Blacks and the Populist* Revolt, 87; *Caucasian*, May 11, 1893, March 14, 28, April 4, 1895.

84. *Caucasian*, August 25, 1892.

85. Ayers, *The Promise of the New South*, 299–304; Anderson, *Race and Politics in North Carolina*, 290; Kousser, *The Shaping of Southern Politics*, 188–93.

86. Woodward, *Origins of the New South*, 348–49.

87. Hunt, *Marion Butler*, 171–73; Anderson, *Race and Politics in North Carolina*, 296–97, 303.

88. Woodward, *Agrarian Rebel*, 385–86, 432; see also Kousser, *The Shaping of Southern Politics*, 139–45; Spriggs, "The Virginia Colored Farmers' Alliance," 201; *National Economist*, April 19, 1890; Hackney, *Populism to Progressivism in Alabama*, 37, 46–47.

89. *Southern Mercury*, June 14, 1888, in Barthelme, *Women in the Texas Populist Movement*, 117–18; *National Economist*, March 1, 1890.

90. *Southern Mercury*, May 28, 1896, in Cantrell, *Limits of Southern Dissent*, 248.

91. *Rockdale Messenger*, May 17, 1900, in Cantrell and Barton, "Texas Populists," 691; see also Kousser, *The Shaping of Southern Politics*, 204–9.

92. "Federal Government's Best Asset," undated letter from John B. Rayner to the *Home Defender*; "The Negro's Heart," undated letter from John B. Rayner to the *Christian Register*, in Rayner Papers; see also Kousser, *The Shaping of Southern Politics*, 238–61.

93. C. Vann Woodward argued in his *Origins of the New South* that voting restrictions were essentially the response of Southern elites to the Populist threat of biracial collaboration among the lower classes. J. Morgan Kousser's *The Shaping of Southern Politics* makes a similar argument, as does Michael Perman's *Struggle for Mastery*. A recent study by Glenn Feldman challenges this framework. He argues that disfranchisement "was a pan-white movement that perhaps engendered various degrees of support among whites of different classes. . . . But in the end, it was a movement aimed by whites at blacks, implemented by whites against blacks, and passed with enough white consensus on the overall goal of black disfranchisement to override white disagreement on specific means." See Feldman, *The Disfranchisement Myth*, 7.

94. Party competition also opened political opportunities for blacks in the North and West. In Kansas, for example, an influential section of black reformers joined the People's party and protested against the lack of resources and patronage for blacks under Republican administrations, while the Populist governor maintained that he would not "countenance any discrimination on account of color" in state appointments. See Cox, *Blacks in Topeka, Kansas*, 111–35; Lorenzo Lewelling to M. A. Householder, July 13, 1893, Lewelling, Governor's Office, Letter Press Books.

95. *National Economist*, March 7, 1891.

96. "The Negro's Opportunity in the South," undated letter from John B. Rayner to the *Houston Post*; "The Negro's Heart," undated letter from John B. Rayner to the *Christian Register*; "Some of J. B. Rayner's Wise Sayings," undated ms., in Rayner Papers.

CHAPTER 7

1. *Southern Mercury*, November 14, 1895.

2. Hicks, *The Populist Revolt*; Goodwyn, *Democratic Promise*, 308–9; McGreevy, "Farmers, Nationalists, and the Origins of California Populism"; Lipow, *Authoritarian Socialism in America*, 97–98; Thomas, *Alternative America*, 5, 36, 332–33, 364–65; Westbrook, "Neorepublican Prophets." Edward Spann's treatment of the Single Tax and Nationalist movements focuses on their "new middle class" following rather than the role that these movements played within Populist coalition. At the same time, his work stands out for its stress on the contemporary and modern impulses—"the striving of Modern Man to improve his social condition"—in nineteenth-century nonconformist movements. See Spann, *Brotherly Tomorrows*, xiv, 8, 47–48, 176–209.

3. Stansell, *American Moderns*, 16, 45–50.

4. Gompers, "Organized Labor in the Campaign," 93; Kleppner, *The Cross of Culture*, 203.

5. Pierce, "The Populist President," 18–23; Wyman, "Agrarian or Working-Class Radicalism?" 827; Greene, *Pure and Simple Politics*, 63–64; Kleppner, *The Cross of Culture*, 190; Jensen, *The Winning of the Midwest*, 257–60; Perlman, "Upheaval and Reorganisation," 512; Robert W. Larson, *Populism in the Mountain West*, 151–52, 156; Schneirov, *Labor and Urban Politics*, 240, 300–301.

6. Scharnau, "Thomas J. Morgan and the Chicago Socialist Movement," 218–32; Destler, *American Radicalism*, 162–211.

7. Jensen, *The Winning of the Midwest*, 245, 257–60; Greene, *Pure and Simple Politics*, 53, 61.

8. Hattam, *Labor Visions and State Power*, 170, and "Economic Visions and Political Strategies," 88–99.

9. Leon Fink, *Workingmen's Democracy*, 13–14; Schneirov, *Labor and Urban Politics*, 237–40; Voss, *The Making of American Exceptionalism*, 234–40; Perlman, "Upheaval and Reorganisation," 482–87.

10. Leon Fink, *Workingmen's Democracy*, 32–33.

11. Swinton, *A Momentous Question*, 246–48.

12. McBride, "Coal Miners," 241–42, 253–54; Gutman, "Coal Miners on the Prairie," in *Power and Culture*, 117–212; Pierce, "The Populist President," *United Mine Workers' Journal*, April 16, 1891.

13. McBride, "Coal Miners," 247.

14. *United Mine Workers' Journal*, May 7, 1891.

15. Ruth A. Allen, *Organized Labor in Texas*, 92, 118; Martin, *The People's Party in Texas*, 31–32.

16. Perlman, "Upheaval and Reorganisation," 487; Pierce, "The Plow and Hammer," 29, 31, 94, 161–79, 205, 209.

17. Ruth A. Allen, *Organized Labor in Texas*, 92, 118; Pierce, "The Populist President," 14.

18. *Coming Nation*, March 30, 1895; see also *United Mine Workers' Journal*, April 16, 23, May 14, 1891; Leikin, *The Practical Utopians*, 72–73.

19. McBride, "Coal Miners," 253–54; see also Bowman, "When Workers Organize Capitalists," 297. As Richard Jensen explains, "Coal cried out for rationalization," and labor organization and strikes were understood by both miners and coal companies as a means to that end. See Jensen, *The Winning of the Midwest*, 246–52.

20. McBride, "Coal Miners," 253–54; see also Brody, "Market Unionism in America: The Case of Coal," in *In Labor's Cause*, 131–74; Bowman, "When Workers Organize Capitalists."

21. Pierce, "The Populist President," 14–16; Brody, *In Labor's Cause*, 139–42.

22. Victoria Hattam quite rightly cites McBride's speech to the AFL convention as evidence of the modernizing visions of the union movement. At the same time, she contrasts this vision to what she describes as "the vision of decentralized economic development" that characterized the "producers' program" of Populist reform. See Hattam, *Labor Visions and State Power*, 158, 170. In reality, McBride articulated the modern vision of labor Populism.

23. Maier, "The Realization of My Boyhood Dream as a Railroad Man"; Chandler, *The Visible Hand*, 1–12.

24. Michael Cassity interprets the modern organizational system of District Assembly 101 as its chief weakness, not its strength. He attributes the defeat of the Knights on the Southwest System to their shift of loyalties "from the traditional to the modern," failing to sustain support of local communities, which viewed the District Assembly 101 as a centralized and remote organizational system no less alien than the similarly organized corporations. See Cassity, "Modernization and Social Crisis," 43, 51, 54, 60.

25. Zlatkovich, *Texas Railroads*, 5–7; Patricia Evridge Hill, *Dallas*, xxiii–xxv. Referring to the burgeoning towns where the Knights took root in the 1880s, Leon Fink notes that "these were not 'island communities' protesting the construction of a bridge to the bureaucratic-industrial mainland. . . . Indeed, the early years of factory-building, quarrying, and railroad construction had been marked by a relative consensus of civic boosterism and popular expectation." See Leon Fink, *Workingmen's Democracy*, 219–20.

26. Stromquist, *A Generation of Boomers*, 46, 196–97; Ruth A. Allen, *The Great Southwest Strike*, 22.

27. Ruth A. Allen, *Organized Labor in Texas*, 25–26, 31–34, 90.

28. Leon Fink, *Workingmen's Democracy*, 119–22; Ruth A. Allen, *Organized Labor in Texas*, 90.

29. Debs, "Martin Irons"; see also *Austin Statesman*, April 27, 1886; *New York Nation*, April 22, 1886; Peck, *Twenty Years of the Republic*, 128.

30. Irons, "My Experience in the Labor Movement"; see also Stromquist, *A Generation of Boomers*, xiii–xv.

31. Irons, "My Experience in the Labor Movement."

32. Irons, "My Experience in the Labor Movement"; Perlman, "Upheaval and Re-organisation," 382–84; Ruth A. Allen, *The Great Southwest Strike*, 42–43.

33. Debs, "Martin Irons." Shelton Stromquist characterizes the Knights' organization on the railroads as "decentralized, rank-and-file, general unionism," which he contrasts to the centralized authority imposed by the Supreme Council of the railway brother-hoods. However, the Knights' organization, whether District Assembly 82 on the Union Pacific or District Assembly 101 on the Southwest System, was an alternative and po-tentially more effective system of centralization, where "the whole working force of the corporation can be controlled at one time and united in common defense." See Stromquist, *A Generation of Boomers*, 76–79; Brundage, *The Making of Western Labor Radicalism*, 113–15.

34. Ruth A. Allen, *The Great Southwest Strike*, 51–52, 90. An unsuccessful strike on the New York Central Railroad in 1890 led to a similar setback for the Knights of Labor in the Midwest and Northeast. See Robert E. Weir, "Dress Rehearsal for Pullman: The Knights of Labor and the 1890 New York Central Strike," in Schneirov, Stromquist, and Salvatore, *The Pullman Strike*, 21–42. For a valuable study of the role of the employer blacklist in the destruction of the Knights of Labor, see Voss, *The Making of American Exceptionalism*.

35. *St. Louis Globe-Democrat*, June 27, 1886.

36. *Galveston Daily News*, April 8, 1886, in Ruth A. Allen Labor Movement in Texas Collection.

37. *Dallas Morning News*, July 4, 16, 17, November 2–7, 1886; Patricia Evridge Hill, *Dallas*, 27–28.

38. *Austin Statesman*, April 7, 1886.

39. *Waco Daily Examiner*, April 3, 1886, in Ruth A. Allen Labor Movement in Texas Collection; *Rural Citizen*, April 29, May 6, 20, 1886.

40. *Fort Worth Gazette*, August 8, 1886, in Ruth A. Allen Labor Movement in Texas Collection; Goodwyn, *Democratic Promise*, 77–80; Garvin and Daws, *History of the National Farmers' Alliance*, 45–47. Leon Fink observes that unlike the Farmers' Alliance, the problems facing the Knights "did not converge nearly so neatly on the public do-main." See Leon Fink, *Workingmen's Democracy*, 32–33. However, for more than most other workers in the private sector, the political demands of the railway workers corre-sponded closely to the regulations and state building sought by the farm reformers.

41. *Southern Mercury*, January 10, 1889.

42. *St. Louis Globe-Democrat*, March 9, 1886, *Galveston Daily News*, April 8, 1886, in Ruth A. Allen Labor Movement in Texas Collection; *National Economist Almanac*, 1890.

43. Jelley, *The Voice of Labor*, 315, 372, 375–400.

44. *Journal of the Knights of Labor*, January 16, 30, 1890; McLaurin, *The Knights of Labor in the South*, 141–42, 148, 175–78.

45. Patricia Evridge Hill, *Dallas*, 35–36; Goodwyn, *Democratic Promise*, 286; John R. Hearle to Ben Owens, August 5, 1940, A. O. Woodward to Ben Owens, January 25, 1940, *Daily Tribune* (Jefferson City (MO), December 17, 1891, interview with John Kept, Bruceville, Texas, June 1938, in Ruth A. Allen Labor Movement in Texas Collection; Terence V. Powderly, *The Path I Trod*, 137.

46. Stromquist, *Generation of Boomers*, 73–84; Weir, "Dress Rehearsal for Pullman," in Schneirov, Stromquist, and Salvatore, *The Pullman Strike*, 36; Salvatore, *Citizen and Socialist*, 145.

47. *Chicago Searchlight*, June 28, 1894; see also Salvatore, *Citizen and Socialist*, 80; Lindsey, *The Pullman Strike*, 115.

48. Lindsey, *The Pullman Strike*, 269.

49. Lindsey, *The Pullman Strike*, 250–61, 277; see also *United States Strike Commission Report*, 434

50. *Chicago Searchlight*, June 7, 28, July 12, 1894; Woeste, *The Farmers' Benevolent Trust*, 68.

51. *Chicago Searchlight*, July 12, 1894.

52. Nugent, *Life Work of Thomas L. Nugent*, 179–205, 255–57.

53. *Chicago Searchlight*, June 21, 1894; see also *Chicago Times*, June 15, 20, 1894; Salvatore, *Citizen and Socialist*, 147.

54. Debs to Frank Holl, May 15, 1895, in Debs Papers.

55. Salvatore, *Citizen and Socialist*, 147; American Railway Union, "Appeal to the American People," in Swinton, *A Momentous Question*, 476–80.

56. *Chicago Searchlight*, August 4, 1894.

57. Debs to Frank Holl, October 3, 1894, in Debs Papers; Debs to *St. Paul Globe*, January 18, 1895, in Debs Papers.

58. Debs to Frank Holl, December 8, 1894, in Debs Papers; Salvatore, *Citizen and Socialist*, 139.

59. "Omaha Platform, July 1892," in Hicks, *The Populist Revolt*, appendix F, 442.

60. Hofstadter, *The Age of Reform*, 46–47.

61. "Omaha Platform, July 1892," in Hicks, *The Populist Revolt*, appendix F, 441; see also Palmer, "*Man over Money*," 3, 8, 14, 18, 199, 214.

62. Watson, *The People's Party Campaign Book*, 220–21.

63. Watson, *The People's Party Campaign Book*, 221; "Omaha Platform, July 1892," in Hicks, *The Populist Revolt*, appendix F, 440. Robert Johnston, in his efforts to restore the good name of the much-disparaged middle class, argues that middling or small proprietors have given rise to radically democratic and anticapitalist populism across the course of American history. Although his study is mainly of middle-class reformers during the Progressive Era, his concept of populism with a small *p* includes the Populists with a capital *P* of the 1880s and 1890s. One of the outstanding theoretical problems

posed by this argument is defining the middle class. Following the lead of E. P. Thompson, Johnston thoughtfully argues that the meaning of "middle class" is best defined by the people who lived their own history. However, any Populist class consciousness in this regard was strikingly undeveloped. See Johnston, *The Radical Middle Class*, 10–17; Thompson, *The Making of the English Working Class*, 9–11.

64. *National Economist*, April 6, 1889, April 19, 26, 1890; *Western Rural*, January 17, 1891; Dunning, *Farmers' Alliance History*, 49; Nixon, "The Cleavage within the Farmers' Alliance Movement."

65. Charles Macune's hand-lettered note for an Indianapolis lecture, in Macune, "National Farmers' Alliance Speeches"; see also Dunning, *Farmers' Alliance History*, 113, 182; Garvin and Daws, *History of the National Farmers' Alliance*, xi, 18–19.

66. *Caucasian*, December 1, 1892.

67. Anna Fader diary, June 17, September 24, 1889, January 24, April 23, 1890, in Haskell Family Papers. Note that although the dates cited are those heading the diary entries, Fader had a "fad" of deliberately placing entries under the wrong date for the sake of "variety." See Anna Fader diary, May 9, 1890.

68. Burnette G. Haskell, "How Kaweah Fell."

69. "News of the Movement, California," *Nationalist* 2(1890), 341–42; see also Walters, "Populism in California," 33–43. The early career of Charlotte Perkins Gilman also provides insights into the social milieu that sustained the reform movement in San Francisco. Although Gilman was deeply involved with literary questions, she was also a prominent lecturer and essayist for the Nationalist and Populist movements in California. Gilman maintained a public image of Victorian respectability that belied the unconventional ideas and practices regarding sex, marriage, and society that prevailed within her reform circle. See Mary A. Hill, *Charlotte Perkins Gilman*, 182–83.

70. Anna Fader diary, November 4, November 17, December 16, 1888, July 13, 1890, and Burnette Haskell's note on the back of Anna's diary signed May 26, 1889, in Haskell Family Papers. Fader's diary reflected a feminist sensibility. However, unlike Charlotte Perkins Gilman and other women attracted to Nationalism, she did not focus her attention on the "woman question."

71. Anna Fader diary, February 10, 11, 25, March 5, April 6, May 10, June 2, August 3, 1889, March 23, April 14, July 13, 1890, in Haskell Family Papers; see also O'Connell, *Co-Operative Dreams*, 26.

72. Anna Fader diary, July 30, September 24, October 26, November 18, December 18, 1889, July 20, 1890, in Haskell Family Papers.

73. Anna Fader Haskell to Nell Haskell, April 26, 1906, in Haskell Family Papers; Donnelly, *Caesar's Column, a Story of the Twentieth Century*, 286–93; Saxton, "'Caesar's Column,'" 224.

74. Anna Fader diary, March 7, 26, April 30, December 4, 1889, July 30, 1890, in Haskell Family Papers; David Brundage, *The Making of Western Labor Radicalism*, 48, 72–73, 90, 105–11; *San Francisco Call*, April 1, 9, 1890, in Cross California Labor Notes.

75. Anna Fader diary, July 26, 1889, in Haskell Family Papers; O'Connell, *Co-*

Operative Dreams, 16, 100; Burnette Haskell to Maria A. Haskell, October 28, 1891, Anna Fader Haskell to Edward W. Haskell, September 5, 1906, in Haskell Family Papers. Edward Spann writes that Bellamyism appealed to the "new middle class of white-collar workers and salaried professionals" squeezed between concentrated capital and "the discontents of the lower classes." Such a characterization makes sense in terms of the intellectual influences on Bellamy and his New England intellectual circle. However, in the Populist strongholds of the Midwest and West, Bellamyism often overran its narrow origins to connect with labor, the unemployed, and other discontents from the lower classes. See Spann, *Brotherly Tomorrows*, 191.

76. Goodwyn, *Democratic Promise*, 308. The Single-Tax idea facilitated powerful multiclass alliances in the 1880s and 1890s, and again in the first decade of the twentieth century. See Johnston, *The Radical Middle Class*, 157–76.

77. Henry George, *Progress and Poverty*, 433–544; see also Henry George, *Social Problems*, 1–9, and "Land and Taxation"; *Chicago Searchlight*, August 2, 9, 16, 1894; *Southern Mercury*, December 6, 1888; *Pacific Rural Press*, May 3, 1890; Leon Fink, *Workingmen's Democracy*, 137; Destler, *American Radicalism*, 13.

78. Destler, *American Radicalism*, 81; Edward W. Thurman to Ira B. Cross, June 11, 1931, in Cross California Labor Notes; Anna Fader diary, December 8, 1888, in Haskell Family Papers; *People's Press*, October 20, 1894; Haskell, "A Plan of Action"; Walters, "Populism in California," 30; Ethington, *The Public City*, 373–77; Saxton, "San Francisco Labor and the Populist and Progressive Insurgencies"; Knapp, "San Francisco and the Civic Awakening."

79. *San Pedro Times*, in *Chicago Searchlight*, August 2, 1894; see also Edward W. Thurman to Ira B. Cross, June 11, 1931, in Cross California Labor Notes; Hall, "California Populism at the Grass-Roots," 197; *Pacific Rural Press*, May 3, 1890.

80. Clarence Darrow to Ellen Gates Starr [c1895], in Ginger, *The Nationalizing of American Life*, 140–43; see also Tierney, *Darrow*, 46–50; McMurry, *Coxey's Army*, 227, 255.

81. *Chicago Searchlight*, July 19, August 9, 16, 1894; Destler, *American Radicalism*, 181, 194, 197.

82. Destler, *American Radicalism*, 168–70, 200–207; *Chicago Searchlight*, July 19, August 2, 9, 1894.

83. *Chicago Searchlight*, August 2, 1894; Destler, *American Radicalism*, 249; Schneirov, *Labor and Urban Politics*, 347; Abbot, "Chicago Populist Campaign"; Leidenberger, "Working-Class Progressivism and the Politics of Transportation in Chicago," viii–xiii.

84. Hamlin Garland to Arthur E. Morgan, February 26, 1940, in Garland Papers.

85. Hicks, *The Populist Revolt*, 161.

86. *Southern Mercury*, December 6, 1888.

87. *National Economist*, December 14, 1889; see also Rice, *The Negro in Texas*, 178.

88. *Southern Mercury*, December 6, 1888.

89. Ronald Yanosky, "The Colored Farmers' Alliance and the Single Tax," in Ali, "Black Populism," 37–38n40; see also *National Economist*, December 14, 1889; December 20, 1890; Woodward, *Origins of the New South*, 220.

90. Nugent, *Life Work of Thomas L. Nugent*, 111–18, 163; see also Winkler, *Platforms of Political Parties in Texas*, 271, 296, 299.

91. Hamlin Garland to Arthur E. Morgan, February 26, 1940, in Garland Papers.

92. Nugent, *Life Work of Thomas L. Nugent*, 73.

93. Bellamy, *Looking Backward*, 27–28, 30–36, 41–42, 56, 62, 73–74, 105. Gillis Harp notes the imprint of the positivism of Auguste Comte on Edward Bellamy's outlook. See Harp, *Positivist Republic*, 96–106. Unlike Spencer, Darwin, or even Henry Thomas Buckle, Comte did not appear as a common reference in Populist discourse. Nonetheless, Comtean positivism either influenced or ran parallel with much of the thinking in Nationalist and Populist circles.

94. *Pacific Rural Press*, January 3, 1891; McGreevy, "Farmers, Nationalists, and the Origins of California Populism," 481; Dodge, *Socialist-Populist Errors*, 5–7, 39, 55–57. Referring to *Looking Backward*, Edward Spann writes: "Not even Gronlund had founded his ideal society on a system so impersonally bureaucratic and so unrelenting in its corporate embrace." See Spann, *Brotherly Tomorrows*, 188–90. Kenneth Lipartito observes that if Bellamy's "brave new world seems a bit frightening to us today it is only because Bellamy carried to logical conclusion the idea of order through the rational allocation of human beings to their most efficient uses." See Lipartito, "The Utopian Corporation," 110–11. Arthur Lipow describes Nationalism as a model of "bureaucratic collectivism" that dreaded a democratic labor movement, and that dismissed the efforts of farmers and other small businesses to resist monopoly. See Lipow, *Authoritarian Socialism in America*, 96–97. The question, therefore, is to explain Nationalism's influence within the Populist coalition.

95. *Nonconformist* (Winfield, KS), starting June 6, 1888.

96. James F. King to Edward Bellamy, September 18, 1892, in Bellamy Papers; see also Blocker, "Edward Bellamy and the Populists."

97. John L. Gilbert to Thomas Cator, January 2, 1892, September 4, November 18, 1893, in Cator Papers; Anna Fader diary, April 21, 23, July 18, 1890, Henry C. Dillon to Burnette G. Haskell, February 19, 1891, in Haskell Family Papers; Walters, "Populism in California," 74.

98. Bellamy, *Looking Backward*, 29, 57, 125–29.

99. Mary A. Hill, *Charlotte Perkins Gilman*, 171.

100. Frances Willard to Lillian [Wald] in Bellamy Papers: May 15, 1888, June 4, 1888; see also Buhle, *Women and American Socialism, 1780–1920*, 78–82.

101. McGreevy, "Farmers, Nationalists, and the Origins of California Populism," 479, 485.

102. Bellamy, *Looking Backward*, 28.

103. Dunning, *Farmers' Alliance History*, 182.

104. *Journal of the Knights of Labor*, March 27, 1890.

105. Nugent, *Life Work of Thomas L. Nugent*, 170–76.

106. Gronlund, "Nationalism."

107. Gronlund, *The Co-operative Commonwealth*, 77, 83–85. Richard Hofstadter held that the "utopia of the Populists was in the past, not the future," and that only the delu-

sional bathos of the agrarian myth pointed farmers away from practical business strategies to Populism's broad ideological agendas. See Hofstadter, *The Age of Reform*, 46–47, 62. However, farm reformers readily understood the connections between modern-day business strategies and the ideological framework of the cooperative commonwealth.

108. Gronlund, *The Cooperative Commonwealth*, 181.

109. Anna Fader diary, April 2, 1890, in Haskell Family Papers; O'Connell, *Co-Operative Dreams*, 25; Haskell, "How Kaweah Fell"; *Commonwealth*, May 17, July 12, 1890. Kenneth Lipartito observes that nineteenth-century utopian experiments typically organized as joint stock companies, and adopted hierarchical and bureaucratic forms of organization that served as "halfway houses in the movement toward modern managerial organization." See Lipartito, "The Utopian Corporation," 98–102.

110. Haskell, "How Kaweah Fell."

111. Anna Fader diary, November 7, 1888, July 14, 1890, in Haskell Family Papers; see also Haskell, "How Kaweah Fell"; Fogarty, *Dictionary of American Communal and Utopian History*, 131, 156.

112. *Commonwealth*, May 24, 1889, in Hine, *California's Utopian Colonies*, 82.

113. Anna Fader Haskell to Maria Haskell, January 21, May 7, 1892, Burnette Haskell to Maria Haskell, October 28, 1891, January 20, 1892, in Haskell Family Papers; Haskell, "How Kaweah Fell"; Roney, *Frank Roney Irish Rebel*, 474–76; Fogarty, *All Things New*, 147–50.

114. Anna Fader diary, August 19, 1890, Burnette Haskell to Edward Haskell, February 22, 1892, in Haskell Family Papers; O'Connell, *Co-Operative Dreams*, 172.

115. W. Fitzhugh Brundage, *A Socialist Utopia*, 2, 13–15, 20–22; Wayland, *Leaves of Life*, 1–33; *Coming Nation*, February 10, 1894. W. Fitzhugh Brundage's thorough study of the Ruskin colony includes this observation: "The Ruskinites should not be dismissed as anti-modern fugitives intent on recreating a lost preindustiral or agrarian past. They viewed their undertaking not as a retreat from modernity but as an exercise in 'business socialism.' . . . Their vision of the cooperative commonwealth, however flawed, was distinctly modern" (p. 9).

116. *Coming Nation*, January 20, 27, February 3, 10, 1894; see also W. Fitzhugh Brundage, *A Socialist Utopia in the New South*, 34.

117. Wayland, *Leaves of Life*, 128–30; see also *Coming Nation*, February 10, 1894; W. Fitzhugh Brundage, *A Socialist Utopia in the New South*, 5, 44, 149.

118. Quintero, "La Colonia de Topolobampo."

119. Albert K. Owen to Dr. Edward Everett Hale, in *Nonconformist* (Winfield, KS), January 9, 1890; see also Spann, *Brotherly Tomorrows*, 169–75.

120. Owen, *Integral Co-Operator*, 22–23; January 16, 30, 1890; *Nonconformist* (Winfield, KS), July 4, 1889; see also Argersinger, *Populism and Politics*, 134, 141, 173.

121. Circular letter signed by George S. Bowen appealing to investors interested in Latin American markets, c1891, in George S. Bowen Papers, Box 53; see also "Platform of the Northern Alliance," in Hicks, *The Populist Revolt*, appendix A, 424–30; *Los Angeles Times*, October 3, 1892.

122. *Nonconformist* (Winfield, KS), July 4, 1889.

123. Lease, *The Problem of Civilization Solved*, 131, 155, 158, 163, 267.

124. Watson, *The People's Party Campaign Book*, 218; see also Hofstadter, *The Age of Reform*, 88–93; Hicks, *The Populist Revolt*, 389–90; Shaw, *The Wool Hat Boys*, 193–94; Hunt, *Marion Butler*, 134–38.

125. Quintero, "La Colonia de Topolobampo," 645–54.

126. Eugene Debs to Frank Holl, March 24, 1896, in Debs Papers; see also Debs, "How I Became a Socialist," *New York Comrade*, April 1902, in *Writings and Speeches of Eugene V. Debs*, 43–47; Ginger, *The Bending Cross*, 184; W. Fitzhugh Brundage, *A Socialist Utopia in the New South*, 183; Salvatore, *Citizen and Socialist*, 156–58; *Coming Nation*, March 16, April 20, 1895.

127. Salvatore, *Citizen and Socialist*, 162–69; Ginger, *The Bending Cross*, 209–16.

128. Alfred Martin Colwick to Ruth A. Allen, undated, in Ruth A. Allen Labor Movement in Texas Collection.

129. Debs, "Martin Irons."

CHAPTER 8

1. Charles C. Post, "Mental Science," in *Freedom: A Journal of Realistic Idealism*, December 1, 1896, in "Notes of J. W. H. Davis," in Rushing Collection.

2. Woodward, *Agrarian Rebel*, 182; Shaw, *The Wool Hat Boys*, 34, 51, 57–60, 67.

3. Argersinger, *The Limits of Agrarian Radicalism*, 65; see also Palmer, *"Man over Money,"* 131; Pollack, *The Just Polity*, 11; McMath, "Populist Base Communities." R. Laurence Moore's observation that the "secular and the sacred are not always easy to separate in American experience" seems especially relevant to American Populism. See Moore, *Touchdown Jesus*, 2. See also Moore, *Selling God*. Commenting on the Chautauqua movement, Andrew Rieser writes of "the erasure and redrawing of the boundaries separating the sacred and the secular" resulting in "a de-Christianized mode of moral authority" for middle-class Americans. In this regard, the Chautauqua and Populist movements had points in common. See Rieser, "Secularization Reconsidered: Chautauqua and the De-Christianization of Middle-Class Authority, 1880–1920," in Bledstein and Johnston, *The Middling Sorts*, 136–50.

4. Gutman, "Protestantism and the American Labor Movement," in *Work, Culture, and Society*, 79–117; Thelen, *Paths of Resistance*, 150–51; Thomas, *Alternative America*, 364–65.

5. Marsden, *Fundamentalism and American Culture*, 20; Grant Wacker, "Religion in Nineteenth-Century American Life," in Butler, Wacker, and Balmer, *Religion in American Life*, 279–86. As James Turner argues, the "mana of science glowed more brightly with each passing day," as science emerged as the "model of new truthfulness" in post–Civil War American intellectual and religious life. See Turner, *Without God*, 190, 201, 213. The authority of science in popular belief expanded in the antebellum years as well.

In what Craig James Hazen describes as the "village Enlightenment," Americans "on the popular level (often, but not always in rural areas and on the frontier) used traditional Enlightenment ideas in new contexts and in new combinations to construct or validate new religious worldviews." See Hazen, *The Village Enlightenment in America*, 1–8.

6. Marsden, *Fundamentalism and American Culture*, 4–5, 80–85; "Fundamentalism," in Lippy and Williams, *American Religious Experience*, 947–62; Carpenter, *Revive Us Again*, 37. R. G. Robins cautions against simple formulas about the antimodern character of the Holiness movement and similar movements. Robins argues that they shared the "progressive" mode of the other denominations and "reflected many of the salient features of modernity and . . . adapted quickly and well to the structural changes reconfiguring American life." Although Holiness leader A. J. Tomlinson ran as a People's party candidate in Indiana, Robins discusses why this was exceptional and why relations between the Holiness movement and Populism remained distant. See Robins, *A. J. Tomlinson*, 5, 11, 59, 105–14. A study of religion and Populism in Texas examines the connections between rural reform and the Holiness evangelicals and other conservative evangelicals. Although the author seeks different conclusions, the data provided indicate that Holiness groups and like groups had weak connections with rural reform, whereas social Christians, spiritualists, and other religious innovators and modernizers were well represented within rural Texas Populism. See King, "Religious Dimensions," 21, 77, 84–85, 94, 112, 153, 164–67, 172.

7. Grant Wacker, "Religion in Nineteenth-Century American Life," in Butler, Wacker, and Balmer, *Religion in American Life*, 286–89.

8. Marsden, *Fundamentalism and American Culture*, 185; Levine, *Defender of the Faith*, 348.

9. Hofstadter, *The Age of Reform*, 288; Kazin, *The Populist Persuasion*, 106; Philips, *Post-Conservative America*, 181; Thomas, *Alternative America*, 333. Ray Ginger stressed the role of regional traditionalism as part of the static "closed society" of the rural South, see Ginger, *Six Days or Forever?* 16, 223.

10. Benjamin Peterson to George S. Bowen, October 24, 1894, in Bowen Papers; Edwards, *New Spirits*, 171–94.

11. Levine, *Defender of the Faith*, 349; Garry Wills, *Under God*, 101; Edward J. Larson, *Summer for the Gods*, 189; Kazin, *A Godly Hero*, 7–9, 292–93; Longfield, *The Presbyterian Controversy*, 58–62; Wayne C. Williams, *William Jennings Bryan*, 22, 28–29; Ashby, *Champion of Democracy*, 1–18; Coletta, *Political Evangelist*, 10.

12. *Caucasian*, June 18, 1891; see also Fox, "The Culture of Liberal Protestant Progressivism"; Hopkins, *The Rise of the Social Gospel*, 123; McGuire, "Liberalism," in Lippy and Williams, *American Religious Experience*, 1129–45; Hutchison, *The Modernist Impulse*, 41, 73–75; Livingstone et al., *Evangelicals and Science in Historical Perspective*.

13. Edward J. Larson, *Summer for the Gods*, 39; see also Kazin, *A Godly Hero*, 15, 273–74; Garry Wills, *Under God*, 101; Wayne C. Williams, *William Jennings Bryan*, 44; Ashby, *Champion of Democracy*, 183–84; Coletta, *Political Evangelist*, 317–18; Levine, *Defender of the Faith*, 222; Longfield, *The Presbyterian Controversy*, 68. Chicago's religious

innovations included the evangelical crusades of D. L. Moody, whom Bryan admired. With his "pluck, push and enterprise," Moody, a moderate in the "religious wars," applied sophisticated business methods and modern mass media campaigns to turn his Chicago revivals into spectacular popular entertainment. See Evensen, *God's Man for the Gilded Age*, 4, 13, 123–63.

14. Garry Wills, *Under God*, 106; see also Tierney, *Darrow*, 63, 104, 120–21; Destler, *American Radicalism*, 194–244; McMath, *American Populism*, 189–91, 195; Darrow, "Nietzsche," 6–16.

15. Darrow, *Resist Not Evil*; Tierney, *Darrow*, 11–12, 15, 80, 142, 169; Darrow, *Closing Arguments*, vii–x.

16. As Michael Kazin persuasively argues, "Bryan had always stuck to a pragmatic view of religion," and was "thus not a fundamentalist, as we now understand that term." See Kazin, *A Godly Hero*, 264. However, in his campaign against the teaching of "evolution as fact," Bryan made common cause with those who were fundamentalist doctrinaires. Hence Darrow's purpose in the Scopes trial was to demonstrate that his erstwhile ally in reform had surrendered to the conservative ideologues.

17. Hubbard, *The Coming Climax*, 202.

18. Grant Wacker, "Religion in Nineteenth-Century America," in Butler, Wacker, and Balmer, *Religion in American Life*, 289; Fox, "The Culture of Liberal Protestant Progressivism"; Hopkins, *The Rise of the Social Gospel*, 123; Hutchison, *The Modernist Impulse*, 41, 73–75; Robert T. Handy, *The Social Gospel in America*; Gutman, "Protestantism and the American Labor Movement," in *Work, Culture, and Society in Industrializing America*, 91–92; McMath, "Populist Base Communities"; King, "Religious Dimensions," 259; Salvatore, *Citizen and Socialist*, 237. Susan Curtis points out that "the social gospel is a key part of the cultural mix that gave birth to modern American culture." She also notes that it developed in the Midwest and South, where "people from small towns and farms first gave it expression." See Curtis, *A Consuming Faith*, 3, 12–13. The Chautauqua movement also suggests that the new liberal religious outlook was not restricted to the big urban churches and had a broad provincial constituency. According to Andrew Rieser, "Chautauqua was a middle-class movement that contributed to modern liberalism," a movement that in rural Illinois and elsewhere intersected with Populism. See Rieser, *The Chautauqua Moment*, 4–8, 112–13.

19. *Coming Nation*, December 2, 1893; see also Argersinger, *The Limits of Agrarian Radicalism*, 65; Ayers, *The Promise of the New South*, 162–63, 172; Fite, *Cotton Fields No More*, 43.

20. King, "Religious Dimensions," 110–11.

21. *National Economist*, March 30, 1889.

22. Isom P. Langley, "Religion in the Alliance," in Dunning, *Farmers' Alliance History*, 313–17.

23. Isom P. Langley, "Religion in the Alliance," in Dunning, *Farmers' Alliance History*, 313–17.

24. *Southern Mercury*, August 21, 1888.

25. *Southern Mercury*, July 5, 12, August 28, 1888; *National Economist*, July 12, 1890.

26. *Caucasian*, June 11, 1891.

27. Creech, *Righteous Indignation*, 44, 71; see also Noblin, *Agrarian Crusader*, 186–89. Although North Carolina's Populist newspapers gave the most extensive coverage to Thomas Dixon, his sermons also appeared in other reform publications in the South and Midwest. Henry Vincent and Julius Wayland, two editors known for their bitter hostility toward organized religion, reported on Dixon's sermons. Wayland described Dixon as a reformer "imbued with the true Christ spirit." See *Coming Nation*, December 2, 1893, April 6, 1895; *Chicago Searchlight*, August 2, 1894.

28. Cook, *Fire from the Flint*, 60, 67, 73–74; Creech, *Righteous Indignation*, 45; Gilmore, *Gender and Jim Crow*, 135–38; Noblin, *Agrarian Crusader*, 164.

29. W. Fitzhugh Brundage, "Thomas Dixon: American Proteus"; see also Hutchison, *The Modernist Impulse in American Protestantism*, 77–109; Wacker, "Religion in Nineteenth-Century America," in Butler, Wacker, and Balmer, *Religion in American Life*, 282–83.

30. Thomas Dixon Jr., "Progress," in *Living Problems*, 129–43; see also *Caucasian*, May 21, 28, 1891, February 11, 18, April 14, 21, 1892.

31. *Caucasian*, June 18, 1891, February 18, June 16, 1892, August 17, 1893.

32. *Caucasian*, June 4, 1891, February 11, March 3, July 7, 1892.

33. Creech, *Righteous Indignation*, 46; Lease, "Mrs. Mary E. Lease"; *Caucasian*, March 3, May 26, July 7, 1892, March 16, 1893, March 28, April 18, 1895.

34. Menand, *The Metaphysical Club*, 89; see also Nugent, *Life Work of Thomas L. Nugent*, 13–14, 34, 54–55; King, "Religious Dimensions," 154–61; Alvord, "T. L. Nugent, Texas Populist."

35. Nugent, *Life Work of Thomas L. Nugent*, 161; see also Griggs, *Parson Henry Renfro*, 117–32.

36. Nugent, *Life Work of Thomas L. Nugent*, 97–98; see also Martin, *The People's Party in Texas*, 117, 232.

37. "Preacher Populists," in *Galveston Daily News*, September 28, 1894.

38. Cantrell, *Limits of Southern Dissent*, 187, 265; John B. Rayner, "Racial Growth," undated letter to the *Dallas Morning News*, "Some of J. B. Rayner's Wise Sayings," undated ms., in Rayner Papers.

39. John B. Rayner, "Good Citizenship and the Negro," undated ms., "Some of J. B. Rayner's Wise Sayings," undated ms., in Rayner Papers.

40. *Southern Mercury*, August 21, 1888.

41. Bode, "Religion and Class Hegemony," 421.

42. Bettie Gay, "Influence of Women in the Alliance," in Dunning, *Farmers' Alliance History*, 308–12.

43. Hubbard, *The Coming Climax*, 23, 208–9.

44. Lengel, "Radical Crusaders and a Conservative Church"; Lease, *The Problem of Civilization Solved*, 7.

45. Lee, "Onward Christian Soldiers," 14–21; see also Jane Addams, *Twenty Years at Hull-House*, 167.

46. London, *Jack London on the Road*, 45. For full accounts of the Industrial Army movement, see Schwantes, *An American Odyssey*; McMurry, *Coxey's Army*.

47. *Coming Nation*, October 21, 1893.

48. *Chicago Searchlight*, June 28, 1894.

49. *Coming Nation*, July 21, 1894; *Chicago Searchlight*, July 26, 1894; Destler, *American Radicalism*, 194–95, 204, 207–8, 223; McGlynn, *Father Lambert, a Priest Who Went to Rome, and What He Got There*; "Social Christianity," in Lippy and Williams, *Encyclopedia of the American Religious Experience*, 917–31.

50. *Topeka Baptist Headlight*, July 18, 1894; *Washington Post*, May 2, 1894; see also *Chicago Record*, March 21, 22, April 3, 6, 17, 18, 24, April 26, May 1, 2, 1894; Schwantes, *An American Odyssey*, 193; *Indianapolis Freeman*, April 7, 28, 1894; *Richmond Planet*, April 7, 21, May 5, 1894; *Washington Evening Star*, May 1, 1894, February 7, 1910; Constance McLaughlin Green, *The Secret City*, 130, 145; *Washington Bee*, May 4, 1894; *Washington Afro-American*, November 5, 1955; Vermont Avenue Baptist Church, "Historical Review of the Origin and Development of the Vermont Avenue Baptist Church"; McMurry, *Coxey's Army*, 246.

51. There were sporadic efforts to set up alternative churches with Populist sympathies. For example, reformers opened a "People's church" in a veterans' hall in Indianapolis that closed after two Sundays as the owners expelled the group from the premises. See *Nonconformist* (Indianapolis), January 26, 1893. In an interpretation of Populism as the revitalization of a radical evangelical tradition, Robert McMath cites the parallels with the Christian base communities of Latin American "Liberation Theology," and the black civil rights movement of the 1960s. See McMath, "Populist Base Communities."

52. Boller, *American Thought in Transition*, 44–46; Turner, "Modern Unbelief," in *Without God*, 171–248.

53. Jacoby, *Freethinkers*, 1, 151, 156, 173–74, 177; *Kansas Farmer*, July 7, 1887; *Farmer and Mechanic*, December 6, 1877, February 7, 1878; *Caucasian*, February 11, 18, 25, 1892.

54. *Nonconformist* (Winfield, KS), October 17, 1889; Denton, "American Nonconformist," 71.

55. French, *Chuca-Choo*; Gutman, *Work, Culture, and Society in Industrializing America*, 91–92; see also *Chicago Times*, July 15, 1894; Ginger, *The Bending Cross*, 161.

56. Debs, "Recollections of Ingersoll"; see also Salvatore, *Citizen and Socialist*, 10; Karsner, *Debs*, 213–15.

57. Eugene V. Debs to Eva Parker Ingersoll, July 23, 1906, in Debs, *Letters of Eugene V. Debs*, vol. 1, 185–86, 229; Ingersoll, *Life and Letters*, 330, 504.

58. Turner, *Without God*, 203; see also Debs, "Recollections of Ingersoll"; Debs, "Martin Irons"; Debs, "John Brown: History's Greatest Hero," *Appeal to Reason*, November 23, 1907, in Debs, *Writings and Speeches of Eugene V. Debs*, 280–81.

59. John W. H. Davis, "Christianity or Socialism," undated ms., clippings from *Progressive Thinker*, clippings from *The New Thought*, clippings from *Freedom*, clippings from *The Social Thought*, in "Notes of J. W. H. Davis"; King, "Religious Dimensions," 169–72.

60. *Southern Mercury*, July 12, 1888. According to Keith Lynn King's study of the religious alignment of Texas Populists, "100 percent of all organized Spiritualists lived in Populist strongholds." See King, "Religious Dimensions" 112, 166–67.

61. Martin, *The People's Party in Texas*, 82, 107; King, "Religious Dimensions," 167; Braude, *Radical Spirits*, 153.

62. *Carrier Dove*, July 21, December 15, 1888, January 5, 1889. R. Laurence Moore writes of the spiritualists: "Everything they said and wrote echoed a widespread nineteenth-century optimism that stemmed from a faith in evolutionary progress and temperate reform." See Moore, *In Search of White Crows*, xiii, 71.

63. Robert S. Cox, *Body and Soul*, 7–18; Moore, *In Search of White Crows*, xiii, 7, 22, 29; Braude, *Radical Spirits*, 2–7, 173–75; *Chicago Searchlight*, August 2, 1894. Craig James Hazen observes that spiritualism and other nineteenth-century American movements that rejected the Bible or tradition often looked to science for cultural authority, as "science became the center and the circumference of their religious thinking and the authoritative foundation on which they built new views of the world." See Hazen *The Village Enlightenment*, 3.

64. *Carrier Dove*, July 18, 1888; see also Braude, *Radical Spirits*, 136–37, 194. See also Moore, "The Spiritualist Medium," 200–21.

65. *Nonconformist* (Winfield, KS), November 11, 1886; see also Wagner, "Farms, Families, and Reform," 26; Walters, "Populism in California," 50; Pierce Burton to George Bowen, October 28, 1894, in Bowen Papers; *Carrier Dove*, January 26, 1889.

66. *Alliance Farmer*, June 25, 1891; "Marion Cannon's Trip East," in Cannon/Walker Family Papers; Obituaries, in Cannon/Walker Family Papers; Walters, "Populism in California," 50.

67. *National Economist*, October 11, 1890; *Pacific Rural Press*, November 29, 1890; Walters, "Populism in California," 27, 50, 83–84; Braude, *Radical Spirits*, 198.

68. Owen, *The Place of Enchantment*, 7–16, 239, 255; see also *Carrier Dove*, July 21, 1888; Robert S. Ellwood, "Occult Movements in America," in Lippy and Williams, *American Religious Experience*, 711–22; Moore, *In Search of White Crows*, 231–32.

69. Hine, *California's Utopian Colonies*, 39–40; Anna Fader diary, November 17, December 16, 1888, July 23, 1890, in Haskell Family Papers; Astaroth Haskell to Ira B. Cross, November 20, 1928, in Cross Papers.

70. *Chicago Searchlight*, June 28, 1894; see also McMurry, *Coxey's Army*, 30–40; Hine, *California's Utopian Colonies*, 39–41.

71. *Caucasian*, September 28, 1893; see also Boller, *American Thought in Transition*, 35; Grant Wacker, "Religion in Nineteenth-Century American Life," in Butler, Wacker, and Balmer, *Religion in American Life*, 286; Edwards, *New Spirits*, 171–74; Barrows, *The World's Parliament of Religions*, vol. 2, 942, 950, 960–61, 978, 1056, 1068, 1209–10, 1234; Muller, "The Real Significance of the Parliament of Religions," 1–14; Seager, *The World's Parliament of Religions: The East/West Encounter*. The World Parliament of Religions received "an immense petition," with hundreds of signatures gathered from Colorado and Utah, urging the gathering to pass resolutions in support of free silver. See Mary Eleanor Barrows, *John Henry Barrows*, 281–82.

72. Levine, *Defender of the Faith*, 349; Longfield, *The Presbyterian Controversy*, 155.

73. *National Economist*, May 25, 1889; see also Clark, "Evolution for John Doe," 1277.

74. Cohen, *Science and the Founding Fathers*, 66, 111, 150, 255.

75. Cator, "Millionaires or Morals?"

76. Cator, "Millionaires or Morals?"

77. Cator, "Millionaires or Morals?"

78. *People's Paper* (Stafford Kans.), November 21, 1895; see also Lester Frank Ward, "Mind as a Social Factor," in Hollinger and Capper, *American Intellectual Tradition*, 39–47; Macleod, "The 'Bankruptcy of Science' Debate."

79. *Southern Mercury*, September 11, 1888.

80. "Some of J. B. Rayner's Wise Sayings," in Rayner Papers.

81. Hubbard, *The Coming Climax*, 472–73.

82. *National Economist*, March 14, 1889, August 3, 1889; Clodd, *The Story of Creation*.

83. *Southern Mercury*, May 10, 1888.

84. *Southern Mercury*, May 10, 1888.

85. *Southern Mercury*, May 10, 1888.

Conclusion

1. Kazin, *A Godly Hero*, 53–65.

2. Woodward, "Populist Heritage and the Intellectual," in *The Burden of Southern History*, 161.

3. Goodwyn, *Democratic Promise*, 387–492.

4. Livingston, *Pragmatism, Feminism, and Democracy*, 25, 46, 105–7, 159–60; Livingston, *Origins of the Federal Reserve System*, 42, 101, 112.

5. Ritter, *Goldbugs and Greenbacks*, 280.

6. Woodward, "Populist Heritage and the Intellectual," in *The Burden of Southern History*, 161; see also Ostler, "The Rhetoric of Conspiracy and the Formation of Kansas Populism."

7. John F. Willits, "Final Address to Populists," and Gasper Clemens, "An Appeal to True Populists," in Populist Party Pamphlets; Summers, *Party Games*, 272–74.

8. *Pacific Rural Press*, October 31, 1891; Ethington, *The Public City*, 373–77; Dematier, McIntosh, and Waters, *The Rumble of California Politics*, 104–22; Dobie, "The Political Career of Stephen Mallory White"; Griffiths, *Populism in the Western United States*, 36–37.

9. Argersinger, *The Limits of Agrarian Radicalism*, 9–16; Argersinger, "Taubeneck's Laws," 101–4.

10. The Populist endorsement of Bryan proved a bitter disappointment to Henry Demarest Lloyd, the muckraking author who saw in the People's party the possibility of a radical anticapitalist reorganization of society. An opponent of fusion, Lloyd de-

scribed free silver as "the cow-bird of the Reform movement," a characterization that has been echoed in the scholarship ever since, most notably in Lawrence Goodwyn's analysis of the so-called "shadow movement." With a different perspective, Robert Durden's *The Climax of Populism* explains why in 1896 both fusion and free silver made sense to a wide spectrum of dedicated Populists. See Durden, *The Climax of Populism*, ix, 6, 14–15. See also Hunt, *Marion Butler*, 82–86.

11. Argersinger, *The Limits of Agrarian Radicalism*, 15.

12. Gasper Clemens, "An Appeal to True Populists," in Populist Party Pamphlets.

13. Hunt, *Marion Butler*, 67–74, 148–55; Shaw, *The Wool Hat Boys*, 140–61; Martin, *The People's Party in Texas*, 238–51; Goodwyn, *Democratic Promise*, 463–69, 477–79.

14. *Houston Daily Post*, August 7, 1896, in Perry, "The Negro in the People's Party," appendix E, 65–66; Martin, *The People's Party in Texas*, 243–44; Pitre, *Through Many Dangers, Toils and Snares*, 124–27.

15. "Copy of a Letter," from John W. Breidenthal, Chairman People's Party Central Committee, to W. D. Vincent, Populist nominee for Congress from the Fifth District, Kasas, October 17, 1896, in Populist Party Pamphlets; John F. Willits, "Final Address to Populists," in Populist Party Pamphlets; see also Summers, *Party Games*, 251–75; Argersinger, "Election Fraud in the Gilded Age."

16. Jeffrey Ostler demonstrates how viable competition between the two established parties proved a key variable in Populist strength in Iowa, Kansas, and Nebraska. See Ostler, *Prairie Populism*, 1–11, 175–79.

17. Macune, "Farmers' Alliance," 59; see also Macune Jr., "Biographical Sketch of C. W. Macune."

18. Danbom, *Born in the Country*, 161–67; Danbom, *The Resisted Revolution*, 3–4; Fite, *Cotton Fields No More*, 21, 84, 91; C. L. Holmes, "Agriculture in Reconstruction," in Schmidt and Ross, *Economic History of American Agriculture*, 529–56.

19. Danbom, *Born in the Country*, 164–66; Fite, *Cotton Fields No More*, 101–2; Sharpless, *Fertile Ground*, 88–89, 196–97.

20. Danbom, *Born in the Country*, 164; Sanders, *Roots of Reform*, 392; Ellsworth, "Theodore Roosevelt's Country Life Commission," 172.

21. Welter, *Popular Education*, 175; Roy V. Scott, *The Reluctant Farmer*, 38, 41, 104–6; Fite, *Cotton Fields No More*, 63–79.

22. Theodore Roosevelt, "Special Message," in *Report of the Country Life Commission*, 75–79; see also Woeste, *The Farmer's Benevolent Trust*, 96–107, 111–17; Sanders, *Roots of Reform*, 287.

23. Woeste, *The Farmer's Benevolent Trust*, 105; Clemens, *The People's Lobby*, 166; Keillor, *Cooperative Commonwealth*, 290–96.

24. Woeste, *The Farmer's Benevolent Trust*, 9, 164–90.

25. Sanders, *Roots of Reform*, 298–310; Ellsworth, "Theodore Roosevelt's Country Life Commission," 172; Woeste, *The Farmer's Benevolent Trust*, 94, 102–6.

26. Sanders, *Roots of Reform*, 391–93; Benjamin Hibbard, "Agricultural Changes during the World War," in Schmidt and Ross, *Economic History of American Agriculture*,

465–95; Edward Wiest, "The Relation of the State to Agriculture," in Schmidt and Ross, *Economic History of American Agriculture*, 504–28; McConnell, *The Decline of Agrarian Democracy*, 22, 30, 47, 59–60; Danbom, *The Resisted Revolution*, 68.

27. Clemens, *The People's Lobby*, 145–83; see also Danbom, *Born in the Country*, 182–83.

28. Davis, *Memoir by Cyclone Davis*, 58–60; Woodward, *Agrarian Rebel,* 467–86. In North Carolina, Marion Butler took a notably different path. Although maintaining his Populist ideas about reform, he was unable to reconcile with the Democratic Party, joined the Republicans, eschewed racial extremism, and languished in political obscurity. See Hunt, *Marion Butler*, 186–257.

29. Friedman and Schwartz, *A Monetary History*, 168–96; Sklar, *Corporate Reconstruction*, 422–24; Livingston, *Origins of the Federal Reserve*, 172–80; Sanders, *Roots of Reform*, 236–59.

30. Charles W. Macune, et al., "Report of the Committee on the Monetary System," in Dunning, *Farmers' Alliance History*, 124–30.

31. Taubeneck, *The Conditions of the American Farmer*, 61.

32. *Caucasian*, May 15, 1890.

33. Livingston, *Origins of the Federal Reserve System*, 17–18, 42.

34. Sanders, *Roots of Reform*, 256–58; Charles W. Macune, et al., "Report of the Committee on the Monetary System," in Dunning, *Farmers' Alliance History*, 124–30.

35. *Report of the Country Life Commission*, 75, 86–87, 91; see also Danbom, *The Resisted Revolution*, viii, 23, 43, 51–62; Roy V. Scott, *The Reluctant Farmer*, 291–92; Ellsworth, "Theodore Roosevelt's Country Life Commission."

36. Roy V. Scott, *The Reluctant Farmer*, 313.

37. Bowers, *The Country Life Movement*, 102–8.

38. *Report of the Country Life Commission*, 118–19, 126; see also Danbom, *The Resisted Revolution*, 62, 84–85; Bowers, *The Country Life Movement*, 103; Handy-Marchello, *Women of the Northern Plains*, 142–49.

39. Galpin, *Rural Social Problems*, 51–64. The extent of popular resentment to elite campaigns for rural hygiene should not be overstated. For example, the Rockefeller Sanitary Commission for the Eradication of Hookworm (1909–14) scored significant successes in the rural South, where "poor families journeyed long distances to hear how they could be saved from the ravages of disease." See, Hoy, *Chasing Dirt*, 130–32.

40. *Report of the Country Life Commission*, 132–35; Galpin, *Rural Social Problems*, 119–30; Wilson, "The Church and the Country Life Movement"; Danbom, *The Resisted Revolution*, 59; Madison, "Reformers and the Rural Church."

41. McGerr, *A Fierce Discontent*, 106–7; Edward J. Larson, *Summer for the Gods*, 31–59; Israel, *Before Scopes*, 130; Keith, *Country People*, 203–10.

42. The Country Life Movement spurred an extensive array of surveys and investigations into rural conditions, the rural community, and the rural mind. According to a review in the *Journal of Social Forces*, fifty noteworthy books of rural sociology were published in 1921 and 1922 alone. See Morse, "Books on Rural Life."

43. W. E. B. DuBois to Liberty Hyde Bailey, November 23, 1908, in Liberty Hyde Bailey Papers.

44. *Report of the Country Life Commission*, 116.

45. "Some of J. B. Rayner's Wise Sayings," undated ms., in Rayner Papers; see also Rice, *The Negro in Texas*, 180–81; Cantrell, *Limits of Southern Dissent*, 248–50, 283.

46. For discussion of the early eugenics and "race betterment" movement, see Seldon, *Inheriting Shame*, 1–9.

47. Barthelme, *Women in the Texas Populist Movement*, 46; Buhle, *Women and American Socialism*, 108, 120; Miller, "Thomas Nugent," 1075; Miller, *Oklahoma Populism*, 173–80; Argersinger, *The Limits of Agrarian Radicalism*, 173; McMath, *American Populism*, 206. See also James R. Green, *Grass-Roots Socialism*.

48. James Scott, *Seeing Like a State*, 89–90.

49. Deborah Fitzgerald, *Every Farm a Factory*, 6–7, 77, and "Accounting for Change," in Stock and Johnston, *The Countryside in the Age of the Modern State*, 189–212. For a different view, see also Gilbert, "Agrarian Intellectuals in a Democratizing State," in Stock and Johnston, *The Countryside in the Age of the Modern State*, 213–39.

50. Watson, *The People's Party Campaign Book*, 220, 222.

BIBLIOGRAPHY

Manuscript Collections

Allen, Ruth A. Labor Movement in Texas Collection. Center for American History, University of Texas, Austin

Bailey, Liberty Hyde. Papers. Division of Rare and Manuscript Collections, Carl A. Kroch Library, Cornell University

Bellamy, Edward. Papers. Houghton Library, Harvard University

Bowen, George S. Papers. Chicago Historical Society

Buda, Texas, Alliance Gin Records, 1890–1915. Center for American History, University of Texas, Austin

Cannon/Walker Family Papers. University of the Pacific

Cator, Thomas V. Papers. Special Collections, Stanford Libraries

Centennial Alliance Minute Book, Bell County, 1891–1897. Center for American History, University of Texas, Austin

Chereno Alliance Ledger. Center for American History, University of Texas, Austin

Cross, Ira B. California Labor Notes, 1815–1960. Bancroft Library, University of California, Berkeley

———. Papers. Bancroft Library, University of California, Berkeley

John Davis Scrapbooks. Kansas State Historical Society, Topeka

Debs, Eugene Victor. Papers. Center for American History, University of Texas, Austin

Farmers' Alliance Clippings. Kansas State Historical Society, Topeka

Garland, Hamlin. Papers. Houghton Library, Harvard University

Gillespie County Alliance Minutes, 1886–1896. Center for American History, University of Texas, Austin

Gove County Farmers' Alliance Minute Book, 1890. Kansas State Historical Society, Topeka

Haskell Family. Papers. Bancroft Library, University of California, Berkeley

Lewelling, Lorenzo D. Correspondence Files. State Archives, Kansas State Historical Society, Topeka

————. Governor's Office, Letter Press Books. State Archives, Kansas State Historical Society, Topeka

Lone Tree Farmers' Alliance, No. 2005, Minute Book. Kansas State Historical Society, Topeka

Macune, Charles W. "National Farmers' Alliance Speeches." Center for American History, University of Texas, Austin

Macune, Charles W. Jr. "Biographical Sketch of C. W. Macune." Unpublished, 1964. Center for American History, University of Texas, Austin

Populist Party Pamphlets. Kansas State Historical Society, Topeka

Rayner, John B. Papers. Center for American History, University of Texas, Austin

Rose, Archibald Johnson. Papers. Center for American History, University of Texas, Austin

Rushing, John B. Collection. Center for American History, University of Texas, Austin

Contemporary Publications

Abbot, Willis J. "The Chicago Populist Campaign." *Arena* 11 (1895): 330–37.

Anonymous. "The Negro's Part." *Nationalist* 2 (1890): 91–97.

Bancroft, Hubert Howe. *History of California.* San Francisco: The History Company, 1890.

Barrows, John Henry, ed. *The World's Parliament of Religions: An Illustrated and Popular Story of the World's First Parliament of Religions, Held in Chicago in Conjunction with the Columbian Exposition of 1893.* 2 vols. Chicago: Parliament, 1893.

Bellamy, Edward. *Looking Backward: 2000–1887.* Boston: Ticknor and Company, 1888. Reprint, New York: Dover, 1996.

Brady, Sue Huffman. "Changing Ideals in Southern Womanhood." In *The Congress of Women*, Mary Eagle, ed. Chicago: International Pub., 1894. Reprint, New York: Arno, 1974.

Bryan, William Jennings. *The First Battle: A Story of the Campaign of 1896.* Chicago: W. B. Conkey, 1896.

Cator, Thomas V. *Millionaires or Morals: Which Shall Rule?* San Francisco: Wm. M. Langton, 1890.

Clodd, Edward. *The Story of Creation: A Plain Account of Evolution.* London: Longman's Green, 1888.

Daniels, Percy. *A Crisis for the Husbandman.* Girard, Kans.: 1889. Quoted in Thomas Frank, "The Leviathan with Tentacles of Steel: Railroads in the Minds of Kansas Populists" *Western Historical Quarterly* 1(1989): 37–55.

Darrow, Clarence S. *Resist Not Evil*. Girard, Kans.: Haldeman-Julius, 1902.

———. "Nietzsche." *Athena* 1 (1916): 6–16.

———. *Closing Arguments: Clarence Darrow on Religion, Law, and Society*. Edited by S. T. Joshi. Athens: Ohio University Press, 2005.

Davis, James H. (Cyclone). *A Political Revelation, in Which the Principles of This Government, the Teachings of Its Founders, and the Issues of Today Are Brought to a Fair and Just Comparison with Each Other, by Means of a Rigid Analysis, a Full and True Description, and Many Happy Illustrations*. Dallas: Advance, 1894.

Davis, John. "Napoleon Bonaparte: A Sketch Written for a Purpose." *Arena* 13–15 (July 1895–April 1896).

Debs, Eugene V. *Writings and Speeches of Eugene V. Debs*. Edited by Arthur M. Schlesinger Jr. New York: Hermitage, 1948.

———. *Letters of Eugene V. Debs*. 2 vols. Edited by Robert J. Constantine. Urbana: University of Illinois Press, 1990.

Diggs, Annie L. "The Women in the Alliance Movement." *Arena* 6 (1892): 161–79.

Dixon, Thomas Jr. *Living Problems in Religion and Social Science*. New York: Charles T. Dillingham, 1889.

Dodge, Arthur H. *Socialist-Populist Errors: An Exposition of Popular Political Theories*. San Francisco: James H. Barry, 1894.

Donnelly, Ignatius. *Caesar's Column, a Story of the Twentieth Century*. Chicago: F. J. Schulte, 1890.

Dunning, Nelson A. *Farmers' Alliance History and Agricultural Digest*. Washington, D.C.: Alliance, 1891.

Emery, Sarah E. V. *Seven Financial Conspiracies Which Have Enslaved the American People*. Lansing, Mich.: Robert Smith, 1887.

French, W. E. P. *Chuca-Choo: Song of the American Railway Union*. St. Paul, Minn: W. J. Dyer & Bro., 1894.

Garland, Hamlin. "Drifting Crane." *Harper's Weekly* 80 (1890): 421–22.

———. *A Spoil of Office: A Story of the Modern West*. Boston: Arena, 1892.

———. *Hamlin Garland's Observations on the American Indian*. Edited by Lonnie E. Underhill and Daniel F. Littlefield Jr. Tucson: University of Arizona Press, 1976.

Garvin, William L., and S. O. Daws. *History of the National Farmers' Alliance and Co-Operative Union of America*. Jacksboro, Tex.: J. N. Rogers, Steam Printers, 1887.

George, Henry. *Progress and Poverty: An Inquiry into the Cause of Industrial Depressions and of Increase of Want with Increase of Wealth, the Remedy*. San Francisco: W. M. Hinton, 1877.

———. "Land and Taxation: A Conversation." *North American Review* 141 (1885): 1–14.

———. *Social Problems*. New York: Henry George, 1883. Reprint, New York: Robert Schalkenback Foundation, 1966.

George, Milton. *The Industrial Struggle: A History of the Farmers' Alliance and Its Work.* Chicago: Western Rural, 1893.

Gilman, Charlotte Perkins. *Women and Economics: A Study of the Economic Relation between Men and Women as a Factor in Social Evolution.* Boston: Small, Maynard, 1898. Reprint, New York: Harper & Row, 1966.

———. *Charlotte Perkins Gilman: Nonfiction Reader.* Edited by Larry Ceplair. New York: Columbia University Press, 1991.

Gompers, Samuel. "Organized Labor in the Campaign." *North American Review* 155 (July 1892): 91–96.

Grady, Henry W. *Life and Labors of Henry W. Grady, His Speeches, Writings, etc.* Richmond, Va.: Franklin, 1890.

Gronlund, Laurence. *The Co-Operative Commonwealth, an Exposition of Modern Socialism.* London: Modern, 1885.

———. "Nationalism." *Arena* 1 (1890): 153–65.

Harvey, William H. *Coin's Financial School.* Chicago: Coin, 1895. Reprint, edited by Richard Hofstadter. Cambridge, Mass.: Harvard University Press, 1963.

———. "A Plan of Action." *Nationalist* 2 (1889): 30–32.

Haskell, Burnette G. "How Kaweah Fell." *San Francisco Examiner,* November 29, 1891.

Hogg, James S. *Speeches and State Papers of James Stephen Hogg Ex-Governor of Texas with a Sketch of His Life.* Edited by C. W. Raines. Austin, Tex.: State Printing, 1905.

Hubbard, Lester C. *The Coming Climax in the Destinies of America.* Chicago: Charles H. Kerr, 1891.

Jelley, Symmes M. *The Voice of Labor.* Philadelphia; Chicago: H. J. Smith, 1888.

Knapp, Adeline. "San Francisco and the Civic Awakening." *Arena* 65 (1895): 241–49.

Lease, Mary Elizabeth. *The Problem of Civilization Solved.* Chicago: Laird & Lee, 1895.

Lloyd, Henry Demarest. *Wealth against Commonwealth.* New York: Harper & Brothers, 1894.

McBride, John. "Coal Miners." In *The Labor Movement: the Problem of Today,* edited by George Edwin McNeill, 241–67. New York: M. W. Hazen, 1887.

McCabe, James Dabney, [Edward Winslow Martin]. *History of the Grange Movement, or the Farmer's War against Monopolies.* Philadelphia: National, 1873. Reprint, New York: Burt Franklin, 1967.

McGlynn, Edward. *Father Lambert: A Priest Who Went to Rome, and What He Got There.* New York: Anti-Poverty Society, 1889.

Miller, Joseph Dana. "The New Woman in Office." *Godey's Magazine* (January, 1896): 59–68.

Morgan, Scott W. *History of the Wheel and Alliance, and the Impending Revolution.* Hardy, Alaska: W. Scott Morgan, 1891.

Muller, Max. "The Real Significance of the Parliament of Religions." *Arena* 11 (1894): 1–14.

"News of the Movement, California." *Nationalist* 2 (1890): 341–42.

Norris, Frank. *The Octopus: A Story of California.* New York: Grosset & Dunlap, 1901.

Norton, Seymour F. *Ten Men of Money Island, or, the Primer of Finance.* Chicago: Chicago Sentinel, 1891.

Nugent, Catherine, ed. *Life Work of Thomas L. Nugent.* Stephenville, Tex.: C. Nugent, 1896.

Ousley, Clarence N. "A Lesson in Co-operation." *Popular Science Monthly* 36 (1890): 821–28.

Owen, Albert K. *Integral Co-Operation; Its Practical Application.* New York: John W. Lovell, 1885.

Peck, Harry Thurston. "Twenty Years of the Republic." *Bookman* 21 (1905): 30–58.

Peffer, William A. *The Farmer's Side: His Troubles and Their Remedy.* New York: D. Appleton, 1891. Reprint, Westport, Conn.: Hyperion, 1976.

———. "Populism, Its Rise and Fall." *Chicago Tribune*, 1899. Edited and with an introduction by Peter H. Argersinger. Lawrence: University of Kansas Press, 1992.

Polk, Leonidas L. *An Address by the Hon. L. L. Polk, of North Carolina, Delivered before the Inter-State Convention of Farmers, Held in DeGive's Opera House, Atlanta, Ga., August 16, 17, 18, 1887.* Atlanta: Jas. P. Harrison, 1887.

Swinton, John. *A Momentous Question: The Respective Attitudes of Labor and Capital.* Philadelphia: A. R. Keller, 1894. Reprint, New York: Burt Franklin, 1971.

Taubeneck, Herman E. *The Conditions of the American Farmer.* Chicago: Schulte, 1896.

Todd, Marion. *Professor Goldwin Smith and His Satellites in Congress.* Battle Creek, Mich.: Wm. C. Cage & Son, 1890.

———. *Railways of Europe and America or Government Ownership.* Boston: Arena, 1893.

———. *Rachel's Pitiful History.* Springport, Mich.: Emery & Emery, 1895.

Tracy, Frank Basil. "Rise and Doom of the Populist Party." *Forum* (1893): 240–51.

Turner, Frederick Jackson. "The Significance of the Frontier in American History." In *The Frontier in American History.* New York: Holt, 1920.

Vincent, Leopold, ed. *Alliance Songster: A Collection of Labor and Comic Songs for the Use of Grange, Alliance or Debating Clubs.* Indianapolis: Vincent Bros., 1891.

Vrooman, Carl S. "Twentieth Century Democracy." *Arena* 22 (1899): 584–98.

Ward, Lester Frank. "Our Better Halves." *Forum* 6 (1888): 266–75.

———. "Mind as a Social Factor." In *American Intellectual Tradition, A Sourcebook*, edited by David Hollinger and Charles Capper, 39–47. New York: Oxford University Press, 1993.

Watson, Thomas E. "The Negro Question in the South." *Arena* 6 (1892): 540–50.

———. *The People's Party Campaign Book, 1892: Not a Revolt: It Is a Revolution.* Washington, D.C.: National Watchman, 1892.

———. *The Story of France: From the Earliest Times to the Consulate of Napoleon Bonaparte* (2 vols.). New York: Macmillan, 1899.

———. *Napoleon: A Sketch of His Life, Character, Struggles, and Achievements.* New York: Macmillan, 1908.

Waugh, Catherine G. *Woman's Wages.* Rockford, Ill.: Daily Gazette Book and Job Office, 1888.

Willard, Frances E. "The Coming Brotherhood." *Arena* 6 (1892): 317–24.

Willard, Frances E., and Mary A. Livermore, eds. *A Woman of the Century: Fourteen Hundred-Seventy Biographical Sketches Accompanied by Portraits of Leading American Women in All Walks of Life.* Chicago: Charles Wells Moulton, 1893.

Wyckoff, Walter A. *The Workers, An Experiment in Reality: The East.* New York: Scribner's, 1897.

Government Documents

Country Life Commission. *Report of the Country Life Commission.* Washington, D.C.: Government Printing Office, 1909.

Ira B. Cross. *Cooperative Stores: Twelfth Biennial Report of the Bureau of Labor and Industrial Statistics.* Madison: State of Wisconsin, 1905–6.

Mayo, Amory Dwight. *Southern Women in the Recent Educational Movement in the South.* Circular of Information, 1892, no. 1., of U.S. Bureau of Education. Washington, D.C.: Government Printing Office, 1892.

Polk, Leonidas L. *Report on the General Condition of the Agricultural Interests of North Carolina, from Returns Made to the Department of Agriculture, Raleigh, N.C., March, 1878.* Raleigh: Farmer and Mechanic Print, 1878.

———. *Report of L. L. Polk, Commissioner of Agriculture, for 1877 and 1878.* Public Document No. 8, Department of Agriculture. Raleigh, N.C., January 6, 1879.

———. *Handbook of North Carolina, Embracing Historical and Physiographical Sketches of the State, with Statistical and Other Information Relating to Its Industries, Resources and Political Conditions.* Raleigh: Raleigh News Steam Book, 1879.

Rust, Irwin W., and Kelsey B. Gardner. *Sunkist Growers, Inc.: A California Adventure in Agricultural Cooperation.* Washington, D.C.: Farmer Cooperative Service, U.S. Department of Agriculture, 1960.

U.S. Department of the Interior. *Abstract of the Eleventh Census: 1890.* Washington, D.C.: Government Printing Office, 1894.

———. *Report on Population of the United States at the Eleventh Census: 1890.* Washington, D.C.: Government Printing Office, 1895.

United States Strike Commission Report. Senate Executive Doc. No. 7. 53rd Cong., 3d sess. Washington, D.C.: Government Printing Office, 1895.

Autobiographies and Reminiscences

Addams, Jane. *Twenty Years at Hull-House.* New York: Macmillan, 1910. Reprint, New York: Signet, 1999.

Barrows, Mary Eleanor. *John Henry Barrows: A Memoir.* Chicago: Fleming H. Revell, 1904.

Davis, James H. *Memoir by Cyclone Davis*. Sherman, Tex.: Courier, 1935.

Debs, Eugene V. "Martin Irons." *Monthly Journal* (February 1901).

———. "Recollections of Ingersoll." *Pearson's Magazine* (April 1917).

Garland, Hamlin. *A Son of the Middle Border*. New York: Macmillan, 1919.

Gilman, Charlotte Perkins. *The Living of Charlotte Perkins Gilman*. New York: Appleton-Century, 1935. Reprint, New York: Ayer, 1987.

Gompers, Samuel. *Seventy Years of Life and Labor: An Autobiography*. New York: Dutton, 1925.

Ingersoll, Robert G. *Life and Letters*. Edited and with a biographical introduction by Eva Ingersoll Wakefield. London: Watts, 1952.

Irons, Martin. "My Experience in the Labor Movement." *Lippincott's Magazine* 37 (1886): 618–27.

Kellie, Luna. *A Prairie Populist: The Memoirs of Luna Kellie*. Edited by Jane Taylor Nelsen. Iowa City: University of Iowa Press, 1992.

Lease, Mary Elizabeth. "Mrs. Mary E. Lease." Unpublished. Kansas State Historical Society, Topeka, 1912.

London, Jack. *Jack London on the Road: The Tramp Diary and Other Hobo Writings*. Edited by Richard W. Etulain. Logan: Utah State University Press, 1979.

Macune, Charles W. "Farmers Alliance." Unpublished. Center for American History, University of Texas, Austin, 1920.

Maier, Charles W. "The Realization of My Boyhood Dream as a Railroad Man." Unpublished. In Ruth A. Allen Labor Movement in Texas Collection. Center for American History, University of Texas, Austin, 1940.

Poe, Clarence Hamilton. *Colonel Leonidas Lafayette Polk: His Services in Starting the North Carolina State College of Agriculture and Engineering*. Raleigh, N.C.: 1926.

Powderly, Terence V. *The Path I Trod*. New York: Columbia University Press, 1940.

Roney, Frank. *Frank Roney Irish Rebel and California Labor Leader: An Autobiography*. Berkeley: University of California, 1931.

Teague, Charles Collins. *Fifty Years a Rancher*. Los Angeles: California Walnut Growers Association, 1944.

Watson, Thomas E. *The Life and Speeches of Thos. E. Watson*. Thomson, Ga.: Jeffersonian, 1911.

Wayland, Julius A. *Leaves of Life: A Story of Twenty Years of Socialist Agitation*. Girard, Kans.: Appeal to Reason, 1912.

NEWSPAPERS AND PERIODICALS

Advocate, Meriden, Kans.

Advocate, Topeka

Alliance Farmer, Los Angeles

American Citizen, Topeka

Ansonian, Polkton, N.C.

Austin Statesmen

Baptist Headlight, Topeka

Carrier Dove, San Francisco

Caucasian, Clinton, N.C.

Chicago Record

Chicago Searchlight

Chicago Times

Comanche Chief, Comanche, Tex.

Comanche Vanguard, Comanche, Tex.

Coming Nation, Greensburg, Ind.

Commonwealth, Visalia, Calif.

Dallas Morning News

Enterprise, Riverside, Calif.

Farmer and Mechanic, Raleigh

Farmers' Voice, Chicago

Fort Worth Gazette

Galveston Daily News

Globe-Democrat, St. Louis

Harper's Weekly

Indianapolis Freeman

Integral Co-Operator, Enterprise, Kans.

Journal of the Knights of Labor, Philadelphia

Kansas Farmer, Topeka

Los Angeles Times

Nation, New York

National Economist, Washington, D.C.

Nationalist, Boston

Nonconformist, Indianapolis

Nonconformist, Winfield, Kans.

Overland Monthly, San Francisco

Pacific Rural Press, San Francisco

People's Advocate, Hill City, Kans.

People's Advocate, Ventura, Calif.

People's Party Paper, Atlanta

People's Press, San Francisco

Pioneer Exponent, Comanche, Tex.

Prairie Farmer, Chicago

Progressive Farmer, Raleigh

Richmond Planet

Rural Californian, Los Angeles

Rural Citizen, Jacksboro, Tex.

San Francisco Call

San Francisco Examiner

Savannah Tribune

Southern Mercury, Dallas

Times-Democrat, New Orleans

Town & Country, Comanche, Tex.

Tribune, Junction City, Kans.

United Mine Workers' Journal, Indianapolis

Waco Daily Examiner

Washington Bee

Washington Evening Star

Washington Post

Western Rural, Chicago

BOOKS

Adams, Jane. *The Transformation of Rural Life: Southern Illinois, 1890–1990*. Chapel Hill: University of North Carolina Press, 1994.

Allen, Robert. *Reluctant Reformers: Racism and Social Reform Movements in the United States*. Washington, D.C.: Howard University Press, 1983.

Allen, Ruth. *Chapters in the History of Organized Labor in Texas*. Austin: University of Texas Press, 1941.

———. *The Great Southwest Strike*. Austin: University of Texas Press, 1942.

Anderson, Eric. *Race and Politics in North Carolina, 1872–1901: The Black Second*. Baton Rouge: Louisiana State University Press, 1981.

Argersinger, Peter H. *Populism and Politics: William Alfred Peffer and the People's Party*. Lawrence: University of Kansas Press, 1974.

———. *The Limits of Agrarian Radicalism: Western Populism and American Politics*. Lawrence: University of Kansas Press, 1995.

Ashby, LeRoy. *William Jennings Bryan: Champion of Democracy*. Boston: Twayne, 1987.

Ayers, Edward L. *The Promise of the New South: Life after Reconstruction*. New York: Oxford University Press, 1992.

Baker, Jean. *Affairs of Party: The Political Culture of Northern Democrats in the Mid Nineteenth-Century*. Ithaca, N.Y.: Cornell University Press, 1983.

Baker, Jean, ed. *Votes for Women: The Struggle for Suffrage Revisited*. New York: Oxford University Press, 2002.

Baker, Paula C. *The Moral Frameworks of Public Life: Gender, Politics, and the State in Rural New York, 1870–1930*. New York: Oxford University Press, 1991.

Bannister, Robert C. *Social Darwinism, Science and Myth in Anglo-American Social Thought.* Philadelphia: Temple University Press, 1979.

Barnes, Donna. *Farmers in Rebellion: The Rise and Fall of the Southern Farmers' Alliance and People's Party in Texas.* Austin: University of Texas Press, 1984.

Barron, Hal S. *Mixed Harvest: The Second Great Transformation in the Rural North, 1870–1930.* Chapel Hill: University of North Carolina Press, 1997.

Barthelme, Marion K., ed. *Women in the Texas Populist Movement, Letters to the Southern Mercury.* College Station: Texas A&M University Press, 1997.

Bederman, Gail. *Manliness and Civilization: A Cultural History of Gender and Race in the United States, 1880–1917.* Chicago: University of Chicago Press, 1995.

Berk, Gerald. *Alternative Tracks: The Constitution of American Industrial Order, 1865–1917.* Baltimore: Johns Hopkins University Press, 1994.

Berman, Marshall. *All That Is Solid Melts into Air: The Experience of Modernity.* New York: Simon & Schuster, 1982. Reprint, New York: Penguin, 1988.

Bledstein, Burton J., and Robert D. Johnson. *The Middling Sorts: Explorations in the History of the American Middle Class.* New York: Routledge, 2001.

Blight, David W. *Race and Reunion: The Civil War in American Memory.* Cambridge, Mass.: Harvard University Press, 2001.

Bloch, Marc. *Historian's Craft.* New York: Knopf, 1961.

Boller, Paul F. Jr. *American Thought in Transition: The Impact of Evolutionary Naturalism, 1865–1900.* Chicago: Rand McNally, 1969.

Bowers, William L. *The Country Life Movement in America, 1900–1920.* Port Washington, N.Y.: Kennikat, 1974.

Braude, Ann. *Radical Spirits: Spiritualism and Women's Rights in Nineteenth-Century America.* Boston: Beacon, 1989.

Brody, David. *In Labor's Cause: Main Themes on the History of the American Worker.* New York: Oxford University Press, 1993.

Brown, Richard D. *Knowledge Is Power: The Diffusion of Information in Early America, 1700–1865.* New York: Oxford University Press, 1989.

Brundage, David. *The Making of Western Labor Radicalism: Denver's Organized Workers, 1878–1905.* Urbana: University of Illinois Press, 1994.

Brundage, W. Fitzhugh. *A Socialist Utopia in the New South: The Ruskin Colonies in Tennessee and Georgia, 1894–1901.* Urbana: University of Illinois Press, 1996.

———. "Thomas Dixon: American Proteus." In *Thomas Dixon Jr. and the Birth of Modern America,* edited by Michele K. Gillespie and Randal L. Hall, 23–45. Baton Rouge: Louisiana State University Press, 2006.

Buck, Solon Justus. *The Granger Movement: A Study of Agricultural Organization and Its Political, Economic and Social Manifestations, 1870–1880.* Cambridge, Mass.: Harvard University Press, 1913.

Buhle, Mari Jo. *Women and American Socialism, 1780–1920.* Urbana: University of Illinois Press, 1981.

Bury, John B. *The Idea of Progress: An Inquiry into Its Origin and Growth*. New York: Macmillan, 1932.

Butler, Jon, Grant Wacker, and Randall Balmer. *Religion in American Life: A Short History*. New York: Oxford University Press, 2003.

Calhoun, Craig. *The Question of Class Struggle: Social Foundations of Popular Radicalism during the Industrial Revolution*. Chicago: University of Chicago Press, 1982.

Campbell, Randolph B. *Gone to Texas: A History of the Lone Star State*. New York: Oxford University Press, 2003.

Cantrell, Gregg. *Kenneth and John B. Rayner and the Limits of Southern Dissent*. Urbana: University of Illinois, 1993.

Carpenter, Joel. *Revive Us Again: The Reawakening of American Fundamentalism*. New York: Oxford University Press, 1997.

Cell, John W. *The Highest Stage of White Supremacy: The Origins of Segregation in South Africa and the American South*. Cambridge: Cambridge University Press, 1982.

Chandler, Alfred D. Jr. *The Visible Hand: The Managerial Revolution in American Business*. Cambridge, Mass.: Harvard University Press, 1977.

Chandler, Alfred D. Jr., and James W. Cortada, eds. *A Nation Transformed by Information: How Information Has Shaped the United States from Colonial Times to the Present*. New York: Oxford University Press, 2000.

Chaplin, Joyce E. *An Anxious Pursuit: Agricultural Innovation and Modernity in the Lower South, 1730–1815*. Chapel Hill: University of North Carolina Press, 1993.

Clanton, O. Gene. *Kansas Populism, Ideas and Men*. Lawrence: University of Kansas Press, 1969.

Clark Christopher. *The Roots of Rural Capitalism: Western Massachusetts, 1780–1860*. Ithaca, N.Y.: Cornell University Press, 1990.

Clemens, Elisabeth S. *The People's Lobby: Organizational Innovation and the Rise of Interest Group Politics in the United States, 1890–1925*. Chicago: University of Chicago Press, 1997.

Clinch, Thomas A. *Urban Populism and Free Silver in Montana, A Narrative of Ideology in Political Action*. Missoula: University of Montana Press, 1970.

Cochrane, William W. *The Development of American Agriculture: A Historical Analysis*. Minneapolis: University of Minnesota Press, 1993.

Cohen, Bernard I. *Science and the Founding Fathers, Science in the Political Thought of Thomas Jefferson, Benjamin Franklin, John Adams, and James Madison*. New York: Norton, 1995.

Coletta, Paolo E. *William Jennings Bryan, Political Evangelist, 1860–1908*. Lincoln: University of Nebraska Press, 1964.

Conzen, Michael P. *Frontier Farming in an Urban Shadow*. Madison: State Historical Society of Wisconsin, 1971.

Cook, Raymond Allen. *Fire from the Flint: The Amazing Careers of Thomas Dixon*. Winston-Salem, N.C.: John F. Blair, 1968.

Cotkin, George. *Reluctant Modernism: American Thought and Culture, 1880–1900*. New York: Twayne, 1992.

Cott, Nancy F. *The Bonds of Womanhood: "Woman's Sphere" in New England, 1780–1835*. New Haven, Conn.: Yale University Press, 1977.

Couchman, Robert. *The Sunsweet Story*. San Jose, Calif.: Sunsweet Growers Inc., 1967.

Cox, Robert S. *Body and Soul: A Sympathetic History of American Spiritualism*. Charlottesville: University of Virginia Press, 2003.

Cox, Thomas C. *Blacks in Topeka, Kansas, 1865–1915: A Social History*. Baton Rouge: Louisiana State University Press, 1982.

Creech, Joe. *Righteous Indignation: Religion and the Populist Revolution*. Urbana: University of Illinois Press, 2006.

Crenson, Matthew A. *The Federal Machine: Beginnings of Bureaucracy in Jacksonian America*. Baltimore: Johns Hopkins University Press, 1975.

Cronon, William. *Nature's Metropolis*. New York: Norton, 1991.

Curtis, Susan. *A Consuming Faith: The Social Gospel and Modern American Culture*. Baltimore: Johns Hopkins University Press, 1991.

Danbom, David B. *The Resisted Revolution: Urban America and the Industrialization of Agriculture, 1900–1930*. Ames: Iowa State University Press, 1979.

———. *Born in the Country: A History of Rural America*. Baltimore: Johns Hopkins University Press, 1995.

Degler, Carl N. *At Odds: Women and the Family in America from Revolution to the Present*. New York: Oxford University Press, 1980.

Destler, Chester McArthur. *American Radicalism, 1865–1901*. New London: Connecticut College, 1946. Reprint, Chicago: Quadrangle, 1966.

Dewing, Arthur S. *A History of the National Cordage Company*. Cambridge, Mass.: Harvard University Press, 1913.

Doyle, Don Harrison. *The Social Order of a Frontier Community: Jacksonville, Illinois, 1825–70*. Urbana: University of Illinois Press, 1978.

Drache, Hiram M. *The Day of the Bonanza: A History of Bonanza Farming in the Red River Valley of the North*. Fargo: North Dakota Institute for Regional Studies, 1964.

DuBois, Ellen Carol. *Feminism and Suffrage: The Emergence of an Independent Women's Movement in America, 1848–1869*. Ithaca, N.Y.: Cornell University Press, 1978.

Dunaway, Wilma A. *The First American Frontier: Transition to Capitalism in Southern Appalachia, 1700–1860*. Chapel Hill: University of North Carolina Press, 1996.

Durden, Robert F. *The Climax of Populism: The Election of 1896*. Lexington: University of Kentucky Press, 1965.

Edwards, Rebecca. *Angels in the Machinery: Gender in American Party Politics from the Civil War to the Progressive Era*. New York: Oxford University Press, 1997.

———. *New Spirits: Americans in the Gilded Age, 1865–1905*. New York: Oxford University Press, 2006.

Ellis, Richard J. *American Political Cultures*. New York: Oxford University Press, 1993.

Erdman, Henry Ernest. *The California Fruit Growers Exchange: An Example of Cooperation in the Segregation of Conflicting Interests.* New York: American Council Institute of Pacific Relations, 1933.

Ethington, Philip J. *The Public City: The Political Construction of Urban Life in San Francisco, 1850–1900.* New York: Cambridge University Press, 1994.

Evensen, Bruce J. *God's Man for the Gilded Age: D. L. Moody and the Rise of Modern Mass Evangelism.* New York: Oxford University Press, 2003.

Faragher, John Mack. *Sugar Creek: Life on the Illinois Prairie.* New Haven, Conn.: Yale University Press, 1986.

Feldman, Glenn. *The Disfranchisement Myth: Poor Whites and Suffrage Restriction in Alabama.* Athens: University of Georgia Press, 2004.

Fields, Barbara. "Ideology and Race in American History." In *Region, Race, and Reconstruction: Essays in Honor of C. Vann Woodward*, edited by J. Morgan Kousser and James M. McPherson, 143–77. New York: Oxford University Press, 1982.

Fink, Deborah. *Agrarian Women: Wives and Mothers in Rural Nebraska, 1880–1940.* Chapel Hill: University of North Carolina Press, 1992.

Fink, Leon. *Workingmen's Democracy, the Knights of Labor and American Politics.* Urbana: University of Illinois Press, 1983.

Fite, Gilbert C. *The Farmers' Frontier.* New York: Holt, Rinehart and Winston, 1966.

———. *Cotton Fields No More: Southern Agriculture, 1865–1980.* Lexington: University of Kentucky Press, 1984.

Fitzgerald, Deborah. *Every Farm a Factory: The Industrial Ideal in American Agriculture.* New Haven, Conn.: Yale University Press, 2003.

Fogarty, Robert S. *Dictionary of American Communal and Utopian History.* Westport, Conn.: Greenwood, 1980.

———. *All Things New: American Communes and Utopian Movements, 1860–1914.* Chicago: University of Chicago Press, 1990.

Foner, Eric. *Politics and Ideology in the Age of the Civil War.* New York: Oxford University Press, 1980.

———. *The Story of American Freedom.* New York: Norton, 1998.

Foner, Phillip S. *Organized Labor and the Black Worker, 1619–1973.* New York: International, 1974.

Fredrickson, George M. *The Black Image in the White Mind: The Debate on Afro-American Character and Destiny, 1817–1914.* New York: Harper & Row, 1971.

Friedman, Jean E. *The Enclosed Garden, Women and Community in the Evangelical South, 1830–1900.* Chapel Hill: University of North Carolina Press, 1985.

Friedman, Milton, and Anna Jacobson Schwartz. *A Monetary History of the United States, 1867–1960.* Princeton, N.J.: Princeton University Press, 1990.

Fuller, Wayne E. *American Mail, Enlarger of the Common Life.* Chicago: University of Chicago Press, 1972.

Gabler, Edwin. *The American Telegrapher: A Social History, 1860–1900.* New Brunswick, N.J.: Rutgers University Press, 1988.

Gaither, Gerald H. *Blacks and the Populist Revolt: Ballots and Bigotry in the "New South."* Tuscaloosa: University of Alabama Press, 1977.

Galpin, Charles Josiah. *Rural Social Problems.* New York: Century, 1924.

Gaston, Paul M. *The New South Creed: A Study in Southern Mythmaking.* New York: Knopf, 1970.

Gilmore, Glenda Elizabeth. *Gender and Jim Crow: Women and the Politics of White Supremacy in North Carolina, 1896–1920.* Chapel Hill: University of North Carolina Press, 1996.

Ginger, Ray. *The Bending Cross, A Biography of Eugene Victor Debs.* New Brunswick, N.J.: Rutgers College, 1949. Reprint, New York: Collier, 1970.

———. *Six Days or Forever? Tennessee v. John Thomas Scopes.* Boston: Beacon, 1958. Reprint, New York: Oxford University Press, 1974.

———. *The Nationalizing of American Life, 1877–1900.* New York: Free, 1965.

Goldberg, Michael Lewis. *An Army of Women: Gender and Politics in Gilded Age Kansas.* Baltimore: Johns Hopkins University Press, 1997.

Goodwyn, Lawrence. *Democratic Promise: The Populist Moment in America.* New York: Oxford University Press, 1976.

———. *The Populist Moment: A Short History of the Agrarian Revolt in America.* New York: Oxford University Press, 1978.

Grant, H. Roger. *Self-Help in the 1890s Depression.* Ames: Iowa State University Press, 1983.

Green, Constance McLaughlin. *The Secret City: A History of Race Relations in the Nation's Capital.* Princeton, N.J.: Princeton University Press, 1967.

Green, James R. *Grass-Roots Socialism: Radical Movements in the Southwest, 1895–1943.* Baton Rouge: Louisiana State University, 1978.

Greene, Julie. *Pure and Simple Politics: The American Federation of Labor and Political Activism, 1881–1917.* Cambridge: Cambridge University Press, 1998.

Griffiths, David B. *Populism in the Western United States, 1890–1900.* Lewiston, N.Y.: Edwin Mellen, 1992.

Griggs, William Clark. *Parson Henry Renfro, Free Thinking on the Texas Frontier.* Austin: University of Texas Press, 1994.

Gutman, Herbert. *Work, Culture, and Society in Industrializing America.* New York: Vintage, 1977.

———. *Power and Culture: Essays on the American Working Class.* New York: Pantheon, 1987.

Hackney, Sheldon. *Populism to Progressivism in Alabama.* Princeton, N.J.: Princeton University Press, 1969.

Hahn, Steven. *The Roots of Southern Populism, Yeoman Farmers and the Transformation of the Georgia Upcountry, 1850–1890.* New York: Oxford University Press, 1985.

———. *A Nation under Our Feet: Black Political Struggles in the Rural South from Slavery to the Great Migration.* Cambridge, Mass.: Harvard University Press, 2003.

Hahn, Steven, and Jonathan Prude. *The Countryside in the Age of Capitalist Transformation: Essays in the Social History of Rural America.* Chapel Hill: University of North Carolina Press, 1985.

Hale, Elizabeth Grace. *Making Whiteness: The Culture of Segregation in the South, 1890–1940.* New York: Pantheon, 1998.

Handy, Robert T. *The Social Gospel in America.* New York: Oxford University Press, 1966.

Handy-Marchello, Barbara. *Women of the Northern Plains: Gender and Settlement on the Homestead Frontier, 1870–1930.* St. Paul: Minnesota Historical Society Press, 2005.

Harp, Gillis J. *Positivist Republic: Auguste Comte and the Reconstruction of American Liberalism, 1865–1920.* University Park: Pennsylvania State University Press, 1995.

Hattam, Victoria C. *Labor Visions and State Power.* Princeton, N.J.: Princeton University Press, 1993.

Hazen, Craig James. *The Village Enlightenment in America: Popular Religion and Science in the Nineteenth Century.* Urbana: University of Illinois Press, 2000.

Hicks, John D. *The Populist Revolt: A History of the Farmers' Alliance and the People's Party.* Minneapolis: University of Minnesota, 1931.

Hill, Mary A. *Charlotte Perkins Gilman: The Making of a Radical Feminist, 1860–1896.* Philadelphia: Temple University Press, 1980.

Hill, Patricia Evridge. *Dallas: The Making of a Modern City.* Austin: University of Texas Press, 1996.

Hine, Robert V. *California's Utopian Colonies.* New Haven, Conn.: Yale University Press, 1953.

Hofstadter, Richard. *Social Darwinism in American Thought.* Philadelphia: University of Pennsylvania Press, 1944.

———. *The Age of Reform, from Bryan to F.D.R.* New York: Random House, 1955.

———. *The Progressive Historians: Turner, Beard, Parrington.* New York: Knopf, 1968.

Holmes, C. L. "Agriculture in Reconstruction." In *Readings in the Economic History of American Agriculture,* edited by Louis Bernard Schmidt and Earle Dudley Ross, 529–56. New York: Macmillan, 1925.

Holt, Marilyn Irvin. *Linoleum, Better Babies, and the Modern Farm Woman, 1890–1930.* Albuquerque: University of New Mexico Press, 1995.

Hopkins, Charles. *The Rise of the Social Gospel in American Protestantism, 1865–1915.* New Haven, Conn.: Yale University Press, 1940.

Horowitz, Daniel. *Jimmy Carter and the Energy Crisis of the 1970s: The "Crisis of Confidence" Speech of July 15, 1979: A Brief History with Documents.* Boston: Bedford, 2005.

Hoy, Suellen. *Chasing Dirt: The American Pursuit of Cleanliness.* New York: Oxford University Press, 1995.

Humphrey, Janet G. *A Texas Suffragist: Diaries and Writings of Jane Y. McCallum.* Austin: Ellen C. Temple, 1988.

Hunt, James L. *Marion Butler and American Populism.* Chapel Hill: University of North Carolina Press, 2003.

Hutchison, William R. *The Modernist Impulse in American Protestantism.* Cambridge, Mass.: Harvard University Press, 1976.

Hyman, Michael R. *The Anti-Redeemers: Hill-Country Political Dissenters in the Lower South from Redemption to Populism.* Baton Rouge: Louisiana State University Press, 1990.

Israel, Charles A. *Before Scopes: Evangelicalism, Education, and Evolution in Tennessee, 1870–1925.* Athens: University of Georgia Press, 2004.

Jacoby, Susan. *Freethinkers: A History of American Secularism.* New York: Henry Holt, 2004.

Jeffrey, Julie Roy. *Frontier Women: The Trans-Mississippi West, 1840–1880.* New York: Hill & Wang, 1979.

Jensen, Richard J. *The Winning of the Midwest: Social and Political Conflict, 1888–1896.* Chicago: University of Chicago Press, 1971.

Jernigan, Jay E. *Henry Demarest Lloyd.* Boston: G. K. Hall, 1976.

Johnston, Robert D. *The Radical Middle Class: Populist Democracy and the Question of Capitalism in Progressive Era Portland, Oregon.* Princeton, N.J.: Princeton University Press, 2003.

Kammen, Michael. *Mystic Chords of Memory: The Transformation of Tradition in American Culture.* New York: Knopf, 1991.

Karsner, David. *Debs: His Authorized Life and Letters.* New York: Boni and Liveright Publishers, 1919.

Kaufman, Jason. *For the Common Good? American Civic Life and the Golden Age of Fraternity.* New York: Oxford University Press, 2002.

Kazin, Michael. *The Populist Persuasion, An American History.* New York: Basic, 1995.
———. *A Godly Hero: The Life of William Jennings Bryan.* New York: Knopf, 2006.

Keillor, Steven J. *Cooperative Commonwealth: Co-ops in Rural Minnesota, 1859–1939.* St. Paul: Minnesota Historical Society Press, 2000.

Keith, Jeanette. *Country People in the New South: Tennessee's Upper Cumberland.* Chapel Hill: University of North Carolina Press, 1995.

Keller, Morton. *Affairs of State: Public Life in Late Nineteenth Century America.* Cambridge, Mass.: Harvard University Press, 1977.

Kerber, Linda K. *Women of the Republic: Intellect and Ideology in Revolutionary America.* Chapel Hill: University of North Carolina Press, 1980.

Kleppner, Paul. *The Cross of Culture: A Social Analysis of Midwestern Politics, 1850–1890.* New York: Free, 1970.

Knapp, Joseph G. *Great American Cooperators.* Washington, D.C.: American Institute of Cooperation, 1967.

Kousser, J. Morgan. *The Shaping of Southern Politics: Suffrage Restriction and the Establishment of the One-Party South, 1880–1910.* New Haven, Conn.: Yale University Press, 1974.

Laird, Pamela Walker. *Advertising Progress: American Business and the Rise of Consumer Marketing.* Baltimore: Johns Hopkins University Press, 1998.

Larson, Edward J. *Summer for the Gods: The Scopes Trial and America's Continuing Debate over Science and Religion.* Cambridge, Mass.: Harvard University Press, 1997.

Larson, Robert W. *New Mexico Populism: A Study of Radical Protest in a Western Territory.* Boulder: Colorado Associated University Press, 1974.

———. *Populism in the Mountain West.* Albuquerque: University of New Mexico Press, 1986.

Lasch, Christopher. *The True and Only Heaven: Progress and Its Critics.* New York: Norton, 1991.

———. "Populism." In *A Companion to American Thought,* edited by Richard Wightman Fox and James T. Kloppenberg, 531–32. Cambridge, Mass.: Blackwell, 1995.

———. *The Revolt of the Elites and the Betrayal of Democracy.* New York: Norton, 1995.

———. *Women and the Common Life: Love, Marriage, and Feminism.* New York: Norton, 1997.

Leikin, Steve. *The Practical Utopians: American Workers and the Cooperative Movement in the Gilded Age.* Detroit: Wayne State University Press, 2005.

Levine, Lawrence W. *Defender of the Faith, William Jennings Bryan, the Last Decade, 1915–1925.* New York: Oxford University Press, 1965.

Lindsey, Almont. *The Pullman Strike: The Story of a Unique Experiment and of a Great Labor Upheaval.* Chicago: University of Chicago Press, 1942.

Lipartito, Kenneth. "The Utopian Corporation." In *Constructing Corporate America: History, Politics, Culture,* edited by Kenneth Lipartito and David B. Sicilia, 94–119. New York: Oxford University Press, 2004.

Lipow, Arthur. *Authoritarian Socialism in America: Edward Bellamy and the Nationalist Movement.* Berkeley: University of California Press, 1982.

Lippy, Charles H., and Peter W. Williams, eds. *Encyclopedia of the American Religious Experience.* New York: Scribner's, 1988.

Lipset, Seymour, and Earl Raab. *The Politics of Unreason: Right-Wing Extremism in America, 1790–1977.* Chicago: University of Chicago Press, 1978.

Litwack, Leon F. *Been in the Storm So Long: The Aftermath of Slavery.* New York: Knopf, 1979.

———. *Trouble in Mind: Black Southerners in the Age of Jim Crow.* New York: Knopf, 1998.

Livingston, James. *Origins of the Federal Reserve System: Money, Class, and Corporate Capitalism, 1890–1913.* Ithaca, N.Y.: Cornell University Press, 1986.

———. *Pragmatism, Feminism, and Democracy: Rethinking the Politics of American History.* New York: Routledge, 2001.

Livingstone, David N., D. G. Hart, and Mark A. Noll, eds. *Evangelicals and Science in Historical Perspective.* New York: Oxford University Press, 1999.

Longfield, Bradley J. *The Presbyterian Controversy: Fundamentalists, Modernists, and Moderates.* New York: Oxford University Press, 1991.

Lustig, R. Jeffrey. *Corporate Liberalism: The Origins of Modern American Political Theory, 1890–1920.* Berkeley: University of California Press, 1982.

MacCurdy, Rahno Mabel. *The History of the California Fruit Growers Exchange.* Los Angeles: G. Rice & Sons, 1925.

Malin, James C. *Winter Wheat in the Golden Belt of Kansas: A Study in Adaption to Subhumid Geographical Environment.* Lawrence: University of Kansas Press, 1944.

———. *Confounded Rot about Napoleon: Reflection upon Science and Technology, Nationalism, World Depression of the Eighteen-Nineties, and Afterwards.* Ann Arbor, Mich.: Edwards Brothers, 1961.

Mallon, Florencia E. *Peasant and Nation, The Making of Postcolonial Mexico and Peru.* Berkeley: University of California Press, 1995.

Marcus, Alan I. *Agricultural Science and the Quest for Legitimacy: Farmers, Agricultural Colleges, and Experiment Stations, 1870–1890.* Ames: Iowa State University Press, 1985.

Marsden, George M. *Fundamentalism and American Culture: The Shaping of 20th Century Evangelicalism 1870–1925.* New York: Oxford University Press, 1980.

Marti, Donald B. *Women of the Grange: Mutuality and Sisterhood in Rural America, 1866–1920.* Westport, Conn.: Greenwood, 1991.

Martin, Roscoe. *The People's Party in Texas: A Case Study in Third-Party Politics.* Austin: University of Texas Press, 1933.

May, Henry E. *The Enlightenment in America.* New York: Oxford University Press, 1976.

McConnell, Grant. *The Decline of Agrarian Democracy.* Berkeley: University of California Press, 1953.

McGerr, Michael. *The Decline of Popular Politics: The American North, 1865–1928.* New York: Oxford University Press, 1986.

———. *A Fierce Discontent: The Rise and Fall of the Progressive Movement in America, 1870–1920.* New York: Oxford University Press, 2003.

McLaurin, Melton A. *The Knights of Labor in the South.* Westport, Conn.: Greenwood, 1978.

McMath, Robert C. Jr. *Populist Vanguard: A History of the Southern Farmers' Alliance.* Chapel Hill: University of North Carolina Press, 1975.

———. *American Populism: A Social History, 1877–1898.* New York: Hill & Wang, 1993.

McMurry, Donald L. *Coxey's Army, a Study of the Industrial Army Movement of 1894.* Boston: Little, Brown, 1929.

McNall, Scott C. *The Road to Rebellion: Class Formation and Kansas Populism, 1865–1900.* Chicago: University of Chicago Press, 1988.

McWilliams, Carey. *Southern California: An Island on the Land.* Santa Barbara, Calif.: Peregrine Smith, 1973.

Menand, Louis. *The Metaphysical Club: A Story of Ideas in America.* New York: Farrar, Straus, and Giroux, 2001.

Miller, Worth Robert. *Oklahoma Populism: A History of the People's Party in the Oklahoma Territory.* Norman: University of Oklahoma Press, 1987.

———. "Thomas Nugent." In *The New Handbook of Texas.* Austin: Texas State Historical Association, 1996.

Mitchell, Theodore R. *Political Education in the Southern Farmers' Alliance, 1887–1900.* Madison: University of Wisconsin Press, 1987.

Monroe, James. *Democratic Wish: Popular Participation and the Limits of American Government.* New Haven, Conn.: Yale University Press, 1998.

Moore, R. Laurence. *In Search of White Crows: Spiritualism, Parapsychology, and American Culture.* New York: Oxford University Press, 1977.

———. *Selling God: American Religion in the Marketplace of Culture.* New York: Oxford University Press, 1994.

———. *Touchdown Jesus: The Mixing of Sacred and Secular in American History.* Louisville: Westminster John Knox, 2003.

Noblin, Stuart. *Leonidas LaFayette Polk: Agrarian Crusader.* Chapel Hill: University of North Carolina Press, 1949.

Noll, Mark A. *God and Mammon: Protestants, Money, and the Market, 1790–1860.* New York: Oxford University Press, 2002.

Novick, Peter. *That Noble Dream: The "Objectivity Question" and the American Historical Profession.* Cambridge: Cambridge University Press, 1988.

Nugent, Walter K. *The Tolerant Populists: Kansas Populism and Nativism.* Chicago: University of Chicago Press, 1963.

Numbers, Ronald L. *Darwinism Comes to America.* Cambridge, Mass.: Harvard University Press, 1998.

O'Connell, Jay. *Co-Operative Dreams: A History of the Kaweah Colony.* Van Nuys, Calif.: Raven River, 1999.

Orsi, Richard J. *Sunset Limited: The Southern Pacific Railroad and the Development of the American West, 1850–1930.* Berkeley: University of California Press, 2005.

Osterud, Nancy Grey. "'She Helped Me Hay It as Good as a Man': Relations among Women and Men in an Agricultural Community." In *"To Toil the Livelong Day": America's Women at Work, 1780–1980,* edited by Carol Groneman and Mary Beth Norton, 87–97. Ithaca, N.Y.: Cornell University Press, 1987.

———. *Bonds of Community: The Lives of Farm Women in Nineteenth-Century New York.* Ithaca, N.Y.: Cornell University Press, 1991.

Ostler, Jeffrey. *Prairie Populism, The Fate of Agrarian Radicalism in Kansas, Nebraska, and Iowa, 1880–1892.* Lawrence: University of Kansas Press, 1993.

Owen, Alex. *The Place of Enchantment: British Occultism and the Culture of the Modern.* Chicago: University of Chicago Press, 2004.

Palmer, Bruce. *"Man over Money": The Southern Populist Critique of American Capitalism.* Chapel Hill: University of North Carolina, 1980.

Parrington, Vernon Louis. *Main Currents in American Thought.* New York: Harcourt Brace, 1927.

Perlman, Selig. "Upheaval and Reorganisation (Since 1876)." In John R. Commons, ed. *History of Labour in the United States,* edited by John R. Commons, 195–537. New York: MacMillan, 1918.

Perman, Michael. *Struggle for Mastery: Disfranchisement in the South, 1888–1908.* Chapel Hill: University of North Carolina Press, 2001.

Peterson, Trudy Huskamp, ed. *Farmers, Bureaucrats, and Middlemen: Historical Perspectives on American Agriculture.* Washington, D.C.: Howard University Press, 1980.

Philips, Kevin P. *Post-Conservative America: People, Politics and Ideology in a Time of Crisis.* New York: Random House, 1982.

Pitre, Merline. *Through Many Dangers, Toils and Snares: The Black Leadership of Texas 1868–1900.* Austin, Tex.: Eakin, 1985.

Pittenger, Mark. *American Socialists and Evolutionary Thought, 1870–1920.* Madison: University of Wisconsin Press, 1993.

Pollack, Norman. *The Populist Response to Industrial America.* Cambridge, Mass.: Harvard University Press, 1962.

———. *The Just Polity: Populism, Law, and Human Welfare.* Urbana: University of Illinois Press, 1987.

———. *The Humane Economy: Populism, Capitalism, and Democracy.* New Brunswick, N.J.: Rutgers University Press, 1990.

Quintero, Filiberto Leandro. "La Colonia de Topolobampo." In *Historia Integral de la Region del Rio Fuerte,* 587–656. Los Mochis, Sinaloa: Edicion de El Debate, 1978.

Rabinowitz, Howard N. *Race Relations in the Urban South, 1865–1890.* New York: Oxford University Press, 1978. Reprint, Athens: University of Georgia Press, 1996.

Rice, Lawrence D. *The Negro in Texas, 1874–1900.* Baton Rouge: Louisiana State University, 1971.

Ridge, Martin. *Ignatius Donnelly: The Portrait of a Politician.* Chicago: University of Chicago Press, 1962. Reprint, St. Paul: Minnesota Historical Society Press, 1991.

Rieser, Andrew C. *The Chautauqua Moment: Protestants, Progressives, and the Culture of Modern Liberalism.* New York: Columbia University Press, 2003.

Ritter, Gretchen. *Goldbugs and Greenbacks: The Antimonopoly Tradition and the Politics of Finance in America.* Cambridge: Cambridge University Press, 1997.

Robins, R.G. *A. J. Tomlinson: Plainfolk Modernist.* New York: Oxford University Press, 2004.

Rogin, Michael P. *The Intellectuals and McCarthy: The Radical Specter.* Cambridge: Massachusetts Institute of Technology Press, 1967.

Rogin, Michael P., and John L. Shover. *Political Change in California: Critical Elections and Social Movements, 1890–1966.* Westport, Conn.: Greenwood, 1969.

Ryan, Mary P. *Womanhood in America: From Colonial Times to the Present.* New York: New Viewpoints, 1975.

Salvatore, Nick. *Eugene V. Debs: Citizen and Socialist.* Urbana: University of Illinois, 1987.

Sanders, Elizabeth. *Roots of Reform: Farmers, Workers, and the American State, 1877–1917.* Chicago: University of Chicago, 1999.

Saxton, Alexander. *The Indispensable Enemy: Labor and the Anti-Chinese Movement in California.* Berkeley: University of California Press, 1971.

Schmidt, Louis Bernard, and Earle Dudley Ross, eds. *Readings in the Economic History of American Agriculture.* New York: Macmillan, 1925.

Schneirov, Richard. *Labor and Urban Politics: Class Conflict and the Origins of Modern Liberalism in Chicago, 1864–97.* Urbana: University of Illinois Press, 1998.

Schneirov, Richard, Shelton Stromquist, and Nick Salvatore, eds. *The Pullman Strike and the Crisis of the 1890s.* Urbana: University of Illinois Press, 1999.

Schwantes, Carlos. *Coxey's Army: An American Odyssey.* Lincoln: University of Nebraska Press, 1985.

Scott, James C. *Seeing Like a State: How Certain Schemes to Improve the Human Condition Have Failed.* New Haven, Conn.: Yale University Press, 1998.

Scott, Roy V. *The Agrarian Movement in Illinois.* Urbana: University of Illinois Press, 1962.

———. *The Reluctant Farmer: The Rise of Agricultural Extension to 1914.* Urbana: University of Illinois Press, 1970.

Seager, Richard Hughes. *The World's Parliament of Religions: The East/West Encounter, Chicago, 1893.* Bloomington: Indiana University Press, 1995.

Seldon, Steven. *Inheriting Shame: The Story of Eugenics and Racism in America.* New York: Teachers College, 1999.

Sellers, Charles. *The Market Revolution: Jacksonian America, 1815–1846.* New York: Oxford University Press, 1991.

Sewell, William H. Jr. "The Concept(s) of Culture." In *Beyond the Cultural Turn*, edited by Victoria E. Bonnell and Lynn Hunt, 35–61. Berkeley: University of California Press, 1999.

Shannon, Fred A. *The Farmer's Last Frontier: Agriculture, 1860–1897.* New York: Holt, Rinehart and Winston, 1945.

Sharpless, Rebecca. *Fertile Ground, Narrow Choices: Women on Texas Cotton Farms, 1900–1940.* Chapel Hill: University of North Carolina Press, 1999.

Sharrer, Terry G. *A Kind of Fate: Agricultural Change in Virginia, 1861–1920.* Ames: Iowa State University Press, 2000.

Shaw, Barton C. *The Wool Hat Boys, Georgia's Populist Party.* Baton Rouge: Louisiana State University Press, 1984.

Singal, Daniel Joseph, ed. *Modernist Culture in America.* Belmont, Calif.: Wadsworth, 1991.

Sklar, Martin J. *The Corporate Reconstruction of American Capitalism, 1890–1916: The Market, the Law, and Politics.* Cambridge: Cambridge University Press, 1988.

Skocpol, Theda. *Protecting Soldiers and Mothers: The Political Origins of Social Policy in the United States.* Cambridge, Mass.: Harvard University Press, 1992.

Spann, Edward K. *Brotherly Tomorrows: Movements for a Cooperative Society in America: 1820–1920.* New York: Columbia University Press, 1989.

Stansell, Christine. *American Moderns: Bohemian New York and the Creation of a New Century.* New York: Henry Holt, 2000.

Steelman, Lala Carr. *The North Carolina Farmers' Alliance: A Political History, 1887–1893.* Greenville, N.C.: East Carolina University Publications, 1985.

Stock, Catherine McNicol, and Robert D. Johnston, eds. *The Countryside in the Age of the Modern State: Political Histories of Rural America.* Ithaca, N.Y.: Cornell University Press, 2001.

Stokes, Melvyn, and Stephen Conway, eds. *The Market Revolution in America: Social, Political, and Religious Expressions, 1800–1880*. Charlottesville: University of Virginia Press, 1996.

Stromquist, Shelton. *A Generation of Boomers, the Patterns of Labor Conflict in Nineteenth-Century America*. Urbana: University of Illinois Press, 1987.

Summers, Mark Wahlgren. *The Gilded Age or, the Hazard of New Functions*. Upper Saddle River, N.J.: Prentice Hall, 1997.

———. *Party Games: Getting, Keeping, and Using Power in Gilded Age Politics*. Chapel Hill: University of North Carolina, 2004.

Sunkist Growers, Inc. *Heritage of Gold: The First 100 Years of Sunkist Growers, Inc.* Los Angeles: Sunkist, Inc., 1994.

Taylor, Elizabeth A. *Citizens at Last: The Woman Suffrage Movement in Texas*. Austin, Tex.: Ellen C. Temple, 1987.

Thelen, David. *Paths of Resistance: Tradition and Dignity in Industrializing Missouri*. New York: Oxford University Press, 1986.

Thomas, John L. *Alternative America: Henry George, Edward Bellamy, Henry Demarest Lloyd, and the Adversary Tradition*. Cambridge, Mass.: Harvard University Press, 1983.

Thompson, Edward P. *The Making of the English Working Class*. New York: Random House, 1963.

Tierney, Kevin. *Darrow: A Biography*. New York: Thomas Y. Crowell, 1979.

Tindall, George Brown, ed. *A Populist Reader: Selections from the Works of American Populist Leaders*. New York: Harper & Row, 1966.

Trattner, Walter I. *From Poor Law to Welfare State: A History of Social Welfare in America*. New York: Free, 1988.

Turner, James. *Without God, Without Creed: The Origins of Unbelief in America*. Baltimore: Johns Hopkins University Press, 1985.

Unger, Irwin. *The Greenback Era: A Social and Political History of American Finance, 1865–1879*. Princeton, N.J.: Princeton University Press, 1964.

Vaught, David. *Cultivating California: Growers, Specialty Crops, and Labor, 1875–1920*. Baltimore: Johns Hopkins University Press, 1999.

Voss, Kim. *The Making of American Exceptionalism: The Knights of Labor and Class Formation in the Nineteenth Century*. Ithaca, N.Y.: Cornell University Press, 1993.

Watkins, Marilyn P. *Rural Democracy: Family Farmers and Politics in Western Washington, 1890–1925*. Ithaca, N.Y.: Cornell University Press, 1995.

Welter, Rush. *Popular Education and Democratic Thought in America*. New York: Columbia University Press, 1962.

Wharton, Vernon L. *The Negro in Mississippi 1865–1890*. New York: Harper & Row, 1965.

Wickett, Murray R. *Contested Territory: Whites, Native Americans, and African Americans in Oklahoma, 1865–1907*. Baton Rouge: Louisiana State University Press, 2000.

Wiebe, Robert H. *The Search for Order, 1877–1920*. New York: Hill & Wang, 1967.

Williams, Wayne C. *William Jennings Bryan*. New York: Putnam, 1936.

Wills, Garry. *Under God: Religion and American Politics.* New York: Simon & Schuster, 1990.

Wills, Jocelyn. *Boosters, Hustlers, and Speculators: Entrepreneurial Culture and the Rise of Minneapolis and St. Paul, 1849–1883.* St. Paul: Minnesota Historical Society Press, 2005.

Winkler, Ernest William, ed. *Platforms of Political Parties in Texas.* Austin: University of Texas, 1916.

Woeste, Victoria Saker. *The Farmers' Benevolent Trust: Law and Agricultural Cooperation in Industrial America, 1865–1945.* Chapel Hill: University of North Carolina Press, 1998.

Woodward, C. Vann. *Tom Watson, Agrarian Rebel.* New York: Macmillan, 1938. Reprint, New York: Oxford University Press, 1970.

———. *The Strange Career of Jim Crow.* New York: Oxford University Press, 1951. Reprint, New York: Oxford University Press, 1974.

———. *Origins of the New South, 1877–1913.* Baton Rouge: Louisiana State University Press, 1951.

———. *The Burden of Southern History.* Baton Rouge: Louisiana State University Press, 1960. Reprint, Baton Rouge: Louisiana State University Press, 1977.

Worster, Donald. *Rivers of Empire: Water, Aridity, and the Growth of the American West.* New York: Oxford University Press, 1985.

Zlatkovich, Charles P. *Texas Railroads: A Record of Construction and Abandonment.* Austin: Texas State Historical Association, 1981.

ARTICLES

Abramowitz, Jack. "The Negro in the Agrarian Revolt." *Agricultural History* 24 (1950): 89–95.

———. "John B. Rayner—A Grass-Roots Leader." *Journal of Negro History* 36 (1951): 160–93.

Aldrich, Mark. "A Note on Railroad Rates and the Populist Uprising." *Agricultural History* 54 (1980): 424–32.

Altenberg, Lee. "Beyond Capitalism: Leland Stanford's Forgotten Vision." *Sandstone and Tile* 14 (1990): 8–20.

Alvord, Wayne. "T. L. Nugent, Texas Populist." *Southwestern Historical Quarterly* 57 (1954): 65–81.

Argersinger, Peter H. "'A Place on the Ballot': Fusion Politics and Antifusion Laws." *American Historical Review* 85 (1980): 287–306.

———. "New Perspectives on Election Fraud in the Gilded Age." *Political Science Quarterly* 100 (1985): 669–87.

———. "Taubeneck's Laws: Third Parties in American Politics in the Late Nineteenth Century." *American Nineteenth Century History* 3 (2002): 93–116.

Beeby, James M. "'Equal Rights to All and Special Privileges to None': Grassroots Populism in North Carolina." *North Carolina Historical Quarterly* 78 (2001): 156–86.

Belknap, Michael R. "The Era of the Lemon, A History of Santa Paula, California." *California Historical Society Quarterly* 47 (1968): 113–40.

Blocker, Jack S. "The Politics of Reform: Populists, Prohibition and Woman Suffrage, 1891–1892." *Historian* (1972): 614–32.

Bode, Frederick A. "Religion and Class Hegemony: A Populist Critique." *Journal of Southern History* 37 (1971): 417–38.

Bowman, John R. "When Workers Organize Capitalists: The Case of the Bituminous Coal Industry." *Politics and Society* 14 (1985): 289–327.

Brown, Richard D. "Modernization and the Modern Personality in Early America, 1600–1865: A Sketch of a Synthesis." *Journal of Interdisciplinary History* 2 (1972): 201–28.

Burkholder, Thomas R. "Kansas Populism, Woman Suffrage, and the Agrarian Myth: A Case Study in the Limits of Mythic Transcendence." *Communications Studies* 4 (1989): 292–308.

Bushman, Richard Lyman. "Markets and Composite Farms in Early America." *William and Mary Quarterly* 55 (1998): 351–74.

Cantrell, Gregg, and D. Scott Barton. "Texas Populists and the Failure of Biracial Politics." *Journal of Southern History* 4 (1989): 659–93.

Carpenter, Daniel P. "State Building through Reputation Building: Coalitions of Esteem and Program Innovation in the National Postal System, 1883–1913." *Studies in American Political Development* 14 (2000): 121–55.

————. "The Political Foundations of Bureaucratic Autonomy: A Response to Kernell." *Studies in American Political Development* 15 (2001): 113–22.

Cassity, Michael J. "Modernization and Social Crisis, The Knights of Labor and a Midwest Community, 1885–1886." *Journal of American History* 66 (1979): 41–61.

Chafe, William. "The Negro and Populism: A Kansas Case Study." *Journal of Southern History* 34 (1968): 402–19.

Clark, Constance Areson. "Evolution for John Doe: Pictures, the Public and the Scopes Trial Debate." *Journal of American History* 87 (2001): 1275–1303.

Craven, Avery O. "The Agricultural Reformers in the Ante-Bellum South." *American Historical Review* 33 (1928): 302–14.

Cross, Ira B. "Co-operation in California." *The American Economic Review* 1 (1911): 535–44.

Crowe, Charles. "Tom Watson, Blacks and Populists Reconsidered." *Journal of Negro History* 55 (1970): 99–119.

Destler, Chester McArthur. "Agricultural Readjustment and Agrarian Unrest in Illinois, 1880–1896." *Agricultural History* 21 (1947): 104–16.

Dobie, Edith. "The Political Career of Stephen Mallory White: A Study of Party Activities under the Convention System." *Stanford University Publications: History, Economics, and Political Science* 2 (1927): 3–266.

Ellsworth, Clayton S. "Theodore Roosevelt's Country Life Commission." *Agricultural History* 34 (1960): 155–72.

Ferkiss, Victor. "Populist Influences on American Fascism." *Western Political Quarterly* 10 (1957): 350–57.

Fox, Richard Wightman. "The Culture of Liberal Protestant Progressivism, 1875–1925." *Journal of Interdisciplinary History* 23 (1993): 639–60.

Frank, Thomas. "The Leviathan with Tentacles of Steel: Railroads in the Minds of Kansas Populists." *Western Historical Quarterly* 1 (1989): 37–55.

Fuller, Wayne E. "The Populists and the Post Office." *Agricultural History* 65 (1991): 1–17.

Goodwyn, Lawrence C. "Populist Dreams and Negro Rights: East Texas as a Case Study." *American Historical Review* 76 (1971): 1435–56.

Hahn, Steven. "A Response: Common Cents or Historical Sense?" *Journal of Southern History* 59 (1993): 2, 243–58.

Hall, Tom G. "California Populism at the Grass-Roots: The Case of Tulare County, 1892." *Southern California Quarterly* 49 (1967): 193–204.

Harrington, Wynne P. "The Populist Party in Kansas." *Collections of the Kansas State Historical Society, Topeka* 16 (1925): 403–50.

Hattam, Victoria. "Economic Visions and Political Strategies: American Labor and the State, 1865–1896." *Studies in American Political Development* 4 (1990): 82–129.

Henretta, James. "Families and Farms: *Mentalite* in Pre-Industrial America." *William and Mary Quarterly* 35 (1978): 3–32.

Higgs, Robert. "Railroad Rates and the Populist Uprising." *Agricultural History* 44 (1970): 291–97.

Holmes, William F. "The Arkansas Cotton Pickers' Strike of 1891 and the Demise of the Colored Farmers' Alliance." *Arkansas Historical Quarterly* 32 (1973): 107–19.

Holt, R. D. "The Introduction of Barbed Wire into Texas and the Fence Cutting War." *West Texas Historical Association Year Book* 6 (1930): 65–79.

Jeffrey, Julie Roy. "Women in the Southern Farmers' Alliance: A Reconsideration of the Role and Status of Women in the Late Nineteenth Century South." *Feminist Studies* 3 (1975): 72–91.

John, Richard R. "Governmental Institutions as Agents of Change: Rethinking American Political Development in the Early Republic, 1785–1835." *Studies in American Political Development* 11 (1997): 347–80.

Kantor, Shawn Everett. "Supplanting the Roots of Southern Populism: The Contours of Political Protest in the Georgia Hills." *Journal of Economic History* 3 (1995): 637–47.

Kantor, Shawn Everett, and J. Morgan Kousser. "Common Sense or Commonwealth? The Fence Law and Institutional Change in the Postbellum South." *Journal of Southern History* 59 (1993): 201–42.

———. "A Rejoinder: Two Visions of History." *Journal of Southern History* 59 (1993): 259–66.

Kernell, Samuel. "Rural Free Delivery as a Critical Test of Alternative Models of American Political Development." *Studies in American Political Development* 15 (2001): 103–22.

Kernell, Samuel, and Michael P. McDonald. "Congress and America's Political Development: The Transformation of the Post Office from Patronage to Service." *American Journal of Political Science* 43 (1999): 792–811.

King, J. Crawford Jr. "The Closing of the Southern Range: An Exploratory Study." *Journal of Southern History* 48 (1982): 53–70.

Kirkendall, Richard S. "The Agricultural Colleges: Between Tradition and Modernization." *Agricultural History* 60 (1986): 3–21.

Koven, Seth, and Sonya Michel. "Womanly Duties: Maternalist Politics and the Origins of Welfare States in France, Germany, Great Britain, and the United States, 1880–1920." *American Historical Review* 95 (1990): 1076–1108.

Kremm, Thomas W., and Diane Neal. "Challenges to Subordination: Organized Black Agricultural Protest in South Carolina, 1886–1895." *South Atlantic Quarterly* 77 (1978): 98–112.

Lee, Matthew C. "Onward Christian Soldiers: The Social Gospel and the Pullman Strike." *Chicago History: The Magazine of the Chicago Historical Society* 20 (1991): 5–21.

Lengel, Leland L. "Radical Crusaders and a Conservative Church: Attitudes of Populists toward Contemporary Protestantism." *American Studies* 13 (1972): 49–59.

Lightfoot, Billy Bob. "The Negro Exodus from Comanche County, Texas." *Southwestern Historical Quarterly* 56 (1953): 407–16.

———. "The Human Party: Populism in Comanche County, 1886." *West Texas Historical Association Year Book* 31 (1955): 28–40.

Lipartito, Kenneth. "When Women Were Switches: Technology, Work, and Gender in the Telephone Industry." *American Historical Review* 99 (1994): 1075–1111.

Macleod, Roy. "The 'Bankruptcy of Science' Debate: The Creed of Science and Its Critics." *Science, Technology, and Human Values* 7 (1982): 2–15.

Madison, James H. "Reformers and the Rural Church, 1900–1950." *Journal of American History* 73 (1986): 645–68.

Magliari, Michael. "Populism, Steamboats, and the Octopus: Transportation Rates and Monopoly in California's Wheat Regions, 1890–1896." *Pacific Historical Review* 58 (1989): 449–69.

Malin, James C. "The Farmers' Alliance Subtreasury Plan and European Precedents." *Mississippi Valley Historical Review* 21 (1944): 255–60.

Marcus, Alan I. "The Ivory Silo: Farmer-Agricultural College Tensions in the 1870s and 1880s." *Agricultural History* 60 (1986): 22–36.

Kevin Mattson. "The Historian As a Social Critic: Christopher Lasch and the Uses of History," *The History Teacher* May 2003 <http://www.historycooperative.org/journals/ht/36.3/mattson.html> (29 Oct. 2006).

McBane, Margo. "The Role of Gender in Citrus Employment: A Case Study of Recruitment, Labor, and Housing Patterns at the Limoneira Company, 1893 to 1940." *California History* 74 (1995): 69–81.

McGreevy, John T. "Farmers, Nationalists, and the Origins of California Populism." *Pacific Historical Review* 58 (1989): 471–95.

McMath, Robert C. Jr. "Southern White Farmers and the Organization of Black Farm Workers: A North Carolina Document." *Labor History* 18 (1977): 115–19.

———. "Populist Base Communities: The Evangelical Roots of Farm Protest in Texas." *Locus* 1 (1988): 53–63.

Merrill, Michael. "Cash Is Good to Eat: Self-Sufficiency and Exchange in the Rural Economy of the United States." *Radical History Review* 3 (1977): 42–71.

Miller, Worth Robert. "A Centennial Historiography of American Populism." *Kansas History* 16 (1993): 54–69.

Montgomery, David. "On Goodwyn's Populists." *Marxist Perspectives* 1 (1978): 166–73.

Moore, R. Laurence. "The Spiritualist Medium: A Study of Female Professionalism in Victorian America." *American Quarterly* 27 (1975): 200–21.

Morse, H. N. "Books on Rural Life: A Summary of Recent Tendencies." *Journal of Social Forces* 2 (1923): 115–17.

Nash, Gerald D. "The California Railroad Commission, 1876–1911." *Southern California Quarterly* 44 (1962): 287–306.

Nixon, Clarence Herman. "The Cleavage within the Farmers' Alliance Movement." *Mississippi Historical Review* 15 (1928): 22–33.

Norton, William, and Leonard Guelke. "Frontier Agriculture: Subsistence or Commercial?" *Annals of the Association of American Geographers* 67 (1977): 463–67.

Nunberg, Geoffrey. "The Curious Fate of Populism: How Politics Turned into Pose." *New York Times*, August 15, 2004.

Orsi, Richard J. "*The Octopus* Reconsidered: The Southern Pacific and Agricultural Modernization in California, 1865–1915." *California Historical Quarterly* 54 (1975): 83–99.

Ostler, Jeffrey. "The Rhetoric of Conspiracy and the Formation of Kansas Populism." *Agricultural History* 69 (1995): 1–27.

Parsons, Stanley B., Karen T. Parsons, Walter Killilate, and Beverly Borgers. "The Role of Cooperatives in the Development of the Movement Culture of Populism." *Journal of American History* 69 (1983): 866–85.

Pierce, Michael. "The Populist President of the American Federation of Labor: The Career of John McBride, 1880–1895." *Labor History* 41 (2000): 5–24.

Raines, Howell. "Winning the Populism PR War." *Washington Post*, July 27, 2004.

Reynolds, Alfred W. "The Alabama Negro Colony in Mexico, 1894–1896." *Alabama Review* 5 (1952): 243–68; 6 (1953): 31–57.

Rogers, Daniel T. "Republicanism: The Career of a Concept." *Journal of American History* 79 (1992): 11–38.

Rosenberg, Charles E. "Science, Technology, and Economic Growth: The Case of the Agricultural Experiment Station Scientist, 1875–1914." *Agricultural History* 45 (1971): 1–20.

Saunders, Robert. "Southern Populists and the Negro." *Journal of Negro History* 54 (1969): 240–61.

Saxton, Alexander. "San Francisco Labor and the Populist and Progressive Insurgencies." *Pacific Historical Review* 34 (1965): 421–38.

———. "'Caesar's Column': The Dialogue of Utopia and Catastrophe." *American Quarterly* 19 (1967): 224–38.

Schwartz, Michael H. "An Estimate of the Size of the Southern Farmers' Alliance, 1884–1890." *Agricultural History* 51 (1977): 759–69.

Scott, Roy V. "Milton George and the Farmers' Alliance Movement." *Mississippi Valley Historical Review* 45 (1958): 90–109.

Simpson, Lee, ed. "Boosterism in the West." *Journal of the West* 42 (2003): 6–62.

Smith, Ralph A. "'Macuneism' or the Farmers of Texas in Business." *Journal of Southern History* 13 (1947): 220–44.

Spriggs, William Edward. "The Virginia Colored Farmers' Alliance: A Case Study of Race and Class Identity." *Journal of Negro History* 64 (1979): 191–204.

Terry, Joe, and Wallace E. Smith. "Mechanization of Lima Bean Threshing." *Ventura County Historical Society Quarterly* 25 (1980): 3–16.

Turner, James. "Understanding the Populists." *Journal of American History* 67 (1980): 354–73.

Voss-Hubbard, Mark. "The 'Third Party Tradition' Reconsidered: Third Parties and American Public Life, 1830–1900." *Journal of American History* 86 (1999): 121–50.

Walters, Donald E. "The Period of the Populist Party." In *The Rumble of California Politics, 1848–1970*, edited by Royce D. Dalmatier, Clarence McIntosh, and Earl G. Waters, 99–124. New York: Wiley, 1970.

Westbrook, Robert B. "Neorepublican Prophets." *Reviews in American History* 11 (1983): 537–42.

Wiest, Edward. "The Relation of the State to Agriculture." In *Readings in the Economic History of American Agriculture*, edited by Louis Bernard Schmidt and Earle Dudley Ross, 465–95. New York: Macmillan, 1925.

Wilentz, Sean. "Populism Redux." *Dissent* (Spring 1995): 149–53.

Wilson, Warren H. "The Church and the Country Life Movement." *Journal of Social Forces* 2 (1923): 23–28.

Wyman, Roger E. "Agrarian or Working-Class Radicalism? The Electoral Basis of Populism in Wisconsin." *Political Science Quarterly* 89 (1974–75): 827.

Dissertations and Papers

Ali, Omar H. "Black Populism in the New South, 1886–1898." PhD diss., Columbia University, 2003.

Beckel, Deborah. "Roots of Reform: The Origins of Populism and Progressivism as Manifest in Relationships among Reformers in Raleigh, North Carolina, 1850–1905." PhD diss., Emory University, 1998.

Blocker, Jack S. "Edward Bellamy and the Populists: A Study of Influence." MA thesis, University of Wisconsin, 1964.

Denton, Richard Charles. "American Nonconformist and Kansas Industrial Liberator: A Kansas Union Labor-Populist Newspaper, 1886–1891." MA thesis, Kansas State College of Pittsburg, 1961.

Destler, Chester McArthur. "The People's Party in Illinois, 1888–1896: A Phase in the Populist Revolt." PhD diss., University of Chicago, 1932.

King, Keith Lynn. "Religious Dimensions of the Agrarian Protest in Texas, 1870–1908." PhD diss., University of Illinois, 1985.

Klepper, Robert. "The Economic Bases for Agrarian Protest Movements in the United States, 1870–1900." PhD diss., University of Chicago, 1973.

Kolnick, Jeffrey David. "A Producer's Commonwealth, Populism and the Knights of Labor in Blue Earth County, Minnesota, 1880–1892." PhD diss., University of California, Davis, 1996.

Leidenberger, Georg. "Working-Class Progressivism and the Politics of Transportation in Chicago, 1895–1907." PhD diss., University of North Carolina, 1995.

Lovett, Laura LeeAnn. "Conceiving the Future: Nostalgic Modernism, Reproduction, and the Family in the United States, 1890–1930." PhD diss., University of California, Berkeley, 1998.

Lutsky, Seymour. "The Reform Editors and Their Press." PhD diss., State University of Iowa, 1951.

Magliari, Michael Frederick. "California Populism, a Case Study: The Farmers' Alliance and People's Party in San Luis Obispo County, 1885–1903." PhD diss., University of California, Davis, 1992.

Perry, Douglass Geraldyne. "Black Populism: The Negro in the People's Party in Texas." MS thesis, Prairie View A & M University, Texas, 1945.

Pierce, Michael Cain. "The Plow and Hammer: Farmers, Organized Labor and the People's Party in Ohio." PhD diss., Ohio State University, 1999.

Scharnau, Ralph W. "Thomas J. Morgan and the Chicago Socialist Movement, 1876–1901." PhD diss., Northern Illinois University, 1969.

Vermont Avenue Baptist Church. "Historical Review of the Origin and Development of the Vermont Avenue Baptist Church." Washington, D.C. (undated).

Wagner, Maryjo. "Farms, Families, and Reform, Women in the Farmers' Alliance and Populist Party." PhD diss., University of Oregon, 1986.

Walker, Philip M. "Un Populiste Californien, Marion Cannon (1834–1920)." PhD diss., Université Paul Valery, Montpellier Université, 1998.

Walters, Donald Edgar. "Populism in California, 1889–1900." PhD diss., University of California, 1952.

Willams, Marshall L. "The Political Career of Cyclone Davis." MA thesis, East Texas State Teachers College, 1937.

Witherspoon, William O. "Populism in Jack County, Texas." MA thesis, North Texas State University, 1973.

INDEX

Adams, Charles Francis, 55
Adams, Herbert Baxter, 324n11
Adams, John, 65
Adams, Sam, 178
Advocate, The, Meriden, Kans., 117, 129–30
African Americans: and American Railway Union, 222–23; and biracial organizing, 39–41; and black Populism, 19, 174, 176, 190–92, 199, 201, 202, 274; churches of, 39–42, 257–58; colonization efforts of, 188, 326n50; and Coxey's Army, 258; disfranchisement of, 200, 201, 203, 279, 284, 327n62, 329n93; economic dependency of, 41, 105, 126, 178; and eugenics, 267, 284–85; and farm cooperatives, 105, 121, 125–26; as farm labor, 39, 52, 105, 106, 183–84, 195, 284; as farm owners, 42, 125, 180, 276, 284; and Farmers' Alliance, 38–41, 86–7, 105–6, 125, 184, 178–79, 300n51; and jury service, 191–92, 327n61; and Knights of Labor, 39–40, 188, 219; and Liberia, 188; and patronage, 199, 329n94; political options of, 19, 173–74, 178–79, 188, 195–97, 199, 201–3, 239, 258, 284; Populist coalition, place in, 14, 18, 19, 181–82, 190–91, 195–96, 284; and

post office employment, 199, 177–78; removal of, 186–88, 200; and segregation, 18, 19, 92, 176–78, 192–93, 203, 258, 284; and slavery, 51, 87, 183–84, 193, 197, 216; terror against, 41, 126, 180, 186–88, 192, 194, 196, 321n89, 328n78; and women's labor, 39, 86–7. *See also* Colored Farmers' Alliance, Farmers' Alliance, Jim Crow laws, lynching, National Farmers' Alliance and Industrial Union, Populism, segregation, white supremacy
African Colonization Club, 188
Agassiz, Louis, 268
agricultural education, 46–8, 50, 53
agricultural experiment stations, 53, 55
Agricultural and Mechanical College of Mississippi, 55
Agricultural Wheel (Arkansas-based), 36; racial attitude of, 29, 39–40
Alabama, 42, 55, 86, 108, 127, 155
Alabama Colored Farmers' Alliance, 232
Alabama Farmers' Alliance, 178, 265
Alabama People's party, 188, 200, 273
Allen, Walter N., 116–17
Alliance Co-operative Milling Co., Santa Clara, Calif., 112
Alliance Packing Co., Tulare County, Calif., 112

Moore, J. L., Rev., 62, 178, 203
Moore, R. Laurence, 338n3, 343n62
Morgan, Thomas, 208, 231
Morgan, W. Scott, 64, 77, 129–30, 154
Morris County, Tex., Alliance, 83
Morrow, S. J., Mrs., 86

Napoleon, 164–67, 274, 322n97. *See also* Thomas Watson
National Alliance Insurance System, 127
National Cordage Company, 127–31
National Council of Women, 235
National Economist, 37, 54, 59, 62–4, 66, 86, 89
National Farmers' Alliance. *See* Northern Farmers' Alliance
National Farmers' Alliance and Industrial Union, 36, 50, 82, 113; Committee on the Monetary System of, 154, 159; Indianapolis convention of (1891), 72, 73, 109; membership of, 14, 26, 33, 36–8, 75–6, 120, 184–85, 197; Ocala, Fla., convention of (1890), 56, 106, 129; St. Louis convention of (1889), 124, 127; and secrecy, 38, 57; Shreveport, La., convention of (1887), 36; whites-only clause of, 36, 38 41, 76, 182, 184–85, 280, 300n51; women membership of, 75–6; on women's suffrage, 94–5. *See also* Farmers' Alliance
National Farmers' Alliance Exchange, 118, 128
nationalism. *See* American nationalism
Nationalist movement: in California Farmers' Alliance, 234–35; class basis of, 207, 215, 226–27, 330n2; and farmers, 234–36; in Populist coalition, 20, 206–7, 225, 288; religious beliefs in, 254, 263–64; San Francisco club of, 226–27; and urban reform, 229. *See also* Edward Bellamy, nonconformists
National Reform Press Association, 62, 63, 72, 129–30
National Union Co. (NUC), 127–31; opposition to, 129–30
"natural monopolies," 146, 148

Nebraska, 31, 82, 132, 161, 263, 269, 273, 307n25
Nebraska Farmers' Alliance, 31, 79, 80, 82, 132
New Braunfels, Tex., Alliance textile mill, 122
New England, 77, 91, 119
New Jersey, 37
New Mexico, 29–30, 184
New Mexico Farmers' Alliance 29–30; and Hispanic People's party, 30
New Orleans, 9, 117, 216
New York City, 9, 21, 55, 106, 107, 128, 129, 133
New York Central Railroad, 332n34
New York, 37, 108
New York Times, 129
Nicaraguan Canal, 111, 147–48, 240
Nietzsche, Friedrich, 248
Nininger, Minn., 157
Nonconformist, 36, 63, 79, 81, 161, 234, 240, 259, 262, 327n68
nonconformists, 12–3, 225, 237; as bohemian moderns, 207; and cooperative models, 237–39, 41; and labor Populism, 225, 236, 241–42; in Populist coalition, 20, 206–7, 225, 286; and urban reform, 207, 253, 242
nonpartisanship, 163, 170, 279; and Farmers' Alliance, 13, 36, 139, 140, 155–56; and People's party, 18, 139, 155–56, 162, 316n10
Norris, Frank, 317n33
North Carolina, 39, 41, 50, 51–3, 56, 59, 130, 147, 155, 167, 187, 197–200, 251–52, 265, 273, 274, 302n27, 314n61, 341n27
North Carolina College of Agriculture and Mechanic Arts (N.C. State University), 53, 252
North Carolina Department of Agriculture, 52
North Carolina Farmers' Alliance, 29, 31, 92, 131; and crop diversification, 107; and education, 61; and internal critics, 168; and manufacturing, 91–2; and state welfare, 93; and white supremacy, 60; and women, 71, 88
North Carolina Farmers' Clubs, 36, 53